New Testament Manuscripts

Texts and Editions

for

New Testament Study

Edited by

Stanley E. Porter and Wendy J. Porter

VOLUME 2

New Testament Manuscripts

Their Texts and Their World

Edited by

Thomas J. Kraus and Tobias Nicklas

BRILL

LEIDEN • BOSTON

2006

This book is printed on acid-free paper.

Library of Congress Cataloging-in-Publication Data

New Testament manuscripts : their texts and their world / edited by Thomas J. Kraus and Tobias Nicklas.
    p. cm. — (Texts and editions for New Testament study, ISSN 1574-7085 ; v. 2)
    Includes bibliographical references and index.
    ISBN 90-04-14945-7 (alk. paper)
    1. Bible. N.T.—Manuscripts I. Kraus, Thomas J., 1965- II. Nicklas, Tobias, 1967- III. Series.

BS1939.N49 2006
225.4'86—dc22

2005058215

ISSN 1574-7085
ISBN 90 04 14945 7

CONTENTS

LIST OF CONTRIBUTORS

MALCOLM CHOAT is a Macquarie University Research Fellow in the Department of Ancient History at Macquarie University, Sydney (Australia). His interests are in papyrology (especially early Christian papyri), Coptic, and monasticism. He is part of the team editing the volume *Papyri from the Rise of Christianity in Egypt* (PCE; forthcoming).

ELDON JAY EPP, Ph.D., Harvard University, is Harkness Professor of Biblical Literature *emeritus* and Dean of Humanities and Social Sciences *emeritus*, Case Western Reserve University (United States of America). He has served recently as Visiting Professor of New Testament at the Harvard Divinity School (2001–2003, 2004–2005) and as President of the Society of Biblical Literature (2003).

MARCO FRENSCHKOWSKI is a scholar of Religious Studies and an outside lecturer of New Testament at the University of Mainz (Germany). His major areas of research are the history of religion in antiquity and early Christianity, matters of the introduction to the New Testament, new religious movements, and the relationship between religion and culture.

KIM HAINES-EITZEN is Associate Professor of Early Christianity in the Department of Near Eastern Studies at Cornell University. She received her Ph.D. from the University of North Carolina, Chapel Hill, in 1997. She is the author of *Guardians of Letters: Literacy, Power, and the Transmitters of Early Christian Literature* (Oxford, 2000) and is currently working on a book project that treats the intersection of gender, asceticism and the transmission of early Christian literature.

PETER M. HEAD is Sir Kirby Laing Research Fellow at Tyndale House and Affiliated Lecturer in New Testament at the Faculty of Divinity, University of Cambridge (United Kingdom). His major research interests are Jesus, the Synoptic Gospels, and the New Testament manuscripts. He participates in the *Early Greek Bible Manuscripts Project* (EGBMP) and concentrates on the publication of papyri with portions of the New Testament.

MICHAEL W. HOLMES is Professor of Biblical Studies and Early Christianity at Bethel College and Seminary in St. Paul/Minnesota (United States of America). His primary research interests are New Testament Textual Criticism and the Apostolic Fathers. He is currently working on the textual history of Paul's letter to the Romans and a commentary on the Martyrdom of Polycarp.

LARRY W. HURTADO is Professor of New Testament Language, Literature and Theology and Director of the Centre for the Study of Christian Origins at the University of Edinburgh (United Kingdom). He specializes on Early Christology, New Testament Textual Criticism, the Gospel of Mark, the Apostle Paul, and the Jewish Background of the New Testament, but is practically interested in anything about earliest Christianity.

DIRK JONGKIND received an MA in Old Testament from Tyndale Theological Seminary in Badhoevedorp (The Netherlands) in 1999 and a year later an MPhil in New Testament from Cambridge University. In 2005 he finished his doctoral work on Codex Sinaiticus with a dissertation entitled *Studies in the Scribal Habits of Codex Sinaiticus* in 2005. In the spring of the same year he worked as curator in the British Library doing preparatory work for the Codex Sinaiticus Digitisation Project. Currently he holds a Fellowship at Tyndale House and St Edmunds College, Cambridge (United Kingdom). He participates in *Early Greek Bible Manuscripts Project* (EGBMP; see Peter M. Head).

THOMAS J. KRAUS is teaching at a grammar school and is a scholar at Classical and Biblical Studies who is participating in several projects (for instance, "Septuaginta Deutsch"; *Novum Testamentum Patristicum* [NTP]; *Oxford Early Christian Gospel Texts* [OECGT], and "Tod in der Antike"). He interests are mainly in (early Christian) papyrology, the Christian Apocrypha, the language and textual history of the Septuagint and the New Testament, and matters of book production and literacy in (late) antiquity.

TOBIAS NICKLAS is Professor of New Testament Studies at Radboud University of Nijmegen, the Netherlands. His major research interests are ancient Christian and Jewish Apocrypha, the textual history and early interpretation of the New Testament, and Reader-Oriented Approaches to the Christian Bible.

STANLEY E. PORTER is President, Dean and Professor of New Testament at McMaster Divinity College in Hamilton/Ontario (Canada). He has taught in post-secondary institutions in Canada, the USA, and the UK. His recent research interests evolve around the language, writings, and texts of the New Testament. Moreover, he developed an interest in papyrology and is writing a commentary on the Book of Romans.

TOMMY WASSERMAN received an M. Div. from Örebro Theological Seminary (Sweden) in 2001, where he works as a part-time teacher in New Testament Greek and Exegesis, and is Ph.D. candidate in New Testament Exegesis at Lund University since 2002. He is currently working on a dissertation upon the textual tradition of the Epistle of Jude and is author of several articles in New Testament Textual Criticism.

ACKNOWLEDGEMENTS

Figs. 1 & 2: P.Ant. II 54 233
Courtesy of the Egypt Exploration Society © (Nikolaos
Gonis, The Oxyrhynchus Papyri Project, Papyrology
Rooms, Sackler Library, Oxford).

Fig. 3: P.Princ. II 107 = *Suppl.Mag.* I 29 239
Princeton University Library. Princeton Papyrus 107.
Manuscripts Division. Department of Rare Books and
Special Collections. Princeton University Library.

Figs. 4 & 5: PSI VI 719 = *Pap.Graec.Mag.* II P19 244
Courtesy of Biblioteca Medicea Laurenziana, Florence

Fig. 6: Louvre MND 5528 247
Réunion des Musées Nationaux (RMN)—Agence
photographique, Paris.

Figs. 7 & 8:—P.Bad. IV 60 249
Holztafel Heidelberg Inv.-Nr. 761—Courtesy of the
University of Heidelberg—Ägyptologisches Institut
(Dina Faltings, curator)

THE WORLD OF NEW TESTAMENT MANUSCRIPTS: 'EVERY MANUSCRIPT TELLS A STORY'

Thomas J. Kraus and Tobias Nicklas

With justification the publication of the first fascicle of the *Aegyptische Urkunden aus den Königlichen* [later *Staatlichen*] *Museen zu Berlin, Griechische Urkunden* (*BGU*) in 1892 can be regarded as the beginning of papyrology as an academic discipline.[1] Today we take it for granted that the massive number of documentary papyri that have been edited since then and those still awaiting publication help to paint a colorful picture of the political, social, and cultural life surrounding their usage and, above all, the people and institutions behind them. In other words, with these documentary papyri, we often get to know far more about living individuals than we do from classical authors or archaeological ruins. However, literary papyri[2] are of no less use and significance—even if the stories they can tell us today sound different in tone, the reality is not different as far as their contents are concerned.

In 1885/86, after their first excavation campaigns in the northeast of the Fayum, an oasis southwest of Memphis, the two friends Bernard P. Grenfell and Arthur S. Hunt[3] from Queen's College,

---

[1] Cf. P. van Minnen in his paper delivered at the 20th International Congress of Papyrologists (Copenhagen, 23–29 August 1992), published as: The Century of Papyrology (1892–1992), *BASP* 30 (1992) 5–18.

[2] Papyrology as a specific discipline is occupied with papyri used in a collective sense for several materials. Thus, classic research tools for the papyrologists refer to papyrus, parchment, ostraca, and tablets, as in J.F. Oates et al., eds., Checklist of Editions of Greek, Latin, Demotic and Coptic Papyri, Ostraca and Tablets (last upd. March 2004 http://scriptorium.lib.duke.edu/papyrus/texts/clist.html; in print form published as J.F. Oates et al., eds., *Checklist of Greek and Latin Papyri, Ostraca and Tablets* (BASP Suppl. 9; Atlanta ⁵2001). This understanding is taken as a basis for the contributions to the present volume. See T.J. Kraus, 'Pergament oder Papyrus?': Anmerkungen zur Signifikanz des Beschreibstoffes bei der Behandlung von Manuskripten, *NTS* 49 (2003) 425–432.

[3] For the story about Grenfell and Hunt's excavation campaigns see the online version of the exhibition *Oxyrhynchus: A City and its Texts* (http://www.csad.ox.ac.uk/POxy/welcome.htm; last access 10/04/05; above all Peter Parsons' story of Oxyrhynchus and its diggers, *Waste Paper City*, and John Rea's *Greek Papyri and Oxyrhynchus*, accessible via 'Intro') and E.G. Turner, *Greek Papyri. An Introduction* (2nd ed.; Oxford 1980; repr. 1998) 27–30.

Oxford, moved south to the ancient county town of Oxyrhynchus (today Behnesa), 120 miles south of Cairo. There together with about one hundred and thirty workers, the two of them started to dig through the rubbish dumps in 1886/87. Soon they found such a massive quantity of papyri that they had to utilize almost any container available, even biscuit tins, to ship them to Oxford—they found documentary papyri but also numerous literary papyri, among them classical and theological ones. However, none of the latter— in the words of Grenfell and Hunt—"aroused wider interest than a page from a book containing Sayings of Jesus and published by us under the title of ΛΟΓΙΑ ΙΗϹΟΥ, *Sayings of our Lord*".[4] This sheet of papyrus with previously unknown sayings, unearthed on 11 January 1897, was supplemented by two further fragments with sayings during their second excavation at Oxyrhynchus, with one written on the back of a survey-list and the other consisting of eight fragments of a papyrus roll.[5] The three pieces were soon understood as parts of the Greek version of the Gospel of Thomas, a collection of sayings of Jesus that had become an apocryphal text in the course of church history. The story of these sensational findings of extra-canonical and quite early manuscripts with portions of the canonical New Testament at ancient Oxyrhynchus—for instance, *P.Oxy.* I 2 (𝔓¹) with a portion of the Gospel of Matthew was also discovered in the course of Grenfell and Hunt's first campaign—caused such a stir that since then the term 'papyrus' has been repeatedly associated with sensationalism or even rumors of conspiracies to keep the apocryphal texts under lock and key.

Nevertheless, other discoveries, acquisitions, and publications added to the great fascination of papyri. In the years 1930–31 Alfred Chester Beatty, who was knighted later on, acquired three biblical papyrus codices (𝔓⁴⁵⁻⁴⁷) now kept in the Beatty Museum in Dublin, Ireland. More than twenty years later, in 1956, the Genevan bibliophile Martin Bodmer succeeded in making the sensational acquisition of

---

[4] B.P. Grenfell/A.S. Hunt, *New Sayings of Jesus and Fragment of a Lost Gospel from Oxyrhynchus* (Egypt Exploration Fund—Graeco-Roman Branch; London 1904) 9. This papyrus was first published by the same scholars under the title mentioned above in 1897 and then as *P.Oxy.* I 1 in 1898.

[5] Both published first in Grenfell/Hunt, *New Sayings* (see note 4)—the small booklet contains the text of *P.Oxy.* I 1 as well—and then as *P.Oxy.* IV 654 and 655.

an ancient library, now in the Bibliotheca Bodmeriana in Cologny/
Geneva, Switzerland, among which there are some invaluable tex-
tual witnesses to the writings of the New Testament ($\mathfrak{P}^{66.72.74.75}$), of
the Old Testament, and of early Christian and classical texts. In
between the excitement among biblical scholars caused by these two
collections, Colin H. Roberts edited P.Ryl. III 457 ($\mathfrak{P}^{52}$) with John
18:31–33, 37–38, the oldest extant witness to any canonical text of
the New Testament to the present, which he dated to 125 CE (± 25
years).[6]

Furthermore, not only papyri—here meaning the writing material—aroused that kind of fascination. Analogously, other materials,
above all parchment manuscripts, caused a stir. Among these are
the spectacular and sometimes even miraculous tales to be told and
retold of those like: Constantin Tischendorf, who by chance read
leaves of a parchment codex later labeled Codex Sinaiticus ($\aleph$) at
the monastery of St. Catharine on Mount Sinai in 1844, and that
finally made its way into the British Museum in London; or of the
thirteen codices with fifty-four different works (most of which otherwise unknown) discovered in a jar by Egyptian peasants near Nag
Hammadi in 1945; or of the Dead Sea Scrolls, the first of them
accidentally found in the area around Khirbet Qumran by a Bedouin
in 1947, which are still in the process of publication.[7]

Each of the manuscripts, libraries, and collections, their texts and
the circumstances of their discovery deserve a full-scale account in
order to tell about their thrilling and sometimes obscure background.
Nevertheless, often scholars concentrate on specific features only,
such as the character and the quality of the text preserved or the
date given and the material used, even if fully aware of that shortcoming. This is legitimate and, of course, sufficient for specific purposes, for example the reconstruction of a reliable critical text of the

---

[6] Even today the time of spectacular findings and/or publications is not over as
demonstrated by the sensationalistic reports that followed publication of the fine
first edition of *P.Vindob.G* 42417 ($\mathfrak{P}^{116}$) by A. Papathomas, A New Testimony to the
Letter to the Hebrews, *JGRChJ* 1 (2000) 18–24, claiming, for instance, that this
papyrus with Hebrews 2:9–11, 3:3–6 from the sixth to seventh century had been
written in Hebrew or was the earliest witness to the Letter to the Hebrews.

[7] The current state of publication of the series *Discoveries in the Judean Desert (DJD)*
can be accessed online by means of the index published by 'The Orion Center for
the Study of the Dead Sea Scrolls and Associated Literature' (http://orion.mscc.
huji.ac.il/resources/djd.shtml; last access 10/04/05).

New Testament or the recognition that there are more than one alternative reading.

However, manuscripts have many more stories to tell if you listen closely to the sounds of the details they preserve for today's world, such as the forms of letters, their layout, their being part of a collection, the other texts written down either on the same or reverse side of a leaf, or the background of their provenance if known, to mention only a few.

This is what this book in general and its essays in particular are meant to do: to retell or even recount for the first time the fascinating tales of the manuscripts of the New Testament and their surroundings, to search for the clues they offer to get to know the people and the world behind them better, and then to assess anew what we have so far considered as common knowledge about those days.

The two opening essays deal with the conditions under which manuscripts from the early days of Christianity were produced and transmitted. Above all, the county town of Oxyrhynchus captures our attention, as it is the origin of many textual witnesses to the New Testament integrated into the famous Gregory-Aland list. Nevertheless, as mentioned above, Oxyrhynchus received a certain reputation for being the place where not only canonical but also apocryphal texts were unearthed. As many papyri found there can be dated to specific periods and the provenance of them is known, a socio-historical pattern may be set up to learn more about their production and transmission. In other words, with the help of semi-literary as well as documentary papyri significant features of the world of Oxyrhynchus and its inhabitants might be reconstructed.

(1)   Eldon J. Epp has regularly put the focus on such specific features in recent years.[8] In his contribution to this volume he adds

---

[8] Cf. E.J. Epp, The New Testament Papyri at Oxyrhynchus in Their Social and Intellectual Context, *Sayings of Jesus: Canonical and Non-Canonical. Essays in Honour of Tjitze Baarda* (ed. W.L. Petersen—J.S. Vos—H.J. De Jonge; NovT.Sup 89; Leiden u.a. 1997) 47–68; Idem, The Codex and Literacy in Early Christianity and at Oxyrhynchus: Issues Raised by Harry Y. Gamble's *Books and Readers in the Early Church, Critical Review of Books in Religion* 11 (1997) 15–37; and Idem, The Oxyrhynchus

new facets to the picture of Oxyrhynchus as a place of writing and reading. With his 'The Jews and the Jewish Community in Oxyrhynchus' he intends to circumscribe the 'socio-religious context for the New Testament papyri', as his subtitle precisely states. However, he immediately points out the trouble with the enterprise of collecting and assessing the testimonies of Jews and/or a Jewish community in Oxyrhynchus from 100 BCE to 600 CE: which sources should be used? Which ones can be identified as being Jewish at all? What about periods of silence, for which no traces of Jewish life have been found (e.g., the impact of the futile Jewish revolt under Emperor Trajan)? Be that as it may, even if aspects of Jewish practice that can be found remain vague, some others continuously run through consecutive periods of time, and others permit selective insights into some individual lives.

(2) The author of the second in this first set of essays, Marco Frenschkowski, concentrates on another town as the home of what was of major significance for the transmission of early Christian literature and the texts of the New Testament: Caesarea and its well-known library. Today we just know many of the early Christian writers and their texts only from quotations in the works of Eusebius of Caesarea, who had direct access to these in the library itself. Besides its uncertain fate, and the quality and quantity of its books, Frenschkowski's 'Studien zur Geschichte der Bibliothek von Cäsarea' also discusses the still unsolved mystery of the total disappearance of the library in the course of the fourth and above all fifth centuries. In contrast to other scholars, who blame war or catastrophes for its end, Frenschkowski utilizes a variety of examples and parallels in order to demonstrate that it is quite plausible to regard the library of Caesarea as a private collection of books. Furthermore, this private collection might have been handed on from Origen to Pamphilos and possibly then to Eusebius, after whose death it was not passed on and thus not used anymore, but dispersed bit by bit. The picture Frenschkowski paints of the ancient library of Caesarea not only is important for the study of its features, background, and end, but may at the same time serve as a model for the problems

New Testament Papyri: 'Not without honor except in their hometown'?, *JBL* 123 (2004) 5–55 (originally his Presidential Address at the Annual Meeting of the Society of Biblical Literature, 2003).

that libraries in general and the New Testament manuscripts in particular have continually faced.

A second group of essays revolves around specific issues to be discussed by means of individual manuscripts. Those specific issues are manifold and extend the scope here from the discovery and publication process of one parchment manuscript, to specific features of a manuscript, such as paleographical particularities, its purpose, and interesting readings of a text, and finally to the question why some texts were bound together in one and the same codex.

(3)   Peter M. Head singles out the recently discovered parchment fragments *de Hamel MS* 386 (Gregory-Aland 0312, abbreviated as *De Hamel Coll. Gk. MS* 2) kept in Cambridge to demonstrate the necessary steps to be taken from its discovery to its identification and publication. In the course of his study, 'A Newly Discovered Manuscript of Luke's Gospel (de Hamel MS 386; Gregory-Aland 0312)', he systematically describes and analyses the fragments, and then reconstructs the original format of the codex and offers a tentative reading of its text of the Gospel of Luke. Head concludes by pointing out the context of the manuscript within the textual history of the New Testament and its significance for a better understanding of the transmission of the New Testament.

(4)   Alongside other studies of the famous *Codex Sinaiticus* (ℵ) performed in the course of an extensive research project, Dirk Jongkind here concentrates on the generally accepted observation that three scribes were involved in the copying process. With 'One Codex, Three Scribes, and Many Books: Struggles with Space in *Codex Sinaiticus*' he puts the focus on the tiny irregularities between the three hands often discernible when there is a change of scribe. After collecting these, he draws some conclusions from scrutinizing these irregularities so that the circumstances of the production of this codex become visible. It is very important to acknowledge the problems a *scriptorium* in late Antiquity was confronted with when instructed to produce a complete Bible.

(5)   More than once a small papyrus fragment with writing on both sides has been the subject of scholarly discussions. *P.Oxy.* XXXIV 2864 ($\mathfrak{P}^{78}$) has been regarded as part of either a codex or an amulet. Tommy Wasserman tries to solve the riddle of this papyrus and argues in favor of the latter alternative. Consequently, to put the

papyrus into the category of 'amulet' provokes further questions to be answered: what does this then imply as far as the value of this as the oldest textual witness to the Letter of Jude? How can the relation between the two terms 'magic' and 'religion' be defined in an appropriate way? Why—according to the title of Wasserman's study, '$\mathfrak{P}^{78}$ (*P. Oxy.* XXXIV 2684)—The Epistle of Jude on an Amulet?'—was this specific text from the Letter of Jude used as an amulet? Based on a paleographic description of the item, Wasserman not only answers these questions, but he reveals the complex inter-action of social, textual and religious aspects by means of a small piece of papyrus.

(6) Tobias Nicklas and Tommy Wasserman then discuss another essential witness to the Letter of Jude, *P.Bodm.* VII + VIII ($\mathfrak{P}^{72}$), which also preserves the First and Second Letter of Peter. Moreover, the two authors widen the scope of their study and concentrate on *Codex Bodmer Miscellani* of the famous *Bibliotheca Bodmeriana*, which probably consisted of a whole set of interesting texts: besides the Letter of Jude and the First and Second Letter of Peter, the fasci-nating collection includes apocryphal texts such as one about Mary's birth (better known as the Proto-Gospel of James), the Third Letter to the Corinthians or the Eleventh Ode of Solomon, two psalms, and writings from authors of the early Christian church (a homily by Melito of Sardis, a fragment of an unknown hymn [by Melito?], and the Apology of Phileas). After an initial description of the codex Nicklas and Wasserman discuss the potential reasons responsible for the formation of this collection of texts alongside possible intertex-tual relationships. Furthermore, the two of them intend to give answers to additional questions motivated by their studies: how was this codex transmitted, how was it read and used? Are there any clearly dis-cernible parallels and allusions to other ancient manuscripts? Con-sequently, they entitle their essay 'Theologische Linien im *Codex Bodmer Miscellani?*'

(7) More than the previous essays, the next essay moves the text as preserved in a particular manuscript into the centre of attention. Michael W. Holmes concentrates on the particularities of one of the *Chester Beatty Biblical Papyry* (*P.Beatty* III[9])—among biblical scholars

---

[9] According to the *Checklist of Editions of Greek, Latin, Demotic and Coptic Papyri*,

well known as *P. Chester Beatty* II ($\mathfrak{P}^{46}$)[10]—and focuses there on Paul's Letter to the Romans. Holmes collects the textual variants in the codex and draws the conclusion that these indicate a tendency to widen and/or explain the text. This observation leads Holmes to assume that this text of Romans might manifest an incipient example of early Christian commentary, or at least an indication of early activities in such a direction, as is expressed in the title of his study, 'The Text of $\mathfrak{P}^{46}$: Evidence of the Earliest "Commentary" on Romans?'.

Special features observed in various manuscripts, that is, more or less general traits of writing and using ancient manuscripts, are the common subject of a last category of essays. By studying many papyri, parchments, ostraca, and tablets specific tendencies become visible, whether they consist of the usage of certain texts with each other, specific writing conventions (e.g., short forms, layout, handwriting), or features of diverse religious backgrounds in some Christian manuscripts, to mention only a few.

(8)   Larry W. Hurtado has often emphasized abbreviated forms of words that scribes regarded as special and significant in his research.[11] Here Hurtado investigates the evolution and the developmental stages of the *staurogram*, which can be found in many of the very early Christian manuscripts and may relate to the early forms of Christian iconography and Christ devotion. Accordingly, his title asks: 'The Staurogram in Early Christian Manuscripts: The Earliest Visual Reference to the Crucified Jesus?' The *staurogram*, a composite form of the Greek majuscule letters *tau* and *rho* with a superimposed ver-

---

Ostraca and Tablets (ed. J.F. Oates et al.; BASP.S 9; Atlanta, fifth ed., 2001) and regularly updated online http://scriptorium.lib.duke.edu/papyrus/texts/clist.html (last access 04/19/05).

[10] Cf. *Kurzgefasste Liste der griechischen Handschriften des Neuen Testaments* (ed. K. Aland et al; ANTT 1; Berlin—New York, second ed., 1994) 9.

[11] L.W. Hurtado, The Origin of the *Nomina Sacra*, *JBL* 117 (1998) 655–673; Id., The Earliest Evidence of an Emerging Christian Material and Visual Culture: The Codex, the *Nomina Sacra* and the Staurogram, *Texts and Artifacts in the Religions of Mediterranean Antiquity: Essays in Honour of Peter Richardson* (eds. S.G. Wilson—M. Desjardins; Waterloo/Ont. 2000) 271–288; Id., $\mathfrak{P}^{52}$ (P.Rylands Gk. 457) and the Nomina Sacra: Method and Probability, *TynB* 54 (2003) 1–14; Id., *Lord Jesus Christ: Devotion to Jesus in Earliest Christianity* (Grand Rapids-Cambridge 2003) 625–627.

tical line of the latter on the first, looks like what we today identify as the symbol for the crucified Jesus. If it really is, the manuscripts will have preserved a reference to Jesus prior to the commonly held start of the depiction of the crucifixion of Jesus.

(9)   In response to the question of which Christian text may be the one most often preserved on papyri, the common answer would be 'the Lord's Prayer'—although the Gregory-Aland list lacks specific entries for papyri with the Lord's Prayer. Thomas J. Kraus collects early Christian manuscripts with verses of the Lord's Prayer, he describes each of them paleographically, he evaluates the data collected in order to assess anew the ways they have been described previously, and finally he compiles the other texts with which the Lord's Prayer is preserved. The many pieces of a massive puzzle fit together to create a picture of the people living in those days and make their world(s) of belief and thought visible. Thus, Kraus demonstrates that each early Christian manuscript is invaluable, even if it has been excluded from the official Gregory-Aland list. So, the title of his essay—'Manuscripts with the *Lord's Prayer*—they are more than simply Witnesses to that Text itself'—is established.

(10)   Not only those manuscripts with extracts from the New Testament writings can and should be accepted as witnesses to the text of the New Testament, however, no matter if they have been integrated into the Gregory-Aland list so important for the creation of the critical editions of the New Testament. Malcolm Choat's 'Echo and Quotation of the NT in Papyrus Letters to the End of the Fourth Century' provides extensive proof for the necessity to take private letters from early Christians seriously. On the one hand, these letters often contain quotations from, allusions to, and echoes of biblical texts; on the other hand, phrases or terms common in the New Testament and its related texts clearly made their way into the everyday language of the senders and addressees of the letters. Additionally, letters offer data regarding their time of writing, their provenance, or even the place to which they were sent. That leads to further insights into the background of a particular word or phrase and, thus, to a circumscription of a scenario of how the world of biblical texts and everyday life interacted on the level of language.

(11)   Although the issue of women's literacy has been treated by a number of scholars, it remains a neglected aspect in biblical studies.

The notion that a specific genre of literature has ever been popular with women—in biblical studies the Apocryphal Acts of the Apostles—manifests a traditional stereotype. Kim Haines-Eitzen links gender studies with the manuscripts of the Apocryphal Acts and, thus, for the first time investigates how far that stereotype can be proved by a close observation of those textual witnesses. Do the manuscripts themselves offer any indications that the Apocryphal Acts of the Apostles are a kind of women's literature? What can be said about their readership and audience? Haines-Eitzen answers these two questions and more in her 'The Apocryphal Acts of the Apostles on Papyrus: Revisiting the Question of Readership and Audience'.

It is not by accident that one essay is set apart from the others as challenging the usual method of how to organize and categorize New Testament manuscripts. Several times reference has been made to the Gregory-Aland list of witnesses to the New Testament, the official and updated list of the Institute in Münster/Germany. Nevertheless, this list has its advantages and disadvantages, in other words its strengths and shortcomings. One of the latter is that it ends up with the exclusion of specific manuscripts or even categories of manuscripts, some overlapping of categories, and a biased treatment of items being classified as 'magic.'

(12)   Only if all manuscripts of the New Testament are taken as what they are, i.e. real artifacts of real people worthy to be respected and accepted as such, will we get a more precise picture of the socio-historical and theological background of early Christianity. Thus, Stanley E. Porter methodologically unfolds a system of how to integrate all witnesses to the New Testament available, be they papyri or parchments, ostraca or tablets. With his 'Textual Criticism in the Light of Diverse Textual Evidence for the Greek New Testament: An Expanded Proposal' he argues for an understanding of textual criticism that allows us to integrate into our textual reconstructions such items as amulets or apocryphal texts, which are necessary for a full-scale knowledge of the situation in which the manuscripts of the New Testaments were written. Furthermore, he pleads for a fresh evaluation of all the entries in the official Gregory-Aland list, because there might be some significant textual witness to the New Testament that has so far been overlooked, only because it was put into the

category of lectionaries. Admittedly, the Gregory-Aland list is practical, but the great variety of extant manuscripts is more complex
than the existing categorical system of the official list of witnesses to
the New Testament. How far and in what respect Porter's proposal
is going to affect the traditional practice of New Testament textual
criticism and the classification of manuscripts will be seen in the next
few years.

THE JEWS AND THE JEWISH COMMUNITY
IN OXYRHYNCHUS: SOCIO-RELIGIOUS CONTEXT
FOR THE NEW TESTAMENT PAPYRI*

Eldon Jay Epp

Introduction

A year ago I explored at some length what can be known from Oxyrhynchus papyri about Christians and Christianity in that city into the early fourth century.[1] The harvest was modest in its extent but of considerable interest for sketching some aspects of Christian worship, liturgy, and homiletics, as well as random aspects of everyday life at one known location within a limited time frame. Exposing the real-life contexts of more than eighty manuscripts of early Christian writings found at Oxyrhynchus, including fifty-nine of what was to become the New Testament, remains my primary goal in the present study also, as in two other earlier articles.[2] Here, however, I

---

* This article is an expanded version of an invited paper presented in a joint session of the Early Jewish Christian Relations Section, the New Testament Textual Criticism Section, and the Papyrology and Early Christian Backgrounds Group at the Annual Meeting of the Society of Biblical Literature, 22 November 2004 in San Antonio, Texas.

As given in my "The Oxyrhynchus New Testament Papyri: 'Not without honor except in their hometown'?" *JBL* 123 (2004) 5 note before n. 1 (*note*) [Presidential Address, Society of Biblical Literature, 2003] and literally repeated here:

> References to Oxyrhynchus papyri will be given as P.Oxy. + papyrus no.; discussions of a papyrus will be indicated by P.Oxy. + vol. no. + pp. All such references relate to *The Oxyrhynchus Papyri* (Graeco-Roman Memoirs; London: British Academy for the Egypt Exploration Society) 1898– [67 vols. to date]. Oxyrhynchus papyri published elsewhere use the appropriate abbreviations, e.g., PSI + vol. + papyrus no. Basic data on papyri (contents, names, date, etc.) are taken from these sources without further acknowledgement.

[1] "The Oxyrhynchus New Testament Papyri: 'Not without honor.'"

[2] E.J. Epp, "The New Testament Papyri at Oxyrhynchus in Their Social and Intellectual Context," *Sayings of Jesus: Canonical and Non-Canonical. Essays in Honour of Tjitze Baarda* (ed. W.L. Petersen—J.S. Vos—H.J. de Jonge; NovTSup 89; Leiden 1997) 47–68; idem, "The Codex and Literacy in Early Christianity and at Oxyrhynchus: Issues Raised by Harry Y. Gamble's *Books and Readers in the Early Church*," *Critical Review of Books in Religion* 11 (1997) 15–37.

shall not dwell on the New Testament manuscripts directly except
to say again that this late antique site offers an ideal—perhaps
unique—opportunity for research of this kind, due to the juxtaposi-
tion of this large number of New Testament and early Christian
manuscripts with an unprecedented array of other literary and documentary papyri.

The present exploration of Jews in Oxyrhynchus is designed to
bring into close proximity New Testament manuscript studies, Jewish-
Christian relations, and papyrology more broadly, in as much as the
Jewish community at Oxyrhynchus was a relevant aspect of the environment of early Christianity there, and, accordingly, part of the
context for the Christian manuscripts in use at that locality. My
specific goal is to determine what can be learned of the Jews, their
community, their religion, and their everyday life at that Egyptian
location from about 100 BCE until around 600 CE—the period covered by documents surviving from the Oxyrhynchus area. This is
not without its difficulties, for the number of clearly Jewish texts
from Oxyrhynchus, at least at present, is small indeed, particularly
letters.[3] This paucity can be illustrated from the three-volume *CPJ*,[4]
which altogether displays 332 documentary papyri and 253 ostraca,
but of the papyri only twenty-eight are strictly Oxyrhynchus papyri,[5]
though five others refer to Oxyrhynchus. These relatively small figures
are the more significant because of the well-recognized penchant of

---

[3] See G.H.R. Horsley, *NewDocs* 3 (1978) 142.

[4] *CPJ* = *Corpus Papyrorum Judaicarum* (ed. V.A. Tcherikover—Alexander Fuks [and
Menahem Stern for vol. 3]; 3 vols.; Cambridge, MA 1957–1964).

[5] P.Oxy. 33 + P.Yale inv.1536 = *CPJ* II 159a+b; P.Oxy. 43 = *CPJ* III 475;
P.Oxy. 100 = *CPJ* III 454; P.Oxy. 276 = *CPJ* II 422; P.Oxy. 335 = *CPJ* II 423;
P.Oxy. 353 = *CPJ* III 482; P.Oxy. 474 = *CPJ* III 475; P.Oxy. 500 = *CPJ* II 448;
P.Oxy. 705 = *CPJ* II 450; P.Oxy. 707 = *CPJ* II 447; P.Oxy. 735 = *CPJ* III 465;
P.Oxy. 816 = *CPJ* II 410; P.Oxy. 899 = *CPJ* II 418e; P.Oxy. 903 = *CPJ* III 457d;
P.Oxy. 1089 = *CPJ* I 154; P.Oxy. 1189 = *CPJ* II 445; P.Oxy. 1205 = *CPJ* III
473; P.Oxy. 1242 = *CPJ* II 157; P.Oxy. 1281 = *CPJ* II 414; P.Oxy. 1429 = *CPJ*
III 477; P.Oxy. 1747 = *CPJ* III 476; P.Oxy. 2019 = *CPJ* III 509; P.Oxy. 2037 =
CPJ III 510; P.Princ. II 42 = *CPJ* II 425; P.Harr. I 142 = *CPJ* III 451; P.Stras.
IV 299 = *CPJ* III 452b; Bodl. Libr. MS. Hebr. d. 86 (P) = *CPJ* III 503; P.Schwartz
ined. = *CPJ* III 516; plus those mentioning Oxyrhynchus: P.Ent. 19 = *CPJ* 127b;
P.Hib. I 90 = *CPJ* 127e; P.Mich. VII 448 = *CPJ* III 463; P.Fay. 39 = *CPJ* III
472a; P.Ryl. IV 603 = *CPJ* III 457a. A number are not relevant, mainly because
the criteria for identifying Jewish/Christian names have changed (see below). Canonical
and deuterocanonical manuscripts known at the time are not included in *CPJ*, nor
are papyri of Philo (or other literary texts).

CPJ to be overly inclusive of presumedly, probably, or possibly Jewish papyri.[6] Of course, this inclusive principle has its positive aspect, for few papyri relevant to Jews are likely to have been missed up to the publication of volume 3 in 1964.[7] The *CPJ*, however, does not include literary papyri, such as biblical manuscripts and those of Philo, though both have relevance for our purposes.[8] A further frustration is that documentary papyri from Oxyrhynchus published since 1964 that are likely to be Jewish are not numerous either, amounting to a mere half dozen, more or less.[9] G.H.R. Horsley succinctly summarizes the situation:

> The major reason for the dearth of Jewish-originated documentary texts in Egypt is the suppression of the Jewish revolt in 115–117 under Trajan, and the decimation of their numbers. . . . Jews very largely had to 'go underground' and though there remained numerically significant communities in a number of larger towns in Egypt . . ., their invisibility in very many others—so far as the evidence indicates—suggests that

---

[6] See Horsley, *NewDocs* 3 (1978) 146; I.F. Fikhman, "L'état des travaux au 'Corpus Papyrorum Judaicarum' IV," *Akten des 21. Internationalen Papyrologenkongresses, Berlin, 13.–19.8. 1995* (APF Beiheft 3; ed. B. Kramer et al.; Stuttgart—Leipzig 1997) 290–296, esp. 291; idem, "Les Juifs d'Égypte à l'époque byzantine d'après les papyrus publiés depuis la parution du 'Corpus Papyrorum Judaicarum' III," *Scripta Classica Israelica* 15 (1996) 223–29, esp. 224–227. Tcherikover, in the "Introduction" to *CPJ* (1, p. xix) does refer to restraint in selecting papyri for inclusion when possibly Jewish *names* constitute the criterion (see below).

[7] On the preparation of a fourth volume, again to contain only documentary texts (papyri, ostraca, etc.) and selected according to revised criteria (over against those of Tcherikover) as to what are surely and what are potentially Jewish texts, see Fikhman, "L'état des travaux," 291.

[8] Manuscripts of the Jewish Greek Bible (including Apocrypha)—whether they are Jewish in origin and use or Christian is a complex issue—are P.Oxy. 403, 656, 845, 846, 1007, 1010, 1073, 1074, 1075, 1076, 1166, 1167, 1168, 1225, 1226, 1351, 1352, 1594, 1595, 1779, 2066, 2386, 3522, 4442, 4443, 4444, P.Harr. I 31, P.Mil.Vogl. I 22, and PSI X 1163. For Philo see P.Oxy. 1173, 1356, 2158; PSI XI 1207; P.Haun. I 8.
    CPJ does include the "semi-literary" "Acts of the Alexandrian Martyrs" (*CPJ* II 154–159, including P.Oxy. 1089, 1242, 33 + P.Yale inv. 1536—from the late second and third centuries), fictional accounts reflecting earlier anti-Jewish sentiments in Alexandria.
    I have not treated these groups of Oxyrhynchus materials in the present paper, due not only to limitations of space, but primarily because of difficulty in determining whether the post-first century CE biblical and related manuscripts were copied and used by Jews or Christians. The same question applies to the Philo manuscripts.

[9] Fikhman, "Les Juifs d'Égypte," 226, points to only three new Oxyrhynchus papyri: P.Oxy. 3203 and 3805, surely Jewish; and P.Oxy. 3314 (Letter of Judas), potentially Jewish. Now P.Oxy. 2745 and CPA VII 2 would be included.

those who survived Trajan had to live near others for solidarity and security.[10]

Oxyrhynchus was one of those larger towns, well known as a location where Jews lived[11] and yielding papyri evidencing Jewish residents from before the Common Era into the late sixth century CE. It must be added immediately, however, that "hardly any evidence remains for any Jews in Egypt from 117 until the end of the third century,"[12] and this general affirmation about Egypt is remarkably accurate for Oxyrhynchus as well, as the ensuing assessment of its papyri demonstrates. This gap in evidence brings into focus a basic, though vexing methodological issue: the differentiation of Jewish documents from others, primarily from Christian materials.

DISTINGUISHING JEWISH DOCUMENTS FROM OTHERS

How do we know which papyri are in fact Jewish—that is, how do we identify papyri written by Jews, referring to Jews, or describing Jewish matters? Naturally, documents with direct reference to someone as a Jew, or other unambiguous indications of Jewish people or practices are the first and obvious objects of our search, but how common are they? Once Jews have been identified with reasonable assurance in our sources—but only then—attempts can be made to discern what the documents' contexts tell us about the Jews, their lives, their culture and religion.

Criteria for identifying Jewish documents—past and present

The excessively inclusive policy of *CPJ* for selecting papyri has been noted, and recently the criteria employed in those volumes have come under renewed scrutiny by Roger S. Bagnall, I.F. Fikhman, and Gideon Bohak, among others. Bohak provides a clear but blunt

---

[10] Horsley, *NewDocs* 3 (1978) 142. See also R.S. Bagnall, *Egypt in Late Antiquity* (Princeton 1993) 276–278.

[11] See Fikhman, "Les Juifs d'Égypte," 227. Other such locations where Jewish papyri of the Byzantine period have been found recently include Apollinopolis Magna, Hermoupolis Magna, Antinoupolis, and perhaps Aphrodito and Heracleopolis.

[12] D. Frankfurter, "Lest Egypt's City be Deserted: Religion and Ideology in the Egyptian Response to the Jewish Revolt (116–117 C.E.)," *JJS* 43 (1992) 203. See Bagnall, *Egypt in Late Antiquity*, 276.278.

critique, after formulating a loose, almost cavalier, and yet essentially accurate paraphrase of the principles employed in *CPJ*:[13]

(1) Anyone identified . . . as a Ἰουδαῖος/-αία is considered a Jew.
(2) Anyone paying a Jewish tax is a Jew.
(3) Anyone bearing a Jewish name is a Jew.
(4) Anyone behaving like a Jew is a Jew.
(5) Anyone who is somehow associated with Jews may be identified as a Jew.

He then evaluates each criterion, in reverse order, with examples to support his points, quite naturally dismissing the last two (numbers 4 and 5) as weak and ambiguous criteria. Numbers 1 and 2, on the other hand, are solid criteria, the first because "in no case can a Ἰουδαῖος/-αία clearly be shown to have been a non-Jew,"[14] and the second because non-Jews considered by tax collectors to be Jews would have "every reason in the world to prove their non-Jewish pedigree and avoid paying."[15] That leaves number 3, the question of Jewish names.

Jewish (and Christian) names

The focus in all the critiques of *CPJ*, then, falls on the middle criterion, "Jewish names," with Bagnall leading the way. For *CPJ*, Victor A. Tcherikover "considered all non-ecclesiastics called by biblical names in the papyrological documents *before* [the death of Constantine— 337 CE] as Jews, *after* it, more probably, as Christians."[16] Yet, basing Jewishness on biblical names is no guarantee of Jewish identity or context after 117 CE, unless other Jewish evidence is present, and this *CPJ* criterion takes us into treacherous territory, as Roger Bagnall has warned.

Bagnall's now frequently cited case begins by seeking "insight into the pace of conversion [to Christianity] in Egypt by examining shifts in patterns of naming"[17] in the papyri. Based on calculations from

---

[13] G. Bohak, "Good Jews, Bad Jews, and Non-Jews in Greek Papyri and Inscriptions," *Akten des 21. Internationalen Papyrologenkongresses* (eds. B. Kramer et al.) 105–112; his list is on 105.

[14] G. Bohak, "Good Jews," 111 n. 21.

[15] G. Bohak, "Good Jews," 111.

[16] *CPJ* I, p. xviii. See his full statement of the name criterion, xvii–xix.

[17] R. Bagnall, "Religious Conversion and Onomastic Change in Early Byzantine Egypt," *BASP* 19 (1982) 108.

names in various identifiable groups of papyri, especially Christian names as he defines them (see below) and Christian and/or pagan names among fathers and sons, he demonstrates that, as the Christianization of Egypt accelerated, Christians began to use biblical names increasingly, especially in the early fourth century. More specifically, the papyri show that biblical and distinctly Christian names were given by converts to their children, then by fathers with Christian names to their sons, as Egypt's Christian population increased. Bagnall calculates that after gradual increases of Christians, there was "a sharp rise ... from about 310 to 360," with Christians constituting 50% of the population around 320–325, 80% shortly after the mid-fourth century, and at least 90% by 400.[18] By this time those bearing Christian names were about 60% of the population.[19]

Bagnall, in the definition of Christian names used in his calculations, assumes that Old Testament and New Testament names in the fourth century are Christian names and not those of Jews. His grounds for excluding Jews are twofold: "the drastic decrease in Jewish population in Trajan's suppression of their revolt" and that all his data are from the country and not from Alexandria[20]—where Jews would be more likely. He admits, of course, that some Jews will be among those with biblical names, but "if a handful are, the results will not be altered in any substantial way"[21]—and it is that very handful of Jewish individuals to which we shall be alert. In short, for Bagnall, after 117 the dearth in non-biblical Jewish names in Egypt is great, and "Biblical names securely attributable to Jews are equally rare."[22]

---

[18] R. Bagnall, "Religious Conversion," 121–23; quotation from 121. E. Wipszycka, "La valeur de l'onomastique pour l'histoire de la christianisation de l'Egypt. A propos d'une étude de R.S. Bagnall," *ZPE* 62 (1986) 173–181, disagrees, noting, e.g., that Christianity did not spread evenly in Egypt; cf. Bagnall's "Conversion and Onomastics: A Reply," *ZPE* 69 (1987) 243–250 [reprinted in his *Later Roman Egypt: Society, Religion, Economy and Administration* (Burlington, VT 2003) nos. VIII and IX, same pagination]. On the entire matter, see Horsley, *NewDocs* 3 (1978) 146–147; idem, "Forfeiture of Jewish Property," *NewDocs* 4 (1979) 210–212; idem, "Name Change as an Indication of Religious Conversion in Antiquity," *Numen* 43 (1987) 8–12.

[19] Bagnall, "Religious Conversion," chart on 124.

[20] Bagnall, "Religious Conversion," 110. See his five categories of Christian names, 110–111.

[21] Bagnall, "Religious Conversion," 110.

[22] Bagnall, "Religious Conversion," 276.

Bohak points out that "many supposed 'Jewish names' actually were common to several Semitic nations,"[23] and insists that "to make sure that a given 'Jewish name' indeed was limited to Jews alone, we must first examine its appearance, in Egypt and elsewhere, among non-Jews,"[24] an eminently reasonable principle. Fikhman suggests a further caution: "The use of onomastics must be more circumspect for later dates [i.e., after the Ptolemaic period] because of mixed marriages, the hellenization of the Egyptian upper strata (also, in part, the Jews), and the assimilation of the lower foreign ethnic element by the local Egyptian population."[25]

Identification of Individual Jews

Jews, of course, certainly used biblical names through the first century CE,[26] and, "in the third century and to a certain measure in the second century BCE, names reflected the ethnic identity of their bearers."[27] Oxyrhynchus records several names from 6 BCE until about 93 CE that—given their first century time frame—might well be Jewish, although in no case is there any other confirmatory information to indicate that they are Jews.[28] These include:

---

[23] Bohak, "Good Jews, Bad Jews, and Non-Jews," 109.

[24] Bohak, "Good Jews, Bad Jews, and Non-Jews," 110.

[25] I.F. Fikhman, "On Onomastics of Greek and Roman Egypt," *Classical Studies in Honor of David Sohlberg* (ed. Ranon Katzoff et al.; Ramat Gan 1996) 405.

[26] One estimate is that ten to fifteen percent of the Egyptian population in the first century CE was Jewish: H.A. Green, "The Socio-Economic Background of Christianity in Egypt," *The Roots of Egyptian Christianity* (ed. B.A. Pearson—J.E. Goehring; SAC; Philadelphia 1986) 110. But see now A. Wasserstein, "The Number and Provenance of Jews in Graeco-Roman Antiquity: A Note on Population Statistics," *Classical Studies in Honor of David Sohlberg* (ed. Ranon Katzoff et al.; Ramat Gan 1996) 307–317, esp. 313–314, who cautions against specific numbers for population or for percentages of Jews in the population, though it is likely to be correct to say that "in some places at some times there were 'many' or 'very many' Jews" and that Jews—due to their prominence in various places—gave an impression of being numerous.

[27] Fikhman, "On Onomastics of Greek and Roman Egypt," 405; see also 413: "For the Ptolemaic period, even for the third century BCE, when . . . names can be taken as a reliable ethnical indicator, many Jews bore Greek names which, without the definition Ἰουδαῖος, Ἰουδαία would never lead us to believe that the bearers were Jews." Fikhman illustrates this with a Fayum papyrus (CPR XVIII = P.Vindob.G. 40618) that lists twenty-four "indisputable Jews" who bear eighteen names that—with one exception—are Greek "or, at best, Greek names favored by Jews because they were a Greek translation of a Jewish name."

[28] Given below are common Jewish names up to the late first century CE. Horsley,

Jesous ('Ιησοῦς) = Joshua (P.Oxy. 816 = *CPJ* II 410; 6/5 BCE), in an account with names and sums of money. Jesous/Jesus/Joshua is a common Jewish name.[29]

Josepos ('Ιωσῆπος) = Joseph (P.Oxy. 1281 = *CPJ* III 414; 21 CE), in a loan agreement, whereby Josepos, in effect, loans money to a weaver for an order of linen cloths, which, when delivered, will cancel the loan. Joseph (in various forms) is an extremely common Jewish name.[30]

Dositheos (Δοσίθεος), Josepos ('Ιωσῆπος[31]) = Joseph, and Bokchoris (Βοκχῶρις) (CPR VII 2, 1st century CE), in a list, perhaps of residents of Oxyrhynchus, including seven people.[32] Dositheos was "perhaps the most common Jewish name in Egypt" and "it appears to be a purely Jewish name,"[33] and Bokchoris could well be Jewish because the name, "Bokchoris son of Josepos," is found on five

---

NewDocs 4 (1979) 211, lists all papyri in *CPJ* that contain common Jewish names but which Horsley views as *possibly* in doubt because of Bagnall's hypothesis—and which *may* be Christian. Included are P.Oxy. 43 = *CPJ* III 475 (after 295 CE), Jacob, guard (see N. Lewis, *BASP* 18 [1981] 76–77); and P.Oxy. 1747 = *CPJ* III 476 (third/fourth century CE), Isak. See also P.Köln III.159 (from Oxyrhynchus, fifth/sixth century) containing Johannes (bis) and Jacob.—Other Oxyrhynchus occurrences of common Jewish/Biblical names in the third and fourth centuries and doubtful as Jewish are P.Oxy. 735 = *CPJ* III 465 (205 CE), Barichius, soldier [but see our discussion, below]; P.Hibeh I 90 = *CPJ* I 127e (222 CE), Dositheos; P.Oxy. 1429 = *CPJ* III 477 (300 CE), Isak, manager; P.Fay. 39 = *CPJ* III 472a (third century CE), refers to Johannes, a donkey-driver from Oxyrhynchus (?); and P.Oxy. 4612 (363 CE), Moses. See also P.Oxy. 2124, Jacob, ex-collector of grain dues in the village of Dositheou, who is identified as Jewish and a descendent of Jewish military settlers there, perhaps in the Ptolemaic period, by Kasher, *Jews in Hellenistic and Roman Egypt*, 93, though the evidence for a Jewish Jacob here is not apparent.

[29] I refer to T. Ilan, *Lexicon of Jewish Names in Late Antiquity: Part I, Palestine 330 BCE–200 CE* (TSAJ 91; Tübingen 2002) 126–133; and also HRCS, ad loc.; and *CPJ*, "Prosopography of the Jews in Egypt," 3, pp. 167–196; esp. 180.

[30] Ilan, *Lexicon of Jewish Names*, 150–68; HRCS, ad loc.; cf. *CPJ*, 3, pp. 182–83.

[31] Read 'Ιωσῆφος rather than 'Ιώσεφος (according to the photograph): E. Boswinkel—W. Clarysse—P.W. Pestman—H.-A. Rupprecht (eds.), *Berichtigungsliste der Griechischen Papyrusurkunden aus Ägypten* (Leiden 1986) 7.45. In Palestine, "Joseph was the second most popular name in the Second Temple period after Simon" (Ilan, *Lexicon of Jewish Names*, 158).

[32] For details, see H. Zilliacus—J. Frösén—Paavo Hohti—Jorma Kaimio—Maarit Kaimio (eds.), *Corpus Papyrorum Raineri, Band VII. Griechische Texte, IV* (2 vols.; Vienna 1979) 1.11–13 + pl. 2. The papyrus, with eleven lines remaining, was edited by J. Kaimio, who gives the provenance as "Oxyrhynchos?"

[33] CPR VII 2, p. 13; see Ilan, *Lexicon of Jewish Names*, 273–276; cf. *CPJ* III, pp. 173–174.

ostraca from Edfu—five receipts—dated 99–102 and 107 CE, one of which (*CPJ* II 196; 102 CE) is for "the Jewish tax."[34]

Jacob (Ἰάκουβος) and Ptollas (Πτολλᾶς) (P.Oxy. 276 = *CPJ* III 422; 77 CE), in a receipt for a shipment of grain by a cargo boat that had three steersmen: the name of the first is missing, but he is the son of Jacob; and the name of the third is damaged, but he is the son of Tryphon (Τρύφων).[35] Jacob is a common Jewish name,[36] and Ptollas also is frequent among Egyptian Jews, with clear instances in a Jewish tax list, not from Oxyrhynchus, but from Arsinoe, that dates within four years of P.Oxy. 276, that is, 73 CE.[37] The editors of *CPJ* II 422 restore the incomplete name of the third steersman as κ[αὶ Σίμ]ων, Simon, but the restoration remains a conjecture.

Jacob (Ἰάκοβος) (P.Princ. II 42 [see pl. VI], from Oxyrhynchus = *CPJ* III 425; 93 CE) occurs twice in an account (col. II, line 21, and col. III, line 32).

Actually, whether these names are Jewish or not turns out to be immaterial for our interests, for the context—actually, the lack thereof—in each case leaves us bereft of any information about them as Jews or as members of the Jewish community of Oxyrhynchus.

It is well known that individuals are identified in documentary papyri, especially in legal documents, by a wide range of descriptive terms, such as official titles (*strategos, gymnasiarch, grammateus*, public doctor, city clerk, etc.); a personal seal; lineage (son/daughter of, father/mother of, etc.); an alias; and socio-political status (citizen, freedman or freedwoman, slave; or Roman, Alexandrian, Egyptian, etc.); but most commonly by age, scars, or other physical features, and by trade or occupation.[38] The most commonly used physical

---

[34] CPR VII 2, p. 13; the others are *CPJ* II 301 (police tax), 306 (dyke tax), 309 and 342 (poll tax). The context offers nothing else Jewish, nor anything informative about this group of residents.

[35] For Tryphon, see Ilan, *Lexicon of Jewish Names*, 308–309. cf. the indexes in *CPJ* I, p. 286; 2, p. 334; cf. 3, p. 194.

[36] Besides a few hundred occurrences in the normal spelling (Ἰάκωβος), Ἰάκουβος occurs once in the LXX and often in other papyri: see *CPJ* III, p. 179; Ilan, *Lexicon of Jewish Names*, 171–174.

[37] See *CPJ* II 421, lines 164, 189, 192; cf. 186. Ptollas occurs five times in B.W. Jones—J.E.G. Whitehorne, *Register of Oxyrhynchites, 30 B.C.–A.D. 96* (ASP 25; Chico 1983) 196; cf. *CPJ* III, p. 188.

[38] E.g., P.Oxy. 4441 (January 315–February 316 CE) contains reports to the *logistes* of Oxyrhynchus from a public doctor and from guilds of builders, with numerous individuals listed with their trades—some fourteen different occupations.

features are age, height, skin color, facial shape, form of the nose, position of the eyes, and scars or spots. A recent study by I.F. Fikhman on the appearance of Egyptian Jews shows only that "Egyptian Jews were generally of medium height, light-skinned and long faced; but [he says] such a result is not too impressive."[39] For one thing, the number of Jews identified by physical appearance is small, and the only relevant Oxyrhynchus papyrus (CPR VII 2, first century CE), discussed above, is a list of seven people, perhaps residents. Four are identified by scars and facial shape—in this case "round-faced" (στρογγυλοπρόσωπος)—and three by scars only. Most of these individuals are without doubt Jewish—given the first century date and several of the names (including Dositheos, Joseph, and Bokchoris)—among them one (perhaps two) of the round-faced quartet. This Oxyrhynchus papyrus, however, is alone in describing Jews as "round-faced" and moves against Fikhman's generalization of Jews as long-faced in Egypt, but this is a matter, after all, of little consequence, for the unclear content and context of this particular papyrus tell us nothing else about these likely Jewish residents of Oxyrhynchus in the first century.

No clearly Jewish individuals appear in records of Oxyrhynchus in the remainder of the second century except an Onias and possibly a couple of Jewish soldiers from or in that city, and some cases of specific identification as a "Jew" from the beginning of the fourth century (Jose), in the fifth (Enoch), and in the sixth century (Lazar [?]) will be treated below.

In summary, the previous use, especially in *CPJ*, of common Jewish names to identify Jews has suffered a severe setback—and rightly so. Three factors appear to be prominent in the lack of Jewish evidence from 117 CE until the end of the third century, namely, (1) the difficulty of ascertaining names that are genuinely Jewish; (2) the decreasing proportion of biblical names among Jews while Christians are rapidly increasing in numbers and co-opting biblical names; and

---

[39] I.F. Fikhman, "The Physical Appearance of Egyptian Jews according to the Greek Papyri," *Scripta Classica Israelica* 18 (1999) 131–138; esp. 136. Reprinted as "La description physique des Juifs égyptiens d'après les papyrus grecs," *Atti del XXII Congresso Internazionale di Papirologia, Firenze 1998* (ed. Isabella Andorlini et al.; 2 vols.; Florence 2001) 1.461–468. Some stereotypical Jewish features, says Fikhman, were not found: hooked nose and sharp nose; at the same time, only among Jews did he find light blue eyes ("Physical Appearance," 135).

(3) the drastic reduction of the Jewish population in Egypt after the devastation of Jews in and following the Revolt of 115–117 CE. Oxyrhynchus provides us with information on that struggle and its long-lasting effects upon Jewish people and their communities.

The Jewish Revolt of 115–117 CE

Two Oxyrhynchus papyri deal with the forfeiture or confiscation of Jewish property following the Revolt. First, P.Oxy. 1189 (= CPJ II 445; ca. 117 CE[40]), a letter (with a copy) from the *strategos* of a neighboring nome, the Heracleopolite, to Apollonius, *strategos* of the Oxyrhynchite nome, referring to "a list of property that belonged to the Jews" (... περὶ γραφῆς τῶν τοῖς Ἰουδαίοις ὑπαρξάντων, lines 9–10) and indicating that the list was attached to the letter (though the concluding portion of the letter is missing). The sender requests that Apollonius should keep one copy of the letter and the list, and send the other one to Sabinus, *strategos* of the Kynopolite nome. Nothing else is preserved, but a *strategos* of Oxyrhynchus named Apollonius is known from P.Oxy. 74 (116 CE) and P.Oxy. 97 (115–116 CE), a virtual guarantee that the letter to him concerns property that had been confiscated (or is to be taken) as a consequence of the Jewish revolt. If so, it is clear that such property was to be found in all three of the nomes mentioned.[41]

Second, P.Oxy. 500 (= CPJ II 448; 130 CE) is a lease of public land, though the document is badly damaged at the relevant point (line 11), so much so that Grenfell and Hunt did not attempt its restoration. A reconstruction to read "Jews who had been killed" (Ἰ]ουδαίω[ν ἀν]ειρη[μ]ένων) was, in turn, altered by changing a single letter to read "Jews who had been stricken by confiscatory measures" or "whose property had been confiscated" Ἰ]ουδαίω[ν ἀφ]ειρη[μ]ένων).[42] Actually, two juridical categories of public land—

---

[40] P.Oxy. 97, though itself undated, is joined to another document, with the date 115–116 CE (P.Oxy. I, p. 169).

[41] CPJ II 445, p. 252.

[42] Grenfell and Hunt later accepted the reading ἀν]ειρη[μ]ένων, as did CPJ II 448. But ἀφ]ειρη[μ]ένων was adopted by J. Mélèze-Modrzejewski, *The Jews of Egypt: From Rameses II to Emperor Hadrian* (tr. R. Cornman; Philadelphia—Jerusalem 5755–1995) 217–218; see his full discussion; a plate of P.Oxy. 500 is on p. 219. Mélèze-Modrzejewski has no footnotes, but his bibliography refers to Anna Świderek, "Ἰουδαικὸς λόγος," JJP 16/17 (1971) 45–62, esp. 60 n. 23; cf. 47 n. 6, who is

land that had reverted to the state—were involved in this lease: first, confiscated land that had belonged to Jewish rebels, and, second, land "that once belonged to Greeks who died without heirs" (line 12), presumably Greek combatants in the war.[43] This double standard was in accordance with Roman law: land of deceased Greeks without heirs reverted to the state, while sedition was punishable by death or deportation and confiscation of property. The effect of this latter regulation was devastating for the Egyptian Jewish population.[44]

A third papyrus from this very time, P.Oxy. 100 (= *CPJ* III 454; 133 CE), also may attest the earlier confiscation of Jewish property, for it preserves an oath by Marcus Antonius Dius, former *strategos* of Alexandria, regarding the sale of „four βίκοι [a square measure[45]] from the remaining open lots that I own in the Cretan street/close and the Jewish [lane/district]" in Oxyrhynchus (lines 8–10). The last phrase reads ἐπ᾽ ἀμφόδου Κρητικοῦ καὶ Ἰουδαϊκῆς . . ., linking the neuter ἄμφοδον with "Cretan," but requiring a feminine noun with "Jewish." Yet, ἄμφοδος, feminine, also exists, and could be the implied noun with "Jewish"; λαύρα was suggested in *CPJ* since Ἰουδαϊκὴ λαύρα is found in a papyrus from Hermoupolis,[46] though the usages of both terms (ἄμφοδον and λαύρα) were debated and recently have been revised.[47] The best translation of ἀμφόδου appears to be "block of houses with surrounding streets," captured in the chiefly British term, "close."

Incidentally, the Jewish area in Oxyrhynchus is attested by P.Oxy. 335 (= *CPJ* II 423), which, around 85 CE, employs the term ἄμφοδον

---

actually responsible for the second proposed reading, and this was fully acknowledged in Mélèze-Modrzejewski's earlier, more detailed discussion of P.Oxy. 500: "ΙΟΥΔΑΙΟΙ ΑΦΗΙΡΗΜΕΝΟΙ: La fin de la communauté juive d'Egypte (115–117 de n.è.)," *Symposion 1985: Vorträge zur griechischen und hellenistischen Rechtsgeschichte (Ringberg, 24.–26. Juli 1985)* (ed. G. Thür; Akten der Gesellschaft für griechische und hellenistische Rechtsgeschichte 6; Cologne—Vienna 1989) 342–351, esp. 348–350. 353–355. 359–360. See also Horsley, *NewDocs* 4 (1979) 210.

[43] Mélèze-Modrzejewski, *The Jews of Egypt*, 217–218.
[44] Mélèze-Modrzejewski, *The Jews of Egypt*, 217–222.
[45] See the same word in P.Oxy. 3334 (line 8) and the note there (p. 64).
[46] *CPJ* III 454: see P.Amh. II 98, line 10; late second/third century (= *CPJ* III 468).
[47] LSJ defined λαύρα as "alley, lane, passage," and ἄμφοδον as "street," "block of houses surrounded by streets," hence, "ward, quarter of a town." But the definitions of both terms have been modified in LSJ, *Revised Supplement* (1996): ἄμφοδον—delete "*quarter of a town*"; λαύρα—add "*district* or *quarter* of a city," in effect reversing their previous defined usages.

in registering the sale of „the sixth part of a house in the Jewish
street/close" (ἐπ᾿ ἀμφόδου Ἰουδα[ι]κ[ου]), which had been sold "to
Nikaia Silbanos (?), the daughter of Psoubios, those among the Jews
of the city of Oxyrhynchus, by Paul" (. . . τῶν ἀπ᾿ Ὀξ(υρύγχων) πόλ(εως)
Ἰου[δ]αίων). Aryeh Kasher, apparently appealing to these two phrases,
draws two conclusions: first, that "the house had passed through the
hands of two Jewish owners at least," and, second, that such a "formal reference" used "in accordance with the legal terminology" of
Roman Egypt implies "that the organized body of Jewish residents
in Oxyrhynchus had won political recognition from the Roman
authorities."[48] Whether or not this is somewhat overdrawn, it is clear
that there was an organized and recognized Jewish community in
Oxyrhynchus around 85 CE. Moreover, from at least 85 until 133
CE, the existence of a Jewish close in Oxyrhynchus is documented,
though that is not to say that many or any Jews lived there from
117 to 133 or even for another century or more.

In addition, an account of a trial held around 136 CE and written on the verso of a roll, P.Oxy. 707 (= *CPJ* II 447), contains on
the recto remnants of a land survey that includes a reference to
"open lots, in which there are buildings burned by the Jews": ψιλ(οὶ)
τόπ(οι) ἐν οἷ[ς] κέλλαι ἐμπ(ρησθεῖσαι) ὑπὸ τῶν Ἰουδαίων)[49] It may be
assumed that the recto of this roll was utilized for a document before
the verso was so used, suggesting that the record on the recto was
written sometime before 136, a date that makes plausible a connection to the Jewish Revolt of 115–117.[50] If the reference to "buildings burned by Jews" was recorded closer to 136 than to 117, P.Oxy.
707 would indicate that "marks of destruction remained for at least
a generation."[51] This connection with the Revolt is supported by
other non-Oxyrhynchus papyri that refer to damage from the war,

---

[48] A. Kasher, *The Jews in Hellenistic and Roman Egypt: The Struggle for Equal Rights*
(TSAJ 7; Tübingen 1985) 150–151; he assumes that Paulus and Nicea Silvanus are
Jews with adopted Roman names, that is, *praenomina* (ibid., 84). (Kasher's material
on Oxyrhynchus was published earlier in his "The Jewish Community of Oxyrhynchus
in the Roman Period," *JJS* 32 [1981] 151–157.)

[49] *CPJ* (and others) accept the reading ἐμπ(ρησθεῖσαι), "burnt by the Jews," rather
than the original editor's ἐμπ(οιούμεναι), "built by the Jews": see F. Bilabel,
Berichtigungsliste der Griechischen Papyrusurkunden aus Ägypten (Heidelberg 1929) I. 326.

[50] P.Oxy. IV 707, p. 169, says "early in the second century," followed by *CPJ*
II, p. 255, where it is placed among papyri relating to the war of 115–117.

[51] Kasher, *Jews in Hellenistic and Roman Egypt*, 152.

especially P. Giss. 41 (= *CPJ* II 443; from Hermoupolis, 28th November 117 CE), an application for a leave from duty:

> For not only are my affairs completely uncared for because of my long absence, but also, because of the attack of the impious Jews, practically everything I possess in the villages of the Hermoupolite nome and in the metropolis needs my attention. (column II, lines 1–9, *CPJ* II 443).[52]

And a mutilated Fayum papyrus (BGU III 889 = *CPJ* II 449) from 151 CE tells—even at that late date—of "properties . . . for the most part waste and disused . . . [here the text is broken] . . . in the Jewish disturbance (ἐν τῷ Ἰουδαϊκῷ ταράχῳ) . . . and is still unfruitful" (καὶ μέχρι νῦν ἄφορος) (lines 22–24)—thirty-four years later![53]

In summary, relying on the revised reading of P.Oxy. 500 and the content of P.Oxy. 1189, J. Mélèze-Modrzejewski described the resulting situation:

> A clear picture of events now emerges: after two years of warfare, much of the land was no longer being tilled, and immediate emergency measures were necessary. The administration of state land took control of the property of the deceased combatants. . . . With all proper reserve due to the approximate nature of our data, it would appear that the losses of the [Jewish] rebels represented all the property once owned by the Jews of Egypt.[54]

> Deprived of their homes and their lands, they could no longer form a nucleus for a possible reconstruction. . . . In Alexandria and in all the rest of the country, the days of Hellenized Jewry had come to an end.[55]

---

[52] Part of the family archive of Apollonios, *strategos* during the Jewish Revolt, containing more than two hundred papyri from Hermopolis: see *CPJ* II, pp. 226–227; more recently, J. Rowlandson (ed.), *Women and Society in Greek and Roman Egypt: A Sourcebook* (Cambridge 1998) 118–124.

[53] *CPJ* III 516 (Oxyrhynchus; 2nd century CE) might be noted: This mutilated papyrus of six lines names two locations that appear to be Oxyrhynchite villages, then has the following text, as best it can be read: "And by supplementary notices . . . debit . . . (year) of Hadrian . . . in respect of the above-mentioned Jews . . . all of them (in all?), 40 (+x?) artabai . . . by Petronius M(amertinus) . . ." (*CPJ* III, p. 108). The final name appears to refer to a prefect of Egypt 133–137, subsequent to the Jewish Revolt, prompting the editor to ask, "Does it refer to some payment imposed upon Jews?" (107).

[54] Mélèze-Modrzejewski, *The Jews of Egypt*, 218. He supports this from SB XII 10892, a long papyrus roll from the Fayum, dating shortly after 188 CE, and recording, in portions of seven surviving columns, four plots of land taken from Greeks compared to eighteen from Jews (for details, see his "ΙΟΥΔΑΙΟΙ," 361 and note 103).

[55] Mélèze-Modrzejewski, *The Jews of Egypt*, 222: See his full discussion and argu-

This bleak assessment may be overly severe, for "there is some evidence for the rudimentary survival of the Alexandrian Jewish population and leadership,"[56] and some Jews undoubtedly remained in Oxyrhynchus and other larger towns after 117,[57] for remnants of at least a modest recovery of the Jewish community can be garnered, over time, from Oxyrhynchus (see below). Yet, for the remainder of the second century and for nearly the entire third century, no evidence of Jews or Jewish presence or activity is extant from Oxyrhynchus, with one or two possible exceptions: the family of a certain Onias and some Hebrew soldiers.

Evidence of Jews following the Revolt of 115–117

The sobering situation described by Bagnall and others means that validating names as Jewish rather than Christian, especially in the second through the fourth centuries CE, will be difficult when no corroborating evidence for one or the other exists. Yet, the attempt must not be repressed, though we shall have to tread cautiously in our search. Naturally, Jewish names will not have been highlighted in the post-117 period.

In 126 CE, a certain Onias is mentioned in an official record of receipts for the Oxyrhynchite village of Sesphtha (P.Harr. I 142 [line 16] = *CPJ* III 451). Yet, his name functions merely as an identifier,

---

ment ibid., 217–22. D. Frankfurter, "Lest Egypt's City be Deserted," *JJS* 43 (1992) 203–220, esp. 204.214–215.219–220, marshals an impressive case that Egyptian priests developed a nationalist "mythology of xenophobia" (ibid., 212) against the Jews, which, after the war, was incorporated into the Oxyrhynchus festival in honor of the victory over the Jews (P.Oxy. 705, discussed below); he points out that the Roman legions apparently were unable to mount the battle, so that "native Egyptian and Greco-Egyptian conscripts" were mobilized, concluding that "these armies must have exterminated practically the entire Jewish population" (ibid., 203–204; cf. 207) and that "Egyptian Jewry itself had become a thing of the past" (ibid., 220). See also Bagnall, *Egypt in Late Antiquity*, 275–276; Fikhman, "Les Juifs d'Égypte," 223 and note 2. For a recent, general description of the Revolt, see R. Alston, *Soldier and Society in Roman Egypt: A Social History* (London—New York 1995) 75–77.

[56] D. Frankfurter, "Lest Egypt's City be Deserted," 204 note 5.

[57] Horsley, *NewDocs* 3 (1978) 142. Kasher, *Jews in Hellenistic and Roman Egypt*, discusses the evidence for Jews—employing papyrological materials—in Ptolemaic (ibid., 29–74) through Roman times (ibid., 75–167). Note particularly the lack of Jews or their lack of participation in the metropolises (ibid., 93–97), especially in the gymnasium (ibid., 98); Jews as farmers (ibid., 98–105); and Kasher's extensive, detailed discussion of Jewish communities in the Egyptian chora—in both Ptolemaic and Roman times (ibid., 106–167).

because the mother of the persons involved in the transaction is
named Herakleia, the "daughter of Onias" ('Ονίας). Whether Onias
is still alive at the time of this document is not clear. Although the
name Onias is not in the Hebrew Bible, four members of a priestly
family, Onias I–IV, were prominent from about 300 BCE to around
160 BCE. Of interest here is that in 164 BCE Onias IV had immi-
grated to Egypt, where he was prominent around the Heliopolite
nome: he built a Jewish temple at Leontopolis, headed a Jewish
army, and served as a general under the Ptolemies, as did his sons.[58]
Due undoubtedly to this history, Onias was a quite common Jewish
name in both Hebrew and Greek in Palestine, but appears to be
found only a few other times in the papyri.[59] Hence, this Oxyrhynchus
Onias, in a record of the early second century, might well meet the
newer criterion on names (discussed above), and he could well have
been a Jew who was living (or had lived) in a village in the
Oxyrhynchite nome, whose daughter and/or her offspring flourished
around 126 CE, though we know nothing else about Onias or the
others in this official record—not even whether the daughter and/or
her children considered themselves Jewish.[60]

Jews are known to have served in the Roman army, though not
in the regular army—the legions—but in the auxiliary forces (auxi-
lia).[61] Two papyri relating to Oxyrhynchus possibly provide such evidence: P.Oxy. 735 (= CPJ III 465; 205 CE) is an account, in Latin,
of a monthly distribution of wheat to a detachment of fifty Roman
soldiers, and it includes a few names that some have taken to indi-

---

[58] See ABD 5.23–24. On "the 'Land of Onias,' the well-known Jewish military
settlement," see Kasher, Jews in Hellenistic and Roman Egypt, 119.

[59] For numerous occurrences, see Ilan, Lexicon of Jewish Names, 377–79; HRCS,
ad loc.; cf. CPJ I 132 [possibly Onias IV]; I 137 (50 BCE), for which an Onias
serves as scribe; III 453 (132 CE). See also SB V 7781, a grave inscription (1st century BCE).

[60] Coincidentally, or otherwise, P.Oxy. 1747 (= CPJ III 476; late 3rd or early
4th century) refers to an Isaac ('Ισάκ), son of Miysis (line 50) of the same Oxyrhynchite
village, Sesphtha, as Onias. This is in a list of people required by the government
to perform work of some kind. Kasher, Jews in Hellenistic and Roman Egypt, 102,
understands Isaac to be one of two Jewish farmers in the list (though he refers to
lines 40 and 52, which do not make sense), and views their inclusion as a clear
sign of "low status." But Isaac is a common name in the papyri. Cf. F. Preisigke,
Namenbuch (Heidelberg 1922); D. Foraboschi, Onomasticon alterum papyrologicum (Milan
1971) and among Christians in this period and later.

[61] See Kasher, Jews in Hellenistic and Roman Egypt, 78–80.

cate Hebrew extraction (Zabdius, Gaddius, Malichus, Barichius). But these are common Semitic names, and "although they sound Semitic, most . . . are not Jewish."[62] The one that might be Jewish is Barichius, since his name appears to be a "typical Hebrew name," and occurs in Jewish inscriptions.[63] It is not clear, however, what this document's connection with Oxyrhynchus might be, other than its discovery there.

The second text, also in Latin, is highly fragmentary and its interpretation is unclear: P.Mich. VII 448 (= *CPJ* III 463; provenance unknown; late second century CE) is some kind of military camp record. It includes the words,]*Oxyrinchis Ebr*[, as line 8, and its editor, Henry A. Sanders, reports that *Ebra* "suggests" *Ebraeus*, namely, Ἑβραῖος,[64] which would be equivalent to Ἰουδαῖος. Hence, the phrase would designate a Jewish soldier from or at Oxyrhynchus,[65] though again in an auxiliary unit.[66]

Finally, an enigmatic papyrus from Oxyrhynchus dating in the second century CE (P.Stras. IV 299 = *CPJ* III 452b) lists various taxes levied—described as "dues" or "additional charges"—including one on the "commerce of the Jews" (ἐμπορίας Ἰουδαίων, line 14). Actually a very small payment was involved, but such a tax is otherwise unknown, and the editor, Menahem Stern, wondered whether this assessment was connected with the 115–117 Revolt, as were the confiscation and sale of Jewish property, etc. This, however, is difficult to know, and perhaps more to the point is Stern's suggestion that this special tax on Jewish commerce might indicate that, though suffering great losses, the Jewish community in Oxyrhynchus continued to exist in the second century and undoubtedly played a roll in the third century recovery.[67]

Yet, for perhaps a century and a half—except for Onias, possibly a "Hebrew" soldier or two, and this special tax—there is silence

---

[62] Kasher, *Jews in Hellenistic and Roman Egypt*, 80. That some might be Jewish, see P.Oxy. IV, p. 227; *CPJ* III 465, p. 25. See some variations in the re-edition by R.O. Fink, *Roman Military Records on Papyrus* (Philological Monographs of the American Philological Association 26; Cleveland, OH 1971) no. 81.

[63] *CPJ* III 465, p. 25. See also Ilan, *Lexicon of Jewish Names*, 84.

[64] P.Mich. VII 448, 81. Sanders notes that *Oxyrinchis* is an ablative of place of the neuter plural name of the town.

[65] Ibid.; *CPJ* III 463, p. 23.

[66] Kasher, *Jews in Hellenistic and Roman Egypt*, 79–80.

[67] *CPJ* III 452b, p. 8.

in Oxyrhynchus regarding the presence or activity of Jews. Of course, this silence is itself based on an argument from silence—it could all be the result of randomness in the survival of papyrus records. Silence, however, still has its voice and makes a point: Jews and Jewish activity have been vastly diminished in Oxyrhynchus.

Festival of victory over the Jews (P.Oxy. 705)

However, any Jews, such as Onias or his family members, who remained in Oxyrhynchus between 117 to around 200 CE had insult added to injury, for via P.Oxy. 705 (= *CPJ* II 450; 199–200 CE[68]) the Emperors Septimus Severus and Caracalla grant a request from Aurelius Horion, an affluent Alexandrian who owned land in the Oxyrhynchite nome, for support to Oxyrhynchite villages that are "utterly exhausted by the burdensome demands of . . . the Treasury" and are "in danger of insolvency and leaving your land uncultivated" (see lines 59–74). Horion's request had included the following statements, among others, about the Oxyrhynchites—obviously intended to flatter the Emperors:

> [The Oxyrhynchites] also possess the goodwill, faithfulness, and friendship to the Romans that they exhibited in the war against the Jews (κατὰ τὸν Εἰουδίαους πόλεμον), giving aid then and even now celebrating the day of victory as a festival every year (καὶ ἔτι καὶ νῦν τὴν τῶν ἐπινεικίων ἡμέραν ἑκάστου ἔτους πενηγυρίτοντας). (Lines 31–35)[69]

It is unclear how long this festival persisted at Oxyrhynchus, but Horion speaks of it, some eighty years after the war, as current even

---

[68] On the date, see Bilabel, *Berichtigungsliste*, II 96, who refers to this dating by J. Hasebroek, *Untersuchungen zur Geschichte des Kaisers Septimius Severus* (Heidelberg 1921) 121–122. H. MacLennan, *Oxyrhynchus: An Economic and Social Study* (Princeton 1935; repr. Chicago 1968) draws conclusions that go beyond the evidence, e.g., Oxyrhynchus "was consistently anti-Jewish" (20; cf. 14).

[69] Translations of these portions of P.Oxy. 705 have been modified slightly from P.Oxy. IV, p. 163 (where the Revolt of 115–117 is not invoked specifically) by use of J.H. Oliver, *Greek Constitutions of Early Roman Emperors from Inscriptions and Papyri* (Philadelphia 1989) 474–481; and Mélèze-Modrzejewski, *The Jews of Egypt*, 223 (who, along with Oliver, assumes the 115–117 war). See Mélèze-Modrzejewski's full discussion, 222–225, where it is noted that a loan from this fund was recorded in an Oxyrhynchus papyrus dating 225 CE. Horion also set up an endowment from which prizes were provided for winners of the annual ephebic games at Oxyrhynchus, which still were active at the outset of the fourth century (ibid., 225). See also K.J. Rigby, "Sacred Ephebic Games at Oxyrhynchus," *ChrÉg* 52 (1977) 147–155, esp. 149–150.

in 200—something not likely to be falsified. And it was exceptional, for among all the Egyptian papyri, this is the only one to speak of a public holiday for a "day of victory."[70]

In addition, any Jews in Oxyrhynchus later in the third century may have faced opposition, not from the Romans as previously, but now from some of the Christians whose numbers had vastly increased.

An anti-Jewish dialogue (P.Oxy. 2070)

As our survey moves into the late third century, it is appropriate to mention the surely Christian and clearly anti-Jewish dialogue found in Oxyrhynchus in an autograph from that period (P.Oxy. 2070). A detailed analysis, given in my SBL presidential address, confirms its anti-Jewish character in a polemical tradition paralleling that of Justin's *Dialogues*.[71] Though badly deteriorated, it uses the name "Jesus," written as a *nomen sacrum* (line 10), and then quotes passages from Isaiah and the Psalms that are found, for example, in Justin's anti-Jewish polemic: Isa 29:13, the people of Israel "honor me with their lips, while their hearts are far from me" (P.Oxy. 2070, lines 24–27), preceded by Ps 18:43–44 [LXX 17:44–45] (lines 5–7); and then, as the culmination—at least in the surviving section—a quotation from Psalm 22:15–22 [LXX 21:16–23]:

> You lay me in the dust of death. For dogs are all around me: a company of evildoers encircles me. . . . They divide my clothes among themselves. . . . Deliver my soul from the sword . . . (P.Oxy. 2070, lines 46–56)[72]

Justin Martyr earlier had used these very quotations in his patently anti-Jewish polemic, introducing Psalm 22 (which he quotes in its entirety) as explicitly disclosing "who they are that rise up against him [Jesus]."[73] Further evidences of anti-Jewish polemic survive in the treatise, leaving no doubt about its general character.[74]

Is this expression of anti-Jewish feeling a continuation of attitudes that developed during the suppression of the Jews in the 115–117

---

[70] Mélèze-Modrzejewski, *Jews of Egypt*, 224.
[71] See Epp, "Oxyrhynchus New Testament Papyri: 'Not without honor,'" 40–42.
[72] The line, following "the sword," namely, "my life from the power of the dog" is not quoted.
[73] Justin, *Dial.* 98.
[74] See Epp, "Oxyrhynchus New Testament Papyri: 'Not without honor,'" 41–42.

Revolt against Rome? Maybe, but more certainly the anti-Jewish treatise represents an extension of a theologically-based polemic virulent in early Christianity, for this particular dialogue—penned in Oxyrhynchus—follows clearly that of Justin Martyr a century and a half earlier. Its presence in the now-numerous Christian community is ominous indeed.[75]

RECOVERY OF JEWRY IN OXYRHYNCHUS

The presence of an anti-Jewish treatise implies, though it does not absolutely require, a visible Jewish community in Oxyrhynchus by the late third century. The preceding survey concerning Jews at Oxyrhynchus after 117 CE, however, shows with reasonable certainty that a Jew named Onias was mentioned in a legal document, but with no assurance that he was alive at the time. Nor is it clear whether or not his adult daughter, or her offspring—those actually named in the account—considered themselves Jews. Yet, Onias and perhaps a soldier appear to be the only Jewish individuals to be named in the records of Oxyrhynchus after 117 until the late third century. To be sure, as we have seen, Jews are very much in the public mind—and in the records of that post-war period—as causing destruction during their rebellion against Rome; as having their property confiscated and that confiscated property being sold to others, even property in the Jewish street or close. And they were further humiliated by a special tax on Jewish commerce; by a long-running festival in Oxyrhynchus celebrating the victory over the Jews; and as the object of Christian anti-Jewish polemic.

It should be noted again that the environment was undergoing changes in the later second and through the third century, for Christians were multiplying rapidly in Egypt and adopting biblical names for their second and succeeding generations. Curiously, orig-

---

[75] P.Oxy. 840, a parchment manuscript of the fourth century, might be introduced here, for it is a "Dispute between the Savior and a Priest in Jerusalem," and therefore would appear to be an anti-Pharisaic polemic present (and presumably used) in Oxyrhynchus alongside the anti-Jewish treatise just discussed. F. Bovon, however, in his "*Fragment Oxyrhynchus 840*: Fragment of a Lost Gospel, Witness of an Early Christian Controversy over Purity," *JBL* 119 (2000) 705–728, demonstrates it is an inner-Christian polemic, reflecting second and third century controversies over purity and baptism. See esp. 721–722.728.

inating at about the same time as the anti-Jewish dialogue, is an onomasticon of Hebrew names.

Onomasticon of Hebrew names (P.Oxy. 2745)

Considerable help on Jewish names might have been expected from an Oxyrhynchus onomasticon (P.Oxy. 2745) of the third/fourth century. It preserves forty Hebrew names, given in Greek transliteration and all beginning with *iota*, with very brief explanations of the nineteen extant in the first column, though the interpretations of the second column of twenty-one names are lacking. The compiler is heavily reliant on the LXX,[76] yet the small surviving portion of the list does not resonate with biblical names encountered at Oxyrhynchus: familiar names such as Jesse, Joab, Joel, and Eleazar[77] occur in the *onomasticon* but not in other records surviving in Oxyrhynchus.

Onomastica of this type go back to the Hellenistic period, and David Rokeah is "inclined to ascribe the first redaction of such a work to the late third or early second century BCE. Of course, a work of this nature is liable to many interpolations and additions, but its ancient character is still distinguishable."[78] Philo used such a resource; Origen appears to have enlarged one by including Christian material; and Jerome translated and elaborated an *onomasticon* as well.[79] Curiously, however, P.Oxy. 2745 contains a *nomen sacrum* ($\overline{\theta \upsilon}$), indicating, as E.G. Turner pointed out, that "this text was copied by a Christian scribe, not a Jewish one, and was probably written in a Christian ambiance," and might even be part of an *onomasticon* compiled by Origen, since "its palaeographical date is entirely suitable."[80] Hence, this papyrus very well may be a version of a much older Jewish document now adopted and elaborated by Christians—whether Origen or another—but one that hardly informs us of Jews in

---

[76] P.Oxy. XXXVI, p. 1, because the onomasticon includes obscure names from the Genesis genealogical lists, at least once in the same sequence. The papyrus was edited by D. Rokeah; see also idem, "A New Onomasticon Fragment from Oxyrhynchus and Philo's Etymologies," *JTS* 19 (1968) 70–82, whose main interests are other *onomastica* and whether Philo knew Hebrew or not.

[77] Apparently spelled Ι[ελιε(?)]ζερ; see P.Oxy. XXXVI, p. 5.

[78] Rokeah, "New Onomasticon Fragment," 81; idem, P.Oxy. XXXVI, p. 2.

[79] Rokeah, "New Onomasticon Fragment," 74–75.81–82.

[80] P.Oxy. XXXVI, pp. 2–3. The *nomen sacrum* was bungled: it should have been $\overline{\theta \varsigma}$: ibid., 4; Rokeah, "New Onomasticon Fragment," 72.

Oxyrhynchus, either in the past or at the time of its copying at the turn of the third/fourth century.

What evidence exists, then, to show a renewed Jewish community in Oxyrhynchus by this period?

Manumission of a Jewish woman[81]

Though virtual silence reigns about specific Jewish people and activities from 117 to the late third century in Oxyrhynchus, a steady—if slow—recovery must have been underway that resulted in an established Jewish community there when P.Oxy. 1205 (= *CPJ* III 473) was drafted in 291 CE. It is a document of manumission *inter amicos*, clearly involving a Jewish woman and her two (or perhaps three) children; the only child's name extant is Jacob, age four (line 5), who is mentioned again later (line 19); another child is ten years old. This mother, Paramone (Παραμονή, lines 4 and 19), age forty and a house-born slave, was freed, along with her children, in Oxyrhynchus by "the community of the Jews" (παρὰ τῆς συναγωγῆς τῶν Ἰουδαίων, line 7) located there[82] for the very large sum of fourteen talents of silver. Given the usual price of an adult slave, this is nearly six times as much,[83] though children are also involved, "suggesting that this is no ordinary case."[84] The funds for this manumission came through two deputies, both Aurelii—Roman citizens—who, in view of the task assigned to them, obviously were important

---

[81] On slaves and freedmen/women in Oxyrhynchus from the first through the seventh century CE, see I.F. Fikhman, "Slaves in Byzantine Oxyrhynchus," *Akten des XIII. Internationalen Papyrologenkongresses, Marburg/Lahn, 2.–6. August 1971* (ed. E. Kiessling—H.-A. Rupprecht; MBPF 66; München 1974) 117–124. His calculations show that "slaves were never numerous" in Oxyrhynchus, that they diminished from the late third century through the seventh, and that during this period emancipation was "characterized by legal facilitation" and by the "most intensive manumission" (121–122; see his chart on 124). He does not discuss P.Oxy. 1205 or any other specific cases.

[82] That the Jewish community of Oxyrhynchus is meant, see *CPJ* III 473, p. 35; the synagogue, as a house of worship, is uniformly described in Egypt as προσευχή, not as συναγωγή (ibid., 35, note on line 7); see also Kasher, *Jews in Hellenistic and Roman Egypt*, 153.

[83] Bagnall, *Egypt in Late Antiquity*, 277 note 104, calculates fourteen talents of silver to be the equivalent of more than 140 *artabas* of wheat, and that an adult slave sold for around twenty-five *artabas*—though the latter price applies to the fourth century.

[84] Rowlandson, Women and Society in Greek and Roman Egypt, 193.

in the Oxyrhynchus Jewish congregation. One, Aurelius Dioscurus, appears to be a local Jew, but the other, Aurelius Justus, is described as "member of the city council of Ono[85] in Syrian Palestine," to which is added immediately, "father of the congregation"[86] (line 8). Aryeh Kasher offers the explanation that Justus, as a city official in Syria-Palestine, was simultaneously an honorary *Pater-Synagogos* in Oxyrhynchus, and in this capacity could serve as deputy for the Oxyrhynchus Jewish community in the manumission.[87]

This manumission transaction and the particulars provided tell us far more than may appear on the surface regarding the recovery of the Jewish community in Oxyrhynchus by the late third century. First, "the formal involvement of the community in such a case implies clearly enough that it represented a legal personality while serving as a juridical party to an official transaction,"[88] and a sign, as Bagnall notes, of the cohesiveness of their community.[89] Second, the payment for the manumission "implies that [the community] possessed public funds and authority to use them, a right reserved exclusively for legal bodies," and that this resulted from communal decisions.[90] And the large sum raised for the ransom suggests a measure of affluence in the community. Third, as noted above, the two intermediaries in the transaction were in the class of Aurelii,[91] indicating something of the civic status of at least some in the Jewish

---

[85] *CPJ* III 473, p. 35, note on line 8: "east of Jaffa, north of Lydda."

[86] The text breaks off after πατρὸς τῆς (line 8), followed presumably by συναγωγή— as restored in *CPJ* III 473; see p. 35, note on lines 8–9, and the frequency of this title, "father of the community," in various inscriptions.

[87] Kasher, *Jews in Hellenistic and Roman Egypt*, 153–154.

[88] Kasher, *Jews in Hellenistic and Roman Egypt*, 153.

[89] Bagnall, *Egypt in Late Antiquity*, 277.

[90] Kasher, *Jews in Hellenistic and Roman Egypt*, 153.

[91] Aurelius and Aurelia were names adopted when Aurelius Antoninus, nicknamed Caracalla, issued the *constitutio antoniniana*, probably in 212 CE, which made all free persons in the empire Roman citizens, including Egyptians (*OCD*³, 221, 383). They placed the nomen Aurelius (the Emperor's *nomen gentilicium*) before their own names, making their own names *cognomina* (Fikhman, "On Onomastics of Greek and Roman Egypt," 407). Controversy remains as to whether all Jews had been granted citizenship: see Kasher, *Jews in Hellenistic and Roman Egypt*, 155–156. Incidentally, "the names Valerius and Flavius were honorific names conferred only on a few people, and denoted a higher status" (Fikhman, "On Onomastics," 408). On changes of Egyptian names to Greek, see Peter van Minnen, "A Change of Names in Roman Egypt after A.D. 202? A Note on P.Amst. I 72," *ZPE* 62 (1986) 87–92, esp. 91–92.

community.[92] Fourth, on grounds not clear, the Oxyrhynchus Jewish community obviously had established a relationship with prominent Jews in Syria-Palestine, at very least with Aurelius Justus, a city councilor there, who also had been honored with the title of "father of the congregation" in Oxyrhynchus. Finally, Kasher has suggested that the manumission document implies that the Jewish community "enjoyed the privilege of living by their ancestral laws,"[93] apparently a deduction from the fact that it was a Talmudic and Mishnaic obligation upon the community to ransom Jewish slaves from Gentile ownership.[94] Arthur S. Hunt, the editor of the papyrus, spoke of "some uncertainty as to the nationality of the manumittors"—whether Jewish or Gentile.[95] All their names are lost, but they consist of a certain Aurelius, his half sister, and her guardian, who is described as "the Admirable" (παράδοξος, line 4),[96] and Jane Rowlandson pointed out that this title, granted to distinguished athletes, musicians, and artists, connected him "with the athletic aristocracy of Oxyrhynchus" and "suggests that the manumittors were Gentiles."[97] Finally, Rowlandson raises the interesting question as to why the Jewish community waited so long—until Paramone was forty—to "discharge its moral obligation to liberate their coreligionists from slavery,"[98] but the answer is clear enough from our previous discussion: In the second and well into the third century—when silence pervades—the Jewish community in Oxyrhynchus was only gradually recovering from the decimation of the Revolt and doubtless found manumissions unfeasible until later in the third century.

Hence, while much can be drawn from this humanitarian action by the Jewish community of Oxyrhynchus near the end of the third century, it stands very much alone in providing solid information on the nature and activity of that community. One can only wish that the rubbish heaps of Oxyrhynchus had been less random and capricious in preserving the city's past and had offered us numerous addi-

---

[92] Kasher, *Jews in Hellenistic and Roman Egypt*, 155–156.
[93] Kasher, *Jews in Hellenistic and Roman Egypt*, 157.
[94] Kasher, *Jews in Hellenistic and Roman Egypt*, 153 note 155; P.Oxy. IX, p. 239; *CPJ* III 473, p. 36, note on line 9.
[95] P.Oxy. IX, pp. 239; 241, note on line 8.
[96] LSJ, ad loc.
[97] Rowlandson, *Women and Society in Greek and Roman Egypt*, 193–194.
[98] Rowlandson, *Women and Society in Greek and Roman Egypt*, 194.

tional glimpses into Jewish life. A few other papyri, following our rough chronological order, may help somewhat.

Hebrew papyrus fragments

The 1905 excavations in Oxyrhynchus turned up several fragments with Hebrew writing, all from the same mound and in the company of Greek papyri dating from the third to fifth centuries. A.E. Cowley, who edited the fragments, dated them around 400 CE, with one perhaps fifty years later.[99] No substantial content can be retrieved, though fragment (a), of the Bodleian Library, MS. Heb. c. 57 (P), preserves the beginning of an official letter to leaders and members of the Jewish community, doubtless in Oxyrhynchus,[100] as follows (with Cowley's reconstructions):

> From the heads of the synagogue [and from your brethren] the mem-
> bers of the synagogue which is in Eg[ypt to our master] A . . . the head
> of the synag[ogue . . .] and to the elders of the synagogue and to [all
> our brethren] the holy congregation which [is in . . .]. Our prayers
> shall [be] for your life and for the welfare of your sons and [your]
> households. . . . And the service of the commandments . . . (Lines 1–8)

Beyond this, two names are recognizable: Joseph (יוסה) and Samuel (שמוא[ל]).

A second fragment (b) may be part of a hymn, since "the lines seem to show a rudimentary rhyme"; and a third (c) "clearly has something to do with Mishna Yoma, suggested by parallels."[101] Another fragment, MS. Heb. d. 86 (P), ca. 450 CE, has the final words of a Greek document, concluding with "as aforesaid Aurelius Samuel," followed by some Hebrew, undoubtedly the "signature of the Jewish witness Samuel."[102]

Even the minimal context recoverable in these Hebrew papyri indicates an organized communal structure involving a head of the

---

[99] A.E. Cowley, "Notes on Hebrew Papyrus Fragments from Oxyrhynchus," *JEA* 2 (1915) 209–213, including 3 pls.

[100] See Cowley's note on line 5: "some form of the Coptic Pemje (= Oxyrhynchus) may have stood at the end" (ibid., 210).

[101] A.E. Cowley, "Notes," 211, though involving only five words of the surviving fragment (Lev 16:30 and 16:9.10, parallel with Yoma iii.8 and iii.9, iv.10, respectively). It might be from a liturgy for the Day of Atonement (ibid.).

[102] A.E. Cowley, "Notes," 213.

synagogue (that is, the Jewish community), elders of the synagogue
(a council or *gerousia*), and members. Also, the use of Hebrew in
these papyri suggests a close connection with and perhaps influence
from Palestinian Jewry[103]—as seen earlier in the manumission document. Moreover, the presence of a hymn, the reference to "service
of the commandments," and the allusion to the tractate Yoma hint
at liturgical practice and Jewish life in accordance with Torah. Should
George Kilpatrick be correct in understanding P.Oxy. 2068 (fourth
century) as a fragment of a Jewish liturgical roll,[104] that would add
another witness to Jewish worship and observance in fourth century
Oxyrhynchus, suggesting that the recovery of the Jewish community
by that period had been substantial. Indeed, these bits of evidence,
few and limited though they are, become significant nonetheless
because without them we would possess virtually no evidence from
Oxyrhynchus of the religious core that was the center of Jewish life.

The Letter of Judas

Jewish private letters in the papyri are scarce, but P.Oxy. 3314 (fourth
century CE) may well preserve one—a letter written by a certain
Judas ('Ιούδας = Judah) to his father, Joses ('Ιωσῆς = Joseph), and
his wife, Maria (μαρία), with a later mention of an Isaak ('Ισάκ, line
23):

> To my lord father, Joses, and to my wife, Maria, Judas. To begin with
> I pray to the divine providence for your [pl.] health, that I find you
> well. Make every effort, my lady sister, to send me your brother, since
> I have fallen ill after a fall from a horse. For when I want to turn
> over to my other side, I cannot do it by myself, unless two other per-
> sons turn me over, and I have no one to give me so much as a cup
> of water. So send help, my lady sister. Make it your serious concern
> to send your brother to me quickly, as I said before. For in straits like
> these a man finds out who his true friends are. You too, therefore,

---

[103] Kasher, *Jews in Hellenistic and Roman Egypt*, 156–157. Again, the same material appeared earlier in idem, "Jewish Community of Oxyrhynchus," 156–157.

[104] G.D. Kilpatrick, "Dura-Europos: The Parchments and the Papyri," *GRBS* 5
(1964) 222 and note 14. He planned a new edition of P.Oxy. 2068, with commentary, to make his case, but I am unaware of such a work. P.Oxy. 2068, however, has three common *nomina sacra* (lines 18, 33, 43), but also an unusual one βϛ
(lines 7, 14), possibly for βασιλεύς, which would favor its Christian origin, as would
its fourth century date—barring some distinctive Jewish context.

please send help to me since I am in a strange place and sick. I searched for a ship to board, but I could not find anyone to search for me; for I am in Babylon. I greet my daughter and all who love us individually. And if you need some money, get it from Isaac the cripple, who lives very near you.

[In the hand of Judas]: I pray you may be well for many years.[105]

On the face of it, this could be a Jewish family—all the names are common Jewish names[106]—or it could be a Christian family, given the fourth century date and the phenomenon of Christians in that period rapidly co-opting biblical names. Judas, of course—for obvious reasons—is unlikely to be used as a Christian name, though some examples can be found;[107] and "divine providence" (ἡ θεία πρόνοια), which occurs here, is not an exclusive marker for either Judaism or Christianity, for it is found both in Jewish writings, such as Philo, *Flacc.* 125, and frequently in Christian letters.[108] Moreover, it occurs as an expression in Greco-Roman religions and philosophy, for not only was it "a fundamental aspect of Stoic thought," but it became "clearly a conventional public formula."[109]

The editor of the Judas letter, John Rea, was inclined, however, toward viewing the family as Christian, not only on the reasonable ground that Christians used biblical names in the fourth century, but that the mention of a "cup of water" (lines 10–11) might be an

---

[105] Translation modified from P.Oxy. XLVI, p. 104; and Horsley, *NewDocs* 3 (1978), 141–142.

[106] See Ilan, *Lexicon of Jewish Names*, 150–168 on Joseph; in Palestine, "Joseph was the second most popular name in the Second Temple period after Simon" (158). On Judas = Judah, ibid., 112–125; on Maria = Mariam, 242–248.

[107] Christians named Judas: (1) "the last bishop of Jerusalem of Jewish origin, martyred under Hadrian," 117–138 (J. Rea, P.Oxy. LV, "Additions and Corrections," p. xix, under 3314) but, as noted, he was a Jew by origin; (2) an early third century chronographer referred to by Eusebius, *Hist. eccl.* vi.7 (J. Rea, P.Oxy. LXVI, p. 103); see also note 116, below. Horsley, *NewDocs* 3 (1978) 146, notes a Christian Judas (Ἰ[ο]ύδα) in P.Iand. VI 132, line 11, but this is sixth/seventh century.

[108] For "divine providence" in official documents; as a basic element in Stoic thought; in Christian and non-Christian letters, prayers for health and safety; and in other ways, see Horsley, *NewDocs* 3 (1978) 143–144, where some two dozen examples from the mid-third through the fourth century are given, including P.Oxy. 1492, 1682, 2156, 2664, 3314, 3396, 3417, to which should be added 3859, 4000, 4001 (bis). Hence, it would be "inconclusive" to use the term on its own to validate a document as Jewish, Christian, or belonging to Greco-Roman religions (144); idem, *NewDocs* 4 (1979) 61.

[109] Horsley, *NewDocs* 3 (1978) 143.

allusion to Mark 9:41.[110] On the latter point, though, a properly broad and cautious view of intertextuality would avoid a rush to judgment as to source and allusion; after all, here only two words, ποτήριον ὕδατος, "cup of water," are parallel to Mark, with nothing else in the context relevant to a New Testament allusion.[111]

Is this famous "Letter of Judas" Jewish or Christian?[112] It would appear so far to be a tossup, but with a tilt toward Christian because of the biblical name phenomenon. Yet, "apart from the names," says E.A. Judge, "there is nothing about the letter that positively suggests Christianity,"[113] and I think that the name, "Judas," is the likely—and obviously—decisive factor. Not only was the name Judas (as in Judas Iscariot) very unlikely to be given to a Christian, it also was unlikely to be used because Christians employed the "curse of Judas" in an anti-Jewish context in the period of the Judas letter (though mostly in Greece, Rome, and Asia Minor), as indicated in this (non-Oxyrhynchus) sepulchral inscription, which is post-Constantine:

> If anyone exhumes it apart from her heirs, let him have the curse of Judas, and of those who say, "Away with him, away with him, crucify him."[114]

The anti-Jewish element appears, of course, in the last clause—a clear allusion to John 19:15, where, in the passion narrative, "Away with him," etc. is, in the Fourth Gospel, explicitly the voice of the Jews (Ἰουδαῖοι). And it should not be overlooked that the anti-Jewish dialogue originating in Oxyrhynchus dates in the late third century, followed by the Letter of Judas at some point in the fourth, suggesting at least a climate in that period conducive to the use of the

---

[110] P.Oxy. XLVI, pp. 103–105.

[111] Rejection of the parallel with Mark is followed also by Horsley, *NewDocs* 3 (1978) 144–145; and E.A. Judge, *Rank and Status in the World of the Caesars and St Paul* (Broadhead Memorial Lecture 1981; University of Canterbury Publications 29; Christchurch, NZ 1982) 30; see his additional evidence.

[112] See Horsley's extensive discussion of the letter: *NewDocs* 3 (1978) 141–148; cf. idem, 4 (1979) 230.

[113] Judge, *Rank and Status*, 30.

[114] From Argos (post-Constantine); I derive the material on the Judas curse from Horsley, *NewDocs* 1 (1976) no. 61, pp. 99–100, who lists numerous other examples from various localities, pre- and post-Constantinian, including one not later than the fourth century. Horsley points out that at Argos, out of a dozen epitaphs extant, three contain the curse of Judas.

Judas curse by Christians, though we have no evidence from Oxyrhynchus that it actually was invoked there.

Now, on the assumption that the letter is Christian, it has been proposed that Judas was a convert from Judaism to Christianity,[115] but this can be little more than speculation. More to the point, is whether the unlikely use of the Judas name by Christians is offset by the increased currency of biblical names among Christians, especially in the fourth century? But the rare Christian uses of Judas[116] do not justify calling P.Oxy. 3314 a Christian letter without some other clear Christian evidence, and the letter has none. But then, common Jewish names, which at this time are likely also to be common Christian names (except for Judas), cannot validate this letter as Jewish either, apart from other Jewish evidence. Of course, the Revolt of 115–117, which vastly reduced the number of Jews and compelled survivors to keep a low profile, clearly requires caution in identifying as Jews individuals with Old Testament names, but it does not mean that all such people are Christians or that Jews were either totally absent from the scene or avoided use of their traditional names.[117] In fact, a well-organized Jewish community existed in the late third century in Oxyrhynchus, as attested in the document of manumission of the Jewish slave, Paramone. As Horsley put it, "If the letter is Jewish names like these [in the letter—including "Judas"] are what we should expect to meet," though Horsley himself inclines toward designating the letter Christian.[118]

---

[115] Horsley, *NewDocs* 3 (1978) 146. His evidence that Judas may have been a Jewish convert to Christianity is that this also "may have been the case with the man [Judas] mentioned in Eusebius" (*Hist. eccl.* vi.7), but again this is at best an inference—one, I would guess, drawn from Eusebius's report that this Judas wrote a discourse on Daniel's seventy weeks and was persuaded that the coming of the antichrist was near. Interestingly, J. Rea (P.Oxy. LXVI, p. 103) says Eusebius's description of this Judas is "in words that make it virtually certain that he was a Christian"—suggesting some doubt (see also the following note).

[116] See notes 107 and 115, above. J. O'Callaghan, in a review of P.Oxy. XLVI, including P.Oxy. 3314 (*Or* 49 [1980] 221), mentions that "the existence of another Judas [the stated author of the Letter of Jude] is also certain," but that is clearly irrelevant and a specious argument, since that Judas is claiming to be the "brother of James," hence the brother of Jesus (see Mark 6:3), and because it involves a figure in the first generation of Jewish Christianity who already was named Judas— and there is no evidence that Jewish Christians named Judas changed names because of Judas Iscariot.

[117] Judge, *Rank and Status*, 31; Horsley, *NewDocs* 3 (1978) 146–147.

[118] Horsley, *NewDocs* 3 (1978) 147.

So, is the letter Jewish or Christian? Though difficult to call, I come down on the side of Judas, a fourth century Jew of Oxyrhynchus, primarily because the name Judas, in a likely climate of anti-Jewish sentiment in Oxyrhynchus and in view of the contemporary wielding of the "Curse of Judas," is so improbable a Christian name. Until further evidence emerges, the only additional support for my position arises from name-dropping: Mélèze-Modrzejewski, G. Tibiletti, Kurt Treu, E.A. Judge, and some others also pronounce the letter to be Jewish.[119] Judge, for example, concluded that:

> Judas may be safely left a Jew. Although the Jews had been in eclipse in Egypt since their suppression in the early second century, the documentary record continues to attest their presence.[120]

But if the letter is Jewish, what do we learn about Jews at Oxyrhynchus? Judas owned a horse (line 7), a sign of some affluence, yet he could find no one to help him (lines 10–11). Still, as indicated by the final prayer for good health in a second hand (lines 24–25), presumably by Judas himself,[121] he found someone to write the rest of the letter for him and someone to deliver the letter. He also located two people to help him turn over (lines 8–10). In addition, he easily identified someone living close to his family who could supply them with cash (lines 22–23), and a curiosity is why, given

---

[119] See I.F. Fikhman, "Les Juifs d'Égypte à l'époque byzantine d'après les papyrus publiés depuis la parution du 'Corpus Papyrorum Judaicarum' III," *Scripta Classica Israelica* 15 (1996) 226, who calls P.Oxy. 3314 "potentially Jewish," and, on the one hand, he gives a list of scholars (228, note 23) who opt for a Jewish provenance, namely, those listed above, plus J.D. Thomas (*CR* 30 [1980] 317); G. Nachtergael (*ChrEg* 56 [1981] 157) and S. Honigman; and, on the other hand, a few who see it as Christian: J. O'Callaghan (*Or* 49 [1980] 221–222), M. Manasse, G.H.R. Horsley (*NewDocs* 3 [1978] 147–148); idem, "Name Change," 8–10; and R.S. Bagnall, *Egypt in Late Antiquity*, 276 n. 102. Horsley very cautiously tips toward the letter as Christian, and Bagnall opines that Horsley's treatment is "better" than Tibiletti's. For E.A. Judge, see his *Rank and Status*, 30–31; for G. Tibiletti, "Appunti su una lettera di Ioudas (P. Oxy. XLVI, 3314)," *Scritti in onore di Orsolina Montevecchi* (ed. Edda Bresciani, et al.; Bologna 1981) 407–411, esp. 409; for K. Treu, "Christliche Papyri XII," *APF* 32 (1986) 95; for Mélèze-Modrzejewski, *SDHI* 47 (1981) 477—a brief endorsement based on Jewish names. For the rest, see Fikhman's references.—O'Callaghan, by the way, says, "... Perhaps it may be convenient to consider the assumption that the letter is Christian. I do not speak about certainty, but only about a serious probability." (221), though later he suggests that "the Christian character of this letter is not improbable" (222).

[120] Judge, *Rank and Status*, 31.
[121] P.Oxy. XLVI, p. 105.

his affluence, he did not have one or more servants accompanying him. Finally, desperate to return home, he was unable to secure help in finding a ship to board (lines 17–19),[122] even though Egyptian Babylon was Egypt's main military base, right on the Nile.[123] Judge pointed out that Jewish communities and Christians both stressed hospitality for strangers, yet Judas found none. Of course, no Jewish settlement is known in Egyptian Babylon, and this might explain why a visiting Jew, such as Judas, found no help.[124] As might be expected, it has been suggested that "Babylon" is used in this letter as a code word—so employed in both Jewish and Christian texts— for exile or wickedness, but the geographical sense is doubtless to be understood.[125] Little if anything, however, is added to our knowledge by this letter, either about Jews or—should Judas have been a Christian—about Christianity.

The second incident to consider concerns a man explicitly identified as a Jew around the year 400:

Jose son of Judas, Jew (P.Oxy. 3203)

Overall, identification of individuals as "Jew" or "Christian" at Oxyrhynchus are rare. As to Christians, the clearest cases are a summons served in 256 upon "Petosorapis, son of Horus, Christian" (P.Oxy. 3035)[126] and a reference to "Sotas the Christian" (PSI XIV.1412, second/third century).[127] Equally scarce—if not more so—

---

[122] Much of this is built on Judge, *Rank and Status*, 30–31, and much of Judge's material is quoted also by Horsley, *NewDocs* 3 (1978) 147.

[123] P.Oxy. XLVI, p. 105.

[124] Judge, *Rank and Status*, 31.

[125] Horsley, *NewDocs* 3 (1978) 147–148, though Horsley rejects the symbolic use.

[126] P.Oxy 3035 reads χρησιανόν (see pl. X), but no alternative to "Christian" is apparent. P.J. Parsons, the editor, in 1974 considered this "by far the earliest use of the word 'Christian' in the papyrus documents" (P.Oxy. XLII, p. 100). The editor calls 3035 an "Order to Arrest," but "arrest orders" are more properly summonses, though often a guard was involved: see T. Gagos in P.Oxy. LXI, pp. 90–91; T. Gagos—P.J. Sijpesteijn, "Towards an Explanation of the Typology of the So-Called 'Orders to Arrest,'" *BASP* 33 (1996) 77–97, esp. 78–79. For a list up to 1986, including some twenty-seven involving Oxyrhynchus, see A. Bülow-Jacobsen, "Orders to Arrest," *ZPE* 66 (1986) 95–98. On P.Oxy. 3035, see Epp, "Oxyrhynchus New Testament Papyri: 'Not without honor,'" 49–50; and in general on identifying Christian letters, 21–27.

[127] PSI XIV 1412, also from Oxyrhynchus, has a spelling similar to P.Oxy. 3035, though the text preserves only χρησια[...] (line 10), restored to χρηστιανοῦ in P.Oxy. XXXVI, p. 84 note 2, by analogy with the restoration in P.Oxy. 3035; cf.

are persons specifically designated as a "Jew" in the Oxyrhynchus papyri.[128] P.Oxy. 3203 (400 CE, lines 7 and 25) speaks of "Aurelius[129] Jose son of Judas, Jew" (Αὐρήλιος Ἰωσὴ Ἰούδα Ἰουδαῖος), who rents rooms from two natural sisters who are also anchorite nuns.[130] Jose (= Joseph),[131] like most of the population, was illiterate, and his lease was signed for him by Aurelius Elias (line 27)—the Greek equivalent of Elijah and frequent in the LXX. Here we have two nuns, property owners presumably living in Oxyrhynchus rather than in a monastery or as hermits,[132] and a Jew, who is a Roman citizen, whose lease was signed for him possibly by another Jew, Elias, also a citizen. At very least, one may deduce from this transaction an occurrence of positive Jewish-Christian relations. Bagnall's two-part comment is interesting:

> The rent is in line with other lease payments for parts of city houses known from the period, and the whole transaction is distinguished by its routineness. All the same, the sight of two Christian nuns letting out two rooms of their house to a Jewish man has much to say about not only the flexibility of the monastic life but also the ordinariness of intersectarian relationships.[133]

But what if the interfaith factor involved more than ordinary business? That would open a door for speculation. What if the anti-Jewish sentiment remained in force from the Revolt and from the Church, as documented in Oxyrhynchus through the second cen-

---

Horsley, *NewDocs* 2 (1977) 173. See the preceding note, and Epp, "Oxyrhynchus New Testament Papyri: 'Not without honor,'" 52–53.

[128] Horsley, *NewDocs* 4 (1979) 212, cites another case in a tax list (*CPJ* III 515, first half of 2nd century, provenance unknown) that three times identifies someone as "Jew," though the first two may be the same person [see *CPJ* III 515]; and four cases in the sixth century, including P.Oxy. 2019: "Enoch the Jew," though in two instances "Hebrew" is used rather than "Jew."

[129] See note 91, above.

[130] P.Oxy. XLIV, pp. 182–184; on monastics owning property and other issues, see Horsley, *NewDocs* 1 (1976) 126–130, and J.E. Goehring, *Ascetics, Society, and the Desert: Studies in Early Egyptian Monasticism* (SAC; Harrisburg, PA 1999) 63.

[131] See Ilan, *Lexicon of Jewish Names*, 150–68, and note 106, above.

[132] Horsley, *NewDocs* 1 (1976) 128; Bagnall, *Egypt in Late Antiquity*, 277; cf. 297 and note 213.

[133] Bagnall, *Egypt in Late Antiquity*, 277–278. Horsley, *NewDocs* 4 (1979) 210, offers a further speculation: The confiscations of Jewish property that followed the Revolt of 115–117 CE "*may* explain why... a Jew is leasing a part of a house from two nuns," that is, if the practice persisted until 400, which is unknown and questionable. On such confiscations, see P.Oxy. 1189 and P.Oxy. 500, discussed above.

tury from the Roman side and in the third from the Christian side? And what if the nuns were showing their own good will toward Jews, who had been seriously put down locally by a series of events over those two centuries? Was the nuns' action perhaps their witness for tolerance? Or were the rental and/or the earlier anti-Jewish dialogue simply two isolated events in the busy multireligious environment of Oxyrhynchus? There is no way to know.

It appears, however, that "Jose son of Judas, Jew" is the only specific identification in this manner of an individual as Jewish in Oxyrhynchus through the fourth century. Two others do survive from the sixth century: P.Oxy. 2019 (= *CPJ* III 509, lines 20–21), an account of numerous receipts for payments (in this case, in grain) to Flavius Apion II, a wealthy Oxyrhynchus landowner, that includes the listing, "From Enoch the Jew, for public land" (line 20),[134] and P.Oxy. 3805, an estate account referring to "Lazar (or Azar?) the Jew, regarding rent for the synagogue" (col. v, line 56). In these two cases, however, nothing substantive is learned about the Oxyrhynchus Jews, except that in the sixth century a Jewish congregation is renting a building for use as their synagogue. Enoch, by the way, is a name not used by Egyptian Jews in the Hellenistic-Roman period, but was rather frequent among Christians, so it is of interest to see the name "Enoch" modified by "Jew" at this late date.[135]

Naturally, one wonders whether identifying someone as a "Jew" in an official record conveys a negative bias, especially when a group is under pressure from authorities or another group. For example, one of the two clear cases (into the fourth century) of individuals being tagged as "Christian" also occurs in an official record—a summons served on "Petosorapis, son of Horus, Christian" (P.Oxy. 3035, 256 CE).[136] Note also the rare appearance of "Christians" in a much

---

[134] See *CPJ* III 509, p. 98. No attempt will be made in this paper to treat cases of individuals specifically identified as Jewish in papyri beyond Oxyrhynchus, though the following might be mentioned: P.Köln III 144 (152 BCE, Arsinoite nome): "Simon, son of Theodoros, and his partners, Jews," (lines 5, 13, 21–22) were apparently soldiers: see B. Kramer et al. (eds.), *Kölner Papyri (P. Köln)* (PapyCol 7; Opladen 1980) 86–94.

[135] *CPJ* III 509, p. 98. Enoch does not appear in Greek, and only once in Hebrew, in Ilan, *Lexicon of Jewish Names*, see p. 98.

[136] The purpose of the summons, headed "Order for an Arrest" (see note 126, above), is unclear, but it is more than a year too early to be a consequence of the Valerian persecution: P.Oxy. XLII, p. 100. But it is a summons nonetheless.

mutilated Oxyrhynchus document (P.Oxy. 3119, 259/260 CE), perhaps of the Valerian persecution, that reads "concerning an investigation," followed in the next damaged line (14) by "Christians."[137]
Such singling out of individuals by religion, race, or nationality is
not common. An interesting instance, however, is P.Oxy. 3197 (111
CE), a declaration dividing up some sixty slaves of their deceased
owner. Of the slaves listed, two are identified by physical characteristics, two by lineage, eleven by various trades, and one by nationality: "Abascantion, Ethiopian" (line 13).[138] Are some or all of these
designations by religion/ethnicity/race matters of prejudice or are
all simply identifiers?

CONCLUSION

This survey of Jews and the Jewish community at Oxyrhynchus from
the first century BCE through the sixth century CE has displayed what
can be discovered from the relatively meager evidence that randomly
has survived at the site. It has been presented in rough chronological order, in full knowledge of the precariousness of palaeographical dating when specific dates or sure signs of their times of
writing are not present. Naturally, only what is available—or reasonably deduced from what survives—can be relied upon with some
confidence, but it may be instructive to note, at the outset of a summary, what has *not* been preserved about the Jews at Oxyrhynchus—
but might have been expected.

First of the title of my paper was changed in the course of research
from "Jews and Judaism in Oxyrhynchus" to "Jews and the Jewish
Community in Oxyrhynchus" for a very simple reason: almost nothing turned up about Judaism—about the worship, the practices,
or the observances of Jewish life, nothing specific about Torah.[139] To

---

[137] On 3035, see P.Oxy. XLII, pp. 99–100; on 3119, XLIII, pp. 77–79; on both,
see Epp, "Oxyrhynchus New Testament Papyri: 'Not without honor,'" 49–50.

[138] P.Oxy. XLIV, pp. 169–74. A late sixth century letter (P.Oxy. 4629, line 7)
refers to "Eutychius the black man" or "dark skinned"; P.Oxy. 3854, 3rd century,
line 1 and back) is a letter to "Horos, the Syrian cameldriver": see P.Oxy. LVI,
pp. 104–105. Though not an identification, a first century letter shows contempt
for Egyptians (P.Oxy. 3061, lines 12–13): "Make sure you look after it. You know
how the Egyptians are."

[139] Curiously, H.I. Bell, *Cults and Creeds in Graeco-Roman Egypt* (Forwood Lectures,

be sure, a fragmented Hebrew document appears to preserve part of a hymn; another carries the phrase, "the service of the commandments"; and a third fragment appears to have language—though fewer than a half-dozen words—parallel to a Mishna tractate. But that is all.

The word Sabbath occurs perhaps twice, but the clear case is in a surely *Christian* legal complaint of an abused wife against her husband, who, when he again did not keep his word, went "to the church on the Sabbath"[140] (line 19, P.Oxy. 903 = *CPJ* VI 457d; fourth century). The other occurrence at Oxyrhynchus is in two surviving words (or, better, one and a half words) in P.Ryl. IV 603 = *CPJ* III 457a; 7 BCE): ἕως Σαμβ[(line 6), "until Sabbath."[141] But there is no context to provide any further information.

Circumcision might also have been expected, and Oxyrhynchus provides at least three instances of circumcision, but the subjects are not Jewish. P.Oxy. 3567 (252 CE) contains a request and confirmation of a circumcision in the "temple of Athena Thoëris, most great goddess"; PSI IX 1039 (Oxyrhynchus, third century CE, see line 39) lists a group of boys who are candidates for circumcision; and PSI V 454 (Oxyrhynchus, 320 CE) is a request to have a son circumcised. This procedure "was equivalent to official admission to the priestly classes in Egypt."[142] But there is no mention of Jewish circumcision.[143]

1952; Liverpool 1957) 28, makes a similar statement about the papyri from the Jewish colony at Elephantine (5th century BCE): "There is no reference in them to the Law, to the Exodus, to Moses or the Patriarchs, to the Sabbath, to the Levites or any tribe, or to any of the Jewish festivals except the Feast of Unleavened Bread and, probably, to the Passover."

[140] See a brief discussion in my "Oxyrhynchus New Testament Papyri: 'Not without honor,'" 51–52. The *editio princeps* read Σαμβαθώ (as if a location), but was revised to σαββάτῳ: see M. David—B.A. Van Groningen—E. Kiessling, *Berichtigungsliste der Griechischen Papyrusurkunden aus Ägypten*, vol. 3 (Leiden 1958) 133. This was based largely on P.Ryl. IV 603 and 613: when P.Ryl. IV 613 (*CPJ* III 457b; 2nd century CE) was published, its Latin phrase (lines 3–4), *propter sambatha* ("because of the Sabbath"), confirmed the reading σαββάτῳ in P.Oxy. 903, rather than a place name. For further evidence from a sepulchral inscription, see H.C. Youtie, "A Parallel for σαμβάθῳ," *CP* 32 (1937) 368; reprinted, with a supplement, in his *Scriptiunculae II* (Amsterdam 1973) 803–804.

[141] See the preceding note.

[142] P.Oxy. L, p. 168; see also Horsley, *NewDocs* 3 (1978) 81.

[143] Just as circumcision and Sabbath are not automatic guarantees of a Jewish context, unless other Jewish evidence is present, neither are the terms synagogue (συναγωγή) or leader of the synagogue (ἀρχισυνάγωγος), for both terms appear in inscriptions that are neither Jewish nor Christian. For non-Jewish use of συναγωγή

More to the point, what can be documented about the Jews and their community in Oxyrhynchus? From just before the Common Era and into the early second century there exist mostly references to individual Jewish residents of Oxyrhynchus with virtually no stories to tell, except for a house sale in the Jewish close. Then, however, the Jewish Revolt against Rome is reflected in references to buildings burned by the Jews; sale of property that had been confiscated from them, including plots in the Jewish close; and the humiliating annual festival celebrating the victory over the Jews—carried on certainly for most of a century after the event. Finally, when the Jewish community had experienced considerable recovery by the late third century, we learn of the manumission of a Jewish slave and her children by an obviously well-organized, well-connected, and apparently affluent Jewish community. The good feelings generated by this action were offset, however, by the appearance—perhaps already earlier—of a Christian anti-Jewish treatise, locally authored. As the fourth century approaches, it becomes increasingly difficult to determine with any certainty whether people with biblical names are Jewish or Christian, though the evidence strongly favors Christian. Yet some Jews with familiar Jewish/biblical names are to be found, including Jose, specified as a Jew in the rental agreement with two nuns, opening speculation about positive—rather than antagonistic—intersectarian relations between Jews in Oxyrhynchus and the now overwhelming population of Christians, amounting to 90% at this time. And, if the Letter of Judas discloses a Jewish man's calamity, we get a glimpse of warm family sentiments when the injured and sick Judas states, philosophically, that "in straits like these a man finds out who his own people really are" (lines 15–16).

This may appear to be a modest harvest indeed from some 5,000 documents retrieved from Oxyrhynchus, a city of some 20,000 residents in Roman times. But this is what we have: reflections of the decimation of the Jewish people as a consequence of their revolt; evidences of a recovery, doubtless gradual over some two centuries;

---

in inscriptions, see Horsley, *NewDocs* 4 (1979) 202 (I.Eph. II.419A [92/3]); ibid., 215, item 21; cf. 219. For non-Jewish examples of ἀρχισυνάγωγος, ibid., 215–17, items 14–19, 21, and others; also 219, where Horsley notes that there are no Christian examples. See also M.H. Williams, "The Structure of Roman Jewry Reconsidered—Were the Synagogues of Ancient Rome Entirely Homogeneous?" *ZPE* 104 (1994) 135.

and a few glimpses into community life, family life, religious practices, and interfaith relations. These results stand on their own, but
for me they also illuminate further the broad context of the eighty-
some copies of early Christian writings discovered and used in
Oxyrhynchus, including fifty-nine papyrus and parchment manuscripts of what was to become the New Testament.

APPENDIX

THE PAPNUTHIS ARCHIVE: JEWISH OR CHRISTIAN? A TEST CASE

Similar to the Judas Letter, the Papnuthis documents from Oxyrhynchus could involve either a Jewish or Christian family, and they
stem from the same period. This extensive archive of two Oxyrhynchus
brothers, Papnuthis and Dorotheus, whose mother was Maria, survives in some fifty documents containing upwards of 1000 lines
(P.Oxy. 3384–3429 [but perhaps not 3427, 3429], 3480, 3875, 1223;
P.Oslo III 88 and 162; SB VI 7756) and dating from 331 to about
376 CE. The family belonged to the class of Aurelii (P.Oxy. 3384,
3386, 3389, 3393–3395), and the two brothers were employed in
various ways, involving management and distribution of goods and
money, but from about 360 on they worked together, primarily as
tax collectors—apparently covering a sizable territory.[144]

The archive's editor, John C. Shelton, in 1981 affirmed that, "So
far as the religion of any persons in these papers can be determined,
they are without exception Christians."[145] This was based on expressions such as "I pray to divine providence" (P.Oxy. 3396, line 3,
and 3417, lines 16–17: θεία προνοία); "by god" (3397, line 5); "for
the sake of god" (3417, line 9) and "in the eyes of god or humans"
(lines 26–27); "god willing" (3418, line 7); "I pray to the all-merciful god" (3421, line 4: ὁ πανελήμων[146] θεός); and "Sunday" (3407,
lines 15–16: ἡ κυριακή).[147]

---

[144] P.Oxy. XLVIII, pp. 74–76. See also Bagnall, *Egypt in Late Antiquity*, 158–159.

[145] P.Oxy. XLVIII, p. 76.

[146] On πανελεήμων, see T.M. Teeter, *Columbia Papyri XI* (ASP 38; Atlanta 1998)
52: the word is rare in literary works, but appears in at least nine other papyri,
including P.Oxy. 3864, lines 5–6 (5th) and 3865, lines 6–7 (late 5th); and P.Wash.
II 108, line 1 (6th) from Oxyrhynchus. Also in P.Edmondstone, line 8 (355 CE; see
the text in P.Oxy. IV, pp. 202–203).

[147] According to the editor, the woman employer writing P.Oxy. 3407 (where

In a recent article,[148] I catalogued most—perhaps virtually all—such references to god in the singular from Oxyrhynchus documentary papyri, concluding, with only several ambiguous instances, that the reference was to a Greco-Roman god unless a *nomen sacrum* or a distinctly Christian connection was present.[149] But there are no *nomina sacra* in the references to god in the Papnuthis archive, and the expression "divine providence," as noted above, is no guarantor of Christian identity, for it is found both in Judaism and frequently in Christian letters, as well as in the other Greco-Roman religions.[150] Moreover, alongside of "I pray to divine providence" in P.Oxy. 3396, the common expression, "May the evil eye not touch them," occurs three times, and this phrase certainly is not a distinctive marker of Christian or Jewish identity, though the phrase was used broadly in the Greco-Roman periods, and, interestingly, the "evil eye" notion has a substantial history in Jewish biblical, Talmudic, and other literature and tradition.[151]

Identification of the Papnuthis family members as Christian presumably was based also on names, such as Dorotheus and Maria (3396, line 2; 3403, line 2); a letter to Dorotheus from an Isak also was found (3413, line 2); and Elias occurs in an order for wheat (P.Oxy. 3388, line 2). These, of course, were common Jewish names,[152] though (as emphasized above) by the period of this archive, Christian use of biblical names was common, while biblical names among Jews were sparse.[153] Yet, as also demonstrated earlier, the Jewish com-

---

κυριακή occurs) "does not hesitate to address two employees as ἀδελφοί." Is this, Shelton asks, "a trace of her Christianity, a sign that their social ranks were indeed about equal, or simply common usage?" (P.Oxy. XLVIII, p. 110). But when Horion in 3391 called Papnuthis "assistant" and then called him "brother" in 3405, Shelton concludes that the latter was a way of addressing a social inferior, of which 3407 "probably gives another example" (P.Oxy. XLVIII, p. 107). Apparently then, Shelton has answered his own question: use of "brother" in these cases represents "common usage" and is not a Christian appellation. Cf. "brotherly" in 3421, line 5.

[148] Epp, "Oxyrhynchus New Testament Papyri: 'Not without honor,'" 21–24, esp. notes 54–61.

[149] Epp, "Oxyrhynchus New Testament Papyri: 'Not without honor,'" 21–27.

[150] See note 108, above.

[151] See *EncJud* VI 997–1000; cf. R. Kotansky, "Incantations and Prayers for Salvation on Inscribed Greek Amulets," in: C.A. Farone and D. Obbink (eds.), *Magika Hiera: Ancient Greek Magic and Religion* (Oxford—New York 1991) 119.

[152] See Ilan, *Lexicon of Jewish Names*, 174; 242–45; 286–87; Elias (Ἡλίας) is common in the LXX, but "does not seem to have been in use for Jews" (63).

[153] See Bagnall, *Egypt in Late Antiquity*, 276.

munity in Oxyrhynchus at this time was well organized and apparently affluent. The names in this family, then, would permit its holders to be designated Jewish or Christian, with an considerable edge toward Christian because of the fourth century date of the documents. In addition, the references to God and to divine providence (as noted) could go either way as well.

The remaining and perhaps decisive evidence is the term "Lord's day" or "Sunday" in P.Oxy. 3407, lines 15–16. A woman employer instructs Papnuthis and his foreman to have bull-drivers prepare rocks on a Saturday because they are to be removed by others "on Sunday (ἐν τῇ κυριακῇ ἡμέρᾳ) that is, tomorrow, the 11th."[154] It might be thought unlikely by many that "the Lord's day" would be used by or with Jews, though that, I think, should not be ruled out in a business document in a multi-religious setting. In fact, strong confirmation that a Jewish—or any other—business letter might refer to "Lord's day" resides in P.Oxy. 3759, dated 2 October 325, in an official record of proceedings before the *logistes*, who postpones a hearing because the next day is Sunday. Four years earlier, in 321, Constantine had issued the edict to "remain quiet on the holy (*or venerable*) day of Sunday," namely *venerabilis dies solis* (= Greek . . . ἡλίου ἡμέρᾳ), which prohibited commercial business and juridical proceedings, but not necessary agricultural work. However, P.Oxy. 3759, the court document, does not use "day of the sun," but twice employs the Christian form, "Lord's Day," (ἡ κυριακή, lines 38–39),[155] indicating that the latter was already in use in secular, official realms.[156] Moreover, parallel to Constantine's formulation, P.Oxy. 3759 appropriately refers to "the *sacred* Lord's day" (ἡ κυριακὴ ἱερά), nullifying any argument that designating the Lord's day as "sacred" could only be done by a Christian.

Therefore, since "Lord's day" is used in official proceedings, there is no reason why it would not have been used in a document of

---

[154] See Shelton's comments on heavy labor on Sunday (P.Oxy. XLVIII, p. 110); and S.R. Llewelyn—A.M. Hobbs, "The Earliest Dated Reference to Sunday in the Papyri," *NewDocs* 9 (1986–87) 109–112.

[155] P.Oxy. LIV, pp. 170–73; R.A. Coles notes that this is the "earliest papyrological reference to Sunday as the Lord's Day" (170), superseding that claim for P.Oxy. 3407: P.Oxy. XLVIII, p. 109. See also the extensive discussion by Llewelyn—Hobbs, *NewDocs* 9 (1986–87) 106–118, esp. 108–112.

[156] P.Oxy. LIV, p. 173, on line 38; *NewDocs* 9 (1986–87) 110.

instructions addressed to a Jewish businessman and his foreman sometime between 331 to 376 CE. In my judgment, therefore, "Sunday,"
that is, the Lord's day, no longer remains the tipping point in deciding whether the Papnuthis family was Christian. Rather, the names
remain crucial, unless there is something else in this large archive
that supports Jewish or Christian identity. One such factor is alleged
from P.Oxy. 3421, but here the editor goes too far when he describes
its first sentence as "a rather florid Christian opening,"[157] for it says
only, "Before all I pray to the all-merciful God concerning your
brotherly attitude that you may receive my letter from me . . . in
good spirit" [i.e., "cheerfully"] (lines 3–8)—language not unconge-
nial with a Jewish or even a secular setting.[158]

It is not unlikely, then that the family was Jewish. Yet, even should
one judge the principals in this archive to be Christian, the case is
interesting for our purposes, for the fifty some documents in the
archive, mostly business or official in nature, except for two or three
that are more personal (3396, 3403, perhaps 3421), reveal virtually
nothing regarding the family's religious faith. Perhaps more should
not be expected of a professional archive, yet the half-dozen references to god and to divine providence (though not necessarily "Lord's
day") lead us to expect some faith elaborations, but there are none.
Nonetheless, given the evidence, the family could very well be Jewish.

---

[157] P.Oxy. XLVIII, p. 133.

[158] Note that "in good spirit" is a passive form of εὐθυμέω and does not involve
πνεῦμα. Also, πανελεήμων (line 4) apparently appears only here and in Papyrus
Edmondstone (line 8, Elephantine, 354 CE) with no Christian context. For the text,
see P.Oxy. IV, pp. 202–203; and L. Mitteis—U. Wilcken, *Grundzüge und Chrestomathie
der Papyruskinde* (2 vols.; Leipzig—Berlin 1912) 2.1, no. 361 (pp. 404–405).

STUDIEN ZUR GESCHICHTE DER BIBLIOTHEK VON CÄSAREA

Marco Frenschkowski

1. Einführung

So wie das ungeklärte Ende der Bibliothek von Alexandrien zu einem Symbol für das Verschwinden antiker Weisheit und Wissenschaft geworden ist, so ist die verschollene Bibliothek von Cäsarea—die erste größere christliche Bibliothek mit wissenschaftlichem Anspruch, von der wir hören—ein Inbegriff für die vielen offenen Fragen in der christlichen Geschichte des 2. und 3. Jh.s. Nach allem, was wir wissen, wäre unser Bild der christlichen Anfänge—wenn auch kaum des 1., aber sicher des 2. und 3. Jh.s—deutlicher, präziser, detailreicher, wenn wir diese Büchersammlung noch besäßen. Obwohl sowohl bibliothekswissenschaftliche[1] als auch patristische[2] Arbeiten in vorbildlicher Weise alle antiken Traditionen über die erste „wissenschaftliche" christliche Bibliothek in *Cäsarea Maritima* gesammelt und manche Hypothese ausgiebig diskutiert haben, bleiben unerquicklich viele Fragen offen. Nicht das geringste Rätsel ist das spurlose Verschwinden dieser Bibliothek nach den letzten expliziten und eindeutigen Zeugnissen bei Hieronymus—über angebliche spätere Spuren wird ausführlich zu handeln sein.

Die folgende Studie versteht sich nicht als umfassende Sichtung all dessen, was wir über die christliche Bibliothek von Cäsarea

---

[1] Zu nennen sind besonders die Arbeiten von C. Wendel, "Das griechisch-römische Altertum," *Handbuch der Bibliothekswissenschaft* 3/1: *Geschichte der Bibliotheken* (begr. v. F. Milkau, 2. Aufl. ed. H. Leyh; Wiesbaden 1955) 51–145, bes. 131–133; Id., "Der Bibel-Auftrag Kaiser Konstantins," *Zentralblatt für Bibliothekswesen* 56 (1939) 165–186; Id., Art. "Bibliothek," *RAC* II (1954) 231–274, und die älteren allgemeineren bibliotheksgeschichtlichen Studien von A. Ehrhardt, H. Leclercq und E. Schwartz.
[2] Die wertvollsten Studien sind A.J. Carriker, *The Library of Eusebius of Caesarea* (VigChr.S 67; Leiden—Boston 2003) 2–36; H.Y. Gamble, *Books and Readers in the Early Church* (New Haven 1995) 154–161; daneben die Textsammlung bei A. von Harnack, *Geschichte der altchristlichen Litteratur bis Eusebius* (Leipzig 1893–1904) I/2 543–550 und II/2, 103–106.

wissen. Insbesondere soll nicht versucht werden, plausibel zu machen, welche Autoren und Werke genau in ihr vertreten gewesen sein mochten. Diese Arbeit ist zuletzt umfassend und vermutlich bei heutiger Quellenlage abschließend von A.J. Carriker geleistet worden. Einige Ergebnisse dieser überaus gründlichen Studie werden verstreut über die folgenden Seiten immer wieder zu referieren sein.[3]

Carriker hat allerdings darauf verzichtet, eine Reihe einfacher Vor- und Nebenfragen zu stellen. Seine Studie ist auch nicht bibliothekswissenschaftlich ausgerichtet. Wir werden im Folgenden versuchen, einige dieser Vor- und Nebenfragen in den Blick zu nehmen. Dabei wird vor allem die bisher nicht ernsthaft problematisierte Frage, wem eigentlich die Bibliothek von Cäsarea rechtlich gehörte, eine Schlüsselrolle einnehmen, aus deren Beantwortung dann eventuell auch neues Licht auf das letztendliche Geschick dieser Büchersammlung im 5. und 6. Jh. fallen könnte. Dieses letzte und wichtigste Problem— was wurde aus der Bibliothek?—werden wir auch nicht mit Sicherheit beantworten können; wie werden aber m.E. eine Reihe von Möglichkeiten auszuschließen haben und ein Alternativmodell vorle-

---

[3] Die wesentlichen Thesen und Beobachtungen der folgenden Studie waren bereits vor Erscheinen der Arbeit von Carriker abgeschlossen. Um größere Überschneidungen zu vermeiden, habe ich auf die Wiedergabe von inhaltlichen Überlegungen zum Bestand der Bibliothek von Cäsarea bis auf einige Details und einige allgemeine Rahmenangaben verzichtet.—Methodisch ist gegen Carriker allerdings einzuwenden, dass er den Bestand der Bibliothek von Cäsarea sozusagen eins-zu-eins mit den von Euseb benutzten Büchern gleichsetzt (vgl. Id., *Library*, 56). Auch wenn wir voraussetzen dürfen, dass Euseb die Bestände der ihm zugänglichen Bibliothek so gut wie möglich genutzt haben wird (vor allem in Bezug auf christliche Quellen), ist das Umgekehrte nicht so sicher. Euseb könnte z.B. auch größere bzw. spezielle eigene Buchbestände besessen haben, deren Auswertung vor allem in seiner *Praeparatio evangelica* (weniger vielleicht in der Kirchengeschichte) dann eventuell nichts Direktes über die Bibliothek von Cäsarea aussagen würde. Außerdem hat Euseb mit Sicherheit auch andere Sammlungen benutzt, z.B. diejenige der kircheneigenen Bibliothek von Jerusalem, die Bischof Alexander schon 212 n. Chr. gegründet hatte (Euseb, *h.e.* VI, 20; vgl. *P.Oxy.* 412). Wir hören, dass er Briefe und Schriften des Beryll von Bostra, Schriften des Hippolyt und den Dialog des Cajus mit dem Montanisten Proklus in Jerusalem in der besagten Bibliothek vorfand, diese also vermutlich in Cäsarea nicht vorhanden waren (Euseb, *l.c.*). Ob die Akten, die in der *Vita Constantini* und andernorts von ihm zitiert werden, in Cäsarea gesammelt worden waren, ist fraglich und wohl eher unwahrscheinlich. Wir werden allerdings sehen, dass diese Einschränkungen wiederum zu relativieren sein könnten, wenn wir versuchen, die Eigentumsverhältnisse der Bibliothek von Cäsarea zu klären. Im Allgemeinen wird man Carriker sicher darin zuzustimmen haben, dass Euseb uns eine ungefähre Vorstellung darüber vermittelt, welche Art von Texten in Cäsarea zugänglich gewesen sein mochten.

gen. Der wesentliche methodische Ansatz dieses Aufsatzes besteht
darin zu versuchen, uns so weit wie irgend möglich vom traditionel-
len und insgesamt recht stabilen Bild der cäsariensischen Bibliothek
in der Sekundärliteratur[4] zu lösen und möglichst die (leider nur spärlichen) Quellen neu in Augenschein zu nehmen. Daneben wird es
nicht fehl am Platze sein, die Geschichte dieser Sammlung mit einigen allgemeinen Beobachtungen in die antike Bibliothekslandschaft
einzuordnen.

2. CHARAKTER UND UMFANG DER BIBLIOTHEK VON CÄSAREA

Die christliche Bibliothek von Cäsarea entstand ursprünglich wohl
aus der Sammlung von Büchern, die Origenes (gest. wohl 253/54)
selbst für seine wissenschaftliche Arbeit und für seinen Unterricht
angelegt hatte.[5] Entsprechend werden philosophische Werke und
Biblica (d.h. Texthandschriften mit biblischen Schriften) den Schwerpunkt ausgemacht haben, daneben Standardwerke und Lehrbücher
für den Unterricht. Eine im engeren Sinn exegetische Literatur war
erst im Entstehen. Origenes war 232 nach seinen Streitigkeiten in
Alexandrien durch Bischof Theoctistus in Cäsarea zum Presbyter
geweiht worden. Pamphilos[6]—der deutlich zwei Generationen jünger

---

[4] Ein extremes Beispiel: J.A. McGuckin spricht von der Suche des Origenes-
Forschers nach „(. . .) the ash and dust that was once his archive and library, and
the reading room where Pamphilus, Eusebius, Euzoius, Hilary of Poitiers, Eusebius
of Vercelli, Gregory Nazianzen, Jerome, and Rufinus once worked" ("Caesarea
Maritima as Origen Knew It," in: *Origeniana Quinta. History—Text and Method—
Biblica—Philosophica—Theologica—Origenism and Later Developments* [ed. R.B. Daly; BEThL
105; Leuven 1992] 3–25, bes. 3). Von diesem verklärten Bild wird wenig kritischer
Nachprüfung standhalten. McGuckin meint auch: „The library, in the 4th century,
was a famous attraction for Christian scholars the world over, and several have left
accounts of their visits and what they found there" (Ibid., 20). Auch das ist so lei-
der nicht zutreffend, wie wir sehen werden, so gerne wir solche Berichte hätten.
[5] Die Verwurzelung in der Arbeit des Origenes wird z.B. stark unterstrichen bei
Carriker, *Library*, XIII. 8 und Wendel, „Das griechisch-römische Altertum," 131.
Vorsichtiger z.B. Gamble, *Books*, 155. Die Quellenaussagen sind hier leider wenig
konkret. Den Forschungsstand zu Origenes insgesamt repräsentiert J. McGuckin
(Hg.), *The Westminster Handbook to Origen* (Louisville 2004). Unangemessen ist es, wenn
Carriker, *Library*, 2–3, selbst Nachrichten über Bücherbestände oder archivierte
Schriftstücke in Cäsarea vor Origenes pauschal auf „die Bibliothek von Cäsarea"
bezieht.
[6] Über ihn vgl. meinen Beitrag M. Frenschkowski, Art. "Pamphilos," *BBKL* 6
(1993) 1476–1478, zu dem die folgenden Zeilen eine Reihe von Verbesserungen

war und von dem durchaus unklar ist, in welchem Kontakt er zu Origenes selbst als ganz junger Mann gestanden haben könnte[7]— wird wohl zum Eigentümer dieser Sammlung, die er ausbaut, katalogisiert und vor allem nutzbar macht, indem er in großem Umfang Handschriften herstellt bzw. herstellen lässt. Wie auch Origenes selbst hatte Pamphilos einen alexandrinischen Bildungshintergrund (Pierius war sein Lehrer gewesen) und genoss erhebliches Ansehen. Πάσης ἕνεκεν ἀρετῆς ἐπιδοξότατος nennt ihn Euseb, *de mart. Palaest.* 7,4, τὸ τῶν Καισαρέων θαῦμα noch der Byzantiner Nicephorus Callistus (*h.e.* VII,17). Mit seinem Engagement ist die christliche Bibliothek von Cäsarea als Institution geboren. Ihre Kontinuität zur persönlichen Arbeitsbibliothek des Origenes wird meist stillschweigend vorausgesetzt, ist aber aus den Quellen nicht direkt zu erheben.[8] In jedem Fall musste Pamphilos erhebliche Mühen aufwenden, um sie auszubauen. Euseb ist ihr wichtigster und unzweifelhafter Nutzer gewesen, während das Ausmaß, in dem Hieronymus sie noch auswerten konnte, im Gegensatz zur Mehrheitsmeinung durchaus fraglich ist (s.u.).

Blicken wir noch einen Augenblick auf das Umfeld der Sammlung. *Caesarea Maritima*, eine Gründung Herodes d. Gr., war im 2. und 3. Jh. eine prosperierende Stadt mit einem Hafen, der dem Athens an Größe nicht nachstand. Josephus schildert sie im 1. Jh. ausführlich (*ant.* XV, 331–341; *bell.* I, 408–415 u.ö.), und auch sonst fließen die literarischen, epigraphischen und archäologischen Quellen nicht spärlich. Noch die *Totius orbis descriptio* 23 spricht von der *civitas deliciosissima* (Text A) bzw. *deliciosior et abundans omnibus* (Text B) (GGM 2,

---

bieten. Vgl. jetzt vor allem SC 464/465 (2 Bde., hg. v. R. Amacker und É. Junod, Paris 2002) und aus den seit meiner Bibliographie erschienen Studien noch R. Williams, "Damnosa hereditas," *Logos. FS. Luise Abramowski* (ed. H.C. Brennecke u.a.; BZNW 67; Berlin—New York 1993) 151–169.

[7] A. v. Harnack und E. Preuschen vermuteten, Pamphilos könnte, weil in Berytus gebürtig, Origenes als ganz junger Mann noch gekannt haben: *Geschichte der altchristlichen Litteratur* II.2, 104.

[8] Das wird in vielen Darstellungen unterschlagen. S. aber insofern ganz richtig A.J. Carriker, *Library*, 10. R. Blum, "Die Literaturverzeichnung im Altertum und Mittelalter: Versuch einer Geschichte der Biobibliographie von den Anfängen bis zum Beginn der Neuzeit," *Archiv für Geschichte des Buchwesens* 24 (1983) 1–256, bes. 84 u. Anm. 24/86 rechnet damit, die Arbeitsbibliothek des Origenes sei nach seinem Tod zerstört oder zerstreut worden, so dass Pamphilos mit seiner Sammlung ganz neu hätte anfangen müssen. Auch das geht aus den Quellen nicht direkt hervor.

517). Ein Theater mit 4500 Plätzen, ein gewaltiges Hippodrom (das
zweitgrößte des Imperiums, erbaut aber wohl erst im 3. Jh.), zahlreiche Tempel und andere öffentliche Gebäude, daneben eine große
jüdische und eine kleinere samaritanische Gemeinde prägten das hellenistische Stadtbild. Vespasian, hier zum Kaiser ausgerufen, hatte
die Stadt zum Status einer römischen Kolonie erhoben (*Colonia prima
Flavia Augusta Caesarensis* bzw. *Caesarea*), Titus ihr die Steuerbefreiung
geschenkt (*digest.* L, 15, 1, 6). Doch waren die sozialen Gegensätze
besonders ausgeprägt, wie wir aus einer Reihe von Indizien wissen.
Metropolis durfte sich die Stadt seit Severus Alexander nennen. Nach
der Dreiteilung Palästinas im 4. Jh. war Cäsarea Hauptstadt von
Palästina prima, d.h. der Küstenregion Judäas und Samariens. Cäsarea
hatte den ersten Platz unter den Kirchen Palästinas nach dem Konzil
von Nizäa inne (*can.* 7), wurde aus dieser Vorrangstellung allerdings
in Chalzedon durch Jerusalem als Sitz des Patriarchates verdrängt
(*sess.* 7). Von der diokletianischen Verfolgung war es neben Ägypten
besonders stark betroffen. Freilich hatte sich die christliche Bevölkerung
in der Stadt früh sehr sicher gefühlt; Porphyrios, der größte Gelehrte
seiner Epoche und Zeitgenosse des Pamphilos, war hier als junger
Mann von christlichem Mob zusammengeschlagen worden (Socrates,
h.e. III, 23, 38 [GCS N.F. 1, 222], wohl aus der verlorenen Schrift
des Euseb gegen den Neuplatoniker). Die Bevölkerungszahl Cäsareas
in frühbyzantinischer Zeit mag 44 000–48 000 Menschen betragen
haben.[9] Seinen Ruhm bis in die Gegenwart hinein allerdings ver-
dankt es der ersten wissenschaftlichen christlichen Bibliothek.

Wir besitzen nur eine einzige Nachricht über die Größe, d.h. den
quantitativen Umfang der Bibliothek von Cäsarea. Isidor von Sevilla
(um 560—636) schreibt in seinen erst von Braulio von Saragossa
nach 636 endredigierten *Etymologiae* oder *Origines*:

> *Qui apud nos bibliothecas instituerunt. Apud nos quoque Pamphilus martyr, cuius
> vitam Eusebius Caesariensis conscripsit, Pisistratum in sacrae bibliothecae studio
> primus adaequare contendit. Hic enim in bibliotheca sua prope triginta voluminum
> milia habuit. Hieronymus quoque atque Gennadius ecclesiasticos scriptores toto orbe
> quaerentes ordine persecuti sunt, eorumque studia in uno voluminis indiculo con-
> prehenderunt.* (*etym.* VI, 6, 1s. ed. W.M. Lindsay).

---

[9] Vgl. Carriker, *Library*, 1–2. McGuckin, "Caesarea Maritima as Origen Knew
It," 11 rechnet für die Zeit des Origenes mit 100 000 Einwohnern, was wohl über-
trieben ist.

Es ist immer schon aufgefallen, dass der Anfang dieser Nachricht aus Hieronymus, *ep.* 34, zu stammen scheint:

> *Beatus Pamphilus martyr, cuius uitam Eusebius Caesariensis episcopus tribus ferme uoliminibus explicauit, cum Demetrium Phalereum et Pisistratum in sacrae bibliothecae studio uellet aequare imaginesque ingeniorum, quae uera sunt et aeterna monumenta, toto orbe perquireret, tunc uel maxime Origenis libros inpensius persecutus Caesariensi ecclesiae dedicauit, quam[10] ex parte corruptam Acacius, dehinc Euzoius, eiusdem ecclesiae sacerdotes, in membranis instaurare conati sunt* (CSEL 54, 259f.).[11]

Aber woher stammt der Rest der Nachricht? Im Kontext spricht der spanische Kirchenvater *de libris et officiis ecclesiasticis* (Inhalt von Buch VI), insbesondere vom Alten und Neuen Testament (VI, 1), *de scriptoribus et vocabulis sanctorum librorum* (VI, 2), *de bibliothecis* (VI, 3), *de interpretibus* (VI, 4), *de eo qui primum Romam libros advexit* (VI, 5; über die ersten Bibliotheken in Rom). Die auf VI, 6 folgenden Abschnitte behandeln *qui multa scripserunt, de generibus opusculorum,* dann die materiellen Aspekte der Buchherstellung etc. Die meisten Nachrichten, die Isidor bringt, sind eher banales gemeinantikes Bildungserbe. Eine durchgehende Quellenbenutzung wird nicht sichtbar und dürfte eher unwahrscheinlich sein.

Auch der Abschnitt über die Bibliothek von Alexandrien enthält eine Rollenzahl:

> *Nam septuaginta milia librorum huius temporibus Alexandriae inventa sunt* (VI, 3, 5 ed. W.M. Lindsay).

Diese ist auffällig, weil deutlich kleiner als die meisten antiken Angaben (s.u.). Zweimal ist von der ersten öffentlichen Bibliotheksstiftung in Athen durch Peisistratos die Rede (VI, 3, 3 und 5),[12] so dass die Anspielung hierauf in VI, 6, 1 einen eindeutigen Rückbezug im Rahmen der Komposition des Isidor darstellt. Auch das spricht vielleicht gegen eine die Einzelnotiz überschreitende Quellenabhängigkeit.[13]

---

[10] Hier ist vielleicht mit E. Klostermann ein *bibliothecam* einzufügen, vgl. CSEL 54, 260 App. z.St.

[11] Die Worte *dedicauit, quam ex parte corruptam Acacius, dehinc Euzoius, eiusdem ecclesiae* fehlen in einem der Textzeugen (*l.c.*).

[12] Zu dieser verbreiteten Überlieferung vgl. Wendel, "Das griechisch-römische Altertum," 55; T. Birt, *Das antike Buchwesen in seinem Verhältnis zur Litteratur* (Berlin 1882 [Ndr. Aalen 1974]) 434, etc.

[13] Wendel, "Das griechisch-römische Altertum," Anm. 2/55, meint, die Nachrichten

An eine Erfindung Isidors ist sicher nicht zu denken; alle Nachrichten im Umfeld sind solides Bildungserbe, und eine intrinsische Unwahrscheinlichkeit hat die Nachricht auch nicht, wie noch gleich zu zeigen sein wird. *Volumina* „must imply rolls",[14] meint Carriker, aber so sicher ist das nicht.

Die Nachricht Isidors wird in praktisch allen kürzeren oder längeren Studien zur Sache erwähnt. Sie ist in zweierlei Hinsicht bemerkenswert: einmal kennen wir die Quelle Isidors nicht. Euseb und Hieronymus, an die man am ehesten denken würde, haben die Notiz nicht, und es ist wenig wahrscheinlich, dass Isidor über für uns verschollene Werke dieser beiden gelehrten Autoren verfügte. Carriker denkt an ein Scholion zu dem genannten Hieronymusbrief oder an eine Notiz in einem verlorenen Lexikon.[15] Das verschiebt das Problem nur. Wendel dachte an die Buchlisten, die Eusebs *Vita Pamphili* beigegeben waren (Euseb, *h.e.* VI, 32, 3).[16] Dagegen spricht aber—wie auch Carriker sieht—dass Isidor kaum diese sonst verlorene Schrift des Euseb gekannt haben wird, und auch überhaupt nur über geringe Griechischkenntnisse verfügte.[17]

Die zweite Auffälligkeit der Nachricht ist die Bescheidenheit des angeblichen Umfangs der Bibliothek. Angesichts der bekannten, auch bei Isidor rezipierten Nachrichten über die Bibliotheken von Alexandrien und Pergamon sind 30 000 Rollen nicht sehr viel. Wenn man etwa 8–10 Rollen für ein modernes Buch ansetzt (umfassendere Bücher wie Lexika und Ähnliches mitberechnet), entsprechen 30 000 Rollen allenfalls 3000–3750 Bänden. Für eine Forschungsbibliothek ist dies eine eher bescheidene Zahl, durchaus auch wenn man antike Vergleichgrößen bedenkt. Die kaiserliche Bibliothek in Konstantinopel hatte 475 n.Chr. 120 000 Bände aufzuweisen (Zonaras XIV, 2). Die Bibliothek von Pergamon besaß zum Beginn der römischen Epoche etwa 200 000 Rollen (Plutarch, *Anton.* 58, 9). Dies

---

des Isidor über Peisistratos gingen wie diejenigen des Aulus Gellius (*noct. att.* VII, 17, 1) auf Varro zurück, ebenso Tertullian, *apol.* 18. Das kann natürlich aus chronologischen Gründen für die Cäsarea-Notiz Isidors nicht gelten und ist auch sonst nur geraten.

[14] Carriker, *Library*, 31.
[15] Carriker, *Library*, Anm. 102/32.
[16] Wendel, "Das griechisch-römische Altertum," 132.
[17] Zu den geringen Griechischkenntnissen Isidors ist mit Carriker auf J. Fontaine, *Isidore de Séville et la culture classique dans l'Espagne wisigothique* 2 (Paris ²1983) 849–851, zu verweisen.

waren große Zentralbibliotheken. Kleinere Sammlungen entsprechen dem, was wir von Cäsarea hören. So hatte die von Trajan gegründete *Bibliotheca Ulpia*, deren Inneneinrichtung wir fast vollständig rekonstruieren können, wohl Platz für etwa 30 000 Rollen.[18] Gebildete Privatpersonen besaßen entsprechend kleinere, zum Teil aber doch sehr beträchtliche Bibliotheken, zumal das Sammeln von Büchern ein gesellschaftlich hoch angesehenes Hobby war (satirisch dargestellt bei Lukian, *adversus indoctum et libros multos ementem*). Die Sammlung des Epikuräers Philodemus in Herculaneum in der *Villa dei Papiri* (die einzige in ihrem häuslichen Umfeld erhaltene Privatbibliothek der Antike) besaß etwa 1700 Rollen.[19] Immerhin umfasste auch die Sammlung des Grammatikers Epaphroditos von Chaironea 30 000 Rollen (*Suda* ed. A. Adler 2, 334f.). Ähnliches hören wir von derjenigen des Cicero-Freundes Tyrannion aus Amisos (mehr als 30 000 Rollen: *Suda* ed. A. Adler 4, 607).[20] Gordian II. erbte—nach einer allerdings nicht über jeden Zweifel erhabenen Nachricht—62 000 Rollen von seinem Lehrer Serenus Sammonicus (*Script. Hist. August.*, Gord. 18, 2f.). Der Dichter Martial nannte 120 Rollen sein Eigen (*ep.* XIV, 190), Persius besaß allein 700 Rollen des Chrysipp, insgesamt also sicher einige tausend Rollen (Sueton, *Pers.* 1).

Etwas anders stünde es, wenn Isidor oder seine Quelle an Codices denken würden. Das scheint aber unwahrscheinlich, denn die reiche nichtchristliche Literatur, die in Cäsarea ja auch vorhanden war und tatsächlich einen Schwerpunkt der Bibliothek ausmachte, wurde im 3. Jh. im Regelfall noch nicht in Codexform tradiert, was vor allem dann relevant ist, wenn die Zahl auf die Zeit des Pamphilos zurückgeht. Sicherheit ist nicht zu gewinnen.

Es muss deutlich gesagt werden, dass die weite geographische und geschichtliche Distanz der Notiz gegenüber ihrem Gegenstand Skepsis wachhalten muss. Schon der sonst nicht übermäßig skeptische Otto Bardenhewer hatte geschrieben:

---

[18] K. Vössing, Art. „Bibliothek," *DNP* 2 (1997) 634–647, bes. 644. L. Casson, *Bibliotheken in der Antike* (Düsseldorf 2002) 121, schätzt den Bestand auf etwa 20 000 Rollen.

[19] Vgl. Carriker, *Library*, 34, mit Literatur.

[20] Der Zahl 30 000 Buchrollen begegnet man in unserer Literatur eigentümlich oft, und in den merkwürdigsten Zusammenhängen. Vielleicht enthält sie eine Anspielung oder einen Vergleich, der uns entgeht. Vgl. als entlegeneres Beispiel D.D. Leslie—K.H.J. Gardiner, *The Roman Empire in Chinese Sources* (Studi Orientali XV; Rom 1996) Anm. 44/90 und 37/206.

eine Zahl, welche freilich auf sich beruhen muß, weil Isidor kaum in der Lage sein konnte, Genaueres in Erfahrung zu bringen.[21]

Wir können nicht sicher sein, ob die Zahl nicht irgendwann einfach geraten, erfunden oder „kombiniert" wurde. Selbst wenn sie auf das 3. oder 4. Jh. und einen Augenzeugen zurückgehen sollte, wovon fast alle Behandlungen des Themas ausgehen, sind einige Einschränkungen erforderlich. Wir besitzen für keine antike Bibliothek vollständige offizielle Kataloge[22] oder differenzierte Zählungen, auch nicht für diejenigen in Alexandrien, Rom oder Pergamon.[23] Alle Zahlen sind vermutlich nur geschätzt, wenn einige auch auf antike Kataloge zurückgehen werden. Wir haben nicht einmal Notizen darüber, dass es jemals Zählungen im strengen Sinn gegeben hat, die z.B. Duplikate ausgesondert hätten und nach Rollen oder Codices und literarischen Werken differenziert hätten. Es ist daher immer fraglich, worauf sich die überlieferten Zahlen genau beziehen. Falls Pamphilos die letzte Quelle der Notiz ist, müsste sie Isidor wohl über eine verschollene Mittelquelle erreicht haben. Von ihm wird ja

---

[21] O. Bardenhewer, *Geschichte der altkirchlichen Literatur* 2 (Freiburg ²1914) 12.

[22] Über antike Buchkataloge vgl. R. Otranto, *Antiche liste di libri su papiro* (Sussidi eruditi 49; Rom 2000). Über die Spätantike sind wir leider in Sachen antiker Bibliothekskataloge nicht gut informiert; auch die erhaltenen kirchlichen Klosterkataloge reichen m.W. nicht über das 8. Jh. zurück (Bobbio z.B. besaß im 9. Jh. etwa 700 Codices). Immerhin besitzen wir aus ägyptischen Klöstern in paar fragmentarische Bücherlisten, die auf Kataloge zurückgehen können (vgl. C. Wendel, „Das griechisch-römische Altertum," 137 mit Lit.; C. Markschies, „Neue Forschungen zur Kanonisierung des Neuen Testaments," *Apocrypha* 12 (2001) 237–262). Aus dem byzantinischen Bereich besitzen wir eine Reihe von Zahlenangaben; am besten fassen können wir die Bibliothek des Photios, der in 280 Beschreibungen 386 literarische Werke bespricht, die natürlich nur einen Teil seiner Sammlung ausmachen. Vgl. weiter N.G. Wilson, "The Libraries of the Byzantine World," *GRBS* 8 (1967) 53–80.

[23] Entsprechend divergieren die Zahlen, wenn wir mehrere Angaben für eine Bibliothek haben, erheblich. Im Fall der Bibliothek des *Museions* in Alexandrien wird zwar in der Sekundärliteratur immer wieder die Zahl 700 000 Rollen genannt, doch besitzen wir in den antiken Quellen auch völlig andere Angaben, z.B. 70 000 bei Isidor und in verschiedenen Gellius-Handschriften, und sogar nur 54 000 bei Epiphanius und al-Qifti. Auf diese Diskrepanzen weist z.B. L. Canfora, *The Vanished Library. A Wonder of the Ancient World* (Berkeley—Los Angeles ²1990) 187 hin. Vgl. die ausführliche Diskussion bei Wendel, „Das griechisch-römische Altertum," 68–69, und D. Delia, "From Romance to Rhetoric: The Alexandrian Library in Classical and Islamic Traditions," *The American Historical Review* 97 (1992) 1449–1467, bes. 1458–1459. Allein an magischer Literatur unter dem Namen des Zoroaster besaß das *Museion* zwei Millionen Zeilen Text (Diogenes Laertios, *prooem.* 8; Plinius, *n.h.* XXX, 4 nach Hermippus).

überliefert, er habe einen Katalog der Bibliotheksbestände zu seiner
Zeit erstellt (Euseb, *h.e.* VI, 32, 3). Aber auch wenn dieser Katalog
mit einer Zählung verbunden gewesen sein mochte, ist bedenklich,
dass diese im 4. und 5. Jh. nirgends sonst überliefert wird, zieht man
in Betracht, wie stolz christliche Autoren auf diese erste wissenschaftliche Bibliothek der Kirche waren (gerade dafür ist noch der späte
Zeuge Isidor ein gutes Beispiel). Zumindest Euseb hätte doch eine
solche Zahl auch in seiner Kirchengeschichte genannt. Insofern ist
die Zuversicht, Isidors Zahl auf Pamphilos zurückführen zu können,
vermutlich fehl am Platze.

   In Cäsarea liegt der Fall also so, dass es offenbar weder Euseb
noch Hieronymus gewesen sind, welche die Zahl überliefern. Wenn
sie aber auf der Schätzung eines beiläufigen, gelegentlichen Besuchers
beruht (z.B. auf einem verschollenen Pilgerbericht), ist sie vielleicht
eher zu klein als zu groß angesetzt. Menschen, die mit Bibliotheken
nicht professionell arbeiten, pflegen die Zahl der Bücher in einem
Zimmer oder einer Bibliothek öfters erheblich zu unterschätzen. Das
wird in der Antike nicht anders gewesen sein. Daher scheint es ange-
zeigt, die Zahl „30 000 Rollen" *cum grano salis* zu nehmen.[24] Die
Bibliothek könnte durchaus größer (oder auch kleiner) gewesen sein.
Erwähnen wir als Indizien für das Vorliegen einer besonderen bibliotheksgeschichtlichen Mittelquelle des Isidor immerhin noch, dass
auch seine Nachricht über das Geschick der großen Bibliothek des
Mithridates Eupator—nach *etym.* VI, 5, 1 nahm sie Lukullus wohl
nach der Eroberung Sinopes 70 v.Chr mit sich als (private!) Kriegsbeute
nach Rom—keine mir bekannte Parallele in sonstiger antiker Literatur
hat, aber durchaus glaubwürdig ist. Weiter kann seine Notiz über
die ersten öffentlichen Bibliotheken Roms (*etym.* VI, 5, 2) nur partiell aus Sueton, *Caesar* 44, stammen. Aber was diese Mittelquelle
gewesen sein könnt, wissen wir nicht.

3. Literarische Zeugnisse nach Eusebius

Es ist meist stillschweigend vorausgesetzt worden, dass die Bibliothek
von Cäsarea Besitz der christlichen Gemeinde gewesen ist. Das würde

---

[24] Gamble, *Books*, Anm. 32/300, ist einer der sehr wenigen Autoren, welche die
singuläre Angabe Isidors hinterfragen, aber auch er bietet keine Diskussion der
Probleme.

bedeuten, dass sie vermutlich in einem Kirchengebäude, wahrschein-
lich in einem Nebenraum oder ähnlich,[25] untergebracht war und der
Jurisdiktion des Bischofs unterlag. Wie sofort noch deutlicher wer-
den wird, führt diese Annahme zu einer Reihe von Aporien. Eine
Reihe von m.E. schwer wiegenden Argumenten zeigt, dass der
Sachverhalt vermutlich komplizierter gewesen ist. Benennen wir einige
der Schwierigkeiten, die sich aus einer Sicht der cäsariensischen
Bibliothek als einer Einrichtung der Gemeinde ergeben:

(1) In den heftigen Streitigkeiten über die Rechtgläubigkeit des
Origenes und über die lateinischen Übersetzungen von dessen Werken
wird niemals auf Autographen oder bessere und ältere Handschriften
in Cäsarea Bezug genommen. Wir hören dagegen von den erheblichen Problemen des Hieronymus und vor allem den Kosten, überhaupt Exemplare der zahlreichen Schriften des Origenes zu erhalten
(*ep.* 84, 3 [CSEL 55, 124]). Dieses Bemühen habe seinen Geldbeutel
vollends geleert. Das klingt nicht danach, als habe er sich in Cäsarea
ohne Umstände Abschriften besorgen können. Entweder gab es in
Cäsarea kein vollständiges Set des Origenes mehr, oder—wahrscheinlicher—der Zugang zu der Bibliothek war schwierig oder gar unmöglich geworden. Auch die Texte der verschiedenen Übersetzungen des
griechischen Alten Testaments konnte sich Hieronymus nur unter
erheblichen Kosten und Mühen ohne Ende beschaffen:

> *Primum enim magnorum sumptuum est et infinitae difficultatis exemplaria posse*
> *habere omnis* (. . .) (Vulgata, prol. in libro Ezrae [ed. Weber, 639]; vgl.
> auch c. Rufin. II, 28 [CCL 79, 66]).

Nach der üblichen Sicht wären ihm diese Texte in Cäsarea in Gestalt
der Hexapla und ihrer Vorlagen frei zugänglich gewesen. Als Rufinus
gegen Hieronymus seine Theorie vertrat, die Schriften des Origenes
seien von Häretikern verfälscht worden—in *De adulteratione librorum*
Origenis,[26] dem *Prologus in Apologeticum Pamphili martyris pro Origene*

---

[25] Alle (freien) Spekulationen darüber, wo die Bibliothek von Cäsarea aufbewahrt
worden sein könnte, beruhen auf der (hier bestrittenen) Annahme, sie sei in
Gemeindebesitz gewesen. Vgl. z.B. Carriker, *Library*, 30–31; Gamble, *Books*, 159–160
mit den Anmerkungen auf S. 301–302.

[26] CCL 20, 1–17 (ed. M. Simonetti) und jetzt v.a. SC 464, 281–323 (ed. R.
Amacker und É. Junod). Die wenig ältere Neuausgabe durch A. Dell'Era (L'Aquila
1983) wurde wegen ihrer vielen überflüssigen Emendationen getadelt; vgl. E. Dekkers,
Clavis Patrum Latinorum (Turnhout ³1995) 64 Nr. 198a.

beigegeben, sowie auch in der *Praefatio* zu seiner Übersetzung von Origenes' *De principiis* (I *praef.* 3 p. 76 ed. H. Görgemanns—H. Karpp, ³1992)—beruft er sich doch niemals auf etwa bessere Exemplare in Cäsarea oder überhaupt auf diese Bibliothek. Die Idee, der ganze Streit um die authentischen Texte des Origenes könnte durch eine Konsultierung von dessen eigener Bibliothek—vielleicht gar mit den Autographen—entschieden werden, scheint keinem der Kontrahenten gekommen zu sein. Das ist mehr als auffällig. M.E. waren die Autographen längst verstreut und in Cäsarea nicht mehr vorhanden.[27]

(2) Dieser eigenartigen Beobachtung korreliert der kontinuierliche Verlust an Originalschriften des Origenes im 4. und 5. Jh., der zwar sicher durch die origenistischen Streitigkeiten mitverursacht war, aber offenbar nicht durch Abschriften aus Cäsarea aufgefangen werden konnte. Gerade der Vergleich zwischen Euseb und Hieronymus ist hier verräterisch:

> Eine Aufstellung der Werke des O(rigenes) bietet Eusebius, h.e. 6, 24. 32. 36; an der Aufzählung in ep. 33 des Hieronymus an Paula läßt sich ablesen, wieviel inzwischen schon von den großen Kommentaren (τόμοι), den Homilien und den sog. Scholien oder Exzerpten (kurzen Notizen) verlorengegangen war.[28]

Das ist kaum erklärlich, wenn beide Gelehrte die gleiche wissenschaftliche Bibliothek in Gemeindebesitz benutzt hätten, die sich gerade der Bewahrung des origenistischen Erbes verschrieben hatte.

(3) Eine größere Zahl bedeutender kirchlich-theologischer Persönlichkeiten des 4. und 5. Jh.s hat in Cäsarea gelebt und studiert, ohne dass wir etwas von einer Benutzung der Bibliothek hören, und vor allem ohne dass aus den erhaltenen Texten und Bruchstücken dieser Autoren wahrscheinlich wäre, dass ihnen die Fülle der Quellen zu Gebote stand, die Euseb noch benutzen konnte.[29]

---

[27] Über Kolophone, die sich auf angebliche Autographen des Origenes berufen (abgesehen von der Hexapla) s. Carriker, *Library*, 238 A. 199. Auf einem Tura-Papyrus (7. Jh.) mag eine solche Angabe glaubhaft sein, schwerlich aber auf einer Handschrift des 13. Jh.s.

[28] H.J. Vogt, Art. „Origenes," *LACL* (²2002) 529; vgl. auch Carriker, *Library*, 235–236.

[29] Selbst Carriker ist irritiert über das Schweigen der in Cäsarea wirkenden Autoren nach Eusebius (*Library*, 23).

Das letztere Argument ist ausschlaggebend. Etwa die Hälfte der von Euseb benutzten frühchristlichen Schriften scheint von keinem anderen Autor des 4.–6. Jh.s gelesen worden zu sein, wie A.J. Carriker ausgerechnet hat.[30] Das wäre schlechterdings rätselhaft, wenn Eusebs Sammlung Teil einer öffentlich leicht und allgemein zugänglichen Bibliothek gewesen wäre, in der unvermindert bis Hieronymus und darüber hinaus hätte kopiert werden können. Wir denken an Gregor von Nazianz, der unter Eusebs Nachfolger Acacius in Cäsarea gemeinsam mit dem späteren Bischof Euzoius Studien betrieb (*or.* 7, 6; vgl. Hieronymus, *de vir. ill.* 113). Sicher hatte ihn vor allem der Ruf des Rhetors Thespesius nach Caesarea geführt (dem er später ein Epitaph schrieb), aber sollte den Verehrer des Origenes sein Weg nicht auch in das Zentrum christlicher Bildung geführt haben, wo vielleicht noch Originale des Meisters aufbewahrt wurden? Gregor erwähnt davon kein Wort. Wie, wenn die Bibliothek ihm nie zugänglich war? Acacius selbst (Bischof wohl 341—365/67) und Euzoius—beide gemäßigte Arianer—waren selbst auch schriftstellerisch tätig, aber es ist zu wenig über ihre Schriften bekannt, als dass wir etwas über einen eventuellen Bezug zur Bibliothek des Pamphilos sagen könnten. Ihre Bemühungen um den Erhalt der Bücher und eine gleich zu diskutierende Passage aus Sozomenos zeigen aber, dass die Bibliothek noch vorhanden war (s.u.). Keinerlei Indizien besitzen wir dafür, dass die Mitte des 4. Jh.s aus dem Westen in den Osten des Imperiums (nach Kleinasien bzw. Skythopolis) verbannten Bischöfe Hilarius von Poitiers und Eusebius von Vercelli, die durch ihre Psalmenkommentare bzw. Übersetzungen zur Rezeption des Origenismus im Westen beitrugen, diesen in der Bibliothek von Cäsarea kennengelernt hatten.[31]

Salamanes Hermeias Sozomenos (380–445) stammte aus Gaza in Palästina, wo er auch die ersten Jahrzehnte seines Lebens gelernt und gearbeitet hat. Erst etwa 425 ging er nach Konstantinopel, wo er bei Gericht als Anwalt tätig war und seine Kirchengeschichte schrieb. Mit griechischer Bildung war er umfassend vertraut. Behandelt wird die Zeit von 324 bis etwa 422 in neun Büchern (das letzte ist nur ein Entwurf). Cäsarea nun wird von Sozomenos öfters erwähnt,

---

[30] Carriker, *Library*, 311.

[31] So zuerst R. Cadiou, „La bibliothèque de Césarée et la formation des chaines," *RevSR* 16 (1936) 474–483, bes. 477–478; dann auch Wendel, „Das griechischrömische Altertum," 132–133. Zurückhaltend Carriker, *Library*, 26.

ebenso die Bischöfe Acacius und Euzoius,[32] aber von einer Nutzung
der Bibliothek durch ihn selbst hören wir kein Wort, obwohl gerade
Sozomenos viele Originalquellen, Aktenstücke u.ä. verwendet hat (vgl.
seine allgemeine Bemerkung über seine Quellen I, 1, 13), über
auffällige Besonderheiten palästinischer Kirchen gut im Bilde ist und
öfters informiert.[33] Das Werk entsprang nicht einem offiziellen Auftrag,
wie das bei Gelasius von Cäsarea durch den letzten Willen Kyrills
von Jerusalem, bei Rufin durch Chromatius von Aquileia und auch
bei Socrates durch Theodoros der Fall war. Die thematische
Konzentration der Kirchengeschichte des Sozomenos, die Rolle, die
einerseits Cäsarea, andererseits griechische und christliche Bildungsgüter
in ihr spielen, macht es überaus auffällig, dass Sozomenos selbst die
Bibliothek offenbar nie besucht hat. Immerhin gibt es in seinem
Werk eine wichtige Stelle, die mit einiger Sicherheit als Anspielung
auf die Bibliothek zu verstehen ist:[34]

> οὐ γὰρ ὁ τυχὼν ἐδόκει Ἀκάκιος, φύσει τε δεινὸς ὢν νοεῖν καὶ λέγειν καὶ τὰ
> βεβουλευμένα εἰς ἔργον ἄγειν καὶ ἐπισήμου προεστὼς ἐκκλησίας καὶ Εὐσέβιον
> τὸν Παμφίλου, μεθ' ὃν τὴν αὐτοῦ ἐπίσκοπον ἤνυε, διδάσκαλον αὐχῶν καὶ τῇ
> δοκήσει καὶ διαδοχῇ τῶν αὐτοῦ βιβλίων πλείω τῶν ἄλλων εἰδέναι ἀξιῶν. καὶ
> ὁ μὲν τοιοῦτος ὢν ῥαδίως ἅ γε ἠβούλετο διεσκεύαζεν (h.e. IV, 23, 2).

Acacius bezog also seinen Ruhm und sein persönliches Selbstbewusstsein
nicht zum Geringsten aus der Tatsache, dass er Erbe nicht nur des
Bischofssitzes des Euseb (vgl. l.c. III, 2, 9; Socrates, h.e. II, 4 [GCS
N.F. 1, 95]), sondern auch einer bedeutenden Büchersammlung war.
Der Bischof meinte auch an theologischem Wissen seinen Gegnern
überlegen zu sein, da ihm die Quellen der Frühzeit umfassender zur
Verfügung standen als diesen. Nebenbei erhalten wir eine erfreuli-
che Bestätigung dafür, wie selbstverständlich die Bücher als die „seinen" (nicht etwa diejenigen der Gemeinde!) bezeichnet werden. Dies

---

[32] Vgl. die Stellen im Register FC 73/4, 1130. 1135 und 1148.

[33] Vgl. etwa seine ausführlichen Berichte über die kirchenöffentliche Lesung der
Petrusapokalypse an Karfreitagen (h.e. VII, 19, 9), über die Mönche Palästinas (h.e. III,
14, 21–28; VI, 32, 1–8 etc.), über den eigentümlichen und faszinierenden interre-
ligiösen Abraham-Kult in Hebron, den Konstantin auf Betreiben seiner Schwieger-
mutter Eutropia unterbinden ließ (h.e. II, 4, 1–8), über andere Volksfeste in Palästina
(h.e. III, 14, 27f.) und überhaupt *passim* über die Verhältnisse in seiner Heimat.

[34] Die folgende Stelle ist sowohl von Harnack in seiner Zusammenstellung der
Zeugnisse als auch von Carriker in seiner Monographie übersehen worden.

dürfte das wichtigste Zeugnis für die Zeit zwischen Euseb und Hieronymus sein. Für die kirchenpolitische Bedeutung des Acacius spricht sein Einfluss bei der Bestimmung des römischen Bischofs Felix, der Liberius ersetzte (Hieronymus, *vir. ill.* 98, 2), und sowohl bei der Einsetzung als auch bei der Absetzung des Kyrill von Jerusalem. Nach Socrates, *h.e.* II, 4 (GCS N.F. 1, 95) hätte Acacius Euseb eine verlorene Biographie gewidmet, ein weiteres Indiz für die enge Verbundenheit beider.

Etwas anders liegt der Fall bei dem älteren Gelasius von Cäsarea, einem Neffen des Kyrill von Jerusalem, mit dem wohl 367 die nizänische Partei vorübergehend den Bischofsstuhl Cäsareas errang (Acacius war noch ein Homöer im Sinne Eusebs gewesen), aber diesen sofort nach 370 durch die Einsetzung des Euzoius wieder verlor.[35] Die von ihm verfasste, bis 395 reichende Euseb-Fortsetzung, die von den Byzantinern noch benutzt wurde (Photios, *cod.* 89) und offenbar erst im 15. Jh. verloren ging, ist teilweise aus Rufins Euseb-Fortsetzung und späteren Zitaten rekonstruierbar. Socrates, Sozomenos und der traditionell „Gelasius von Cycicus" genannte Autor haben Gelasius von Cäsarea in unterschiedlichem Umfang benutzt; die Bibliothek wird indes in der noch erkennbaren Tradition nirgends eigenständig thematisiert.[36] Insgesamt gewinnen wir den Eindruck einer im 4., 5. und 6. Jh. nicht abreißenden theologischen und historischen Schriftstellerei in Cäsarea, die neben und nach Hieronymus nicht ein einziges Mal Bezug auf eine eigene und selbständige Benutzung der Bibliothek des Pamphilos nimmt und auch die Fülle der dort nach Ausweis des Euseb vorhanden frühchristlichen Literatur nicht mehr kennt. Das ist in hohem Maße erklärungsbedürftig.

Die gerade in Cäsarea heftigen Christenverfolgungen scheinen die Bibliothek nicht in Mitleidenschaft gezogen zu haben. Bezeugt sind in Cäsarea selbst Auswirkungen der Verfolgungen des Maximinus 235 n. Chr., des Decius 250 n. Chr., des Valerian 257/58 n. Chr.,

---

[35] Hieronymus, *vir. ill.* 130, erwähnt überhaupt nur seinen Episkopat nach Euzoius.

[36] Ob der trinitätstheologisch interessierte Grammatiker „Johannes von Cäsarea", den wir zuerst etwa um 515 n. Chr. literarisch fassen können, aus Cäsarea Maritima oder Cäsarea in Kappadokien stammt, wissen wir leider nicht (vgl. G. Röwekamp, Art. „Johannes von Cäsarea, Grammatiker," *LACL* (²2002) 376). Sein Schweigen wiegt daher nicht schwer. Das gleiche gilt für den Verfasser etymologischer Lexika Orion von Theben, der im 5. Jh. längere Zeit in Cäsarea wirkte, u.a.

des Gallienus 260 und des Diokletian 303–311.[37] Wir hören aber in keinem Fall davon, dass der Bestand der Bibliothek in Gefahr gewesen sei, wie es zu erwarten wäre, wenn sie in einem kirchlichen Gebäude untergebracht oder überhaupt in gemeindlichem Besitz gewesen wäre.[38] Allerdings wissen wir nichts Sicheres über die meist angenommene Kontinuität zwischen der persönlichen Sammlung des Origenes und der eigentlichen Bibliotheksgründung durch Pamphilos, die wir nicht genauer datieren können, die aber wohl in die Jahre zwischen Gallienus und Diokletian gefallen sein wird. Gerade Diokletian hatte in seinem Verfolgungsdekret besonderen Wert auf die vollständige Vernichtung des christlichen Schrifttums gelegt (Euseb, *h.e.* VIII, 2, 4), das nur in Privathäusern überdauern konnte.[39] Bald nach dem Ende der Verfolgungen ergeht der berühmte Auftrag des Konstantin an Bischof Euseb, 50 Prachthandschriften in Cäsarea herzustellen. Dies alles deutet darauf hin, dass die materielle Sicherheit der Bibliothek nicht unmittelbar von den Verfolgungen der Gemeinde betroffen war. Das aber ist am ehesten denkbar, wenn sie sich gar nicht in Gemeindebesitz befand, sondern als wissenschaftliche Einrichtung—wie in der Antike meist (s.u.)—in Privatbesitz war.

4. Das Zeugnis des Hieronymus

Die Autoren des 4. und 5. Jh.s scheinen die zahlreichen christlichen Autoren des 2. Jh.s, die Eusebius zitiert, nur noch über diesen zu

---

[37] Zu allen Details vgl. L.I. Levine, *Casearea under Roman Rule* (Studies in Judaism in Late Antiquity 7; Leiden 1975) 131–134. Levine unterstreicht die durchaus nicht selbstverständliche Schwere der Verfolgungen in Cäsarea. Für die diokletianische Verfolgung haben wir das ausführliche Zeugnis der beiden Fassungen (eine kürzere griechische und eine längere syrische) von Eusebs *De martyribus Palaestinae*. Neben allein 83 Hinrichtungen wurden zahlreiche Christen durch Ausbrennen eines Auges, Abhacken eines Fußes und Deportation misshandelt (vgl. *h.e.* VIII, 12, 10). Pamphilus wurde wohl Nov. 307 inhaftiert und am 16. Febr. 310 (oder 309) durch Enthauptung hingerichtet.

[38] Unter Missachtung solcher Plausibilitäten meint dagegen McGuckin, "Caesarea Maritima as Origen Knew It," 20, die Bibliothek sei von Anfang an sicher in einem Kirchengebäude untergebracht gewesen.

[39] Vgl. Wendel, „Das griechisch-römische Altertum," 129, mit Belegen.—Bekannt sind die Vorgänge 303 im nordafrikanischen Cirta, wo die kaiserlichen Häscher die Gebäude der Gemeinde (*ad domum, in qua Christiani conviebant*) nach Büchern durchsuchten (*gesta apud Zenophilum* 18a–19a, abgedruckt in den Werken des Optatus von Mileve, CSEL 26, 186–188), danach freilich auch vor Privatwohnungen nicht Halt machten. Doch waren in privaten Häusern die Chancen zur Rettung von Buchbeständen sehr viel größer.

kennen, von wenigen Ausnahmen wie Justin und Clemens abgesehen. Das spricht nicht dafür, dass diese Autoren in einer leicht zugänglichen Bibliothek noch vorhanden waren und kopiert werden konnten. Autoren wie Papias, Meliton, Quadratus und manche anderen scheinen bis auf Reste verschollen. Man müsste doch damit rechnen, dass gerade diese wertvollen Autoren, auf die Hieronymus in seiner ersten christlichen Literaturgeschichte mit großem Stolz verweist, auch sonst noch Interesse gefunden hätten. Autoren mit fragwürdiger Wahrheitsliebe wie Philippus von Side kommen hier kaum in Betracht (zu seiner Bücherleidenschaft s. Socrates, *h.e.* VII, 27f.). Aber selbst Hieronymus scheint die christlichen Schriftsteller des 2. und 3. Jh.s meist nur über Euseb zu kennen. Was *vir. ill.* 1–78 über die Anfänge einer eigenständigen christlichen Literatur steht, stammt weitestgehend in neuer Anordnung aus Euseb, wie schon oft beobachtet,[40] und nicht etwa aus eigener Lektüre. *De viris illustribus* entstand wohl Frühjahr 393,[41] als Hieronymus schon einige Jahre in Bethlehem gelebt und drei Frauenklöster sowie ein Männerkloster gegründet hatte.[42] Damit haben wir ein entscheidendes Gegenargument gegen die Auffassung, Hieronymus habe die Bibliothek von Cäsarea in ihrem ursprünglichen Bestand noch nur Verfügung gehabt. Was aber ist mit seinen scheinbar expliziten Aussagen zur Sache? Diesen müssen wir uns jetzt etwas eingehender zuwenden. Hieronymus schreibt in seinem Tituskommentar:

> *Unde et nobis curae fuit omnes veteris legis libros, quos vir doctus Adamantius in Hexapla digesserat, de Caesariensi bibliotheca descriptos, ex ipsis authenticis emendare, in quibus et ipsa Hebraea propriis sunt characteribus verba descripta; et Graecis litteris tramite expressa vicino* (in *Tit.* 3, 9 [PL 26, 630]).

Was steht hier mehr, als dass Hieronymus ein Exemplar der Hexapla besaß?[43] Aber es soll ja gar nicht bestritten werden, dass Hieronymus

---

[40] Vgl. A. Fürst, *Hieronymus. Askese und Wissenschaft in der Spätantike* (Freiburg u.a. 2003) 62 und schon z.B. G. Grützmacher, *Hieronymus: Eine biographische Studie zur alten Kirchengeschichte* 2 (ND Aalen 1986) 128.133 und Harnack, *Die Geschichte der altchristlichen Litteratur* I/2, 545.

[41] Vgl. z.B. Fürst, *Hieronymus*, 61 und 64 zur Titelform (Augustin lernte den Katalog noch ohne Titel kennen und fragte bei Hieronymus eigens nach dem Titel nach); Grützmacher, *Hieronymus* 2, 139 etc.

[42] Der Beginn des Bethlehem-Aufenthaltes ist auf 386 anzusetzen.

[43] In Untersuchungen über die exegetische und übersetzerische Arbeit des Hieronymus sind in der jüngeren Forschung erhebliche intrinsische Zweifel daran

gelegentlich in Cäsarea selbst arbeitete. Leider wird er nie wirklich deutlicher. Zum 1. Psalm schreibt er:

> ... *nam* ἐαπλοῦς *Origenis in Caesariensi bibliotheca relegens semel tantum scriptum repperi* (*in Ps.* 1, 4 [CCL 72, 180 ed. G. Morin]).

Anlässlich seines Konfliktes mit Rufinus heißt es einmal:

> (. . .) *in Caesariensi bibliotheca sex Eusebii uolumina repperi* Ἀπολογίας ὑπὲρ Ὠριγένους (*c. Rufin.* III, 12 (CCL 79, 84 ed. P. Cardet)).

An der wohl wichtigsten Stelle, aus der viele Autoren die eifrige Benutzung der cäsariensischen Bibliothek herauslesen wollen, ist genau dieses mit keinem Wort aussgesagt:

> *Pamphilus presbyter, Eusebii Caesariensis episcopi necessarius, tanto bibliothecae diuinae amore flagrauit, ut maximam partem Origenis uoluminum sua manu descripserit, quae usque hodie in Caesariensi bibliotheca habentur. Sed in duodecim prophetas uiginti quinque* ἐξηγήσεων *Origenis manu eius exarata repperi, quae tanto amplector et seruo gaudio, ut Croesi opes habere me credam. Si enim laetitia est unam epistulam habere martyris, quanto magis tot milia uersuum, quae mihi uidetur sui sanguinis signasse uestigiis* (*vir. ill.* 75, 1f.).

Diese Sätze sind ganz eindeutig. Hieronymus besitzt persönlich eine Handschrift mit dem Zwölfprophetenkommentar des Origenes, die Pamphilos noch mit eigener Hand abgeschrieben hatte. Dies betrachtet er als spektakulären und wertvollen Besitz, so dass er sich—wie wir sagen würden—„wie ein Krösus" vorkommen mochte. Die Handschrift hat er offenbar auf dem antiquarischen Buchmarkt erworben. Von einer persönlichen Beziehung nach Cäsarea sagt Hieronymus an dieser Stelle nichts;[44] nur, dass die Bibliothek zu seiner Zeit noch bestand und weitere Autographen des Pamphilos besaß (von solchen des Origenes ist nicht die Rede, nur von Abschriften des Origenes,

---

laut geworden, ob dem Kirchenvater je ein vollständiger Text der Hexapla zu Händen war. Vgl. P. Nautin, *Origène: sa vie et son oeuvre* (Paris 1977) 329; J.M. Dines, "Jerome and the Hexapla: The Witness of the Commentary on Amos," *Origen's Hexapla and Fragments: Papers Presented at the Rich Seminar on the Hexapla, Oxford Centre for Hebrew and Jewish Studies, 25th July–3rd August 1994* (ed. A. Salvesen; TSAJ 58; Tübingen 1998) 421–436, bes. 421–422; G. Cavallo, "Scuola, scriptorium, biblioteca a Cesarea," *La biblioteche nel monde antico e medievale* (ed. G. Cavallo; Rom—Bari 1988) 67–78, bes. 71.

[44] Fälschlich verweist E. Plümacher, Art. „Bibliothekswesen II," *TRE* 6 (1980) 414, gerade auf diese Stelle als Hauptbeleg für eine Nutzung der Bibliothek in Cäsarea durch Hieronymus.

die Pamphilus angefertigt hatte). Dieser Autor ist ja das Thema des ganzen Abschnitts, nicht etwa die Bibliothek, so dass die Nebeneinanderordnung beider Sätze Sinn macht. Es ist daher m.E. verfehlt, wenn diese Stelle unter jenen angeführt wird, die eine wissenschaftliche Arbeit des Hieronymus mit den Beständen von Cäsarea belegen sollen.[45] Davon ist ja mit keinem Wort die Rede. Über den Buchhandel des 4. Jh.s, den Hieronymus offenbar eifrig zu nutzen wusste, besitzen wir insbesondere aus dem syrischen Antiochien (leider nicht aus Cäsarea oder Jerusalem) eine Reihe von Nachrichten.[46]

Zu diesen Auffälligkeiten treten weitere Beobachtungen, die einen freien und ungetrübten Zugang zu der Bibliothek von Cäsarea fragwürdig machen. Um 375 schreibt Hieronymus nach dem Zeugnis von *ep.* 5, 2 (CSEL 54, 22f.) aus der syrischen Wüste an den Mönch Florentinus, der in Jerusalem ein Hospiz für Palästinapilger betreibt, einen Brief mit einer Liste von Büchern, die dieser für ihn kopieren lassen soll (nicht etwa an ein Skriptorium im näher gelegenen Cäsarea). Die dem Brief ursprünglich beiliegende Liste ist leider nicht erhalten. Im Tausch bietet Hieronymus Abschriften biblischer Texte aus seinen eigenen Beständen an. (Der Tausch wertvoller Bücher ist auch heute unter Bibliophilen ein gegenüber dem Kauf vielfach bevorzugtes Verfahren).[47] Von gegenseitigen Geschenken zwischen Bibliophilen, ja geradezu von dem Versuch des Hieronymus, sich Bibliotheksbesitzer durch kleine Gaben zu verpflichten, um Zugang zu ihren Büchern zu haben, zeugt sein Briefverkehr mit Paulus in Concordia (*ep.* 10, 3 [CSEL 54, 37f.]).[48] Auch als er in Bethlehem wohnte, nutzte er Skriptorien in Jerusalem, um sich Buchabschriften (z.B. der Dialoge

---

[45] Fürst, *Hieronymus*, 71. In anderer Weise missverstanden hat die Stelle Grützmacher, *Hieronymus* 2, 115.

[46] A.F. Norman, "The Book Trade in Fourth Century Antioch," *Journal of Hellenic Studies* 80 (1960) 122–126, der u.a. darauf aufmerksam macht, dass der Präfekt Strategius Musonianus zwischen 354 und 358 Probleme hatte, in der Stadt 10 Kalligraphen ausfindig zu machen, um Kopien des ihm gewidmeten Panegyricus des Libanius anzufertigen. Libanius sagt, das kalligraphische Potential der Stadt wäre damit ausgelastet gewesen. Vgl. auch S. Mratschek, „Codices vestri nos sumus. Bücherkult und Bücherpreise in der christlichen Spätantike", *Hortus litterarum antiquarum. FS H.A. Gärtner* (ed. A. Haltenhoff & M.F.H. Mutschler; Heidelberg 2000) 369–380.

[47] Zu einem antiken Fallbeispiel vgl. auch T.J. Kraus, „Bücherleihe om 4. Jh. n.Chr.: P.Oxy. LXIII 4365—ein Brief auf Papyrus und die gegenseitige Leihe von apokryph gewordener Literatur," *Biblos* 50 (2001) 285–296.

[48] Vgl. Fürst, *Hieronymus*, 66–67.205.

Ciceros) zu besorgen (Rufinus, *c. Hieron.* II, 11 [CCL 20, 91f.]).
Natürlich hatte er auch selbst Schreiber zur Hand (*ep.* 84, 3).
Hebräische Bibeltexte verschafften ihm jüdische Partner; offenbar
kann er sie sich nicht einfach in Cäsarea abschreiben lassen (*ep.* 36,
1 [CSEL 54, 268]). Das könnte natürlich auch daran liegen, dass
dort zwar vielleicht noch das Original der Hexapla und eventuell
auch hebräische Texte vorhanden waren, aber keine des Hebräischen
kundigen Schreiber (Origenes selbst hatte nach Euseb, *h.e.* VI, 16,
1; Hieronymus, *vir.ill.* 54, 6 zwar Hebräisch gelernt, aber das Ausmaß
seiner Kenntnisse ist umstritten).[49] Schreiber aus den jüdischen Schulen
in Cäsarea, über die wir recht gut unterrichtet sind, werden vermutlich keine Aufträge von Christen angenommen haben. Insgesamt bietet Hieronymus gute Belege für das, was Kim Haines-Eitzen jüngst
als „private scribal networks" der Alten Kirche beschrieben hat.[50] Er
musste alle Findigkeit aufwenden, um eine Bibliothek der für seine
exegetische und übersetzerische Arbeit benötigten Schriften zusam-
menzukaufen. Von der Existenz einer kirchlich-öffentlichen Bibliothek
in Cäsarea, deren Skriptorium Exemplare aller relevanten Bücher
hätte herstellen können, wird bei all den diversen und breit gestreu-
ten Nachrichten, die wir über die Buchbeschaffungen des Hieronymus
besitzen, nichts direkt sichtbar; ja wir hören abgesehen von den oben
genannten zwei Stellen aus seinen Kommentaren zu Titus und zum
1. Psalm nicht einmal, dass er diese Bibliothek für sich benutzt habe,
nur, dass bestimmte Bände dort zu finden seien.[51]

In dieser Hinsicht noch sehr viel erstaunlicher sind die Passagen
des Hieronymus zum aramäischen Matthäusevangelium. Er meint
ja, dieses nur von Judenchristen benutzte Werk sei das Original des
kanonischen Matthäus:

> *Mattheus qui et Leui, ex publicano apostolus, primus in Iudea propter eos qui ex
> circumcisione crediderunt euangelium Christi hebreis litteris uerbisque conposuit; quod
> quis postea in graecum transtulerit, non satis certum est. Porro ipsum hebraicum
> habetur usque hodie in Caesariensi bibliotheca, quam Pamphilus martyr studiosis-
> sime confecit. Mihi quoque a Nazareis qui in Veria, urbe Syriae, hoc uolumine
> utuntur, describendi facultas fuit (vir. ill. 3, 1f.).*

---

[49] Vgl. noch E.F. Sutcliffe, "St Jerome's Hebrew Manuscripts," *Bib.* 29 (1948)
195–204.
[50] K. Haines-Eitzen, *Guardians of Letters. Literacy, Power, and the Transmission of Early
Christian Literature* (Oxford 2000) 77–104 und 163–175.
[51] Wir hören auch nie von einem *bibliothecarius* o.ä. in Cäsarea (dieses Wort nebenbei bemerkt zuerst bei Fronto, *ep.* IV, 5).

Ein Exemplar dieses „Ur-Matthäus" sei also in der Bibliothek von Cäsarea vorhanden (so auch *adv. Pelag.* III, 2 (MPL 23, 597f.): *quod et in Caesariensi habetur bibliotheca*), er selbst habe sich aber eine Abschrift bei den Nazaräern (Judenchristen) in Beröa verschaffen können, die er dann auch übersetzt habe (*comm. in Matth.* 12, 13 [CCL 77, 90] u.ö.). Das ist gelinde gesagt erstaunlich, wenn wir uns—wie viele Autoren sich das vorstellen—Hieronymus als eifrigen Nutzer der cäsariensischen Bibliothek zu denken hätten. Die Passage bietet noch viele Probleme—was genau für eine Art von Matthäus-Derivat hat Hieronymus in Händen gehabt?[52]—aber hier interessiert nur die auffällige Buchbeschaffung, auf die Hieronymus offenbar besonders stolz ist. Er rekurriert ja noch öfters auf diesen Evangelientext, als dessen Entdecker für die Großkirche er sich offenbar profilieren will.[53] Dazu passt, dass er ihn von einer kleinen, versprengten, sonst unbekannten und isolierten judenchristlichen Splittergruppe erhalten zu haben beansprucht. Was aber soll dann die Nachricht, das Buch wäre in der Bibliothek des Pamphilos vorhanden—*wenn diese frei zugänglich und allgemein nutzbar war?*[54] Wir haben hier eine Diskrepanz, die uns auch gegenüber anderen Aussagen skeptisch macht. Allerdings ist es ja traurige Gewissheit, dass sich Hieroynmus die Tatsachen so zurecht bog, wie er sie in seiner oft maßlosen persönlichen Eitelkeit und Polemik brauchen konnte.[55] *Vir. ill.* 75 weiß er genau, dass

---

[52] Zu allen weiteren Problemen vgl. die bei Fürst, *Hieronymus*, 67–69 angegebene Literatur. Fürsts These, Hieronymus habe den semitischen Matthäus während seines Aufenthaltes in der Wüste von Chalkis kennengelernt (*Hieronymus*, 68), ist nicht möglich, wenn dieser, wie A.F.J. Klijn, *Jewish-Christian Gospel Tradition* (VigChr.S 17; Leiden u.a. 1992) 18, wahrscheinlich gemacht hat, das Buch erst um 392, also in Bethlehem, kennen gelernt hat.

[53] Alle Anspielungen auf ein judenchristliches Evangelium und auf judenchristliche Auslegungen bei Hieronymus sind mit Text und Übersetzung gesammelt bei A.F.J. Klijn—G.J. Reinink, *Patristic Evidence for Jewish-Christian Sects* (NT.S 36; Leiden 1973) 198–229.

[54] Zu bedenken ist auch, dass der Besitz häretischer oder potentiell häretischer Bücher (wozu der aramäische Matthäus nach Hieronymus natürlich nicht gehörte) als nicht unproblematisch galt, vor allem unter der totalitären Politik Theodosius I. Der 39. Osterfestbrief des Athanasius von 367 n. Chr. hatte vor der Lektüre solcher Schriften gewarnt, und es war offenbar eher eine Ausnahme, wenn sie in kirchlichen Bibliotheken aufbewahrt wurden. Was die zunehmende Reglementierung der Lektüre für eine Bibliothek wie diejenige in Cäsarea bedeutet haben mochte, entzieht sich unserer Kenntnis.

[55] Fürst u.a., die Hieronymus gegenüber diesen alten Vorwürfen möglichst rehabilitieren möchten, können dies nur erreichen, in dem sie die zahlreichen und offenbar wissentlichen Falschaussagen des Hieronymus nie zusammen betrachten,

Pamphilos fünf der sechs Bücher der Apologie für Origenes geschrieben hat (das 6. Buch stammt von Euseb), was er dann zehn Jahre später ableugnete (*c. Rufin.* I, 8–10; II, 23 [CCL 79, 7–9. 59f.]), um Origenes nicht durch den angesehenen Märtyrer Pamphilos verteidigt zu sehen und damit Rufin stärker entgegen treten zu können.[56] Man wird auch nur schwer vergessen können, wie Hieronymus behauptet, exegetische Details von jüdischen Informanten zu besitzen, die wörtlich aus Werken des Origenes übernommen sind.[57] Damit soll seinem Verdienst kein Abbruch getan werden; aber singuläre Einzelinformationen müssen immer kritisch gesichtet werden, vor allem, wenn sie mit seiner eigenen Person zusammenhängen. Kleine Detailbeobachtungen stabilisieren meine Skepsis. Von den Briefen des Pamphilos scheint Hieronymus nur über die Biographie Eusebs zu wissen (*adv. Rufin.* I, 9; II, 23 [CCL 79, 8.59]), was merkwürdig ist, wenn diese doch wohl in Cäsarea vorhanden waren (denn daher kannte sie ja Euseb; oder ist aus *adv. Rufin.* I, 9 zu folgern, dass sogar Euseb die Briefe des Pamphilos nicht mehr direkt gesehen hat?).[58] Schriften wie die vier Bücher des Dionysios von Alexandrien *contra Sabellium* und die Briefe des Origenes—zu Zeiten des Euseb in Cäsarea vorhanden—waren Hieronymus offenbar nicht zugänglich.[59]

Dies alles spricht dafür, dass die Bibliothek zur Zeit des Hieronymus zwar noch existierte und von ihm auch gelegentlich aufgesucht worden sein mag (das soll nicht bestritten werden), aber längst keine Arbeitsbibliothek auf neuerem Stand mehr und offenbar auch nicht frei zugänglich war. Dies ist ein übliches Geschick von Privatbibliotheken nach dem Tod derer, die sie zusammengetragen haben. Ihre Bedeutung für Hieronymus war offenbar viel geringer, als meist angenommen wird.[60]

---

sondern immer nur isoliert zur Sprache bringen, um sie im jeweiligen Kontext zu verharmlosen. Harnack hatte hier mit Recht weniger Vorbehalte gegenüber Hieronymus. Der entscheidende Punkt ist dabei, dass es ja nicht um entschuldbare Sachfehler geht, sondern um Falschaussagen, die Gegner grob verunglimpfen oder die eigene Bedeutung und Wichtigkeit herausheben sollen.

[56] Vgl. É. Junod, „L'auteur de l'Apologie pour Origène traduite par Rufin: les témoignages contradictoires de Rufin et de Jérôme à propos de Pamphile et d'Eusèbe," *Recherches et tradition. FS H. Crouzel* (Paris 1992) 165–179.

[57] Vgl. z.B. Fürst, *Hieronymus,* 131.

[58] Das vermutet Harnack, *Geschichte der altchristlichen Literatur* II/2, Anm. 3/105–106.

[59] Vgl. Carriker, *Library,* Anm. 84/27, mit Literaturangaben.

[60] Vgl. die gegenüber theologiegeschichtlichen Arbeiten viel vorsichtigeren

Hieronymus, *ep.* 34, sagt nun allerdings, Pamphilos habe die Bibliothek der Gemeinde dediziert. Wir haben die Stelle oben bereits kurz in Augenschein genommen:

> *Beatus Pamphilus martyr, cuius uitam Eusebius Caesariensis episcopus tribus ferme uoliminibus explicauit, cum Demetrium Phalereum et Pisistratum in sacrae bibliothecae studio uellet aequare imaginesque ingeniorum, quae uera sunt et aeterna monumenta, toto orbe perquireret, tunc uel maxime Origenis libros inpensius persecutus Caesariensi ecclesiae dedicauit, quam <bibliothecam> ex parte corruptam Acacius, dehinc Euzoius, eiusdem ecclesiae sacerdotes, in membranis instaurare conati sunt* (CSEL 54, 259–260).

Diese Aussage wäre eventuell ein deutliches Gegenargument gegen die hier vertretene Sicht. Aber was genau besagt sie, und trifft sie überhaupt zu? Wir sind bereits schwer wiegenden Einwänden begegnet, so dass Hieronymus hier einem Missverständnis unterlegen sein könnte, welches aus der Lebenszeit des Euseb stammt und in jedem Fall erst etwa 90 Jahre nach dem Tod des Pamphilos niedergeschrieben wurde. Vielleicht wurde die Sammlung nach dem Tod des Pamphilos in die Wohnräume des Bischofs gebracht, was bei Außenstehenden als Schenkung an die Gemeinde missverstanden wurde. Merkwürdig ist auch, dass die beiden Bischöfe Acacius und Euzoius *ecclesiae sacerdotes* heißen; wüssten wir es nicht besser, würden wir aus dem Wortlaut schließen, zwei Priester hätte in Cäsarea als ein gemeinsames Projekt das Umschreiben organisiert oder gar selbst durchgeführt (s.u.). Das Ganze macht keinen sehr verlässlichen Eindruck, und gehört eben vielleicht doch nur in die ja auch sonst immense Zahl von Sachirrtümern und Flüchtigkeitsfehlern des Hieronymus. Im Widerspruch zur (m.E. sachlich unzutreffenden) Angabe des Hieronymus steht übrigens auch die durch keinerlei Quellenindizien gestützte Vermutung A.J. Carrikers, unter Bischof Theotecnus (ab 260 n. Chr., also noch vor Pamphilos) sei die Bibliothek „under direct episcopal authority"[61] gelangt. Auch Harry Gamble spekuliert völlig unabhängig von der Aussage des Hieronymus:

Formulierungen bei dem Althistoriker Casson, *Bibliotheken in der Antike*, 184: „Eusebios (. . .) gehörte zu ihren Benutzern wie *wohl auch Hieronymus* in seinen späteren Jahren" (meine Kursivierung).

[61] Carriker, *Library*, 12 und 21. In direktem Widerspruch hierzu vermutet er S. 14, der familiäre Hintergrund des Pamphilos, d.h. der Reichtum seiner Familie, habe den Ankauf so vieler Bücher ermöglicht. Wenn Pamphilos nur Bibliotheksangestellter der Gemeinde war (was Carriker faktisch voraussetzt), ist das wenig plausibel.

Since the library of Pamphilus at Caesarea was not a congregational library of liturgical and archival material but an actual research library, it is a question what relation it had to the Caesarean church. During Pamphilus's time it must have been under his direct supervision, although, since he was a presbyter and not a bishop, it would ultimately have been under episcopal control. It appears to have come directly under episcopal control with Eusebius and his successors. It is unclear also where the library was located in relation to the church. Since the library at Caesarea escaped the persecution of Diocletian, it has been suggested that it was housed in a building not associated with the church.[62]

Dies ist eine lange Folge von *Non sequiturs* und kirchenrechtlichen Anachronismen: wie kommt Gamble auf die Idee, der Besitz eines Presbyters wäre im 3. Jh. automatisch unter bischöflicher Verfügungsgewalt gewesen? Das ist rechtsgeschichtlich (in heidnischer Zeit!) nicht denkbar. Und wenn Gamble im Folgenden gar spekuliert, die Bibliothek sei deshalb nicht zerstört worden, weil die Christenverfolgung in Cäsarea nur oberflächlich und flüchtig gewesen sei, so steht dies in eklatantem Widerspruch zum gegenteiligen expliziten Zeugnis der Quellen (s.o.). Immerhin sieht er deutlicher als Carriker die Aporien, die entstehen, wenn wir die Bibliothek als Einrichtung der Gemeinde verstehen wollen.

5. Wem gehörte die Bibliothek von Cäsarea?

Wenn die Bibliothek aber vielleicht doch niemals förmlicher Besitz der Gemeinde gewesen sein sollte, wem gehörte sie dann? Wir müssen in Hinsicht auf die sich abzeichnende Alternative zumindest prüfen, ob sie die bekannten Tatsachen besser zu erklären geeignet ist. Dazu ist eine Vorbemerkung erforderlich. Zwar hat die Antike durchaus in erheblicher Zahl öffentliche Bibliotheken gekannt. Auch mittelgroße Städte wie Korinth (Dio Chrysostomus, *or.* 37, 8) oder Karthago (Apuleius, *flor.* 18, 1–4; vgl. CIL VIII 997 über das Asklepiosheiligtum) besaßen solche Einrichtungen, und viele genossen großen Ruhm (in Kleinasien wird man z.B. an die bekannte Celsos-Bibliothek in Ephesus zu denken haben).[63] Kirchliche Biblio-

---

[62] Gamble, *Books*, 159–160.
[63] Vgl. weiter T.K. Dix, *Private and Public Libraries at Rome in the First Century BC:*

theken konnten, wenn sie das wollten, an diese etablierte Kultur öffentlicher Bibliotheken anknüpfen, zumal Bibliotheken oft in Tempeln
untergebracht waren.[64] Aber die größten und bedeutendsten, insbesondere wissenschaftlichen Sammlungen waren im Gegensatz zu heutigen Verhältnissen oft gerade *keine* öffentlichen Einrichtungen. Das
gilt selbst für die berühmteste aller antiken Bibliotheken, diejenige
des *Museions* in Alexandrien, wie zuletzt D. Delia herausgearbeitet
hat.[65] Ein kurzer Blick auf die Verhältnisse in Alexandrien ist lehrreich, um nicht vorschnell moderne Verhältnisse in die Antike zu
projizieren. Es ist völlig falsch, sich die Bibliothek von Alexandria
sozusagen nach dem Muster einer modernen Universitätsbibliothek
mit freiem Zugang und fleißig ein- und ausgehenden Studenten vor-
zustellen.[66] Eine Analogie sind eher die Fürstenbibliotheken der
Renaissance,[67] die wesentlich auch Prestigeobjekte waren, oder die
frühe griechische Bibliothek des Peisistratos. Seneca, *de tranquillitate
animi* 9, 5 hebt diesen Aspekt fürstlichen Prestigegewinns für die beiden Bibliotheken in Alexandrien stark hervor. Forschung geschah als
persönliche Vergünstigung durch den Fürsten, der sie finanzierte,
aber auch reglementierte. Ähnlich war es in Alexandrien: die beiden
Bibliotheken waren rechtlich Privateigentum des Königs bzw. später
Kaisers. Eine Ausleihe von Büchern gab es grundsätzlich nicht,[68]

A Preliminary Study in the History of Roman Libraries (Ann Arbor 1986); K. Vössing,
„Bibliothek," 643–645. Dion von Prusa schenkte seiner Heimatstadt eine Bibliothek,
über deren gleichzeitige Verwendung als Familiengrab sich ein Rechtsstreit erhob
(Plin. min., *ep.* X, 81, 7). Ob Cäsarea in heidnischer Zeit eine öffentliche Bibliothek
besaß, ist nicht bekannt. Zumindest die Rechtsschule, an der Gregor Thaumaturgos
studierte (*or. paneg. in Originem* 64 [FC 24, 146]), besaß sicher eine eigene wissenschaftliche Sammlung.

[64] Vgl. Delia, "From Romance to Rhetoric," Anm. 10/1451–1452.

[65] Delia, "From Romance to Rhetoric."

[66] Vgl. auch N. Lewis, "The Non-Scholar Members of the Alexandrian Museum,"
Mn. 16 (1963) 257–261.

[67] Doch war die Aufbewahrungsweise eher schlicht und anspruchslos. Die prunk-
vollen Bücherschränke der Renaissance sind der Antike noch unbekannt. Vgl. Wendel,
„Das griechisch-römische Altertum," 86–88.

[68] Das scheint in antiken öffentlichen oder halböffentlichen Bibliotheken der
Regelfall gewesen zu sein. Vgl. allgemein Wendel, „Das griechisch-römische Altertum,"
141–142, und speziell etwa die Benutzungsordnung einer Athener Bibliothek aus
der Zeit um 100 n.Chr., die inschriftlich erhalten ist (*Hesperia* 4, 1935, 330–332; 5,
1936, 42 [T.L. Shear]) und wo es heißt: βυβλίον οὐκ ἐξενεχθήσεται, ἐπεὶ ὠμόσαμεν·
ἀνυγήσεται ἀπὸ ὥρας πρώτης μέχρι ἕκτης) Auch den in heutigen Bibliotheken bekannten „Giftschrank" mit öffentlich nicht zugänglichen Büchern kennt die Antike bereits
(Sueton, *Caes.* 56).

während eine solche in Cäsarea zur Zeit des Pamphilos—nach einem
bei Hieronymus erhaltenen Zeugnis des Euseb (*c. Rufin.* I, 9)—zumindest im Fall biblischer Texte möglich zu sein schien. Es ist sehr
merkwürdig und vielleicht geradezu verräterisch, dass sich Hieronymus
nicht auf seine eigene Gegenwart bezieht. Die kleinere Bibliothek
des *Serapeions* (mit 42 800 Rollen nach Tzetzes, dessen letzte Quelle
Kallimachos gewesen sein wird) war möglicherweise eine leichter
zugängliche Zweigstelle der großen Sammlung des *Museions*, die auch
eine Art „Publikumsverkehr" gekannt haben könnte. Beide Bibliotheken
hatten keine eigenen Gebäude, sondern waren in Tempeln untergebracht.[69] Nach einer bei Tertullian überlieferten (*apol.* I, 18, 8), später von Johannes Chrysostomus (*adv. Iud.* I, 6 [MPG 48, 851])
wiederholten Nachricht lag das Originalmanuskript der Septuaginta
in dieser kleineren Bibliothek aus, was wohl Legende sein wird.
Natürlich dienten beide Bibliotheken der griechischen Kultur-
propaganda, aber wohl mehr durch ihre bloße Existenz als durch
leichte Nutzbarkeit in einem modernen Sinn. Diese Beobachtungen
sind deshalb so wichtig, weil sich aus ihnen der allmähliche Ruin
der Bibliothek von Alexandrien im 3. Jh. zwanglos erklären lässt.
Caracalla strich sowohl den beiden Bibliotheken als auch den in ihr
arbeitenden Gelehrten alle finanziellen Privilegien und jede staatli-
che Unterstützung (Dio Cass. LXXVIII, 7, 3). Damit war der
Untergang nicht mehr aufzuhalten. Der Redner Aphthonius, der
Alexandrien wohl um 315 besuchte, beschreibt in einer exemplari-
schen Ekphrasis die letzten Rollen in den Regalen und den Verfall
der Bestände (*progymnasmata* 12).[70] Was der Zahn der Zeit übrigge-
lassen hatte, zerstörten fanatische Christen in groß angelegten
Vernichtungsaktionen.[71]

Praktisch alles, was wir an antiker Wissenschaft kennen, geschah
unter primärer Benutzung privater Buchsammlungen. Was wurde

---

[69] Vgl. Delia, "From Romance to Rhetoric," 1459.

[70] Vgl. zu allen Details Delia, "From Romance to Rhetoric," 1463–1464. Die
Zerstörung der Bibliotheken unter den Arabern ist eine erst im 13. Jh. belegte
Legende (ibid., 1465–1466). Auch der Brand unter Cäsar ist historisch fragwürdig
(weil zeitgenössisch nicht bezeugt) und führte jedenfalls nicht zum Ende der beiden
Bibliotheken.

[71] Rufinus, *h.e.* II, 23–30; Theodoret, *h.e.* V, 22; Socrates, *h.e.* V, 26–27; Sozomenos,
h.e. VII, 15. 20; Zosimus V, 23; Eunapios, *vit. soph.* 472; Orosius, *hist. adv. pagan.*
VI, 15, 32. Vgl. auch *Suda* 3, 638–639; s.v. Ἰοβανός ed. A. Adler.

(und wird) aus solchen Privatbibliotheken? Der Besitzwechsel nach
dem Tod eines Besitzers pflegt einen erheblichen Einschnitt zu bedeuten. Wenn die neuen Besitzer kein Interesse an den Beständen haben,
wachsen sie nicht weiter und verwahrlosen in wenigen Jahrzehnten.
Oft werden sie einfach verkauft. Aber auch andere Faktoren tragen
zum Schwund bei: Wasser, Licht, Feuer, Mäuse—die großen Feinde
aller älteren Bibliotheken. Bücher werden ausgeliehen und nicht
zurückgegeben. Sollte das von Pamphilos' eigener Hand geschrie-
bene Exemplar des Origenes in der Sammlung des Hieronymus (s.o.)
vielleicht gar ein solcher Fall gewesen sein?

Nun ist die Bibliothek von Cäsarea weiter in vieler Hinsicht mit
den Bibliotheken antiker Philosophenschulen zu vergleichen.[72] Es ist
insofern aufschlussreich, dass auch diese offenbar in gewissem Umfang
persönlicher Besitz des Schulhauptes waren und auch im Erbfall blie-
ben. Das einschlägige Material hierzu ist noch nicht umfassend gesichtet worden; das kann hier nicht geleistet werden. Berühmt ist immerhin
das Schicksal der Bibliothek des Aristoteles.

> Sie wurde nicht als Bestandteil der Schule, d. h. des Grundstücks und
> der auf ihm errichteten Baulichkeiten, verwaltet und vererbt, sondern
> blieb persönliches Eigentum ihres jeweiligen Besitzers.[73]

Nach dem Tod des Philosophen ging sie auf Theophrast über, der
sie seinerseits Neleus aus Skepsis in der Troas vermachte, einem
Sohn des ehemaligen Platon-Schülers Koriskos. Die Wahl zum Haupt
der peripatetischen Schule fiel jedoch auf Straton, womit die Bibliothek
nicht mehr in der Verfügung durch die Schule war. Die Quellen-
angaben über das weitere Geschick der Sammlung sind wohl so zu
interpretieren, dass Neleus einen Teil an Ptolemaios Philadelphos
verkaufte, der damit Teil des alexandrinischen *Museions* wurde, den
wertvolleren Teil aber—insbesondere die Autographen des Aristoteles
und des Theophrast—behalten und mit sich nach Skepsis genommen hat. Dort wurden sie von Erben in einem Keller verstaut (angeblich, um sie vor dem Besitzeifer der Attalidenfürsten zu schützen)
und dann offenbar vergessen. Fast zwei Jahrhunderte später waren
die Handschriften von Feuchtigkeit und Würmern stark beschädigt;
ganze Passagen waren zerstört. Der reiche Bibliophile und Münzmeister

---

[72] Vgl. zu diesen Wendel, „Das griechisch-römische Altertum," 58–62.
[73] Wendel, „Das griechisch-römische Altertum," 60.

Apellikon, der sich in Athen niedergelassen hatte, bekam von der
Sache Wind und kaufte die Sammlung auf.[74] Seine Bibliothek wurde
von Sulla nach der Eroberung Athens als persönliche Beute (also
wiederum als Privatbesitz!) nach Rom gebracht (84 v. Chr.). Zwanzig
Jahre später ließ der Grammatiker Tyrannion unter der Hand—
ohne Wissen des privaten Besitzers—Abschriften herstellen, die er
dem zu dieser Zeit wirkenden Schulhaupt des Peripatos (Andronikos
von Rhodos) zur Verfügung stellte (Strabon XIII, 54). Durch Erbschaft
ging die Sammlung an Faustus Cornelius Sulla. Zu dieser Zeit nutzte
Cicero sie eifrig für seine philosophische Arbeit im nahegelegenen
Cumanum—wohlgemerkt als Privatbibliothek eines Freundes (*ep. ad
Atticum* IV, 10, 1). Ähnlich hat Cicero ja auch die Sammlungen des
T. Pomponius Atticus, seines Bruders Quintus Cicero, des Grammatikers Servius Claudius, die ihm dann dessen Erbe L. Paporius
Paetus im Jahr 60 v. Chr. zum Geschenk machte, u.a. benutzen
können. Wir erhalten hier Einblick in das Netzwerk, in dem in der
Antike Wissenschaft und Philosophie zu erheblichen Teilen nur möglich waren. Schulden nötigten Faustus schließlich zu einer Versteigerung
der Bücher, wobei Cicero erhebliche Bestände aufgekauft zu haben
scheint (Plutarch, *Cicero* 27).

Diese Ereignisse sind für uns nicht nur deshalb lehrreich, weil aus
ihnen das nicht untypische Schichsal einer Gelehrtenbibliothek ohne
interessierte Erben in schmerzlicher Weise kenntlich wird, sondern
weil wir deutlich sehen können, wie die Existenz einer philosophi-
schen Schule von den Besitzverhältnissen der Forschungsbibliothek
losgelöst zu sehen sein kann. Wir haben noch weitere Indizien, dass
Forschungsbibliotheken von Philosophenschulen jeweils Privatbesitz
waren: Straton, den wir eben als Nachfolger des Theophrast in der
förmlichen Schulleitung erwähnt haben, vermacht explizit die während seiner Zeit als Leiter der Schule neuerlich angesammelte Literatur
einem gewissen Lykon (Diogenes Laertios V, 62). Zwar wurde Lykon
dann auch Schulhaupt des Peripatos, aber die eigene Erwähnung
der Bücher im Testament zeigt, dass über diese jeweils gesondert
verfügt werden konnte (vgl. auch das Testament des Favorinus von
Arelate bei Philostrat, *v. soph.* I, 8, 3). Auch die Bibliothek des Zenon

---

[74] H. Gottschalk, Art. „Apellikon," *DNP* 1 (1996) 830, hält die Überlieferung für
fiktiv. Zwingende Argumente hierfür kann ich nicht sehen.

von Kition war sicher dessen Privatbesitz, wurde aber von Antigonos Gonatas insofern „gesponsort", als dieser dem Philosophen Schreibsklaven zur Verfügung stellte (Diogenes Laertios VII, 31). Ganz ähnlich kann man sich die Förderung der Bibliothek des Pamphilos durch die Kirche von Cäsarea vorstellen. Proklos aus Naukratis, ein Sophist des 2. Jh.s. n.Chr., verfügte in seinem Testament, dass seine Privatbibliothek auch nach seinem Tod von seinen Schülern genutzt werden dürfe (Philostrat, *v. soph.* II, 21, 3),[75] was sich also nicht von selbst verstand. Auch Augustin traf testamentarisch die spezielle Verfügung, dass seine Bibliothek in seiner Gemeinde weiter genutzt werden sollte (Possidius, *v. Augustini* 31, 5). Solche Regelungen entsprachen den Realitäten des antiken Unterrichtes, der wenig institutionell abgesichert war und sich in vielen Städten weitgehend privat organisierte, selbst auf einem Niveau, das wir heute universitär nennen würden. Der Fall der Bibliothek des Aristoteles könnte auch in Hinsicht auf Cäsarea von großer Bedeutung sein. Das Geschick der aristotelischen Sammlung könnte in manchem demjenigen der Bibliothek des Pamphilos etwa ab dem Ende des 4. Jh.s gleichen, und auch Licht auf andere ähnliche wissenschaftliche Sammlungen werfen.

Es ist lehrreich, von dieser Analogie her auf die Bezeichnungen der Bibliothek von Cäsarea zu blicken. Isidor hatte geschrieben:

> *Pamphilus (. . .) enim in bibliotheca sua prope triginta voluminum milia habuit.* (*etym.* VI, 6, 1).

Das weist sehr deutlich und unmissverständlich darauf hin, dass die *Bibliothek von Cäsarea zu Zeiten des Pamphilos dessen Privatbesitz war.* Er hatte sie offenbar als Schüler bzw. Nachfolger von Origenes geerbt, vielleicht über Zwischenglieder, oder auch einfach selbst zusammengetragen. Auch Hieronymus nennt sie noch *bibliotheca Origenis et Pamphili* (*vir. ill.* 113). Natürlich war sich der Gelehrte Pamphilos der Bedeutung dieser Sammlung bewusst und nutzte sie für seine wissenschaftliche und editorische Arbeit im Sinne des Origenismus. Das ändert aber

---

[75] Im römischen Recht wurde u.a. unter Tiberius diskutiert, inwiefern mit dem Vermächtnis eines Landgutes auch die Bücher bzw. mit dem eines Schrankes auch die darin befindlichen Bücher inbegriffen waren. Vgl. Corpus Iuris Civilis, *digest.* XXXIII, 7, 12 §34; XXXII, 52 §7 und XXX, 41 §9; Iulius Paulus, *sentent. recept.* III, 6, 51 sowie weiter Wendel, „Das griechisch-römische Altertum," 52.116.

nichts daran, dass er dies nicht sozusagen als Bibliotheksangestellter einer Gemeinde tat,[76] sondern als angesehener Gelehrter, der eine bedeutende Buchsammlung (vielleicht) geerbt hatte und sie (in jedem Fall) weiter ausbaute.[77] Euseb und Pamphilos standen in einem sehr engen persönlichen Freundschafts– und Lehrverhältnis. Zwar beruht die gelegentliche Behauptung einer leiblichen Verwandschaft zwischen beiden (Nikephoros Kall., *h.e.* VI, 37) auf einem Missverständnis des von Euseb frei gewählten Beinamens ὁ τοῦ Παμφίλου (eine Verwandschaft ist wegen Euseb, *h.e.* VII, 32, 25 unmöglich; vgl. Sokrates, *h.e.* III, 7). *Necessarius* des Pamphilos nennt Hieronymus Euseb (*vir. ill.* 75), woraus Photios (*ep.* 73) einen Sklaven macht. In Wahrheit ist ὁ τοῦ Παμφίλου wohl einfach eine ehrende Reverenz.[78] Ich halte es für plausibel, dass Euseb die Bibliothek von ihm erbte (zu der scheinbar widersprüchlichen Nachricht bei Hieronymus s.u.). Als Euseb dann Bischof von Cäsarea war, mochte der Eindruck entstehen, die Sammlung wäre eine Einrichtung der Gemeinde, zumal sie damals sicher in einer für Euseb leicht erreichbaren Form untergebracht war. Wahrscheinlich wurde aus ihren Beständen ein Skriptorium unterhalten, das dem Bischof und der Gesamtgemeinde zur Verfügung stand, wie es auch sonst mehrfach für größere antike Bibliotheken bezeugt ist. Aber mit dem Tod des Euseb musste sich dies ändern—und genau zu dieser Zeit beginnt es auffällig leise um

---

[76] Ohne Anhalt an den Quellen und gegen jede historische Plausibilität vermutet McGuckin, "Caesarea Maritima as Origen Knew It," 20, die diversen Reisen des Origenes seien zumindest partiell im Auftrag der Gemeinde zum Zweck der Buchbeschaffung für die Gemeindebibliothek (!) durchgeführt worden. Vgl. auch Carriker, *Library*, 21.

[77] Es ist ein Vorurteil zu meinen, Wissenschaft geschehe immer primär unter Benutzung öffentlicher oder akademischer Bibliotheken. Nach wie vor gibt es Forschungsgebiete, zu denen fast alle ernst zunehmende Arbeit weithin auf privaten Sammlungen und z.T. bedeutenden Privatbibliotheken beruht, die für befreundete und interessierte Forscher offenstehen. In der Antike spielte der private Austausch von Büchern eine größere Rolle als die Benutzung der öffentlichen Bibliotheken, die nach allem, was wir wissen, ohnehin in erster Linie „Klassikerausgaben" sammelten.

[78] So z.B. schon Harnack, *Geschichte der altchristlichen Litteratur bis Eusebius* II/2, Anm. 3/103–104, sowie auch 1, 2, 550; auch Frenschkowski, "Pamphilos," und vor allem die sorgfältige Diskussion bei A.J. Carriker, *Library*, 19–21. H. Lapin, "Jewish and Christian Academies in Roman Palestine: Some Preliminary Observations," *Caesarea Maritima: A Retrospective after Two Millenia* (ed. K.G. Holum—A. Raban; DMOA 21; Leiden u.a. 1996) 496–512, bes. 504, deutet als "intense personal relationship".

die Bibliothek zu werden. Diese Beobachtung wäre sonst schwer zu erklären. Hieraus mag sich schließlich auch die erwähnte Aussage des Hieronymus erklären, Pamphilos habe die Bibliothek der Gemeinde dediziert. Sie könnte nach dem Ende der Verfolgungen längere Zeit in Gemeinderäumen gestanden haben. Aber eine Institutionalisierung der Bibliothek in der ja nicht eben kleinen und kirchlich hoch angesehenen und viel beachteteten Gemeinde von Cäsarea ist praktisch unvereinbar mit ihrem späteren spurlosen Verschwinden, zumal sie auch noch mit den großen Namen des hochverehrten Mäyrtrers Pamphilus (der einen lokalen Kult hatte; s.u.) und des Euseb verbunden war. Es scheint mir daher sehr erwägenswert, dass Hieronymus die Besitzverhältnisse missverstanden hat. Nur wenn die Bibliothek Privatbesitz war, ist es verständlich, dass sie später so völlig aus den insgesamt nicht spärlichen Nachrichten über die kirchlichen Einrichtungen von Cäsarea verschwindet, ohne dass ihr Verlust jemals thematisiert wird. Auch Hieronymus selbst nennt sie ja gelegentlich noch *bibliotheca Origenis et Pamphili* (*vir. ill.* 113) und hebt auf diese Weise ihre primär personale Anbindung hervor.[79] Das ist auch die übliche Sprachregelung der Handschriftenkolophone (s.u.), die daneben Eusebius öfters nennen.

Ein weiteres interessantes mögliches Gegenargument ist zu bedenken. Das Umschreiben der Papyri auf Pergamente, das ausdrücklich auf die Initiative der beiden Bischöfe Acacius (340–366) und Euzoius (369–380) zurückgeführt wird, scheint auf eine gemeindliche Verantwortung für die Bibliothek zu weisen. Der Fall liegt aber doch nicht so eindeutig. Wir haben für diesen Vorgang nur zwei direkte Zeugnisse: Hieronymus, *ep.* 34, 1 (CSEL 54, 260) und *vir. ill.* 113, die praktisch identisch sind (zu eventuellen Spuren in einem Handschriftenkolophon s.u.). Vielleicht ist die Aussage in *ep.* 34 sogar erst nachträglich aus *vir. ill.* glossiert.[80] Merkwürdig ist schon die

---

[79] Entsprechend hatte die Bibliothek von Cäsarea viele Eigentümlichkeiten privater Sammlungen. Die Auswahl der vorhandenen Bücher war manchmal recht zufällig und jedenfalls merkwürdig, wenn man hier aus Euseb Rückschlüsse ziehen darf. Platon und Porphyrios werden hochgeschätzt, aber Jamblich ist noch unbekannt (Carriker, *Library*, 314). Ein Exemplar des platonischen *Parmenides* scheint gefehlt zu haben (ibid., 108). Aristoteles war gar nicht vertreten (ibid., 84); auch von dem verehrten Philon fehlte einiges (ibid., 175). Sehr auffällig ist das Fehlen jedes Zitates aus dem Diatessaron, von dem Euseb explizit zu sagen scheint, dass es ihm nicht zur Hand ist (ibid., 259–260).

[80] Vgl. nach dem Vorgang älterer Carriker, *Library*, Anm. 70/23.

Zuschreibung der Aktion an zwei zu verschiedenen Zeiten amtierende Bischöfe (die *ep.* 34 aber nicht als solche gekennzeichnet werden)—als ob das Projekt mehrfach in Angriff genommen worden wäre, oder über gute Vorsätze und bescheidene Anfänge nicht hinausgekommen sei. Beide Bischöfe waren gemäßigte Arianer; Euzoius wurde 380 nach dem Religionsedikt Theodosios I. exkommuniziert (Hieronymus, *vir. ill.* 113). In der Sekundärliteratur wird er oft mit dem etwa gleichzeitigen Bischof Euzoius von Antiochien, der Constantius II. 361 auf seinem Totenbett taufte und ebenfalls Arianer war, verwechselt.[81] Eine Identität beider ist aber unmöglich, da sie verschiedene Bischofssitze hatten. Welchen Einfluss das Religionsedikt Theodosius I. von 380 auf die Verhältnisse in Cäsarea hatte, ist schwer zu sagen: jedenfalls ging die episkopale Gemeindeleitung wie in Antiochien und in so vielen Gemeinden des Ostens aus arianischen in katholische Hände über. Dieser Prozess—und mit ihm die Zurückdrängung der Arianer und ihrer Splittergruppen—dauerte mehrere Jahre lang.[82]

Das Umschreiben einer ganzen Bibliothek—in der Antike ohne mir bekannte Parallele[83]—wäre ein Unternehmen, das eines erheb-

---

[81] So von T.P. Halton in den Anmerkungen zu seiner Übersetzung *Saint Jerome, On Illustrious Men* (The Fathers of the Church 100, Washington, D.C. 1999) 147. Unterschieden werden beide ganz richtig z.B. von M. Simonetti, Art. "Euzoïus d'Antioche" und Art. "Euzoïus de Césarée," in: *Dictionnaire encyclopédique du Christianisme ancien* 1 (1990) 930 bzw. 930–931. Eine Charakteristik des Mannes steht neben den bekannten Passagen bei Hieronymus, Sozomenos etc. auch bei Epiphanius, *pan.* 73, 37, 5–6, der Euzoius von Cäsarea als aggressiven, gewaltbereiten Arianer schildert.

[82] Nur in einer Anmerkung möchte ich die spekulative Möglichkeit äußern, dass die Exkommunikation des Euzoius den entscheidenden Bruch in der Geschichte der Bibliothek mit sich brachte. Wenn sie—wie ich denke—aus dem Privatbesitz des Pamphilus in jenen des Euseb und später in jenen des Acacius übergegangen ist, könnte Euzoius ihr letzter bischöflicher Besitzer gewesen sein. (Der Nizäner Gelasius war natürlich nicht von Acacius zum Erben eingesetzt worden, und kommt als Besitzer nicht in Betracht). Nach seiner Exkommunikation und seinem Tod (und der Rückkehr des Gelasius) fiel sie vielleicht in außerkirchliche, nicht weiter interessierte Hände. Sie war dann zwar noch ein paar Jahre vorhanden und wegen ihres ehemaligen Ruhmes unvergessen, stand aber der theologischen Arbeit nicht mehr zur Verfügung. Schließlich verfiel sie. Diese spekulative Vermutung hat den Vorteil, dass sie alle bekannten Fakten zur Nutzung der Bibliothek vollständig erklären kann. Es macht keine besondere Mühe zu verstehen, dass Hieronymus nicht erwähnen will, wenn sich die Bibliothek zu seiner Zeit im Besitz einer nicht-rechtgläubigen (faktisch arianischen) Familie befand. Das passt gut dazu, dass er die Bibliothek immer wieder als Referenzgröße erwähnt, aber seine eigenen Kontakte zu ihr niemals näher ausführt (z.B. in seinen zahlreichen autobiographisch so detailreichen Briefen nie von einem konkreten Besuch spricht!).

[83] Vgl. Birt, *Das antike Buchwesen*, 100–101.

lichen finanziellen, zeitlichen und logistischen Aufwandes bedurft hätte. Es wäre vielleicht doch zu erwarten, dass dieser Aufwand mehr Spuren hinterlassen hätte, bedenkt man zudem, dass wir von Bibelaufträgen über 50 Exemplare sehr wohl hören, und gerade Acacius in den nachnizänischen Streitigkeiten eine oft erwähnte, einflussreiche Persönlichkeit im gemäßigt arianischen Lager war. Vielleicht bezog sich die Aktion ja nur auf wenige schadhaft gewordene Exemplare. Die Haltbarkeit und Unempfindlichkeit von Papyrus dürfen aber auch nicht unterschätzt werden.[84] Die gerade in der deutschen Forschung gelegentlich noch anzutreffende Behauptung von der Fragilität bzw. Brüchigkeit des Papyrus ist heute definitiv widerlegt.[85] Dringender Bedarf wird also wohl eher für einzelne Bücher bestanden haben. Wurde das Projekt überhaupt in größerem Umfang durchgeführt? Ich erlaube mir trotz des gleich zu besprechenden Kolophons einige Skepsis.[86]

Von einer nun etwa einsetzenden breiteren Nutzung der Bibliothek kann jedenfalls keine Rede sein: Geradezu das Gegenteil ist der Fall. Außer Hieroynmus erwähnt diese aufwändige Aktion—*oder eine Nutzung der Bibliothek selbst*—kein anderer Autor, und Cäsarea ist ein bedeutendes Zentrum christlichen Lebens und christlicher Bildung gewesen. Diese massive Diskrepanz muss erklärt werden. Bei einer frei zugänglichen kircheneigenen Bibliothek wäre das sehr erstaunlich— man kontrastiere etwa, was Paulinus von Nola über die im Kirchenraum selbst untergebrachte Bibliothek seiner Gemeinde schreibt (*ep.* 32, 16 [FC 25/2, 782]).[87] Die allmähliche Bevorzugung des haltbareren Pergaments für Bücher können wir natürlich auch sonst im 4.

---

[84] Zur Haltbarkeit von Papyri vgl. H. Blanck, *Das Buch in der Antike* (München 1992) 82 und schon Birt, *Das antike Buchwesen*, 364–366.

[85] Vgl. auch T.C. Skeat, "Early Christian Book Production," *The Collected Biblical Writings of T.C. Skeat. Introduced and Edited by J.K. Elliott* (NT.S 113; Leiden—Boston 2004) 33–59, bes. 55–56.

[86] Übrigens las Hieronymus selbst den Origenes in Form von *Alexandrinae chartae*, also auf Papyrus, wie er *ep.* 84, 3 (CSEL 55, 124) schreibt. Auch das steht etwas merkwürdig neben der Aussage, dass er in Cäsarea auf Pergament umgeschrieben worden sei. Natürlich spricht Hieronymus hier aber von seinen privaten Exemplaren.

[87] Vgl. A. von Harnack, „Die älteste Inschrift über einer öffentlichen Kirchen-Bibliothek," in: Id., *Reden und Aufsätze* (Gießen 1916) 39–44. Die Kirchen knüpften mit der Aufbewahrung von Büchern im Kirchengebäude an den (vor allem ägyptischen, aber auch sonst bezeugten) Brauch an, in Tempeln Bibliotheken zu unterhalten. Vgl. Wendel, „Das griechisch-römische Altertum," 107–108.

und 5. Jh. beobachten, selbst in Ägypten (z.B. sind auch die im oxy-
rhynchitischen Dialekt des Koptischen geschriebenen Codices Glazier,
Scheide und al-Mudil auf Pergament geschrieben).[88] Der Codex hatte
sich Ende des 4. Jh.s auch in Palästina im kirchlichen Gebrauch
natürlich gegenüber der Rolle längst durchgesetzt, wovon u.a. der
Reisebericht der Egeria in deutlicher Weise Zeugnis gibt (*itin.* 10, 7;
33, 2), aber über das Verhältnis von Rollen und Codices in Cäsarea
wissen wir nichts Sicheres. Wahrscheinlich bestand auch die Sammlung
zu Zeiten des Euseb sowohl aus Rollen als auch aus Codices, nur
eben solchen auf Papyrus.[89] An unkompliziertesten ist die Deutung,
dass schadhafte Papyrusrollen und Papyruscodices auf Pergamentcodices
transferiert werden sollten.

Meine Vermutung ist, dass es sich um eine in ihrer Größenordnung
überschaubare Rettungsaktion für eine begrenzte Zahl von verschlis-
senen Handschriften handelt, welche die beiden Bischöfe finanzierten
oder dieses zumindest versprachen, um die immerhin berühmte
Bibliothek nicht verkommen zu lassen. Aber genau das scheint leider im Folgenden geschehen zu sein.

6. Spätere Zeugen für die Bibliothek von Cäsarea?

Keine Möglichkeit, die späteren Geschicke der Bibliothek von Cäsarea
zu klären, bieten nach der hier vertretenen Auffassung die Kolophone
spätantiker und mittelalterlicher Bibelhandschriften. Hier werden zwar
sowohl (gelegentlich) die Bibliothek als auch (öfter) Pamphilos, Origenes
und Euseb erwähnt, aber die Angaben sind nicht verifizierbar, vage
und wurden vor allem offenbar regelmäßig von einer Handschrift in
die nächste Abschrift übernommen, so dass wir gar nicht wissen,

---

[88] Vgl. zusammenfassend L. Casson, *Bibliotheken der Antike*, 173–176 und besonders T.C. Skeat, "Early Christian Book-Production," 53–58.

[89] Der Gebrauch von σωμάτια in einem gleich zu diskutierenden Kolophon weist
eher auf ein Umschreiben von Rollen in Codexform. Aber das Zeugnis ist zu spät
und zu singulär, um etwas beweisen zu können. Vgl. T.D. Runia, "Caesarea Maritima
and the Survival of Hellenistic-Jewish Literature," *Caesarea Maritima: A Retrospective
after Two Millenia* (ed. K.G. Holum—A. Raban; DMOA 21; Leiden u.a. 1996)
476–495, bes. Anm. 14/481. Interessanterweise wurde auch Philon schon im 3. Jh.
und frühen 4. Jh. in Codexform tradiert (was für literarische pagane Texte zu dieser Zeit noch durchaus unüblich war, wenn auch wohl meist von Christen. J. van
Haelst, *Catalogue des papyrus littéraires juifs et chrétiens* (Paris 1976) Nr. 695 und 696.

worauf sie sich tatsächlich beziehen.[90] Das Material müsste freilich neu gesichtet werden, was hier nicht zu leisten ist. Aber einige Beispiele werden die Probleme verdeutlichen und meine Skepsis in Bezug auf den Wert dieser speziellen Angaben der Kolophone begründen.[91]

Codex Vindobonensis gr. 29 (saec. XI) enthält nach dem Inhaltsverzeichnis (fol. 146v) die in Kreuzform angebrachte Notiz: Εὐζόϊος ἐπίσκοπος ἐν σωματίοις ἀνενεώσατο) Ohne Frage ist ἐν σωματίοις ἀνενεώσατο das gleiche wie *in membranis instaurare* (so auch Sophronius in seiner Übersetzung von *de vir. ill.*). Fraglich ist, ob wir ein von Hieronymus unabhängiges Zeugnis vor uns haben. Oder sollten wir die Abschrift (über wie viele Zwischenglieder, wäre immer noch unbekannt) eines Codex besitzen, der zu den in Cäsarea unter Euzoios erneuerten gehört hat? Das ist gut möglich, wenn auch der erhebliche zeitliche Abstand (4. und 11. Jh.) keine sicheren Aussagen erlaubt.

Im Codex Sinaiticus fügt eine Hand wohl des 6. Jh.s (C[Pamph] nach T.C. Skeat) am Ende von Εσδρας β (= Esra u. Nehemia in der LXX-Fassung) hinzu:

αντεβληθη προς παλαιωτατον λιαν αντιγραφον δεδιορθωμενον χειρι του αγιου μαρτυρος παμφιλου οπερ αντιγραφον προς τω τελει υποσημειωσεως τις ϊδιοχειρος υπεκειτο εχουσα ουτως· μετελημφθη και διορθωθη προς τα εξαπλα ωριγενους αντωνινος αντεβαλεν· παμφιλος διορθωσα (fol. 13),

dazu am Ende von Esther:

αντεβληθη προς παλαιωτατον λιαν αντιγραφον δεδιορθωμενον χειρι του αγιου μαρτυρος παμφιλου. προς δε τω τελει του αυτου παλαιωτατου βιβλιου οπερ

---

[90] Insbesondere müssten die paläographischen Datierungen der verschiedenen Texte, die ja öfters gar nicht von den Schreibern der Handschrift selbst stammen, überprüft werden. Ich folge hier nur der vorliegenden Literatur, ohne eigene Datierungen vornehmen zu können. Vgl. zum Problem G. Zuntz, *Lukian von Antiochien und der Text der Evangelien*, hg. von B. Aland und K. Wachtel (AHAW.PH 1995/2; Heidelberg 1995) 52–53.

[91] Alle im Folgenden genannten Kolophone sind nach der Sammlung bei Harnack, *Geschichte der altchristlichen Litteratur bis Eusebius* I/2, 543–545 und den (leider sehr viel unvollständigeren) Angaben bei Carriker, *Library*, 14–15, zitiert. Eine Kontrolle anhand der Ausgaben (zum Großteil des 19. Jh.s) bzw. von Handschriftenfaksimiles bzw. -fotografien ist mir im Augenblick nicht möglich, dürfte aber am Gesamtbild schwerlich etwas ändern. Vgl. auch H. von Soden, *Die Schriften des Neuen Testaments* I/1 (Berlin 1902) 680–682; A. Ehrhard, "Die griechische Patriarchalbibliothek von Jerusalem. Ein Beitrag zur griechischen Paläographie," *Römische Quartalschrift für christliche Altertumskunde und für Kirchengeschichte* 5 (1891) 217–265, bes. 225–243; G. Mercati, *Nuove note di letteratura biblica e cristiana antica* (Studi e Testi 95; Rom 1941) 7–48.

αρχην μεν ειχεν απο της πρωτης των βασιλειων. εις δε την εσθηρ ελεγεν τοιαυτην τις εν πλατει ϊδιοχειρος υποσημειωσις του αυτου μαρτυρος υπεκειτο εχουσα ουτως. μετελημφθη και διορθωθη προς τα εξαπλα ωριγενους· υπ αυτου διορθωμενα· αντωνινος ομολογητης αντεβαλεν. παμφιλος διορθωσατο τευχος εν τη φυλακη δια την του θεου πολλην και χαριν και πλατυσμον και ειγε με βαρυ ειπειν τουτω τω αντιγραφω παραπλησιον ευρειν αντιγραφον ου ραδιον (fol. 19).[92]

Man hatte also Teile der Handschrift (1. Kön. bis Esther) anhand einer älteren kollationiert, die ihrerseits auf eine solche aus der Werkstatt des Pamphilos zurückging. Der Abstand zu Pamphilos ist groß, und zeigt *ex negativo*, dass solche Kontrollmöglichkeiten für andere Teile des Textes nicht mehr zur Verfügung standen.

Näher an Cäsarea werden wir scheinbar durch ein Kolophon der sogenannten Euthalius-Handschrift H[Paul] (Coislianus 202 = H 015 Gregory-Aland aus dem 6./7. Jh.) geführt:

αντεβληθη δε η βιβλος προς το εν Καισαρια αντιγραφον της βιβλιοθηκης του αγιου παμφιλου χειρι γεγραμμενον (fol. 14).[93]

Unter dem Judasbrief ist zu lesen:

αντεβληθη δε των πραξεων και καθολικων επιστολων το βιβλιον προς τα ακριβη αντιγραφα της εν Καισαρεια βιβλιοθηκης ευσεβιου και παμφιλου.

Auch das besagt m.E. nicht unbedingt, dass die vorliegende Handschrift aus Cäsarea stammt, sondern vielleicht nur, dass ein älteres Exemplar aus dem dortigen Skriptorium zu Kontrollzwecken verwendet wurde (die Bibliothek heißt nach wie vor „die des Euseb und Pamphilos"), was uns keinerlei Information über den Bestand der Bibliothek nach Hieronymus vermittelt. Das gilt *mutatis mutandis* auch für das Zeugnis des Marchalianus (Vaticanus gr. 2125 = Q aus dem 6. Jh.):[94]

---

[92] T.C. Skeat, "The Codex Sinaiticus, The Codex Vaticanus and Constantine," in: *The Collected Biblical Writings of T.C. Skeat* (NT.S 113; Leiden—Boston 2004) 193–237, bes. 229, will daraus schließen, Codex Sinaiticus sei noch Jahrhunderte lang in Cäsarea selbst aufbewahrt worden. Dabei setzt er voraus, was erst noch bewiesen werden müsste: dass die Bibliothek so spät noch bestand. Aus dem Text der Kolophone folgt nur eine Benutzung von Exemplaren der Hexapla-LXX.

[93] Zu dieser Handschrift und ihrer Bedeutung vor allem für die Geschichte der Kapiteleinteilung vgl. C.R. Gregory, *Textkritik des Neuen Testaments* 1 (Leipzig 1900) 114–116 (mit Korrekturen 3 [1909], 1041) und die reichen Literaturangaben bei J.K. Elliott, *A Bibliography of Greek New Testament Manuscripts* (MSSNTS 109; Cambridge ²2000) 57–58.

[94] Die Handschrift ist berühmt als ältester Textzeuge der frühjüdischen *Vitae pro-*

μετελήμφθη ἀπὸ τῶν κατὰ τὰς ἐκδόσεις ἐξαπλῶν καὶ διορθώθη ἀπὸ τῶν
ὠριγένους αὐτοῦ τετραπλῶν ἅτινα καὶ αὐτοῦ χειρὶ διορθῶτο καὶ ἐσχολιο-
γράφητο ὅθεν εὐσέβιος ἐγὼ τὰ σχόλια παρέθηκα πάμφιλος καὶ εὐσέβιος
διωρθώσαντο (fol. 280 zu Ez.; ähnlich fol. 84 zu Is.).

Fast identische Behauptungen bieten eine ganze Reihe noch späterer griechischer Handschriften alttestamentlicher Texte.

Verdacht muss hier schon die späte Bezeugung erregen. Stünden
solche Sätze in erster Hand in einer der großen Majuskeln des 4.–5.
Jh.s, wäre die Beweiskraft höher, aber dafür gibt es m.W. keinen
Beleg. Wir erfahren etwas über das Ansehen der Bibliothek Cäsareas
(die nach wie vor „Bibliothek des Pamphilos und Eusebius" o.ä.
heißt, sich also nicht etwa mit aus Sicht der Handschriften zeitgenössischen Namen verbindet!). Vielleicht haben wir in einigen Fällen
sogar einfach ein Zeugnis frühmittelalterlicher Hieronymusrezeption
vor uns. Der Gelehrte beherrscht ja wie kein zweiter das mittelal-
terliche Wissen um die Bibel und wird zum Gegenstand einer reichen Legendenbildung—als eine Art Schutzpatron der exegetischen
Wissenschaften.[95] Gerade *De viris illustribus* ist im Mittelalter allgemein bekannt, wohl im 7. Jh. auch—sehr mangelhaft—ins Griechische
übersetzt (der schon erwähnte *Sophronius*, hg. von O. von Gebhardt,
TU 14/1b, Leipzig 1896) und von den byzantinischen Lexikographen
(Photios, *Suda*) gerne benutzt worden. Die Notiz des zitierten
Vindobonensis-Kolophons etwa eignete sich daher auch zur Wertsteigerung
einer Handschrift: Sie erhält das Flair alter Tradition. Es gibt ja
durchaus zahlreiche Kolophone bzw. *subscriptiones*, die sich aus der
Legende (etwa über die apostolischen Autoren des Neuen Testaments
und ihre Schüler) nähren. Natürlich spricht andererseits nichts dagegen, dass eine Vorlage oder Vorvorlage des *Vindobonensis* gr. 29 tatsächlich aus dem mittleren 4. Jh. stammt. Solange keine Zeugnisse
aus älteren Manuskripten auftauchen,[96] können wir kaum Rückschlüsse

---

phetarum, die dort nach der Prophetenliste des Euseb und vor dem eigentlichen
Prophetentext (dem Hauptinhalt der Handschrift) stehen, und als einer der wich-
tigsten Zeugen der Propheten-Hexapla. Vgl. die Beschreibung bei H.B. Swete, *An
Introduction to the Old Testament in Greek* (Cambridge 1914) 144–145, und weiter A.M.
Schwemer, *Studien zu den frühjüdischen Prophetenlegenden Vitae Prophetarum 1* (WUNT 49;
Tübingen 1995) Anm. 43/13.
[95] Schon zu Lebzeiten wurde er viel gelesen: *Hieronymus per totum orbem legitur*
(Sulpicius Severus, *dialogi* I, 8).
[96] Weitere Belege bei Harnack, *Geschichte der altchristlichen Litteratur bis Eusebius*, l.c.

ziehen—verdächtig stimmt in jedem Fall, dass wir keine einzige Information über die Bibliothek hören, die nicht aus Hieronymus oder Euseb geschöpft sein könnte. Dabei ist außer den schon genannten Stellen besonders noch an *adv. Rufin.* II, 27 zu denken:

> *Alexandria et Aegyptus in Septuaginta suis Hesychium laudat auctorem. Constantinopolis usque Antiochiam Luciani martyris exemplaria probat. mediae inter has provinciae palaestinos codices legunt, quos ab Origine elaboratos Eusebius et Pamphilus vulgaverunt.*

Die aus der Hexapla derivierte Septuagintaausgabe bot also den regulären Text in den Kirchen Palästinas.

Öfter finden sich Verweise auf den Text des „Euseb" bzw. des „Pamphilos und Euseb" weiter in den syrischen Glossen und Subskriptionen der Syrohexapla, der sehr wortgetreuen syrischen Übersetzung der Septuaginta aus dem Griechischen, die mit dem Namen des Paulus von Tella verbunden ist und vor 619 entstand (vgl. die Belege bei Fr. Field, Origenis Hexaplorum quae supersunt I, Oxford 1875, XCIX–CI, bes. A. 6).[97] Aber soweit ich sehen kann, deutet keine dieser Angaben auf eine direkte Benutzung der Bibliothek, nur auf die solide Kenntnis des (separat abgeschriebenen und zu Kontroll- und Vergleichszwecken verwendeten) hexaplarischen LXX-Textes, während einige der weitergehenden Angaben („aus dem Exemplar des Origenes") m.E. unglaubwürdige Fiktionen sind, welche der legitimierenden Absicherung des Textes dienen. Auch diese Notizen verdienen sicher eine weitergehende Analyse, werden aber schwerlich zu neuen Informationen über die Bibliothek von Cäsarea führen, die offenbar nur als vage Referenzgröße für die Textüberlieferung der Hexapla-LXX Erwähnung findet. Und die immense Bedeutung der hexaplarischen Arbeiten des Origenes und Pamphilos steht ja außer Frage. Sie darf aber nicht mit einer Benutzung der Bibliothek von Cäsarea selbst verwechselt werden. Zeugnisse aus neutestamentlichen Handschriften sind seltener, fehlen aber nicht völlig.[98]

---

[97] Vgl. auch Carriker, *Library*, 14–15, und v.a. Mercati, *l.c.*, der eine Typologie der betreffenden Kolophone entwirft.

[98] Vgl. oben zu H[Paul] (Coislianus 202 = H 015 Gregory-Aland) und weiteres bei Carriker, *Library*, Anm. 46/15–16. Für die Annahme eines eigenen etwa auf Pamphilos zurückgehenden Texttyps reichen die vorliegenden Indizien nicht aus.

Leider beweist keines der genannten Zeugnisse—oder macht es auch nur wahrscheinlich—, dass die Bibliothek von Cäsarea nach Hieronymus noch über ein aktives Skriptorium verfügte. Dass manche früher dort hergestellte Handschrift noch umlief, ist nicht unwahrscheinlich. Diese Zeugnisse können aber nicht tragen, was ihnen gelegentlich aufgebürdet wurde: die Bibliothek von Cäsarea als Ort aktiver Produktion von Manuskripten nach Hieronymus, ja im Grunde genommen nach Euzoius zu erweisen.

7. CODEX SINAITICUS, CODEX VATICANUS UND DER BIBELAUFTRAG KAISER KONSTANTINS

Last not least bleiben die vielfachen Bemühungen Spekulation, unsere Majuskeln Sinaiticus (ℵ) und Vaticanus (B) auf den bekannten Bibelauftrag Konstantins zurückzuführen. Diese These ist m.W. zuerst von Constantin v. Tischendorf[99] und in jüngerer Zeit vor allem von T.C. Skeat,[100] aber auch von G. Zuntz[101] vertreten worden. Dabei sind es einige sehr wenig zwingende Beobachtungen zu singulären Lesarten (Sinaiticus zu Mt 13,54 und Apg 8,5), vor allem aber allgemeine Plausibilitätserwägungen, welche diese These begründen. Skeat unterschätzt dabei m.E. die Zahl der ehemals vorhandenen Handschriften und vielleicht eben doch auch Vollbibeln.[102] Die geringe Zahl aus der Spätantike erhaltener Vollbibeln sagt nichts über deren grundsätzliches Vorhandensein, sondern nur über ihren in der Tat noch für lange Zeit geringen Anteil an der gesamten Produktion biblischer Handschriften. Deren Umfang aber kennen wir schlechterdings nicht. Vor Unterschätzungen müssen Nachrichten wie die bekannte Theodorets warnen, er habe bei einer Razzia allein in den Dörfern seiner Diözese 200 Exemplare des Diatessarons vernichten

---

[99] C. von Tischendorf, *Novum Testamentum Sinaiticum* (Leipzig 1863) XVIII. XXXI–XXXIV.
[100] Skeat, "The Codex Sinaiticus, The Codex Vaticanus and Constantine." Carriker, *Library*, Anm. 49/16, hat sich seiner Sicht ohne weitere Diskussion angeschlossen.
[101] Zuntz, *Lukian*, 42–45, der ganz den Argumenten von Skeat folgt.
[102] Konstantins Auftrag hatte mit einiger Sicherheit Vollbibeln im Blick. Vgl. Skeat, "The Codex Sinaiticus, The Codex Vaticanus and Constantine," Anm. 28/216–217, gegen die konkurrierenden Deutungen von Barnes (Handschriften des Neuen Testaments) und Gamble (Vierevangeliencodices).

lassen und durch die getrennten Evangelien ersetzt (*h.e.* I, 20).[103] Auch vom privaten Besitz von Prunkbibeln hören wir im 4. und 5. Jh. mehrfach.[104] All dies spricht gegen eine eindeutige Zuordnung von Sinaiticus und Vaticanus.[105] Die Diskussion anderer Details der (ohne Frage wichtigen und sorgfältigen) Studie Skeats ist an dieser Stelle nicht möglich, insbesondere auch nicht der speziellen These, Codex Sinaiticus sei noch Jahrhunderte lang in Cäsarea aufbewahrt worden (also gar nicht zur Versendung nach Konstantinopel gelangt). Konsens dürfte darüber bestehen, dass dies allenfalls eine kodikologische Denkmöglichkeit ist.

Der Bibel-Auftrag Konstantins erging auch nicht etwa direkt an die Bibliothek von Cäsarea, sondern an den dem Kaiser persönlich verbundenen Bischof Eusebius (Euseb, *v. Const.* IV, 36 f.; III, 1). Der Wortlaut des kaiserlichen Briefes macht dies völlig deutlich.[106] Der Kaiser hat sich schwerlich um Fragen der Textherstellung oder der Qualität von Skriptorien gekümmert, sondern hat sich an ihm bekannte kirchliche *Persönlichkeiten* gehalten, um den Mangel an Bibelhandschriften in seiner neuen Hauptstadt auszugleichen. Dies wird m.E. schlagend aus dem zweiten Großauftrag zur Herstellung von Bibeln deutlich, von dem wir im 4. Jh. hören. Er erging einige Jahre später durch Kaiser Constans an den hoch angesehenen (wenn auch umstrittenen) Athanasius von Alexandrien (*apol. ad Constant.* 4, 2 [MPG 25, 600C]).[107] Der Bibelauftrag an Eusebius, dessen Durchführung diesem offenbar erhebliche Probleme bereitete, da er ihn nur in Etappen erfüllen konnte, ist viel weniger ein Zeugnis für den Ruhm der Bibliothek von Cäsarea als für den des Eusebius. Unvoreingenommene Lektüre des kaiserlichen Briefes macht dies m.E. völlig deutlich. Von der Bibliothek, ihrer Arbeit oder ihren Skriptorien ist mit keinem

---

[103] Man vergleiche auch etwa Augustin, *conf.* VI, 5, 7; Optatus von Mileve, *c. Parmen.* VII, 1.

[104] Vgl. A. v. Harnack, *Über den privaten Gebrauch der heiligen Schriften in der alten Kirche. Beiträge zur Einleitung in das Neue Testament* V (Leipzig 1912) 69.

[105] Kritisch zu der von Skeat u.a. vertretenen These z. B. auch Gamble, *Books,* 80; S. Jellicoe, *The Septuagint and Modern Study* (Oxford 1968) 176–182.

[106] Der Brief ist mit einer Begründung seiner Echtheit auch abgedruckt bei Skeat, "The Codex Sinaiticus, the Codex Vaticanus and Constantine," 215–217 (unter Benutzung textkritischer Vorschläge von A.H.M. Jones).

[107] Diesen Auftrag wird man am ehesten in die Zeit zwischen der Rückkehr des Athanasius aus dem Trierer Exil November 337 und dem Beginn des zweiten Exils in Rom April 339 zu datieren haben.

Wort die Rede, was umso auffälliger ist, als der Brief ja eine detaillierte Sondergenehmigung zur Benutzung der kaiserlichen Schnellpost *Cursus velox* (die für Privatpersonen nicht zur Verfügung stand) und auch sonst einige Wünsche zur Qualität des Ergebnisses enthält. Konstantin hatte sich an Euseb als angesehene kirchliche Führungspersönlichkeit gewandt, nicht an eine Bibliothek, von deren Qualität er etwa gehört hätte. Als Euseb verstorben war, wandte sich der Hof entsprechend an einen anderen Kirchenfürsten—die Frage, über welche Skriptorien dieser dann den Auftrag ausführt, ist m.E. völlig jenseits des kaiserlichen Blickes gewesen.[108] Es ist im Übrigen gut denkbar, dass auch andere Bischöfe ähnliche kaiserliche Aufträge erhalten haben, von denen wir nur zufällig nichts wissen. Von den an Euseb und Athanasius ergangenen wissen wir ja auch nur über ihr eigenes Zeugnis. In diesem Kontext mag noch abschließend Erwähnung finden, dass bei den erheblichen Bemühungen Theodosius II. (408–450), in Konstantinopel eine Art kaiserlicher Reichsbibliothek aufzubauen (vgl. Niceph. Call., *h.e.* IV, 3), Cäsarea ebenfalls keine Rolle gespielt zu haben scheint. Diese Bibliothek umfasste bei ihrem Brand 475 n.Chr. 120 000 Codices (Zonaras, *epit. hist.* XIV, 2 Bd. III S. 256 ed. Dindorf, was nach *Suda* 3, 315 ed. A. Adler aus den Βυζαντιακά des Malchos stammt), wurde aber bald darauf wieder hergestellt, bis vermutlich der erste ikonoklastische Kaiser Leo der Isaurier sie 726 zerstörte.

8. Modelle für den Untergang der Bibliothek von Cäsarea

Welche Möglichkeiten sind in Hinsicht auf eine gewaltsame Zerstörung zu bedenken? Man hat gelegentlich an die Verwüstungen erinnert, welche räubernde Nomadenbanden im Palästina des 5. und 6. Jh.s angerichtet haben. Hieronymus selbst schreibt 405 oder 406:

> <*Quod*> *tardius beatitudini tuae Latino sermone translatum librum tuum remitterem, multa in medio inpedimenta fecerunt: Isaurorum repentina eruptio, Phoenicis Galilaeaeque uastitas, terror Palaestinae, praecipue urbis Hierosolymae, et nequaquam librorum, sed murorum extructio, ad hoc asperitas hiemis, fames intolerabilis nobis praesertim, quibus multorum fratrum cura inposita est* (*ep.* 114, 1 (CSEL 55, 394).

---

[108] Das Gegenteil vermutet—gegen den Wortlaut des Briefes Konstantins—Carriker, *Library*, 16.

Man vergleiche auch *ep.* 77, 8:

> (. . .) *ecce subito discurrentibus nuntiis oriens totus intremuit, ab ultima Maeotide inter glacialem Tanain et Massagetarum inmanes populos, ubi Caucasi rupibus feras gentes Alexandri claustra cohibent, erupisse Hunorum examina, quae pernicibus equis huc illucque uolantia caedis pariter ac terroris cuncta conplerent. (. . .) avertat Iesus ab orbe Romano tales ultra bestias!* (CSEL 55, 45; vgl. den Kontext).

Im Jahr 412 entschuldigt er sich in einem anderen Brief bei Augustinus für das langsame Voranschreiten seines Ezechielkommentars:

> *Hoc autem anno, cum tres explicassem libros, subitus impetus barbarorum, de quibus tuus dicit Vergilius: ,Lateque vagantes Barcaei' (. . .) sic Aegypti limitem, Palaestinae, Phoenices, Syriae percucurrit ad instar torrentis cuncta secum trahens, ut vix manus eorum misericordia Christi potuerimus euadere. quodsi iuxta inclitum oratorem ,silent inter arma leges', quanto magis studia scripturarum, quae et librorum multitudine et silentio ac librariorum sedulitate, quodque uel proprium est, securitate et otio dictantium indigent!* (*ep.* 126, 2 [CSEL 56, 144] zitiert werden Vergil, *Aen.* 4, 42f. und Cicero, *Mil.* 11).

Das wird man *cum grano salis* zu lesen haben; wir hören aus keiner anderen Quelle von diesem angeblich weit reichenden Überfall.[109] Schon 395 hatte Hieroynmus ja seine Angst vor den vorrückenden Hunnen artikuliert, wie aus den zitierten Passagen hervorgeht. Das Bild des bedrohten Gelehrten, das Hieroymus zeichnet, korreliert mit seinen Befürchtungen um Rom und seiner ambivalenten Wahrnehmung von Reich und Stadt.[110]

416 wurde Bethlehem von räubernden Horden geplündert. Hieronymus und die Mitbewohner seines Klosters überlebten in einem Wehrturm, doch ein Diakon wurde getötet. Das Kloster wurde ausgeraubt, zwei der Gebäude in Brand gesteckt.[111] Später deutet

---

[109] Beobachtet bei Fürst, Anm. z. St. in: FC 41/2 (2002) Anm. 574/340.

[110] Vgl. O. Zwierlein, „Der Fall Roms im Spiegel der Kirchenväter," *ZPE* 32 (1978) 45–80; J. Doignon, „Oracles, prophéties, 'on-dit' sur la chute de Rome (395–410). Les reactions de Jérôme et d'Augustin," *REAug* 36 (1990) 120–146.

[111] Das berichtet Hieronymus nicht selbst, wohl aber Augustin, *gest. Pelag.* 66 (CSEL 42, 121–122) und *serm.* 348A, 7 (Edition: F. Dolbeau, "Le sermon 348A de Saint Augustin contre Pélage, Édition du texte intégral," *RechAug* 28 [1995] 37–63, bes. 57). Merkwürdig und schon Papst Innozenz in seiner Korrespondenz mit den Betroffenen als bedenklich aufgefallen ist die Zurückhaltung sowohl des Hieronymus als auch seiner reichen Gönnerinnen, darüber Auskunft zu geben, wer eigentlich die Räuber waren. Es wurde allgemein auf pelagianische Häretiker geraten. Vgl. J.N.D. Kelly, *Jerome, his Life and his Controversies* (London 1975) 322–323, mit den

Hieronymus allerdings an, er und die bald darauf verstorbene Eustochium hätten zu dieser Zeit Bethlehem verlassen gehabt (*ep.* 138 [CSEL 56, 266]; 154, 2 [CSEL 56, 367f.]); wir begegnen hier vielleicht wieder der für ihn so typischen Widersprüchlichkeit der Behauptungen. Die Faktizität der Plünderungen wird man gewiss nicht bezweifeln dürfen. Dabei könnte, wie schon oft vermutet wurde, auch seine private Bibliothek zerstört oder zumindest in Mitleidenschaft gezogen worden sein.[112] So etwas ist nicht selten vorgekommen: der gelehrteste aller Römer, Terentius Varro, verlor große Teile seiner Bibliothek durch Plünderung im Bürgerkrieg (Aul. Gell., *noct. Att.* III, 10, 17). Immerhin überstand z.B. Augustins Bibliothek in Hippo unbeschadet die Einfälle der Vandalen.[113]

Sollten in ähnlicher Weise räubernde Horden auch etwas mit dem Ende der Bibliothek in Cäsarea zu tun haben? Das ist nicht unmöglich, aber doch eher unwahrscheinlich. Wenn man bedenkt, welche Bedeutung die Bibliothek für Pamphilos, Euseb und Hieronymus hatte, wäre das Schweigen unserer Quellen für eine datierbare gewaltsame Zerstörung schwer verständlich, gerade wenn man vergleicht, welche erheblichen Reaktionen von ganz verschiedener Seite wir auf den begrenzten Überfall auf Hieronymus' Kloster in Bethlehem besitzen. Ohne Frage hat es räubernde Banden im Palästina des 5. Jh.s tatsächlich in großer Zahl gegeben. Meist hören wir von Überfällen durch arabische Beduinen, die in der zeitgenössischen Literatur im allgemeinen Sarazenen genannt werden (vgl. auch schon Hieronymus, *comm. in Ez.* 25, 1–3 [MPL 25, 244] und *comm. in Ierem.* 3, 2 [MPL 24, 699f.], dazu den Sarazenenexkurs bei Sozomenos, *h.e.* VI, 38, 10–16).[114] Wenn Sarazenen aber je zu Lebzeiten des Hieronymus

---

Belegen. Ich halte es für möglich, dass der Verdacht absichtlich auf Pelagianer gelenkt werden sollte, ohne diese Unwahrheit explizit auszusprechen. Man beachte, wie pauschal Augustinus und Innozenz Bestrafung der Pelagianer forderten, ohne dass es irgendeinen Beweis für ihre Beteiligung gab, oder dass je klare Indizien genannt worden wären.

[112] Vgl. zur Bedeutung dieses Ereignisses für Hieronymus Fürst, *Hieronymus*, 70.118; Wendel, „Das griechisch-römische Altertum," 136, der mit Zerstörung der Privatbibliothek rechnet.

[113] Possidius setzt *vita Augustini* 18, 9 ihr Bestehen voraus; er schreibt aber nach der Eroberung Hippos. Zur Bibliothek Augustins vgl. dessen *de haeresibus* 88 sowie Possidius, *op. cit.* 18, 9; 31, 5. 7.

[114] Die Befestigung des Katharinenklosters wurde durch Justinian finanziert, um das Kloster vor den regelmäßigen Araberüberfällen zu schützen. In Palästina scheint die Zahl der Plünderungen vom 5. bis zum 7. Jh. ständig gestiegen zu sein. Am

etwas so Dramatisches wie die Zerstörung der bekanntesten christlichen Bibliothek bewerkstelligt hätten, würden wir dies wissen. Der fanatische Bücherliebhaber und Sammler großen Stils Hieronymus hätte darüber an mehr als einer Stelle geklagt, und auch für die spätere Zeit wäre ein Schweigen der Historiker ungewöhnlich. Außerdem war Cäsarea anders als das kleine Bethlehem, in dem Hieronymus lebte, eine große, vielfach militärisch abgesicherte Stadt, deren Geschichte uns gut bekannt ist. Für die spätere Zeit wäre am ehesten noch an die verlustreichen und blutigen Samaritaneraufstände zu denken, von denen Palästina 451, 484, 529 und 578 und dabei öfters auch speziell Cäsarea schwer betroffen war (vgl. z.B. Johannes Malalas XV, 8, p. 382; XVIII, 119, p. 487 Dindorf, etc.; noch Bar-Hebräus erwähnt sie). Wir hören von der Zerstörung von Kirchen und der Ermordung vieler Christen, aber wenig Spezielles (selbst in Konstantinopel gab es noch im Jahr 580 Straßenkämpfe mit Samaritanern). Die Aufstände waren jedoch jeweils rasch niedergeschlagen. Damit sind Möglichkeiten benannt und nicht mehr als dies.

Hieronymus bleibt der letzte Zeuge der Bibliothek von Cäsarea.[115] Manche Gelehrte haben es dabei bewenden lassen und nicht weiter gefragt:

> Wann die Bibliothek untergegangen ist, steht dahin.[116]

Spätere Autoren schweigen über die Bibliothek von Cäsarea. So wissen wir aus den Schriften Prokops von Cäsarea (geb. um 500 in Cäsarea Maritima) nur, dass er die Bibliotheken in Konstantinopel für seine Arbeiten herangezogen hat (vgl. zu seiner Heimatstadt bes. *anecdota* 11, 25). Freilich hatte Prokop eine primär juristische und rhetorische Ausbildung absolviert und war an kirchlichen Quellen weniger interessiert, so dass aus seinem Schweigen wenig folgt. Im 6. Jh. erlebte Cäsarea noch einmal eine kurze Blüte, nachdem um 502 unter Anastasius der Hafen wiederhergestellt worden war, wor-

---

bekanntesten waren die bis nach Phönizien reichenden Raubzüge der arabischen Fürstin Mavia (um 372), die 378 mit Valens Frieden schloss und ihre Tochter mit einem römischen *Magister equitum* verheiratete (Socrates, Sozomenos und Theodoret berichten ausführlich über sie). Vgl. weiterführend M. Gil, *A History of Palestine 634–1099* (Cambridge 1992) 17–18. Auch Plünderungen durch isaurische Banden sind im 4. und 5. Jh. bis weit hinab nach Phönizien bezeugt.

[115] So auch z.B. Fürst, *Hieronyms*, 71.

[116] Bardenhewer, *Geschichte der altkirchlichen Literatur* 2, 12.

über Prokop von Gaza berichtet. Es ist kaum vorstellbar, dass wir nichts über die Bibliothek hören würden, wenn sie noch greifbar und im städtisch-kirchlichen Bewusstsein präsent gewesen wäre. Auch die Pilgerberichte schweigen. Um 570 besucht der Piacenza-Pilger Palästina und dabei auch Cäsarea Maritima (*Antonini Placentini Itinerarium* 46). Er betet an den Gräbern der Heiligen Pamphilus, Procopius (gemeint ist ein Märtyrer der diokletianischen Verfolgung) und Cornelius (der Zenturio von Apg 10). Mehr wird zu der Stadt nicht gesagt, die er zudem fälschlich mit Cäsarea Philippi identifiziert. Keinem Zweifel unterliegt jedoch, dass er Cäsarea Maritima besucht hat, und dort Pamphilus Gegenstand eines lokalen Kultes gewesen ist, eine wichtige, meist übersehene Notiz.[117] Von der Bibliothek hören wir nichts. Und auch Hieronymus selbst schreibt 404 in seinem Bericht über die Pilgerfahrt der Paula und ihrer Tochter Eustochium (*Epitaphium S. Paulae, ep.* 108 *ad Eustochium* 6–14 [CSEL 55, 310–325]) über den Aufenthalt der beiden Pilgerinnen in Cäsarea Maritima. Hier handelt es sich um hochgebildete, literarisch interessierte Frauen, die sowohl gegenüber kirchlichen als auch säkularen Sehenswürdigkeiten voller Aufmerksamkeit waren. Sie besuchen in Cäsarea das angebliche Haus des Cornelius, das zur Kirche umgebaut worden war, das Häuschen des Philippus (Apg 21,8ff.) und die Zelle seiner vier prophezeienden jungfräulichen Töchter. Es ist—schon angesichts ihrer Beziehungen zu Hieronymus—praktisch undenkbar, dass sie nicht einen Blick in die berühmte Bibliothek geworfen hätten, *wenn das möglich gewesen wäre*. Weniger aussagekräftig ist das Schweigen späterer Pilger (Arkulf und Adomnanus z. B. erwähnen um 680 Cäsarea nur *en passant, Adamnani de locis sanctis* 20). Insgesamt ergibt sich der Eindruck, dass die Bibliothek schon im 5. Jh. nicht mehr zugänglich oder vorhanden gewesen ist. Aber von einer Zerstörung oder einem Verlust erfahren wir nichts, auch von Hieronymus nicht. Also wird das Schweigen andere, vielleicht banalere Gründe haben.

Es bleiben allerdings noch kurz zwei wesentliche Möglichkeiten gewaltsamer Zerstörung zu bedenken, die in der Literatur immer

---

[117] Sein Name wird auch in Menologien der Hauptstadt u.ä. erwähnt (*Leonis Diaconi menologium Graecorum, Basilii Porphyrogeniti Imperatoris iussu editum* [MPG 117] 315; *Synaxarium ecclesiae Constantinopolitanae*, ed. H. Delehaye, 467–468). Pamphilos' jugendlicher Schüler Porphyrios (nicht mit dem Neuplatoniker zu verwechseln) hatte es mit dem Tode bezahlen müssen, den Statthalter nach dem Leichnam des Märtyrers gefragt zu haben (Euseb, *de mart. Palest.* 11, 15–19).

wieder einmal genannt werden:[118] Erdbeben, Feuer und ähnliche Naturkatastrophen einerseits, und die schließliche Eroberung Palästinas durch die Araber bzw. Perser andererseits. Hier sind nur einige allgemeine Wahrscheinlichkeitserwägungen möglich. Von Bibliotheksbränden hören wir ausgesprochen oft. Die von Augustus nach einer Anregung Cäsars und nach dem Vorbild des Asinius Pollio in der Porticus des Apollon-Tempels auf dem Palatin errichtete öffentliche Bibliothek z.B. ist vermutlich 363 n.Chr. durch einen Brand zerstört worden (*Amm. Marcell.* XXIII, 3, 3), nachdem sie schon früher mehrfach gebrannt hatte. Die Möglichkeiten zu solchen Ereignissen waren groß: Rom besaß zur Zeit Konstantins 28 öffentliche Bibliotheken.[119] Aber Feuer war natürlich zu allen Zeit ein Hauptfeind von Bibliotheken (vgl. auch die persönlichen schmerzlichen Erfahrungen Galens, ed. Kühn XV p. 24 und mehrfach in *De libris propriis*, ed Kühn XIX, p. 19. 41, dazu *de comp. med.* I, 1 ed. Kühn XIII p. 362; ed. Kühn XIII p. 66 und *Dio Cass.* LXXII, 24, 1f.). Stadtbrände waren in der Antike weitaus häufiger als heute. Die Bibliothek des *Museions* von Antiochien hat sowohl unter Tiberius als auch unter Jovian gebrannt (Joh. Malalas X, 10 p. 235f. Dindorf). Hieronymus selbst erwähnt noch ein Feuer, das eine sonst nicht bezeugte Bibliothek auf dem Kapitol unter Commodus 188 n.Chr. zerstört habe (*Chron. a. Abrah.* 2204 [GCS Eusebius 7 ed. R. Helm, 3. Aufl. 1984, 209]).[120] Aus der stadtrömischen Geschichte sind überhaupt zahlreiche antike Bibliotheksbrände überliefert (insgesamt annähernd 20), die offenbar immer vielbeachtete Ereignisse waren.[121]

Neben Feuer sind Erdbeben die massivsten Naturereignisse, die zu bedenken sein könnten. Palästina und gerade auch Syrien und

---

[118] Allgemein über die leichte unabsichtliche Vernichtung von privaten Büchern und auch Bibeln vgl. Optatus v. Mileve, *c. Pirmin.* VII, 1 (CSEL 26, 166–167; die Stelle auch bei Harnack, *Über den privaten Gebrauch der heiligen Schriften*, 72).

[119] Wendel, „Das griechisch-römische Altertum," 125.—Legende wird es freilich sein, wenn Zosimos von Askalon (Rhetor in Gaza um 500 n.Chr.) in seinem βίος Δημοσθένους vom Brand der Bibliothek von Athen erzählt, bei der das Geschichtswerk des Thukydides zerstört worden sei, welches Demosthenes danach aus dem Gedächtnis wiederhergestellt habe (*Oratores Attici* ed. C. Müller, II p. 523).

[120] Am Tag, da ich dies schreibe (2. Sept. 2004), ist in Weimar die Herzogin-Anna-Amalia-Bibliothek, die zum UNESCO-Weltkulturerbe gehört, zu erheblichen Teilen ein Raub der Flammen geworden, wenige Wochen bevor die unersetzlichen Buchbestände in eine feuersichere neue Bibliothek umgelagert werden sollten. Etwa 40 000 Bände sind zerstört oder durch Löschwasser beschädigt worden.

[121] Vgl. P. Werner, *De incendiis urbis Romae* (Diss. Leipzig 1906).

die Küste gehören zudem zu den erdbebenreichsten Gebieten der Erde. Mehrfach hören wir von der Zerstörung ganzer Regionen, von Beben mit Tausenden, z.T. sogar Zehntausenden von Toten und der Verwüstung ganzer Dörfer und Städte.[122] Am 15. 08. 502 wurde z.B. die Küstenregion von Beirut bis in die Schefela erschüttert, während am 09. 06. 551 ein Beben katastrophalen Ausmaßes für ganz Palästina und Syrien bezeugt ist (völlige Zerstörung Petras). In einem solchen Fall könnte der Verlust der Bibliothek sozusagen nebenbei zu beklagen gewesen sein. So scheint es der Celsos-Bibliothek in Ephesus ergangen zu sein, deren Bausubstanz dann von benachbarten Wohnhäusern genutzt wurde. Aber konkrete Indizien für eine solche Annahme (Zerstörung durch Feuer oder Erdbeben) gibt es für Cäsarea nicht.

Da in der Sekundärliteratur—wenn auch ohne bestimmte, etwa aus den Quellen abgestützte Argumente—immer wieder auf die arabische Invasion rekurriert wird, müssen wir diese Möglichkeit etwas eingehender diskutieren. Viele antike Bibliotheken sind ja bei Kriegseinwirkungen vernichtet worden, in der uns interessierenden Zeit z.B. die *Bibliotheca ad clivum Scauri* des Papstes Agapet im Jahr 546 anlässlich der Rückeroberung Roms durch Totila.[123] Cassiodor, *inst.* II, 5, 10 spricht wenig später ganz allgemein von der hohen Wahrscheinlichkeit, dass Bücher durch Barbareneinfälle (*gentili excursione*) unwiederbringlich verloren gehen. Aber solche allgemeinen Möglichkeiten ersetzen keine konkreten historischen Nachrichten. Manche Autoren haben sich hier mit einer angesichts der Quellen völlig unverständlichen Zuversicht geäußert:

> The great library of Caesarea probably functioned until the Persians conquered the city in 614 or possibly until the Arabs devastated Caesarea in 640[124]

---

[122] Für den syrischen Raum sind alle literarisch bezeugten Beben aufgelistet bei W. Capelle, Art. „Erdbebenforschung," *PW.Supp.* 4 (1924) 344–374, bes. 355–357; speziell für Palästina ist noch das ältere Buch von B. Willis, *Earthquakes in the Holy Land* (Stanford 1928) zu vergleichen; dazu auch M. Gil, *History*, 78.89–90; aus naturwissenschaftlicher Sicht siehe u.a. die zahlreichen einschlägigen Arbeiten des Geophysikers Amos Nur [Bibliographie unter: http://srb.stanford.edu/nur/].

[123] P. Courcelle, *Les lettres grecques en occident. De Macrobe à Cassiodor* (Paris 1948) 315–415, bes. 316.

[124] J. McRay, Art. "Caesarea," in: *Encyclopedia of Early Christianity* (1997) 199–201, bes. 201.

schreibt ein Autor noch 1997 in einem weitverbreiteten patristischen Nachschlagewerk.[125] Aber schon Adolf von Harnack äußerte sich mit nicht weniger sicherem Tonfall:

> Die Bibliothek, deren Schätze in Abschriften uns z.T. noch heute zugute kommen, wurde von den Arabern i. J. 653 zerstört.[126]

Was spricht für diese Sicht?

Cäsarea blieb auch in den Wirren des 5. und 6. Jh.s eine bedeutende Stadt Palästinas. 614 wurde die gesamte Region bis nach Ägypten von den Persern eingenommen und gehörte damit erneut in das Konfliktfeld des Jahrhunderte währenden Konkurrenzkampfes zwischen den beiden Großmächten, dem byzantinischen und dem sassanidischen Reich. Die mühsame Rückeroberung unter Heraclius (*reg.* 610–641), in den Jahren 626–628 bot keinen dauerhaften Erfolg: rasch folgte die islamische Invasion, der Byzanz wenig entgegenzustellen hatte. Gegenüber den Arabern widerstanden Cäsarea und Jerusalem am längsten. 638 (nach anderen, weniger wahrscheinlichen Quellen 636 oder 637) fiel Jerusalem. Die Belagerung Cäsareas—begonnen wohl schon Juli 634[127]—war kurzfristig aufgehoben worden, um die Truppen bei Jerusalem zu konzentrieren, aber nach dessen Fall konnte auch Cäsarea trotz seines Zuganges zu Meer (über das viele aus der Stadt flohen) nicht mehr lange Widerstand leisten. 640 (nach anderen erst 641) nahm die Armee Mu'āwiyas die Stadt ein.

---

[125] Sachlich identisch z.B. D. Stiernon, Art. „Césarée de Palestine I. Origines du Christianisme," in: *Dictionnaire encyclopédique du Christianisme ancien* 1 (1990) 453–454, bes. 454; G. Bönig, Art. „Kaisareia am Meer," in LThK² 5 (1960) 1244; vorsichtiger in diesem Sinn z.B. Fürst, *Hieronymus*, 71; Gamble, *Books*, 160 und z.B. auch schon Swete, *An Introduction to the Old Testament in Greek*, 75. Runia, "Caesarea Maritima and the Survival of Hellenistic-Jewish Literature," 477, meint gar, die Bibliothek „was preserved at least until the sixth century" (unter Berufung auf das oben diskutierte Kolophon aus Coislianus 202).

[126] A. v. Harnack, *Die Mission und Ausbreitung des Christentums in den ersten drei Jahrhunderten* (Leipzig ⁴1924; ND Wiesbaden 1981) Anm. 1/640. Man beachte, wieviel zurückhaltender sich der Bibliothekswissenschaftler Wendel ausdrückt: „Über das weitere Schicksal der Bibliothek liegen keine Nachrichten vor." ("Das griechisch-römische Altertum," 133). Ähnlich zurückhaltend E. Plümacher, Art. "Bibliothekswesen II," *TRE* 6 (1980) 414.

[127] Vgl. Gil, *History*, 59. Gil ist überhaupt zu allen hier interessierenden Fragen der islamischen Invasion zu vergleichen. Vgl. auch K.G. Holum u.a., *King Herod's Dream. Caesarea on the Sea* (New York 1988) 203–206; R. Schick, *The Christian Communities of Palestine from Byzantine to Islamic Rule: A Historical and Archaeological Study* (Studies in Late Antiquity and Early Islam 2; Princeton 1995) 276–279.

Die Eroberung selbst wird in den islamischen Quellen ausführlich beschrieben. Ṭabarī (gest. 923), ein meist glaubwürdiger Autor, der mehr Ansätze eines kritischen Umganges mit seinen Quellen zeigt als jeder byzantinische oder lateinische Schriftsteller seiner Zeit, berichtet, bei der Belagerung seien 80 000 Bewohner ums Leben gekommen, später bei der Einnahme noch einmal 20 000 weitere (*Taʾrīkh al-rusul waʾl-mulūk* I, 2396f.). Die Verwüstungen müssen immens gewesen sein. Ich halte es für nicht unwahrscheinlich, dass Ṭabarī, der selbst ein Büchersammler ganz großen Stils war, eine in irgendeiner Weise spektakuläre Bibliotheksvernichtung erwähnt hätte, wenn sie in den ihm vorliegenden Quellen zur Sprache gekommen wäre, aber Sicherheit ist hier nicht zu gewinnen. Keiner der durchaus nicht spärlichen Berichte über die arabische bzw. persische Invasion Palästinas berichtet hierzu etwas, während wir über das Geschick z.B. von Kirchengebäuden eine ganze Reihe von Nachrichten besitzen.[128] So beschreiben *Vita und Martyrium Anastasius' des Persers* (gest. 628) ausführlich jene Kirchen der Stadt, die auch unter sassanidischer Okkupation in den 620er Jahren noch in Betrieb waren[129] (erst 484 hatte Kaiser Zenon die große Prokop-Kirche nach ihrer Zerstörung durch Samaritaner neu errichten lassen).

Wenn die Bibliothek in späterer Zeit, nach der islamischen Invasion noch bestanden hätte, dürften wir außerdem erwarten, dass sich Männer wie *Anastasius bibliothecarius* (ca. 800—ca. 879), der *bibliothecarius Romanae Ecclesiae*, und ähnliche dafür interessiert und Nachforschungen angestellt hätten—von dem immer auf seltene Bücher begierigen Photios ganz zu schweigen. 1102 eroberten dann die Kreuzfahrer die Stadt.[130] Damit dürfte ein plötzliches gewaltsames Ende der Bibliothek von Cäsarea eher ausscheiden. Es bleibt der langsame, schleichende Tod im späten 4. und frühen 5. Jh., den wir zuvor wahrscheinlich gemacht haben.[131]

---

[128] Vgl. W.E. Kaegi, "Some Seventh-Century Sources on Caesarea Maritima," *IEJ* 28 (1978) 177–181.

[129] Die Edition dieses interessanten Textcorpus von H. Usener, *Acta martyris Anastasii Persae* (Bonn 1894) ist leider nur in wenigen Bibliotheken vorhanden.

[130] Zur Geschichte Cäsareas in frühislamischer Zeit s. Gil, *History*, 80–81.107.217–218 u.ö.; M. Sharon, Art. "Kaiṣariyya, Kaiṣariyyā," *EI*² 4 (1978) 841–842, der auch die weiteren arabischen Quellen zur Invasion diskutiert.

[131] Carriker, *Library*, 29, meint, die Bibliothek sei vielleicht von den vor den Arabern flüchtenden Christen partiell mitgenommen worden. Dann wäre aber zu erwarten, dass sie weitaus mehr kodikologische Spuren hinterlassen hätte.

9. RÜCKBLICK UND FORSCHUNGSDESIDERATE

Nach der hier begründeten Theorie war die erste wissenschaftliche christliche Bibliothek eine sukzessiv gewachsene Sammlung mehrerer bedeutender Gelehrter, die mit einiger Sicherheit auch anderen befreundeten Theologen zur Verfügung stand. Ihre Bestände wurden von Skriptorien zur Herstellung von Handschriften verwendet.[132] Unsicher ist, wie sich diese Skriptorien zur Bibliothek verhielten; einiges spricht dafür, die Beziehung nicht zu eng zu sehen. Vielleicht zu Lebzeiten des Hieronymus und jedenfalls kaum sehr viel später (vielleicht aber auch schon früher) könnte sie auf dem Wege der Erbschaft (vermutlich nach der Absetzung des letzten arianischen Bischof Euzoius) in uninteressierte Hände geraten und dann durch Verwahrlosung allmählich unbrauchbar geworden sein. Der wohl von der Gemeinde gesponserte Rettungsversuch mit einer Umschreibung schadhafter Texte auf Pergamente hat jedenfalls nicht zu einer Intensivierung des Gebrauchs geführt; im Gegenteil hören wir danach fast nichts mehr von der Sammlung. Die Wege des Verlustes dieser bedeutenden Bibliothek sind nicht mehr eindeutig zu klären. Dies hat die Sammlung des Pamphilos z.B. mit einer der bedeutendsten westlichen antiken Kirchenbibliotheken gemeinsam, derjenigen im Vivariense Cassiodors im heutigen Kalabrien, von der wir immerhin eine umfassende Beschreibung besitzen.[133]

In keinem Fall darf man sich die Bibliothek Cäsareas nach dem Vorbild heutiger größerer organisierter Bibliotheken vorstellen. Ihre Bestände waren überschaubar und primär von den persönlichen

---

[132] Skriptorien spielten in antiken Bibliotheken auch insofern eine Rolle, als diese ihre Bestände offenbar weniger durch Käufe, sondern eher durch das organisierte Anfertigen von Abschriften—auch aus den Beständen anderer Sammlungen—ergänzten. So jedenfalls Casson, *Bibliotheken in der Antike*, 140. Natürlich ist hier größere Sicherheit nicht zu gewinnen. Weitergehende Spekulationen über den Einfluss von Skriptorien in Cäsarea finden sich u.a. bei Cavallo, *Scuola, scriptorium, biblioteca a Caesarea*, der aber m.E. zu unkritisch das Zeugnis der Kolophone verwendet. Interessant sein Hinweis 70 auf Vaticanus gr. 1288, eine Cassius Dio-Handschrift, die vielleicht aus Cäsarea stammt. So zuvor schon C.M. Mazzucchi, „Alcune vicende della tradizione di Cassio Dione in epoca bizantina," *Aevum* 53 (1979) 94–114. Kritisch hierzu Carriker, *Library*, Anm. 56/154.

[133] Vgl. W. Bürsgens, in: FC 39/1, 30–31. Man beachte übrigens, dass auch Cassiodor durchaus von seiner Sammlung als *bibliotheca mea* spricht (*inst.* II, 2, 10), obwohl er natürlich voraussetzt, dass sie nach seinem Tod den Mönchen zur Verfügungen stehen würde.

Forschungsinteressen der Besitzer geprägt. Wahrscheinlich waren kaum mehr als ein oder zwei große Räume erforderlich, sie unterzubringen, vor allem wenn es tatsächlich zu einer vollständigen Umschreibung auf Pergamentcodices gekommen sein sollte (was ich für eher unwahrscheinlich halte). An eine förmliche Zerstörung durch Kriegseinwirkung oder Naturkatastrophen ist kaum zu denken. Im 4. oder auch noch im 5. Jh. wäre ein Schweigen unserer grundsätzlich nicht spärlichen Quellen über ein solches Ereignis in Cäsarea schwer vorstellbar. Natürlich hat es auch bewusste und planmäßige Bibliotheksvernichtungen gegeben, in erster Linie freilich heidnischer Sammlungen durch christliche Kaiser. Julians Nachfolger Jovian ließ die Bibliothek verbrennen, die der „Apostat" in Antiochien, in einem von Hadrian errichteten Tempel gegründet hatte (Johannes Antiochenus *frg.* 181 = FHG IV, 607; *Suda* s.v. Ἰοβιανός [ed. A. Adler 2, 638]). Auch Justinian ließ heidnische Bibliotheken vernichten, sogar in Konstantinopel selbst (Joh. Malalas XVIII, 136 p. 491 Dindorf). An die planmäßigen Zerstörungen heidnischer Bildungsgüter durch Patriarch Theophilos im Alexandrien des Jahres 391—eines der schmachvollsten Kapitel altkirchlicher Geschichte—muss nur *en passant* erinnert werden.[134] So etwas war aber insgesamt doch eher die Ausnahme, und kommt für die Zeit des Hieronymus in Cäsarea nicht in Betracht.[135]

Auch die immer wieder geäußerte These einer Vernichtung zur Zeit der Araberinvasion findet keinen Anhalt an den Quellen, die hier durchaus nicht spärlich fließen. Viel eher wird also ein allmähliches „Versickern", eine Verwahrlosung und ein langsamer Schwund der Bibliothek über einen längeren Zeitraum (z.B. etwa ein Jahrhundert) anzunehmen sein. Ein solcher Prozess ist am leichtesten denkbar, wenn sich die Bibliothek wie andere wissenschaftliche und philosophische Samlungen, auch wenn sie mit Schulen verbunden waren, in privatem Besitz befand, der zur Zeit des Hieronymus (kaum später)

---

[134] Vgl. unter bibliotheksgeschichtlichen Gesichtspunkten Wendel, „Das griechisch-römische Altertum," 78–79, und allgemeiner W. Speyer, *Büchervernichtung und Zensur des Geistes bei Heiden, Juden und Christen* (Stuttgart 1981).

[135] Von manchen heidnischen Bibliotheken hören wir auch später noch. So scheint diejenige des Athenäums in Rom—an dem Augustin und Hieronymus studiert hatten, und die sowohl eine griechische wie eine lateinische Abteilung besaß—erst 602 unter Kaiser Phokas aufgelöst worden zu sein. Vgl. Wendel, „Das griechisch-römische Altertum," 105.

den Kontakt zur wissenschaftlichen Arbeit verloren hatte. Dies entspricht dem düsteren Bild, welche Ammianus Marcellinus in einer viel zitierten Passage vom generellen Geschick der Bibliotheken im 4. Jh. zeichnet (er denkt primär an private Sammlungen und den allgemeinen Niedergang der Bildung):

> *Quod cum ita sit, paucae domus studiorum seriis cultibus antea celebratae/nunc ludibriis ignauiae torpentis exundant uocabili sonu perflabili tinnitu fidium resultantes. Denique pro philosopho cantor et in locum oratoris doctor artium ludicrarum accitur et bibliothecis sepulchrorum ritu in perpetuum clausis organa fabricantur hydraulica et lyrae ad speciem carpentorum ingentes tibiaeque et histrionici gestus instrumenta non leuia* (XIV, 6, 18; geschrieben zwischen 383 und 391).

Das Bild der wie Gräber geschlossenen und verfallenden Bibliotheken berührt auch heute noch.[136] Damit ist ein eher trauriges Ende auch für jene Bibliothek zu vermuten, die vor den Klostergründungen von Bobbio, St. Gallen, Fulda etc. mit ihren Sammlungen im 7. Jh. den reichsten Schatz altchristlicher Literatur bewahrt hatte, und die Hieronymus einst schlicht die *bibliotheca divina* genannt hatte (*vir. ill.* 81, 1).

---

[136] Vgl. zu diesem Text auch Blanck, *Das Buch in der Antike*, 165–166; Houston, "A Revisionary Note on Ammianus Marcellinus 14.6.18: When Did the Public Libraries of Ancient Rome Close?" *Library Quarterly* 58 (1988) 258–260.

A NEWLY DISCOVERED MANUSCRIPT OF LUKE'S GOSPEL (DE HAMEL MS 386; GREGORY-ALAND 0312)

Peter M. Head

1. Introduction: The Manuscript and its Identification

Early in 2003 a private collector purchased a collection of small pieces of vellum from a London dealer in old books and manuscripts. These were originally described as 'tiny scraps, in Greek, on vellum' and were part of a group with some Latin texts (which were the focus of interest for the collector). He sent me a photocopy of the pieces with the suggestion that I might be interested in looking at the Greek pieces, which, he thought, were 'likely to be Christian texts' on the basis of a mention of 'deacons' in one of them, and with the fervent hope that 'some, at least, might be biblical'. The collection of small pieces of vellum turned out to contain portions of six different manuscripts of the Greek Bible.[1]

Evidence of provenance for individual pieces is lacking, although it was reported to me that the dealer 'believes they [i.e. the whole collection] were part of a pre-War Armenian collection of antiquities and Armenian manuscripts in France'. From the nature of the manuscripts—all in small pieces with glue and other damage—it is pretty clear that they were cut up into small pieces some time in the distant past (with a pattern of wear after the cutting) and used in the repair or bindings of other manuscripts (hence the glue marks, generally on the hair side). It might be therefore that the fragments were extracted at some point from Armenian bindings, but there is no solid evidence for their original provenance, nor is there definite proof that the separate pieces are related in their provenance. The

---

[1] For a preliminary report based on a presentation to the Cambridge Senior New Testament Seminar see: P.M. Head, "Fragments of Six Newly Identified Greek Bible Manuscripts in a Cambridge Collection: A Preliminary Report," *TC: A Journal of Biblical Textual Criticism* [see http://purl.org/TC] 8 (2003). For the NT manuscripts see P.M. Head, "Five New Testament Manuscripts in a Cambridge Collection" [forthcoming].

Greek manuscripts range in date from the 5th to the 8th century. They differ considerably, not only in date and extant text, but also in style, original format (large format, single column, double column, etc.) and textual features (spelling, text-type broadly defined etc.). Beyond their presence in the same collection there is no obvious evidence which would connect the pieces.[2]

One of these fragments stood out immediately from the others, a very small piece of thin vellum (16 × 1–1.5 cm) with damaged edges, tiny letters, a central fold line, and a text which could immediately be identified as part of Luke 7 even though much of the rest was quite unclear to the naked eye. After further study, detailed analysis using ultra-violet and infra red lamps, various levels of magnification and long exposure ultra-violet photographs, the information which emerged still left this particular manuscript uniquely important compared with the others and deserving of a fuller treatment than the publication in the *editio princeps* could provide.

It is probably worth laying down the different stages in the process of identification and study explicitly. There was a complex interaction between advances in transcription and advances in identification and understanding of the manuscript as a whole.

(1)   The first stage, on the basis of a photocopy of the manuscript provided by the new owner, involved the reading of the name of John and the mention of the disciples in the most legible column of the manuscript. This quickly led to Luke 7:18 and the rest of the left hand column could immediately be identified and almost completely transcribed (including material as well from verse 17). This column is now designated as page D (containing Luke 7:17–18).

(2)   The second stage, on the basis of the first visual inspection of the manuscript, involved the initial transcription and identification of a further column as containing Luke 7:9–10 (now designated as page C).

(3)   The third stage involved the initial transcription and unsuccessful attempts at identification of the other two columns.[3] At this

---

[2] P.M. Head, "A New Manuscript of Jeremiah in Greek according to the Lucianic Recension (de Hamel MS 391; Rahlfs 897)," *BIOSCS* 36 (2003) 27–37 [publication date 2004] (the opening two paragraphs cover similar ground).

[3] Thanks to Dr L. McFall who, without advancing the identification directly, made a careful independent transcription at this stage (4.3.03).

stage the significance of the middle fold mark as evidence for the initial format of the codex was not yet recognized and I was really trying (unsuccessfully) to fit the extant text into Luke 7 somewhere. It is perhaps worth admitting that with a difficult to read manuscript whose basic content has been identified one is basically proposing various hypotheses and then seeking to test the hypotheses against the evidence ('Is this an alpha?'—because if this is a copy of the text I think it is it should be an alpha). Effectively this stage involved unsuccessful testing which served to problematise the hypothesis that these columns probably contained material from Luke 7.

(4)   The fourth stage involved the inspection of manuscript with UV light and hand-held magnification (12/3/03). This provided additional information on the two columns already identified and enabled the production of corrected transcriptions of these, followed by the identification of the other two columns as portions of Luke 5.[4] This in turn led to recognition of the importance of the fold and the whole question of the format of the codex represented by this small piece. Once the initial hypothesis—that the two columns represented two columns on each page—has been rejected it is necessary to gain more information by observation and then construct a new hypothesis which fits all the available evidence—the manuscript provides evidence for four small pages with internal margins and fold.

(5)   The final stage involved procuring high-quality long-exposure UV photographs which were studied alongside further visual inspection of the manuscript using UV light and hand-held magnification.[5] This allowed for the completion of the transcript as it has now been published and the final identification of the extant portions of the manuscript.

To summarise briefly, what emerged is a relatively early majuscule manuscript of Luke in an interesting format with an unusual text. The remainder of this paper will fill out the details on these three features.

---

[4] Thanks are due to G. Waller and the staff in the manuscript room of the Cambridge University Library for the use of their facilities.

2. Page Layout: Analysis and Reconstruction

First, the page layout. As I have already noted, on first viewing the fragment appeared to be a portion of a two-columned manuscript page (although not many letters and practically no complete words could be read on the back with the naked eye, the two columns were easily seen). This initial assumption had to be rejected once all the material could be read. Then the fold in between the two columns could be recognized as the original fold in the codex. What we have is not two columns on two pages, but individual columns on four pages—the surviving fragment represents a portion of a complete sheet of the original manuscript. The four pages can then be labeled as pages A (Luke 5:23–24), B (Luke 5:30–31), C (Luke 7:9), and D (Luke 7:17–18), with the following portions of text extant on each page:

Page A: Luke 5:23–24 (hair)
σοι αι αμαρτιαι σου η ειπε(ι)ν [εγει
ρε και περιπατει· ινα δε ειδητε
οτι ο υιος του ανθρω[π]ου εξουσι[αν

Page B: Luke 5:30–31 (flesh)
. . .] εσθιεται· και αποκρι
θεις ο $\overline{ις}$ ειπεν προς αυτους ου χρει
αν εχουσιν οι [υγιαι]νοντες ιατρου

Page C: Luke 7:9 (flesh)
ακουσας δε ταυτα ο $\overline{ις}$ εθαυμασ[εν
και ειπεν τω ακολουθουντι οχλω
λεγω υμιν ουδε ν τω [ισραηλ τοσαυ
την πιστιν ευρον· [. . .

Page D: Luke 7:17 (end)—18 (hair)
και εν παση τη περιχωρω <blank>
και απηγγειλαν ϊωαννη οι μαθη
ται αυτου περι παντων τουτων
και προσκαλεσαμενος δυο τινας

The next stage in analyzing the format of the manuscript was to calculate how large the pages were and what type of page layout was represented in this manuscript. This can then be used for comparative purposes—what other manuscripts are similar?—and for then further calculations about how many pages there might be between page B and page C, which might in turn prompt reflections on the potential size and scope of this manuscript in its original format.

As can be seen on the transcript the lines average c. 26 letters. Between Luke 5:24 (assuming the next line after the extant text begins with εχει of Luke 5:24) and 5:30 (assuming that και πινετε was read at the start of the extant line) there are 609 letters (counted using NA²⁷ and allowing for *nomina sacra*), suggesting that there would have been 24 lines between the two texts.[6] Similarly, between Luke 7:10 (assuming a short line for the final extant line) and 7:17 (assuming a line ending with περι αυτου preceding the extant line) there are 615 letters (again NA²⁷ assuming *nomina sacra*), confirming that there would probably have been 24 lines between the two texts.[7]

Both these calculations confirm the picture of a page of 28 lines (+/−1), averaging around 26 (+/−1) letters on each line. Although we lack outer margins, we have complete lines of text which are 6.5–7.0 cm wide, with an inner margin of 1.0–1.5 cm. Given that each page had approximately 27 lines of text; because of the closeness of the writing—3 lines per cm—the height of the text column on each page would be around 9 cm. So text occupies 9×7 cm on each page with probably at most 2 cm of margin at any edge (it would be rather anomalous for such a compact text to have spacious margins; rather I am assuming that the external margins would be congruent with the obvious space constraints of the text layout). We might therefore estimate that the each page measured approximately 12 (+/−1) $\times$ 10 (+/−1) cm.

Layouts of this type were very common for parchment codices of literary texts from the third to the sixth century.[8] Among Christian texts in particular we find a number of close parallels in terms of

---

[5] Thanks for the photographs are due to M. Scudder of the photographic department of the Cambridge University Library.

[6] 609 letters at an average of 26 (+/−1) letters per line gives 23.4 (22.6–24.4). Averaging up (to allow for occasional short lines) suggests 24 lines (+/−1). This is clearly only an approximation—assuming a certain type of text and a relatively uniform layout and a normal distribution of narrow and wide letters. As a point of comparison we might note that Codex Bezae has 612 letters in the same (assumed) gap.

[7] 615 letters at an average of 26 (+/−1) letters per line gives 23.7 (22.8–24.6). Once again averaging up suggests 24 lines (+/−1). Codex Bezae has 618 letters in the same (assumed) gap.

[8] E.G. Turner attempted (somewhat arbitrarily it must be said), to group early codices by size patterns in his *The Typology of the Codex* (Haney Foundation Series 18; Pennsylvania 1977). This manuscript corresponds to Turner's Group XI—

size and content, details of which will be found in the following table.[9] In addition to date and content, the three later columns provide information on the size of the codex (if available through pagination on the extant page or by simple calculation), the size of each page and the number of lines per page (they are all single column codices).

Designation	Date	Text	Pagination	Size	Lines
0232 = P.Ant. I 12[10]	III–IV	2John	164, 165	9.9 × 8.8	20
0206 = P.Oxy. XI 1353[11]	IV	1Peter 5.5–13	229	13.5 × 10.1	17
P.Oxy. XV 1783[12]	IV	*Herm., Mand.* 9		13 × 9.3	14
P.Oxy. VI 849[13]	IV	*Acts of Peter*	167, 168	9.8 × 9	19
0169 = P.Oxy. VIII 1080[14]	IV	Rev 3:19–4:2	33, 34 [c. 170 p.]	9.5 × 7.8	14
0163 P.Oxy. VI 848[15]	V	Rev 16:17–20	[c 200 p.]	10 [+ mg] × 9	17
0176 = PSI III 251[16]	V	Gal 3:16–25		c. 12 × 7	22

breadth of 11/10 cm and 'square' (*Typology*, 29)—which he describes as a common format (*Typology*, 25; cf. 29–30 for a list of evidence). Cf. also M.J. Kruger, "P. Oxy 840: Amulet or Miniature Codex?," *JTS* 53 (2002) 81–94, esp. 89–92, who focuses on Turner's (related) group XIV—those with a breadth of less than 10cm (*Typology*, 29–30).

[9] Kruger notes that 47 of the 55 miniature codices collected by Turner were Christian: "it was a favoured format among private Christian book-owners" (Kruger, "P. Oxy 840: Amulet or Miniature Codex?," 90). For further discussion of the Christian appropriation of the miniature format, see, C.H. Roberts, *Manuscript, Society and Belief in Early Christian Egypt* (London—New York 1979) 10–12; H.Y. Gamble, *Books and Readers in the Early Church: A History of Early Christian Texts* (New Haven—London 1995) 235–236.

[10] C.H. Roberts, *The Antinoopolis Papyri. Volume One* (London 1950) 24–26: "the volume was of considerable compass" (24).

[11] B.P. Grenfell—A.S. Hunt, *The Oxyrhynchus Papyri* XI (London 1915) 5–6.

[12] B.P. Grenfell—A.S. Hunt, *The Oxyrhynchus Papyri* XV (London 1922) 15–17.

[13] B.P. Grenfell—A.S. Hunt, *The Oxyrhynchus Papyri* VI (London 1908) 6–12.

[14] B.P. Grenfell—A.S. Hunt, *The Oxyrhynchus Papyri* VIII (London 1911) 14–16. A single page of this manuscript (counting from line 2 recto = Rev 3.19—20 (νοησον ιδου εστηκα επι) to line 1 verso = Rev 4:1 (ταυτα ιδον και ιδου θυ) corresponds to 7 lines of text in NA[27]. Revelation takes up approximately 1,200 lines, hence this manuscript would probably have had around 170 pages.

[15] Grenfell—Hunt, *The Oxyrhynchus Papyri* VI, 6. A single page of this manuscript (counting from line 3 recto = Rev 16:17–18 (γεγονεν και εγε) to line 2 verso = Rev 16:19 (πιον του θυ δου) corresponds to 6 lines of text in NA[27]. Revelation takes up approximately 1,200 lines, hence this manuscript would probably have had around 200 pages.

[16] E. Pistelli, *Papiri Greci e Latini Volume Terzo (III)* (*PSI*; Firenze—Roma, 2004 reprint of 1914) 108–110 (No. 251).

It is firstly notable that these codices made up of small pages could nevertheless be quite thick; indeed, all but one of the parallel samples we noted provide evidence for quite large codices, some comprising multiple books, others comprising single volumes of quite large books (*Acts of Peter*, Revelation).[17] None of these comparable manuscripts have writing as small and compact as that exhibited in our manuscript—typically the manuscripts listed above might have 2 lines of writing per centimeter, whereas we have calculated that this manuscript had around 27 lines of text per page, or (for 9 cm of writing space), 3 lines of writing per centimeter. Indeed, among the compact writing evident in Christian texts, very few manuscripts contain writing smaller than 2 lines per centimeter: taking account of the margins, P.Ant. I 12, P. Oxy. VI 849 and PSI III 251, all listed above, manage more than 2 lines per centimeter, as does Codex Vaticanus Gr 1209 (B 03), which has 42 lines of text within columns of 18 cm in height (set within very wide margins). Among NT papyrus manuscripts, we find some examples at the 2 lines per centimeter rate, but none smaller. These include $\mathfrak{P}^{75}$ (P. Bodmer XIV & XV), where a column of text around 21 cm in height has between 38—45 lines (average 42); and others such as $\mathfrak{P}^4$ (18 cm height with 36 lines per column);[18] $\mathfrak{P}^{27}$ (P.Oxy. XI 1355, frag. 1 is 10cm in height with 19 lines);[19] $\mathfrak{P}^{48}$ (c. 25 cm in height with 42–47 lines);[20] and $\mathfrak{P}^{110}$ (c. 22 cm in height with 40–43 lines).[21]

Smaller writing is found, but not, as far as my searches have located, among biblical manuscripts. One impressive example is P.Oxy. VI 840, a non-canonical gospel manuscript from the fourth century, which—in a vellum page measuring 8.8 × 7.4 cm—has 22 lines of writing on one side and 23 lines on the other. The height

---

[17] Cf. Kruger: "Despite their small size, some [miniature codices] could contain a surprising number of pages" in "P. Oxy 840: Amulet or Miniature Codex?," 89 and referring to P. Oxy 849 (*Acts of Peter*) and the *Mani Codex* which has 192 pages measuring only 3.5 × 4.5 cm (see note 38 on pp. 89–90).

[18] K. Aland, *Kurzgefasste Liste der griechischen Handschriften des Neuen Testaments* (ANTTF 1; Berlin—New York ²1994) 3 (similar, although not identical, figures are given for $\mathfrak{P}^{64+67}$, which is sometimes thought to belong to the same original manuscript: c 20 cm high with 38–39 lines; *Liste*, 12).

[19] Grenfell—Hunt, *The Oxyrhynchus Papyri* XI, 9–112; fr. 1, recto in Plate 1.

[20] Aland, *Liste*, 10.

[21] Aland, *Liste*, supplement.

measurement of 8.8 cm includes upper and lower margins; and the 22 lines of text take up only 5.5 cm or four lines per centimeter.[22]

All of this suggests that while the format of our manuscript is not unusual, and could be used for fairly thick codices exceeding two hundred pages, the small size of the writing is unusual, even unique, among biblical manuscripts. We shall need to bear this comparative information in mind as we attempt to reconstruct the codex format of the original manuscript represented by our small fragment.

3. Codex Format: Calculation and Exploration

If we return to our general conclusion that a page in our manuscript would have contained 28 lines (+/−1), averaging around 26 (+/−1) letters on each line, we can calculate that each page would, on average, have around 728 (+/−50) letters. The space between the extant text on page B (Luke 5:31) and that on page C (Luke 7:9) is approximately 6,450 letters (c. 150 lines of NA at c. 43 letters per line). 6,450 letters corresponds to nine pages of content on this scale.[23] These nine pages would comprise two portions amounting to one whole page on the bottom of page B and the top of page C, and eight additional pages, between page B and page C. This is an extremely plausible solution, since eight pages would comprise four leaves of vellum or two whole sheets.

The most likely conclusion to be drawn from this is therefore that the eight missing pages would have comprised the two innermost sheets of a quire, while our four page sheet would represent the third sheet from the inside of the quire. Since most codices are made up from four sheet quires it follows that the most likely scenario would have an outer sheet, our sheet as the second sheet, and two internal sheets making up the quire. Confirmation of this view of things comes from the observation that in this case pages A&D are written on the hair-side of the vellum, while pages B&C are on the

---

[22] B.P. Grenfell—A.S. Hunt, *The Oxyrhynchus Papyri* V (London 1908) 1–10; verso in Plate 1; cf. Kruger, "P. Oxy 840: Amulet or Miniature Codex?"

[23] 6,450 divided by our page size of 728 (+/− 50) letters equals 9 pages of intervening material [more precisely: 8.9 [range 8.3–9.6]].

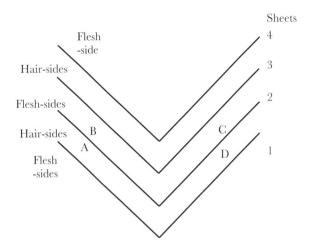

flesh-side.[24] This corresponds to what would be expected, since most quires come to have a standard format, known as Gregory's rule, whereby the outside of the quire consists of the flesh-side of the external vellum sheet and the sheets are laid on top of each other matching hair-sides and flesh-sides and leaving a flesh-side opening in the center—this results in each opening alternating between hair-sides and flesh-sides, providing a consistency of colour and texture within each opening.[25] As the second sheet of a four-sheet quire our sheet fits with the expected format: pages A and D are hair-side (and would presumably have faced the hair-side of the external sheet), while pages B and C are flesh-side (and would presumably have faced the flesh-side of the third sheet). A simple diagram may demonstrate the structure of the quire on this understanding:

If we were to take this attempted reconstruction one step further we could calculate that such a quire, incorporating sixteen pages of text, would have around 11,650 letters (+/–800). If for the sake of

---

[24] It is notable that although in antiquity the flesh-side of vellum seems to have been the prestige side—with the best surface for writing and reading; it is normally the hair side which preserves the text best.

[25] For Gregory's rule see C.R. Gregory, "Les cahiers des manuscrits grecs," *Comptes rendus de l'Académie des Inscriptions et Belles-Lettres* (Paris 1885) 261–268; Id., "The Quires in Greek Manuscripts," *American Journal of Philology* 11 (1886) 27–32; also cf. Id., *Canon and Text of the New Testament* (Edinburgh 1907) 324: "I like to tell about this law because I discovered it".

argument we assume for a moment that our piece comes in the middle of a page then the portion of text taken up on this quire would be around 1,800 letters before and after the extant portions of pages A and D (two and a half pages). Mapping this against the NA²⁷ text of Luke (taking 1,800 letters as corresponding to c. 42 lines of text in NA²⁷), suggests that the quire would have extended from around Luke 5:6 through to 7:38.

Further extrapolation becomes increasingly speculative. If a four-sheet quire contains 11,650 (+/–800) letters and Luke's Gospel contains approximately 97,714 letters, then this would suggest that the whole of Luke's Gospel would need between eight and nine quires (calculation gives: 8.4 quires with range: 7.85–9.0). Eight quires would require 128 pages, while nine quires would require 144 pages—both of these are well within the range for this type of codex and suggest that the most likely scenario is a multiple quire but small format codex containing the whole gospel of Luke. Indeed the space requirements for Luke are so far within the range provided by the other examples that it would not be impossible to rule out the presence of some other text with Luke in such a codex—another gospel like John (à la 𝔓⁷⁵) which on these figures would require six quires (range: 5.6—6.5) or 96 further pages, or perhaps the Acts of the Apostles which would require eight quires (range: 7.55–8.65) or 128 further pages—although a four-gospel codex would seem to be ruled out as requiring in total an unparalleled twenty-seven quires or 432 pages.[26]

4. Palaeographical Analysis: Dating

To some extent this discussion has already provided some comparative evidence for dating our manuscript. Ultimately any dating depends on the palaeographical analysis of the hand or script of the

---

[26] We have used the following figures for the number of letters in each book: Matthew: 89,925; Mark: 55,550; Luke: 97,714; John: 70,210; Acts: 94,000, supplied by E. Nestle, *Introduction to the Textual Criticism of the Greek New Testament* (ET E. Edie; London 1901) 48–49 (this material additional to the German second edition) on the basis of counting by Graux (in *Revue de Philologie*, II) reported by Zahn. It should be obvious that the approach we are taking does not hinge on the absolute accuracy of these figures.

manuscript.[27] In this connection the small size of the hand creates some difficulties.

The hand is a 'biblical majuscule'—the letters are upright and formally produced, most of the letter forms can fit within squares, there are contrasts between thick strokes for vertical lines downward diagonals to the right and thin strokes for horizontal lines and upward diagonals, *rhos* and *upsilons* have tails that descend below the line. There are some decorative elements at the tips of horizontal lines (in *tau* and *gamma*, but not in *pi*), and on *upsilon*. The *kappa* remains attached.

In terms of dating the crucial clues are the decorative elements and the pronounced contrasts between thin and thick strokes, both of which characterize the 'biblical majuscule' in the fifth century. We have a manuscript from early in the sixth century, the *Vienna Dioscurides*, dated to AD 513, which provides the major chronological marker to the end of this period. Compared to our manuscript, the Vienna manuscript has a rather more stylized and elaborate presentation, the arms of the *kappa* are detached from the vertical line, decorative elements are more prevalent (at the bottom of descenders in *rho*, *phi*, *upsilon*; at the end of horizontal lines in *pi*, *zeta*, *delta*, *xi*; and at the end of curved strokes in *eta* and *sigma*).[28] Our manuscript must clearly be dated earlier than this.

A fairly close parallel in terms of size and subject matter is NT manuscript 0176, already mentioned in our list of similar sized codices above, and generally dated to the fifth century.[29] In many ways this is a close match, as 0176 also has decorative elements, but they are

---

[27] Comparable manuscripts are cited from the following collections: F. de Cavalieri—J. Lietzmann, *Specimina codicum graecorum vaticanorum* (Bonn 1910); G. Cavallo, *Ricerche sulla maiuscola biblica* (Firenze 1967); G. Cavallo—H. Maehler, *Greek Bookhands of the Early Byzantine Period AD 300–800* (BICS Supp. 47; London 1987); B.M. Metzger, *Manuscripts of the Greek Bible: An Introduction to Greek Palaeography* (New York—Oxford 1991 [corrected edition]); W.H.P. Hatch, *The Principal Uncial Manuscripts of the New Testament* (Chicago 1939); R. Barbour, *Greek Literary Hands, AD 400–1600* (Oxford Palaeographical Handbooks; Oxford—New York 1981); E.M. Thompson, *An Introduction to Greek and Latin Palaeography* (Oxford 1912).

[28] Cavallo—Maehler, *Greek Bookhands*, 25b (p. 59); Thompson, *Palaeography*, facs. 47 (p. 210); Barbour, *Greek Literary Hands*, No. 1; Cavallo, *Ricerche*, plate 84.

[29] Pistelli, *Papiri Greci e Latini Volume Terzo (III) (PSI)*, 108–110 (No. 251): fifth century. Plate of verso (Gal 3:20–25) in Cavallo—Maehler, *Greek Bookhands*, 18b (pp. 44–45): mid-fifth century. Plate of recto (Gal 3:16–19) in Cavallo, *Ricerche*, plate 62a.

less distinct and less common than in our manuscript; and in general there is less clear cut distinctions between the thickness of strokes
than in our manuscript, which is probably later than this example.

Among manuscripts in this style generally placed in the second
half of the fifth century there are two which appear close enough
to our manuscript to support this dating. The "Cotton Genesis"
(British Library, Cod. Cotton Otho B.VI) and the Vatican manuscript of Cassius Dio (Vat Gr. 1288), although both represent much
larger and more formal books than our small codex, nevertheless
represent a basically similar stage in the development of the 'biblical majuscule'.[30]

We might thus conclude that as far as palaeographical compar-
isons go, our manuscript is to be dated in the second half of the
fifth century.[31]

5. Textual and Other Questions

Scribal Features: The scribe uses a dieresis over the initial *iota* in ιωαννη
(7:18); but otherwise there is no evidence of accentuation. Evidence
of *punctuation* is present on each of the surviving pages of the manuscript—four examples involving two different levels of punctuation
or text division. In three places (at the ends of Luke 5:23; 5:30 and
7:9 corresponding to the modern verse division) a middle point is
visible. These all correspond to minor breaks in the thought of the
passage—5:24 introduces a parenthetical remark; 5:31 introduces a
saying of Jesus (involving a change of speaker); while 7:10 represents
a transition from Jesus' words to narration—and are normally punc-

---

[30] For Brit. Lib, Cod. Cotton Otho B.VI see Cavallo—Maehler, *Greek Bookhands*,
24a (pp. 56–7) or K. Weitzmann—H.L. Kessler, *The Cotton Genesis* (Princeton
Monographs in Art and Archaeology 45; Princeton 1986); for Vat. Gr. 1288 see
Cavalieri—Lietzmann, *Specimina codicum graecorum vaticanorum*, 2; Cavallo, *Ricerche*, plate
67. Other comparable biblical manuscripts from this period include Codex Alexandrinus
(Brit. Lib., Royal I.D.v–viii), see Metzger, *Manuscripts*, 18 (pp. 86–87); Thompson,
Palaeography, facs. 46 (pp. 206–7); Cavallo, *Ricerche*, plates 64–65; Hatch, *Principal
Uncial Manuscripts*, plates XVII–XIX; and the *Freer Manuscript* of Deuteronomy and
Joshua (Washington, Freer Gallery, Cod. Wash. 1), see Metzger, *Manuscripts*, 17 (pp.
84–85); cf. also T.J. Kraus, "*P.Vindob.G* 39756 + *Bodl. MS Gr. th. f.* 4 [P]: Fragmente
eines Codex der griechischen Petrus-Apokalypse," *BASP* 40 (2003) 45–61, esp. 50.
[31] In a letter dated 4 Sept 2003 Prof. Herwig Maehler suggested 'late V rather
than early VI'.

tuated as new sentences in modern editions. The fourth example involves a more major paragraph division marker in which the end of the line is left blank after the completion of 7:17. This corresponds to a relatively major transition of thought in the text and corresponds to the end of a paragraph in other ancient manuscripts, the Ammonian-Eusebian Sections, and in modern editions. Given that these four examples correspond to widely recognized text-divisions, and that they represent all the potential punctuational points in the entire textual sample, it seems fair to conclude that our manuscript was thoroughly and conventionally punctuated throughout.

Nomina sacra are used for the name of Jesus (the two letter form—5:31; 7:9); but not for 'the Son of Man' in Luke 5:24.[32] Abbreviations for 'the Son of Man' can and do vary a lot both within and between manuscripts. At this point, for example, while many manuscripts abbreviate both of the key words (e.g. C f [1] 𝔐), others abbreviate only one of the two words (e.g. 01 has $\overline{υς}$ with ανθρωπου in full; Γ Θ and f [13] have υιος in full and $\overline{ανου}$), and some others, like our manuscript, have the two words written out in full here at this point (so B and W).[33] A single example is insufficient to prove that this was the standard practice throughout the manuscript—B never abbreviates 'the Son of Man' in Luke's Gospel; while W varies between the full form and one using $\overline{ανου}$ in a pattern that is not obvious.[34]

There is only one *singular reading* in the extant material. This is the omission of στραφεις in 7:9. A single singular reading hardly allows any generalizing deductions, especially since this occurs in the context of a passage in which our manuscript has several readings

---

[32] For a recent general orientation see L.W. Hurtado, The Origin of the *Nomina Sacra*: A Proposal, in: *JBL* 117 (1998) 655–673.

[33] R.J. Swanson, *New Testament Greek Manuscripts: Variant Readings Arranged in Horizontal Lines against Codex Vaticanus: Luke.* (Sheffield—Pasadena 1995) 85 provides information about the *nomina sacra* in different manuscripts in apparatus B (thanks to Bruce Prior for helping me on this point).

[34] Although initial soundings were taken using Swanson, the situation was confirmed (for Luke) at least using facsimiles of the two manuscripts: C.M. Martini, *Novum Testamentum e Codice Vaticano Graeco 1209 (Codex B) tertia vice phototypice expressum* (Vatican City 1968) and H.A Sanders, *Facsimile of the Washington Manuscript of the four Gospels in the Freer Collection* (Ann Arbor 1912). For W we find the full form in 5:24; 6:5.22; 7:34; 9:22.26.44; then with $\overline{ανου}$ in 9:58; then the full form in 11:30; 12:8.10.40; then with $\overline{ανου}$ in 17:22.24.26.30; 18:8.31; 19:10; 21:27; then the full form in 21:36; using $\overline{ανου}$ in 22:22; the full form in 22:48; then using $\overline{ανου}$ in 22:69 and 24:7.

which have only relatively minor support. The passage reveals a paraphrastic tendency with some parallels with Codex Bezae. 7:9 in our manuscript seems to read as follows:

ακουσας δε ταυτα ο ι̅ς̅ εθαυμασεν και ειπεν τω ακολουθουντι οχλω
λεγω υμιν ουδε εν τω [ισραηλ] τοσαυτην πιστιν ευρον·

With this we might compare two other versions of the verse:[35] Codex Vaticanus (with wide-ranging support including 𝔓[75], although fragmentary at this point, and Sinaiticus, reflected in NA):

ακουσας δε ταυτα ο Ιησους εθαυμασεν αυτον,
και στραφεις τω ακολουθουντι αυτω οχλω ειπων,
λεγω υμιν, ουδε εν τω Ισραηλ τοσαυτην πιστιν ευρον

Codex Bezae:

ακουσας δε ταυτα ο ιης εθαυμασεν και στραφεις ειπεν τω ακολουθουντι οχλω αμην λεγω υμιν ουδεποτε τοσαυτην πιστιν ευρον εν τω
ισραηλ

To summarise the evidence of this verse, we find that our manuscript agrees in the omission of αυτον with only D Θ and 700, and then uniquely omits στραφεις. It then fronts ειπεν and omits αυτω in the following clause, resulting in a close parallel with Codex Bezae (which agrees almost uniquely in both these respects): ειπεν τω ακολου-θουντι οχλω.[36] In the final part of the verse, the saying of Jesus, our manuscript definitely doesn't follow the text represented by Bezae, rather following the text represented by Vaticanus. Our text therefore represents a somewhat paraphrastic rendering of the introduction, with connections to the text of Codex Bezae. But how significant are the connections with Codex Bezae?

On the positive side we could note that three agreements in close context, two of which are paralleled only in Bezae (in a four-word agreement that has hitherto been regarded as a singular reading in Bezae), are definitely suggestive.[37] But a direct literary connection

[35] Evidence drawn initially from Swanson, *Luke*, 118; then checked against the two facsimiles.

[36] W lacks τω ακολουθουντι αυτω, thus coincidentally agreeing in the omission of αυτω.

[37] In 7:17 we have a further agreement with Bezae—και εν παση τη περιχωρω—albeit here the reading is also shared among other important supporting witnesses: A D 𝔐.

with Codex Bezae seems unlikely given the lack of agreement with several other Bezan readings in the saying of Jesus in 7:9 and in the other texts extant in our manuscript. In this respect we should note the following:

(1) in 5:23 0312 has σοι αι αμαρτιαι σου (with B, A, C, L, U, Δ Λ 𝔐 f^1 f^{13} 33.1346, etc.), against σου αι αμαρτιαι (01 D W Θ);

(2) in 5.31 0312 has και αποκριθεις (with all other witnesses) against αποκριθεις δε (D—a singular reading);

(3) in 7:18a 0312 has και απηγγειλαν ϊωαννη οι μαθηται αυτου περι παντων τουτων (with other witnesses) against εν οις και μεχρι Ιωανου του βαπτιστου ος (D—a singular reading);

(4) in 5.18b 0312 also reads τινας against Bezae.

As in other respects, but more so in relation to the actual text, if we possessed more we could know. The agreements could easily be the coincidental product of similarly paraphrastic tendencies: fronting the verb of speech and dropping the redundant pronoun. On the other hand we know that a text sharing many characteristics of the Bezan text had a relatively wide distribution in the early church, so it would not be surprising to find other evidence for it. The question remains intriguing but we cannot really expect to resolve it decisively given the amount of extant text available for study. In my opinion the general divergences from the text of Codex Bezae make it more plausible to think of this as a coincidentally parallel paraphrastic rendering of the passage.

Some other evidence that might offer support for a paraphrastic or free tendency in 0312 is found in 5:30. Unfortunately the text is pretty obscure, but it is quite clear that this verse ends here in 0312 with εσθιεται (the previous word or two should be present but are obscured by glue and general wear and are indecipherable). This suggests that 0312 either lacked και πινετε (an agreement with K), or had a different word order from other texts.

CONCLUDING REFLECTIONS

It is inevitable that the discovery of small fragments of a NT manuscript will leave many questions unanswered and unanswerable. Nevertheless it is also obvious that the small fragments add to our knowledge of the NT text and its transmission incrementally. In addition, we were able to deduce a fair bit about the layout, format and structure of our manuscript, and from that other deductions could follow. For example, one feature of the small codex format that we have not previously noted is the fact that a relatively high proportion of such small codices contain texts from beyond the edge of the canon.[38] Is this relevant to the question of care of copying? Perhaps this format, apparently for personal use rather than public reading, was also characterised by somewhat paraphrastic or free textual renderings. But that is a question for further study and cannot be entered into here.

---

[38] Kruger, "P.Oxy 840: Amulet or Miniature Codex?," noted that of the 45 miniature codices listed in Turner (*Typology*, 29–30), most of them were Christian, and they included texts such as *Hermas*, *Acts of Peter*, an apocryphal Gospel, *Acts of Paul and Thecla*, *Protevangelium of James*, *6 Ezra*, *Didache*.

ONE CODEX, THREE SCRIBES, AND MANY BOOKS: STRUGGLES WITH SPACE IN *CODEX SINAITICUS*

Dirk Jongkind

When the British Museum acquired Codex Sinaiticus in the 1930's, it was decided that a thorough study of the paleographical and codicological features should be made. The task was assigned to H.J.M. Milne and T.C. Skeat and resulted in the 1938 monograph *Scribes and Correctors of the Codex Sinaiticus*.[1] The study of the scribal hands led to the identification of three main scribes; this was in contrast to Tischendorf, who determined four different hands.[2] The work originally attributed to scribe C was assigned to scribes A and D, with the result that the remaining labels of the scribal hands were A, B, and D.[3] Also the numerous corrections of the text were reassigned by Milne and Skeat, resulting in all the early corrections (pre'C corrector') being attributed to one of the scribes of the main text.

The codicological description of the *Sinaiticus* is an invaluable aspect of *Scribes and Correctors*. As it was decided that the codex should be rebound into two volumes, part of the evidence regarding earlier bindings and the formation of the quires was destroyed. Consequently,

---

[1] H.J.M. Milne—T.C. Skeat (with contributions by D. Cockerell), *Scribes and correctors of the Codex Sinaiticus* (London 1938).

[2] The original publication of most of the Septuagint part and the complete New Testament was made by C. v. Tischendorf in 1862, three years after he had taken the manuscript to St. Petersburg: *Bibliorum codex Sinaiticus Petropolitanus: Ex tenebris protraxit in Europam transtulit ad juvandas atque illustrandas sacras litteras edidit C. Tischendorf*. 4 vols. (St. Petersburg 1862). Earlier he had published the content of the 43 folios he had procured on his first visit to Mt. Sinai, which contain part of 1 Chronicles and II Esdras, Esther and the first verses of Tobit, most of Jeremiah and part of Lamentations: *Codex Friderico-Augustanus: sive fragmenta Veteris Testament e codice Graeco omnium qui in Europa supersunt facile antiquissimo in oriente detexit in patriam attulit ad modum codicis edidit C. Tischendorf* (Leipzig 1846). The first verses of the New Testament were not published by Tischendorf but by the archimandrite Porfiri Uspenski who has included a plate of parts of 1 Corinthians 13 in a book on his travels to the Middle East (P. Porfiri, *Vostok khristianskii: Egipet i Sinai; bidy, ocherki, plany i nadpisi.* 2 vols. [St. Petersburg 1857]).

[3] Cf. H.J.M. Milne—T.C. Skeat, *Scribes and Correctors*, 22–24.

in some cases we have to rely upon the description by Milne and
Skeat as the original data cannot be checked any longer. However,
where the information can be checked, the data presented in *Scribes
and Correctors* are almost always vindicated. *Codex Sinaiticus* is a large
manuscript written on fine vellum with four (prose) or two (poetic
books) columns per page. The pages are always ruled and each column has 48 lines. The basic physical unit of the codex is the *quater-
nion*, a gathering or quire of four sheets folded together. Thus, each
quire consists of four sheets and eight folios, what makes 16 pages.[4]
Assuming that *Hermas* was the last book included in the original
codex, it must have contained around 95 quires, of which 50 survive almost completely. Not all the extant quires are regular. Three
quires, which started their life as standard eight-folio quires, have
their last one or two folios cut out, apparently because these were
left blank.[5] Three other quires have less folios, because they were
formed by using only one, two or three sheets.[6] Despite the occasional glitch, the original design of the codex has been consistently
followed throughout. The almost monotonous feel of page after page
of the same lay-out is only broken by the transition from one book
to the other and by the many corrections, most of which derive from
a period of time two or three centuries after the writing of the original text.

---

[4] For the making of quires and the various types see E.G. Turner, *The Typology
of the early codex* (University of Pennsylvania Press, 1977), 55–71. *Codex Sinaiticus* is
also mentioned in the list of consulted codices, p. 134.

[5] Quire 58 (the end of the Dodekapropheton; two folios removed), quire 78 (the
end of Luke; one folio removed), and quire 80 (the end of John; two folios removed).
In the New Testament the count of the secondary quire numbering, which was
added a few centuries after the making of the manuscript, is one number lower
than the original numbering. Though this suggests that one quire was lost between
Job and Matthew, Milne and Skeat have argued that this so-called 'missing quire'
never existed but was only intended to be included later on. In this paper we follow the secondary quire numbering. See Milne—Skeat, *Scribes and Correctors*, 7–9.
Throughout this paper, individual folios of *Sinaiticus* are numbered according to
their place in a quire and the numbering in the two facsimile volumes by Lake
*Codex Sinaiticus Petropolitanus: the New Testament, the Epistle of Barnabas and the Shepherd
of Hermas, preserved in the Imperial Library of St. Petersburg, now reproduced in facsimile from
photographs by Helen and Kirsopp Lake* (Oxford 1911) and Eid., *Codex Sinaiticus Petropolitanus
et Friderico-Augustanus Lipsiensis: The Old Testament. Preserved in the public library of Petrograd,
in the library of the society of ancient literature in Petrograd, and in the library of the university
of Leipzig, now reproduced in facsimile from photographs by Helen and Kirsopp Lake* (Oxford
1922).

[6] Namely quires 40, 90 and 91.

One suggestion by the authors of *Scribes and Correctors* which has caused some discussion ever since was that *Sinaiticus* was not copied from a model manuscript but written by dictation.[7] According to Milne and Skeat, the most probable solution to the widely different spelling patterns of the three scribes was to assume that the scribes wrote a text that was dictated to them. The quality of the spelling of the resulting text therefore depended on the ability and skill of the individual scribe. Scribe D was a reasonably good speller, scribe A particularly prone to interchange the vowels ι—ει and ε—αι, while scribe B committed all sorts of orthographic sins.[8] In books that were copied by more than one scribe, it is possible to distinguish the contributions by the various scribes simply by looking at the type and frequency of spelling errors.

DIVIDING THE WORK

The identification of the three main hands in the text by Milne and Skeat is nowadays undisputed and is corroborated by textual features such as the distinct spelling patterns of each scribe. That more than one scribe worked on a single codex is in itself nothing extraordinary; in almost all the early large codices more than one hand can be identified. The reasons for this are obvious: copying a complete Bible is a daunting task. By splitting the work up among more people the whole project became more manageable and could be finished more quickly.[9] What sets *Sinaiticus* apart from other manuscripts is the nature of the distribution of the tasks among the scribes.

---

[7] Cf. Milne—Skeat, *Scribes and Correctors*, chapter VII: Orthography and the Dictation Theory, 51–59. See also T.C. Skeat, "The Use of Dictation in Ancient Book Production" and Id., "The 'Codex Sinaiticus', the 'Codex Vaticanus' and Constantine," *The Collected Biblical Writings of T.C. Skeat* (ed. J.K. Elliott; NT.S 113; Leiden—Boston 2004) 3–32, 193–237.

[8] For the issue of itacism in general and the common occurrence of the ει—ι and αι—ε interchange see e.g. F.T. Gignac, *A grammar of the Greek papyri of the Roman and Byzantine periods* 1: Phonology (Milano 1976) 189–193; E. Mayser, *Grammatik der griechischen Papyri aus der Ptolemäerzeit mit Einschluss der gleichzeitigen Ostraka und der in Ägypten verfassten Inschriften I Laut- und Wortlehre; I. Teil Einleitung und Lautlehre*, 2. Auflage bearbeitet von Hans Schmoll (Berlin 1970) 66–70 and 85–87. For the role of itacism in the transmission of the text of the New Testament see C.C. Caragounis, *The Development of Greek and the New Testament: Morphology, Syntax, Phonology, and Textual Transmission* (WUNT 167; Tübingen 2004) 496–502.

[9] Speed of execution cannot be the only reason for splitting the work up: two people working on the same codex take as much time to produce two codices as two people working each on their own project.

Let us first consider the sections of the codex that are written by scribe B. This scribe wrote all the prophetic books of the Old Testament[10] as well as *Hermas*, at the end of the codex. He started both these sections with a new quire and ended the prophetic section with a quire from which the last two folios were cut off.[11] According to Milne and Skeat, he also corrected his own work and wrote all the superscriptions and running titles. Taking all these observations together, the contribution of this scribe to the total codex is self-contained and could have been carried out at the same time as that of the other two scribes; no close interaction with the other scribes was needed. In this way, scribe B's work is an example of the modular approach to the copying of a manuscript which one would expect when more scribes work on the same codex.

The work of the other two scribes, scribe D and A, does not show the same independence. In the book of Psalms, for example, scribe A continued the work of scribe D from the *verso* of the third folio of quire 62 onwards,[12] which is halfway through Psalm 97:3, and he subsequently finished all the poetic books. The New Testament, which follows upon the poetic books, is also done by scribe A's hand, except for six folios which, for reasons that should not distract us here, have been replaced by scribe D. Curiously, on the *verso* of folio 89.1 (NT 126) scribe D starts Revelation and stopped after he had written the first 34.5 lines of column 1. Scribe A takes over on this line and writes the remainder of the book.

In the closing stages of the historical books in the Old Testament the situation is even more complex, as is shown by diagram 1.

Diagram 1

35		36		37		38		39		40		41	42		43
SCRIBE A					SCRIBE D				SCRIBE A			D	A	SCRIBE B
2 Esdras			Esther	Tobit		Judith			1 Maccabees			4 Macc		Isaiah

---

[10] Seven quires (quires 50–56) are missing, containing the end of Lamentations, Ezechiel, and the start of the Dodekapropheton. There is no reason to assume that the missing part was not written by the same scribe.

[11] We do not know the quire composition of the ending of *Hermas*, as that part of the manuscript has not been preserved.

[12] Folio 62.3 (OT 160).

Scribe A wrote 2 Esdras, the first surviving book of this section, followed by scribe D who produced Tobit and Judith, after which scribe A added 1 Maccabees. Then scribe D penned the first seven pages of 4 Maccabees, and scribe A finished with the remaining nine. Clearly, these two scribes had a much closer working relationship with one another than with scribe B. Their combined work fits neatly into that of scribe B, but their individual work was in all likelihood not executed independently. The frequent changes of hand between scribe A and D in a relatively short distance calls for closer examination.

DIVIDING THE TASKS

The transition from Judith to 1 Maccabees is a very interesting one. The two pages on which Judith ends and 1 Maccabees starts are relatively poorly preserved as the lettering has faded considerably. However, more than enough can be discerned to identify some remarkable features.

In order to understand the problems of this quire, it is important to know how a quire was prepared for ruling out the lines. After a quire was folded together, tiny holes were pricked through the folded sheets to function as anchor-points for the ruling. The ruling was then made on each opening of the quire that showed the flesh side of the parchment. In order to keep the sheets of a single quire in exactly the same position to one another, they were either glued or stitched together.[13] In practice, this means that it is impossible for two scribes to work on the same quire simultaneously; the sheets of a quire formed already a physical unit at the time the scribe started to copy on the first page. The text of 1 Maccabees starts on the third folio of quire 39. It seems natural to assume that the scribe of 1 Maccabees, scribe A, could only start 1 Maccabees after Judith was completed by the other scribe. Yet, this may not have been the case when we consider the other irregularities surrounding this transition.

First of all, the first column of folio 39.3 is left blank though the previous book ends of the last column of folio 39.2. Occasionally an

---

[13] See Milne—Skeat, *Scribes and Correctors*, 73.

empty column follows the end of a book as the last column on a page, so that the next book can start on a new page. However, an empty column in between books that end and start on the same opening never occurs elsewhere in *Codex Sinaiticus*. Secondly, the superscription above 1 Maccabees is not written by scribe A, the scribe of the main text, but by scribe D, the scribe of the previous book. Superscriptions were not always added by the scribes themselves and this may be one of such instances,[14] but as a rule a scribe wrote the title of the text he was working on. However, the strongest clues for a proper reconstruction of what happened come from the closing pages of Judith where we find clear indications that the text was stretched.

First, the outside column of both the *recto* and *verso* of folio 39.2 has only 46 lines, whereas the remaining full columns have 47 lines. In the case of these last columns the actual text ignores the original ruling for 48 lines, which is still clearly visible.

Secondly, on the last pages of Judith we also find many more instances of the *diple*, the wedge-shaped sign used as a filler-mark at the end of slightly shorter lines. The *recto* of folio 39.1 (OT 36) has 14 of these wedges, the *recto* of 39.2 (OT 37) 39 plus three double ones. The last page, which comprises only three and a half columns, has still 31 filling signs.

Thirdly, if one looks at the number of paragraph breaks per folio, the number of new paragraphs rises dramatically in the last pages of Judith. This is not only an indication that the scribe inserted such paragraph breaks at his own discretion, but also that he uses paragraph breaks as a means to stretch the text.[15] As a result of these last two measures the average number of letters per line decreases. Though the average number of letters per line on 39.2 *recto* drops only one or two letters, down from 12.7 on 39.1 *verso* and 13.6 in the first eight columns of the book to 11.7, this drop still amounts to four to six lines of text per column. Taking all these phenomena together, it seems fair to conclude that scribe D wanted to stretch the text of the end of Judith.

---

[14] Scribe D added the superscription to scribe A's Romans, Galatians, and Ephesians, while scribe B added the superscription to scribe A's Acts.

[15] In *Sinaiticus*, a new paragraph is normally indicated by leaving the remainder of the previous line blank and projecting the first line of the new paragraph slightly into the left margin.

Given that scribe D stretched the text, and that his section is followed by a blank column, it is most likely that the text of 1 Maccabees had already been written by scribe A before Judith was finished by scribe D. In the process of deciding beforehand where Judith would end and 1 Maccabees had to commence an error was made, so that scribe A wrote 1 Maccabees starting in the wrong column; two columns too late. It may well be that the Title '1 Maccabees' was added by scribe D not after scribe A wrote the main text, but before, as an indication where to start. When scribe D, whilst finishing Judith, noticed the error (either on the *verso* of 39.1 [OT 36] or the first column of 39.2 [OT 37]), he tried to stretch the remaining text in order to cover as much of the superfluous space as possible. In the end, he succeeded only partially.

Can we say more about the moment when the calculation for the starting point of 1 Maccabees was made? It is most probable that this was done well before scribe D had to use quire 39 for himself. The earliest possible point is the start of scribe D's section, which is the start of Tobit on the recto of folio 37.3 (OT 22), but it is more likely that scribe D was already working on Judith. This means that the calculation where to start 1 Maccabees was made somewhere between folio 38.2 (OT 30) and 38.8 (OT 35). It is impossible to narrow this window further down.[16]

The precise relationship between scribe D and A remains vague, but it follows that at least at this stage both were involved in copying different sections of the main text at the same time. We only know this because of the error that was made: it may well be that the previous transition between these scribes, from Esther to Tobit, was made using a similar procedure, but then without the error. If it can be argued that these two scribes worked concurrently in the actual copying process, the same becomes even more likely for the third scribe, scribe B, who produced the neat and self-contained modules.

---

[16] Part of the last leaf of quire 38 was recovered from a binding by V.N. Beneshevich and published in 1911; most of the remainder of the folio is lost. However, the error in determining the start of 1 Maccabees cannot be the result of an omission of two columns on this folio, not only because one would expect that the calculation was made earlier than this, but also because the amount of text that is supposed to be on this leaf matches exactly the available space (roughly 4.900 letters according to the text of Rahlfs).

FITTING THE PARTS TOGETHER

Although the phenomena surrounding the Judith—1 Maccabees transition are relatively easy to explain, the situation from 1 Maccabees to 4 Maccabees is much harder to understand. In itself it is not remarkable that 1 and 4 Maccabees are included in a Septuagint codex. But it is slightly peculiar that only these two books were included and that 2 and 3 Maccabees were left out.[17] 1 and 4 Maccabees are the last two books before the Prophets, written by the third scribe, scribe B, and it is well possible that this scribe was already working on this section, or had even finished it. In that case, the necessity existed to ensure that the books of the Maccabees would fit neatly into the space available before Isaiah started.

When scribe A had reached the end of quire 40, he did not continue with a regular quire consisting of four folded sheets, but with one of only two sheets, which contains four folios. The text of 1 Maccabees that still needed to be copied, fitted neatly on these four folios so that the book boundary coincided with the quire boundary.[18] The next book, 4 Maccabees, starts therefore on a new quire. Scribe D writes the first three and a half folios of this new quire (quire 42), after which scribe A takes over on the *verso* of folio 42.4 (OT 59), and finishes the remainder of the book on the space left on this quire. In total, 4 Maccabees occupies exactly eight folios, which is a single quire; only 11 lines are left over on the last column of the last page of this quire.

It is not only the change in hand in the middle of a book that is remarkable, but also the specific circumstances. Scribe D had started to write 50 lines per column from the *verso* of folio 42.3 (OT 58) and increased this number to 51 in the last two columns of the

---

[17] In *Sinaiticus*, the books bear the title MAKKABAIΩN A and MAKKABAIΩN Δ, indicating that the books were already considered to be part of a collection of books of the Maccabees.

[18] One does wonder why the scribes started to trouble themselves with changing the quire format when one can also simply cut away the superfluous leaves, as was done later in the manuscript. An answer may be found in the way the quires were fastened together. Milne—Skeat, *Scribes and Correctors*, 72, inform us that "in the earlier part of the book" a quire was held together by some stitches with thin vellum, while in the later part of the book the sheets of the quire were glued together. It is possible that it may have been easier to remove superfluous sheets from a glued quire then from a quire that was provisionally stitched together.

recto of 42.4 (OT 59). Scribe A, who takes over on the *verso*, continues with the 50 lines per column format on the first one and a half folio, only to return to the regular column length of 48 lines from folio 42.6 (OT 61) onwards. This action—to increase the number of lines—was deliberate: it is still visible that the parchment was prepared as usual to contain the normal 48 lines but that seperate action was undertaken to accomodate the extra lines. Of course, these measures were taken to ensure that 4 Maccabees would neatly fit onto a single quire, and the scribes made a correct estimation of the amount of extra space they needed. What is remarkable, though, is that they started to make these adjustments six folios before the actual end of the book and were satisfied that enough space was left three folios before the end. It can also be concluded that, as the space-increasing measures start with scribe D and continue with scribe A, these scribes wrote one after the other. Therefore, the situation here is different from that seen in the transition from Judith to 1 Maccabees.

But why was the effort made to keep both books within their own quire limits? If the section of historical books had to fit unto the already written quires of Isaiah, why already adjust the quire format in 1 Maccabees? Three possible scenarios can be considered.

First, scribe D had started 4 Maccabees already on a new quire, so scribe A had to make sure that his 1 Maccabees would fit in seamlessly. 4 Maccabees had to fit onto a single quire for the obvious reason that Isaiah had been already written. This explanation has the advantage of explaining the change of hand from 1 to 4 Maccabees, but supposes also that scribe A was more or less left on his own to sort out the problems of space when he was writing 1 Maccabees, unless the strategy for both books was planned in advance.

A second scenario is that the section of historical books was originally supposed to end with 1 Maccabees, and 4 Maccabees was added only as an afterthought and subsequently had to be squeezed in. Perhaps no exemplar of this book was available at the original time of writing, or the plans were changed while scribe A was already finishing 1 Maccabees on the adjusted quire. This hypothesis accounts for most of the irregularities, but is only a partial explanation for the strange combination of books. Why select only 1 and 4 Maccabees for inclusion and not just 1 Maccabees or all four books?

A third scenario can be constructed, which removes the weakness of the second, by assuming that 1 Maccabees was restricted to quire boundaries in order that the other two books of the Maccabees could be inserted in between 1 and 4 Maccabees. As both were limited to their own quires it would be physically possible to insert new quires at a later stage.

It is impossible to prove any of the three explanations above empirically. Yet the common element in each of these suggestions is that *Sinaiticus* does not display a level of professionalism that one would expect in a scriptorium that produces such volumes on a regular basis.

BOOK TRANSITIONS AND SPACE

The closing stages of the New Testament display their own set of irregular phenomena. It has been already noted that at the start of Revelation scribe D limits himself to just under 35 lines, after which scribe A writes the remainder of the book.[19] Revelation is followed by *Barnabas*, also by scribe A, and by the *Shepherd of Hermas* from the hand of scribe B. This last book starts on a new quire and, like the other section written by scribe B, may have been completed before scribe A had finished *Barnabas*. Yet, it is not so much the inclusion of these two books in the codex that is remarkable, but rather the irregular quire composition of quire 90, a quire of three sheets (a *ternion*) containing the end of Revelation and half of *Barnabas*, and quire 91, a quire consisting of a single folded sheet (*bifolium*) containing the remainder of *Barnabas*.[20]

Quire 91 has always been a *bifolium*, there are no sheets or folios missing, as assumed in the 19th century by Scrivener. These two irregular quires are followed by a regular one containing the first part of *Hermas*. There is only a single blank column at the end of the second quire (91). All the remaining space has been used up by the letter of *Barnabas*.

---

[19] It was Tischendorf himself who noted the section by scribe D at this point. This identification was made slightly easier by the spelling of the name John as ιωανης in contrast to scribe A's preference ιωαννης. The difference between the two hands is only very slight: two of the differences are that scribe D's letters tend to tilt more to the left and that the two arms of the *kappa* are attached much higher to the vertical than is the case with scribe A.

[20] Turner did not know of any parchment codex consisting entirely of quires formed by only one folded sheet (*uniones*) but notes their existence in codices where the gatherings are normally larger. E.G. Turner, *Typology*, 60–61.

Diagram 2

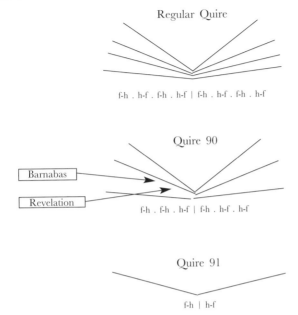

Regular Quire

f-h . h-f . f-h . h-f | f-h . h-f . f-h . h-f

Quire 90

Barnabas

Revelation

f-h . f-h . h-f | f-h . h-f . h-f

Quire 91

f-h | h-f

The *ternion* (quire 90) violates a rule that has been strictly observed in the rest of the manuscript, and is known as *Gregory's Law*.[21] Gregory noticed that the quires of most Eastern manuscripts have always the flesh side of the parchment at the outside (as is also true for quires 90 and 91 in *Sinaiticus*) and that, faces like, *i.e.* the flesh side of a page is always matched by a flesh side on the opposite page on any opening of the codex. The only violation of this rule in the whole codex is found in quire 90, where the first sheet is laid out as expected, the second and third are laid out correctly in relation to one another, but the first and second sheet show a mismatch.[22] The result is that the opening showing the *verso* of folio 90.1 (NT 134) and the *recto* of folio 90.2 (NT 135), as well as the opening of the *verso* of folio 90.5 (NT 138) and the *recto* of folio 90.6 (NT 139), show different sides of the parchment.

---

[21] C.R. Gregory, "The Quires in Greek Manuscripts," *American Journal of Philology* 7 (1886) 27–32.
[22] In the case of quire 78, the end of Luke and start of John, there is also a mismatch in that hair side faces flesh side, but there it is not caused by an irregular quire make-up but by the removal of the last, empty, folio.

The transition from Revelation to *Barnabas* takes place on the *recto* of folio 90.2 (NT 135). The first column contains the last verses of Revelation with the normal subscription, the second column starts with *Barnabas*. There is no sign whatsoever that the scribe intended to indicate that a new section of books was about to begin or that *Barnabas* belonged to a different category of books than Revelation. Elsewhere in the codex this happens frequently, with or without a change of the scribe. We have seen this already in the transition from the historical books to the prophets, to which can be added the transition from Job to Matthew (new quire), from John to the Pauline letters (new quire), and from Paul to Acts (a blank column and a blank page).[23] What can be said about the lack of a 'break' between Revelation and *Barnabas*?[24] Is it an indication for a similar 'canonical status' of these books at the time the codex was compiled or are there other factors at play?[25] And do the two irregular quires have anything to do with this?

The first possible solution to the problem posed by the two irregular quires is that scribe A, coming to the end of his daunting task, simply used some left-over sheets to construct a *ternion*, and, noticing that he needed more space for *Barnabas*, added a *bifolium* as well. This assumes a remarkable error in estimating the length he needed for *Barnabas*: he needed two folios more than he had prepared and which he would have had available if he had made a regular quire. The unique irregularity in quire 90, the hair side of the parchment facing the flesh side, is then simply part of the abnormal circumstances of producing this quire. Though possible, this reconstruction explains none of the irregularities, but simply acknowledges their existence.

---

[23] Irrespective of the situation of *Barnabas*, the *Shepherd* is set apart from the previous section by means of its start on a new quire and the change of scribe. Though, this does not tell us anything about a possible lesser status of the book, it does inform us that it did not belong to the same group of books as *Barnabas*.

[24] The opposite impression, *viz.* that the New Testament and *Barnabas* are two distinguishable entities in the codex, might be created by a statement such as 'It [*viz.* the epistle of Barnabas] stands after the New Testament in the fourth-century codex Sinaiticus of the Greek Bible.' (B.M. Metzger, *The Canon of the New Testament: its Origin, Development, and Significance* [Oxford 1997] 188).

[25] The dating of *Sinaiticus* becomes an issue here as well; towards the end of the fourth century, the canon of the New Testament was much more an outspoken and agreed upon concept than in the first quarter of the century. *Sinaiticus* has been dated anywhere in this century.

A second solution starts with assuming that quire 90 started of as a normal quire of four regularly folded sheets. If one removes the second sheet from such a quire, one ends up exactly with the irregularity that can presently be seen. This is a more plausible explanation for the current quire make-up than the assumption that this quire was composed with the gross irregularity of hair facing flesh.[26] In this case, enough space was availabe in quire 90 to contain the whole text of *Barnabas*. After the removal of the sheet from quire 90, the scribe ran short of two folios, which were subsequently added as the single-sheet quire 91. The scribe could have foreseen this, of course, and ought to have replaced the second sheet with a new one, instead of simply removing it and adding the missing sheet as a new quire.

But what can be the reason for the removal of the second sheet? One can only speculate about this, but it is tempting to relate the absence of a break between Revelation and *Barnabas* in the current state of the codex to this irregularity, which happens to occur on the irregularly placed sheet in quire 90. What if scribe A had started *Barnabas* originally on the *verso* of the true folio 90.2 (a proper break) instead of on the second column of the *recto*, immediately after Revelation? If he were confronted with the necessity to write *Barnabas* within the quire boundaries, he would have to squeeze in three extra columns of text into the six and a half folios available to him. Although this does not seem impossible, it would result in a tightly written text. The only major problem is that we must assume that the scribe realised this only while he had written upon the *verso* of folio 90.2, but before he had started the *recto* of 90.3. If he had written only a few lines on the *verso* of 90.2 he could have washed this text away, and if he had started already on 90.3, it would have been necessary to remove two sheets. As it stands now, he chose not to wash the text away, but simply took the sheet out and restarted on the former third sheet, which had now become the second one.

Both solutions suggested above assume at least two mistakes on the scribe's side in order to account for all the phenomena; and none of them can be proven beyond the point of speculation. In

---

[26] Irregularities and miscalculations do happen of course in many manuscripts. However, as *Codex Sinaiticus* is mostly very consistent this irregularity stands out more prominently than it would have in more irregularly formed manuscripts.

any case, it seems clear that the scribe was seriously struggling to write the text of *Barnabas* within the limits of a quire. The absence of a break between Revelation and *Barnabas* tells us very little about their respective canonical status. It is rather part of a pattern of confused transitions from the text written by scribe A to that written by scribe B.

CONCLUSION

In this essay, I have been looking at some irregularities in the make-up of the quires and the change of scribal hand in *Codex Sinaiticus*. Concentrating on the irregularities in order to deduce some insights into the making of this codex is only justified because of the overall regular apprearance of this codex. Some surviving early codices, such as the *Freer Gospels*, are strikingly irregular in their quire format, while others seem to contain hardly any exception at all, like *Codex Vaticanus*. But what are the implications of the reconstructions offered above?

Despite the fact that the three scribes of *Codex Sinaiticus* individually write in a bookhand that is extremily similar to one another and by doing so betray their professional training, some tension exists between the appearance of the script and the actual physical composition of the codex as a whole. The division of work among the three scribes caused some problems when it came to the point of fitting the various parts of the main text together. Quires were shortened, and text was condensed so that it would fall within the quire boundaries. The alternation between scribes A and D in the historical books of the Old Testament proved very risky and caused some serious problems for scribe D when he had to finish Judith. Also, the situation surrounding the end of the New Testament is muddled, and it seems that at least two errors on the side of scribe A need to be supposed in order to explain the resulting situation.

The picture that emerges from our brief enquiry into the relationship between quires and changes of scribal hands is that, as would be expected, the scribes worked concurrently on various parts of the manuscript, but that this splitting up of the work was not executed with the fluency one might expect in an established and experienced scriptorium (as we know it, e.g. from early medieval monasteries). This can be explained in two ways: either the phenomenon of producing a codex of this size was so new that the scriptorium was still experimenting with the correct approach,[27] or the codex was produced outside a major centre and at a locality where there was demand for a large Bible but where one lacked the experience to produce one. The rather peculiar choice of including only 1 and 4 Maccabees may lend some weight to the latter option, especially if one accepts the suggestion that manuscripts of 2 and/or 3 Maccabees were simply unavailable at the time of writing.

The obvious efforts made in 4 Maccabees to write the book onto a single quire, as well as the deliberate stretching out of the text in Judith, brings up the question whether the dictation theory can still be uphold. Is it likely that a scribe, while listening to the reader, also had time to keep a close eye on the amount of space still available, let alone time to roughen up the parchment in order to add two or three extra lines to a column? Also, one could ask whether the fact that one scribe wrote 1 Maccabees on the third folio of a quire while the previous book had not been finished yet, might be easily reconcilable with copying by dictation. Although the dictation theory provides a very neat solution for the spelling differences between the three scribes, it may well be that this theory leaves some of the many other peculiarities of *Sinaiticus* not addressed.

The division of tasks between the three scribes did not stop with the actual copying process. The text had to be corrected, running titles were to be added, and various numbering systems were incorporated. As these tasks were also carried out by the same three scribes, the actual nature of their working relationship could be spelled out in much greater detail than what is done in this brief study. However, this would not substantially alter the picture that emerges from our study. Even in the case of a well-known and well-studied manuscript (certainly true in comparison to e.g. *Codex Vaticanus* or *Alexandrinus*) such as *Codex Sinaiticus*, plenty of phenomena are still waiting for a good description.

---

[27] This view is more or less implied in Skeat, "The 'Codex Sinaiticus', the 'Codex Vaticanus' and Constantine," 583–598.

𝔓78 (*P.OXY.* XXXIV 2684):
THE EPISTLE OF JUDE ON AN AMULET?

Tommy Wasserman

In the *editio princeps* of *P.Oxy.* xxxiv 2684, known among biblical scholars as 𝔓78, the first editor, Peter Parsons, suggested, that "most probably we have to do with an amulet."[1] However, he pointed out that
the textual content of this double leaf preserving four verses from the
Epistle of Jude, is an odd choice of text for an amulet. During the
years to follow, several scholars have concurred with the judgment
that the MS was probably an amulet, but there has been disagreement about the range of verses in relation to the number of quires
once extant; Kurt Treu concluded that the Epistle of Jude was too
long for a single-quire codex, but, on the other hand, the whole
text would not be necessary for an amulet.[2] However, Kurt Aland
assumed that it was a single-quire codex and stated, "[Der Codex]
diente vermutlich als Amulett, umfaßte aber wohl den ganzen
Judasbrief."[3] Winfried Grunewald, in his work on the papyrus witnesses of the Catholic Letters, also agreed that 𝔓78 could be an
amulet, but, like the first editor, he expressed his surprise of the fact
that this particular text would have been used for the purpose in
question.[4] It was perhaps for this reason that he suggested the alternative function of a "Schmuckcodex."[5] An amulet could of course
be worn for both purposes. However, the very mundane nature of

---

[1] L. Ingrams—P. Kingston—P. Parsons—J. Rea, *The Oxyrhynchus Papyri XXXIV*
(London 1968) 5.

[2] K. Treu, "Christliche Papyri IV," *APF* 22 (1973) 373. In regard to the choice
of this text for an amulet, Treu stated (373): "Der Abschnitt nicht ganz abwegig,
wenn auch eher apotropäisch."

[3] K. Aland (ed.), *Repertorium der griechischen christlichen Papyri I: Biblische Papyri: Altes
Testament, Neues Testament, Varia, Apokryphen* (PTS 18; Berlin—New York 1976) 314
(NT 78).

[4] Cf. K. Junack—W. Grunewald, *Die katholischen Briefe, Das Neue Testament auf
Papyrus 1* (ANTF 6; Berlin—New York 1986) 29: "Überraschend ist jedoch die
Tatsache, daß überhaupt der Text oder Textteile gerade dieses Briefes für einen
solchen Zweck ausgewählt sind".

[5] Junack—Grunewald, *Die katholischen Briefe*, 29.

this particular item speaks in favour of the religious or magical purpose rather than the decorative. One should of course also note the possibility that the function of a manuscript may shift over time.

In this study, I will first describe the manuscript itself—its physical and textual features—and then very briefly the historical context in which it once filled its function, probably as an amulet. Finally, I will attempt to offer an explanation as to why this particular text was chosen for the occasion. Why would an individual, the scribe or someone else, want to produce and carry around an amulet with verses from the Epistle of Jude? Can the text itself offer any explanation as to its specific function?

1. Description of 𝔓[78]

The extant portion of the manuscript, today kept in the Sackler Library in Oxford, consists of a *bifolium*, a double leaf, from a papyrus codex with one column per page. The size and especially the proportions of this miniature codex are unusual as it is much broader than high (5,3 × 2,9 cm).[6] There is a visible fold in the middle with two small holes approximately 7 and 9 mm from the upper edge.[7] The presence of visible folds is a characteristic feature of amulets, since they were often single sheets rolled or folded into compact form and worn upon the person.[8] However, in this case we have to do with a codex, and, therefore, the evidence is inconclusive since there is always a folding in the middle of a codex. The two holes

---

[6] E.G. Turner reserved the term "miniature" for codices less than 10 cm broad (*The Typology of the Early Codex* [University of Philadelphia 1977] 25). In his list of miniature codices (table 1, group 11), which needs an updating, there are no comparable items (ibid., 22; cf. C.H. Roberts, "The Codex," *Proceedings of the British Academy* 40 [1954] 198–199). For recent discussions of the terms involved, see M.J. Kruger, "P. Oxy. 840: Amulet or Miniature Codex?," *JTS* 53 (2002) 81–94; and T.J. Kraus, "*P.Oxy.* V 840—Amulett oder Miniaturkodex? Grundsätzliche und ergänzende Anmerkungen zu zwei Termini," *ZAC* 8 (2005) [485–97].

[7] On the facsimile it looks like there are three holes, but Parsons, *The Oxyrhynchus Papyri XXXIV*, 4, indicates two holes.

[8] The compact form is applicable also in the case of miniature codices used as amulets. Cf. L. Amundsen, "Christian Papyri from the Oslo Collection," *SO* 24 (1945) 128: "The reasons for using the diminuitive book may be partly economical; it may, however, be considered too, that such a tiny volume was a handy thing to carry along in one's pocket, and also easy to conceal if necessary (cf. the μαντική and the amulet!)."

probably carried a thread for binding. It is impossible to say if there was a pair of holes in the corresponding area at the foot, since this part is broken away. Sometimes amulets of a single sheet were provided with a string used to hang, for instance, around the neck of the owner,[9] but in this case involving several sheets (see below), the function of binding is the most natural explanation of the presence of the holes.[10]

The hand has been described as "leisurely half-cursive" (Parsons) or "semi-uncial with elements of cursive" (Grunewald) and the manuscript has been dated to the 3rd or 4th century.[11] The form and size of the letters are consistent, but the number of lines are irregular; folio 1 has three lines on recto and verso, whereas folio 2 has five lines on verso; on the fifth line only the last three letters of ενὕπνειαδομενοι followed by a middle stop are squeezed underneath the word to be completed that way.[12] The recto has four lines. Of lectional signs are found only the *diaeresis* (fol. 1↓, line 4 and 5; fol. 2↓, line 4) and the middle stop (fol. 1↓, line 4; fol. 2↓, line 5). *Nomina sacra* occur in usual forms: ιην, κν, χρν (fol 1→, line 3). The orthography reflects common itacisms: ι for ει (fol. 1→ line 1); ει for ι (fol. 2↓, line 4; fol. 2→, line 7); and ε for αι (fol. 1↓, line 6).[13] However, the confusion of δ and ζ (fol. 2↓, line 4) is quite remarkable. The extraordinary format, the strange spelling, the remarkable layout and the irregular hand give the impression of an untrained scribe.

---

[9] See for example Chrysostom, *Hom.* 19.14.

[10] Grunewald, *Die katholischen Briefe*, 28–29, thinks that the two holes were used for both purposes; first he refers to them as "eine wichtige Angabe für die Zweckbestimmung . . . Das Format und das Vorhandensein der beiden Löcher am oberen Rand (van Haelst, s.o.), durch die ein Faden gezogen werden konnte, lassen den Schluß zu, daß es sich bei 𝔓⁷⁸ um ein Amulett bzw. einen Schmuckcodex handelt, der um den Hals getragen wurde." Secondly, he refers to "zwei kleine Löcher in dem Knick, die wohl für die Heftung bestimmt waren".

[11] Parsons, *The Oxyrhynchus Papyri XXXIV*, 4, assigns it to the 3rd or earlier 4th century CE; Grunewald, *Die katholischen Briefe*, 29, points out that a specific date is difficult to indicate because of the very individual outlook of the hand, but he finds the nearest equivalents in 𝔓⁹ (3rd cent.), and 𝔓¹⁷ (4th cent.), and so dates the MS to the 3rd–4th century.

[12] Perhaps this was done in order to avoid a possible confusion, had the last three letters begun a new page, with the dative form of νοῦς ("mind"), as opposed to the next word σάρξ ("flesh"), i.e. νοΐ σάρκα μὲν μιαίνουσιν ("with their minds they defile the flesh," or "they defile the flesh for the sake of the mind").

[13] Cf. E. Mayser, *Grammatik der griechischen Papyri aus der Ptolemäerzeit. Band I: Laut- und Wortlehre. 1. Teil: Einleitung und Lautlehre* (rev. by H. Schmoll; Berlin ²1970) §8.3; §9.2–3; §14.3.

All margins are intact and the two leaves must have contained at least 176 letters. The leaves are not consecutive—c. 335 letters (without punctuation) from the text of Jude are missing between them.[14] In the following I shall try to reconstruct the possible extent of the missing leaves of the codex. This can only be an approximation, due to the irregularity of writing and format, and to the fact that we do not know exactly the textual character and extent of the missing parts of the original manuscript.

> Fol. 1, recto (Jd 4) contains three lines and 35 letters (12+ 11+12)
>
> Fol. 1, verso (Jd 4–5) contains three lines and 39 letters (13+ 12+14)
>
> Fol. 2, recto (Jd 7–8) contains five lines and 56 letters (12+ 15+14+12+3)
>
> Fol. 2, verso (Jd 8) contains four lines and 46 letters (10+ 13+13+10)

We do not know which portions of Jude were copied in the original codex, but since the text on the first folio commences in the middle of a word and sentence in v. 4 (the itacistic γιαν, in ἀσέλγειαν), we may conclude that there was at least one leaf on the outer side of the extant leaf, or possibly in another preceding quire. Moreover, v. 5 breaks off in the middle of a sentence (before εἰδότας) and commences again in the end of v. 7 (αιωνιου), so we conclude that there was at least one leaf on the inside of the extant leaf. As mentioned above, the missing portion of text in between (Jd 5–7) consists of c. 335 letters, which would occupy two double leaves. These leaves would then contain an average of 42 letters per page, which makes good sense if we consider the tendency of the scribe to increase the number of lines and letters progressively. Possibly, the scribe had to condense his text in consideration of the extent of his writing material (especially if the codex was made up of one single quire, which is likely, and brought forward by Parsons in his *editio princeps*).

It seems reasonable to assume that there were more than one leaf on the outer side, or another preceding quire with several leaves, since the complete sentence of v. 4 would require at least two leaves—

---

[14] For convenience sake, the text of the standard edition of the Greek New Testament is used in the reconstruction of the missing portions.

there are c. 125 letters from παρεισεδυσαν to [ασελ]γιαν. If Jude was copied from the very beginning, it would require approximately six outer leaves (12 pages), or three leaves in a preceding quire (12 pages), since there are c. 390 letters in the missing portion of vv. 1–4. This would make an average of c. 33 letters per page, which is consistent with the pattern above. However, six outer leaves would not be enough to hold the latter part of Jude, provided that we have to do with a single quire codex—thus, Kurt Aland's assumption of a single-quire codex holding all of the text is wrong.[15] From [βλ]ασφη-μουσιν to the end of the letter there are c. 1,450 letters, and six outer leaves would only hold about enough space for vv. 8–13, i.e. c. 600 letters, which means c. 50 letters per line (12 pages), in consistence with the pattern above.

Thus three main possibilities remain:

(a) the letter was copied in more than one quire (the whole letter would require 13–14 leaves);

(b) another text (e.g. a prayer) preceded Jude, if the complete text was copied in a single quire;

(c) only a part of Jude was copied, possibly vv. 1–13 considering both the pattern of the extant leaf in terms of letters per line, and the natural sense divisions of the letter.

The first alternative is least attractive, since it does not explain the described tendency on the part of the scribe, to increase the number of lines, and letters per line. The choice between the two latter alternatives is best resolved by appealing to Occam's razor; the second alternative brings in the notion of another text, of which there is no extant evidence, and, therefore, the last alternative seems to be best explanation.[16]

For the benefit of the readers, I include a transcription of the text:

---

[15] Aland's assumption could still be correct if the MS contained some other text preceding Jude, but this fact was not expressed, nor can it be evidenced. Cf. Aland, *Repertorium*, 314.

[16] The fact that only a part of Jude would have been copied cannot be used as evidence for or against the last alternative since many amulets record short extracts from works of various lengths. If this MS was used as an amulet, it is perhaps even easier to imagine that only the first part of the epistle was copied (see below).

Fol. 1→

v. 4 γιαν και τον μο   1
      νον δεϲποτην
      κ̄ν̄ ημων ιην χρν   3

Fol. 2↓

v. 7 αιωνιου δικην   1
v. 8 επεχουϲαι ομοιωϲ
      μεντοι και αυτοι   3
      ενϋπνειαδομε

Fol. 1↓

v. 5 αρνουμενοι· ϋπο   4
      υνηϲαι δε ϋμαϲ
      βουλομε αδελφ[οι   6

Fol. 2→

v. 8 ϲαρκα μεν μι   6
      αινουϲιν κυρει
      οτητα δε αθετου
      ϲιν δοξαν δε[. . .   9

It will be noted that my transcription differs slightly from that found in the *editio princeps*, as far as uncertain or extant letters are concerned.[17] Moreover, Parsons indicated "two unique" and "three rare readings" (repeated by Treu with the remark "ohne kritisches Gewicht") in the four extant verses of Jude, whereas Grunewald indicated that five readings deviated from NA[26], three of which were "Singulärlesarten."[18] Actually, there is only one singular reading, and four other rare readings.[19] Below is a selective apparatus showing these five peculiar readings, in which $\mathfrak{P}^{78}$ constitutes the base text (in the left margin):[20]

---

[17] Differences from Parsons' transcription (*The Oxyrhynchus Papyri XXXIV*, 5): v. 4: δεϲποτην; ημων (uncertain letters not indicated by Parsons); v. 5 αδελφ[οι (the ending is not visible and could be either -οι or -ε as indicated by Parsons in a note; ibid. 6); v. 8 αθετουϲιν (uncertain letters not indicated); δοξαν (final ν is visible); δε[.. (there is room for two letters, the first of which there is a trace). Differences from Grunewald, *Die katholischen Briefe*, 60–63: v. 4: the letter π in δεϲποτην is visible; v. 5: αδελφ[οι (the ending is not visible and could be either -οι or -ε); v. 8: ενϋπνειαδομενοι (the letter ε is only partly visible but can be nothing else); δοξαν (final ν is visible); δε (ε is partly visible and can be nothing else).

[18] Parsons, *The Oxyrhynchus Papyri XXXIV*, 5; Treu, *Christliche Papyri*, 373; Grunewald, *Die katholischen Briefe*, 29.

[19] E.C. Colwell, "Method in Evaluating Scribal Habits: A Study of $\mathfrak{P}^{45}$, $\mathfrak{P}^{66}$, $\mathfrak{P}^{75}$," *Studies in Methodology in Textual Criticism of the New Testament* (NTTS 9; Leiden—Grand Rapids 1969) 106–124, was the first to use singular readings in order to isolate the scribal tendencies in individual MSS. See also E.J. Epp, "Toward the Clarification of the Term 'Textual Variant'," *Studies in the Theory and Method of New Testament Textual Criticism* (SD 45; Grand Rapids 1993) 47–61; and J.R. Royse, "Scribal Tendencies in the Transmission of the Text of the New Testament," *The Text of the New Testament in Contemporary Research. Essays on the Status Questionis* (eds. B.D. Ehrman—M.W. Holmes; SD 46; Grand Rapids 1995) 239–252. Royse describes Colwell's method and results and gives examples of a number of more recent studies based upon his method.

[20] My apparatus is based on the textual apparatuses found in C.A. Albin, *Judasbrevet. Traditionen, Texten, Tolkningen* (Stockholm 1962) and NA[27].

Peculiar readings

v. 4: δεσποτην κν ημων: so 38
  δεσποτην και κυριον ημων ℵ A B C 0251 33 81 323 1241 1739 *al*
  δεσποτην θεον και κυριον ημων P Ψ 𝔐
  ημων δεσποτην και κν 𝔓⁷²
  θεον και κυριον ημων 378 2147
  θεον και δεσποτην τον κυριον ημων 42 51 *pc*

v. 5: αδελφοι (in consistence with υμας or else, αδελφε; in each case a singular reading)

v. 7: δικην επεχουσαι: so 378 630 876 1505 1611 1765 2138 2243 2495
  δικην υπεχουσαι 𝔓⁷² B C Ψ 0251 33 81 323 1241 1739 𝔐
  δικην υπερεχουσαι A
  δικην ουκ εχουσιν ℵ*
  δικην υπεχουσιν ℵᶜ

v. 8: αυτοι: so 92 1885
  omit 142
  ουτοι *rell*

v. 8: δοξαν: so 3 5 90 796 1799 1831
  δοξας *rell*

It may be argued that a discussion of the text proper does not belong in a paleographical description as such. However, the singular reading in v. 5 deserves a brief comment here, since it has bearing on my judgment on the original range of verses of the MS: The address in the nominative (vocative), αδελφ[οι] is superfluous—especially if the personal pronoun ὑμᾶς was repeated a second time as in some witnesses, which is impossible to say since the text is not extant— and may be an indication that the manuscript did not contain v. 3, where Jude has used the address, ἀγαπητοί (as in v. 17). However, the address in v. 5 is more likely an influence from 2 Pet 1:10 (ἀδελφοί, σπουδάσατε), which is a parallel to Jude 3 (ἀγαπητοί, πᾶσαν σπουδὴν ποιούμενος), in which case 𝔓⁷⁸ probably included v. 3 with the same substitution. The scribe might then have repeated the word a second time in order to create a greater sense of immediacy or gravity to the warnings.

Nevertheless, it is clear from the relatively large number of peculiar variants in only four verses, that we have to do with an "eccentric text," to use Parsons' words.[21] This feature may be due to the

---

[21] Parsons, *The Oxyrhynchus Papyri XXXIV*, 5. The text of 𝔓⁷⁸ is categorized by

inexperience and carelessness of the scribe, but it can also be interpreted in connection with the purpose and function of the MS.

In regard to the question of the purpose and function of $\mathfrak{P}^{78}$, we
must return to another important issue briefly touched in the introduction; is it possible that the function of this manuscript shifted
over time? G.H.R. Horsley has offered a detailed reconstruction of
the prehistory of another manuscript, *P.Vindob.* G 29831.[22] The manuscript is another double leaf of a presumed miniature codex, originally devoted to the Gospel of John (presumably John 1:1–18), and
the extant portion contains a passage from John 1:5–6 on the first
folio and an amulet formula on the second folio. In his reconstruction Horsley suggests that the arrangement of sheets was binary, and
that the scribe, after completing John 1:1–5 on two sheets (not surviving), took out a third (the surviving leaf) by mistake and proceeded with the rest of v. 5—possibly because he was used to work
with larger gatherings (ternios, quaternios, etc.)—and realized his
error only after having copied the full folio on both sides. Since this
sheet did not fit into the codex and he did not want to waste his
effort, he reused it by adding a standard amulet formula on the second folio (which is written in the same hand). Horsley's suggestion
is tempting, but there are of course other possibilities.[23]

---

the Alands as "free text, category I". Cf. K. Aland—B. Aland, *The Text of the New
Testament* (Grand Rapids ²1989) 101. The textual categorization of this MS is of
course somewhat problematic due to its fragmentary nature. For a general critique
of Alands' categories, see B.D. Ehrman, "A Problem of Textual Circularity: The
Alands on the Classification of New Testament Manuscripts," *Bib.* 70 (1989) 377–388.

[22] G.H.R. Horsley, "Reconstructing a Biblical Codex: the Prehistory of MPER
n.s. XVII. 10 (*P.Vindob.* G 29831)," *Akten des 21. Internationalen Papyrologenkongresses,
Berlin, 13.–19.8.1995* (2 vols.; eds. B. Kramer et al.; APF Beihefte 3; Stuttgart—
Leipzig 1997) 473–481.

[23] Significantly, the point of departure for Horsley is the question what relevance
the content of this passage (John 1:5–6) would have for the wearer, since the content does not speak of health or safety, nor is a text of the popular kind such as
LXX-Ps 90. This rather contradicts Horsley's own conclusion—that the scribe after
having realized his mistake, did see the text as fit for an amulet, even in spite of
the fact that the text is broken off in mid-phrase at the end (v. 6). Moreover,
Horsley does not mention the fact that Gospel incipits, sometimes extended to more
than the initial verse, were very common on amulets and were often copied in
sequences where other incipits would precede John (cf. University of Chicago MS
125 which contains Mark 1:1–8; Luke 1:1–7; John 1:1–17; and some other texts),
which could be the case here. For example, if the codex was made up of binios,
a number of preceding gatherings could have contained other incipits, plus the missing part of John 1:1–5, and inside the extant leaf there could have been another

As a "preliminary investigation," Horsley also appended a list of other potential manuscripts intended for codices but then reused as amulets.[24] Interestingly, he included 𝔓⁷⁸ in the list of items. However, the possibility that the extant folio of 𝔓⁷⁸ represents a sheet, intended for a codex, but rejected because of erroneous copying in relation to the arrangement of the gatherings can be firmly excluded; 𝔓⁷⁸ comprises text from Jude on both folios, which means that the copying process was not interrupted in the same way as Horsley tried to demonstrate in the case of *P.Vindob.* G 29831. There are of course other ways of reusing a manuscript. Recently, Peter Arzt-Grabner and Michael Ernst have convincingly demonstrated how *P.Bingen* 16 (= *P.Vindob.* G 39205) was once part of a parchment codex, but then cut or torn out and reused as an amulet.[25] However, this possibility too can be excluded in the case of 𝔓⁷⁸ since the margins are intact and the text continues from fol. 1 recto to verso (vv. 4–5), and fol. 2 verso to recto (vv. 7–8), which means that the format is original.

In conclusion, a theory of reuse in the case of 𝔓⁷⁸ is unnecessary since it demands additional and purely hypothetical explanations. The evidence suggests that our manuscript was intended for the use of an amulet in the first place. Nevertheless, the main question remains: why was this text chosen for an amulet?

---

one perhaps containing John 1:5–8 (c. 70 letters per folio), thus forming the concluding binio. There is also the possibility that the extant manuscript does not preserve the complete amulet formula—it ends somewhat abruptly with επι τον φορουντα τουτο (the existence of any punctuation is not mentioned by Horsley). Horsley suggests that τὸ φυλακτήριον is implied, which is of course possible, but the more common version of the formula explicitly includes τὸ φυλακτήριον. Cf. R. Kotansky, *Greek Magical Amulets. The Inscribed Gold, Silver, Copper, and Bronze "Lamellae": Text and Commentary. Part I: Published Texts of Known Provenance* (ARWAW PapyCol 22.1; Opladen 1994) 345. A presumed longer formula continuing into another folio would of course open up further possibilities. Cf. K. Treu—J. Diethart, "MPER NS XVII 10" [*P.Vindob.* G. 29831]," *Griechische literarische Papyri christlichen Inhalts II* (MPER N.S. 17; Wien 1993) 23: "Obwohl der Text auf IIv 12 (Folio 2, verso l. 12; Anm. d. Verf.) mitten im Satz abbricht, folgte vielleicht nicht mehr."

[24] See G.H.R. Horsley, "Reconstructing," 480–81.

[25] P. Arzt-Grabner—M. Ernst, "*P.Bingen* 16. *Ps.*, 43, 21–24.27 und *Ps.*, 44, 1–2 LXX," *Papyri in Honorem Johannis Bingen Octogenarii* (ed. H. Melaerts; Studia Varia Bruxellensia 5; Leuven 2000) 79–84 (+ plate 9).

2. Magic and the Use and Function of Amulets in Early Christianity

"Magic" is a very difficult word to define. In many societies magic is an integral part of religious thought and behavior, whereas in others, especially in the Western world, it is generally thought of as mere superstition. Traditionally, it has been thought to mark a distinction between so-called primitive and advanced cultures, or even between non-Christian and Christian religions. In the 19th century it was common among scholars to contrast magic with religion as well as science.[26] Today, however, there is a consensus, in particular among anthropologists and sociologists, that the old dichotomy between magic and religion is false; magic is increasingly acknowledged as being a general substructure of all religions.[27] However, it is still possible to distinguish magic and religion, if not in essence, at least in the empirical sense. Sociologists regard religion, including magic, as a social fact; while religion is a collective practice, there being no religion without a "church," magic is an individual affair unauthorized by the religious collectivity, and often regarded as abnormal or at least suspect.[28] Indeed, as we shall see, such a negative attitude was prevalent towards amulets on the part of the early church and its official representatives.

---

[26] So the early and influential anthropologists Edward B. Tylor (1832–1917) and James G. Frazer (1854–1941); see for example E.B. Tylor, *Primitive Culture: Researches into the Development of Mythology, Philosophy, Religion, Language, Art, and Custom* (London 1871); J.G. Frazer, *The Golden Bough: A Study in Magic and Religion* (London ²1922).

[27] E.E. Evans Pritchard, also an anthropologist, was among the first to criticize the theories of Tylor and Frazer, and dismissed the view of "magic" and "religion" as mutually exclusive phenomena capable of clear definition. See his *Theories of Primitive Religion* (Oxford 1965).

[28] The French Sociological School pioneered this view; see É. Durkheim, *Les formes élementaires de la vieu religieuse: le système totemique en Australie* (Paris 1911); L. Lévy-Bruhl, *Les fonctions mentales dans les societés inférieures* (Paris 1910); H. Hubert—M. Mauss, "Esquisse d'une théorie génerale de la magie," *Année sociologique* 7 (1904) 1–146. In his study of magic in early Christianity, D.E. Aune offers a non-dichotomous, sociological definition of the nature and function of magic in relation to religion: "[M]agic is defined as that form of religious deviance whereby the individual or social goals are sought by means alternate to those normally sanctioned by the dominant religious institution". See D.E. Aune, "Magic in Early Christianity," *ANRW* II.23.2 (1980) 1515. For similar discussions and definitions, see J. Bremmer, "The Birth of the Term 'Magic'," *ZPE* 126 (1999) 1–12, esp. 9–12; G. Luck, *Arcana Mundi. Magic and the Occult in the Greek and Roman World. A Collection of Ancient Texts* (Baltimore 1985) 3–61, esp. 7–9.46–53; and F.A.M. Wiegemann, "Magie I," *RGG* V, 661–662.

From the second through the fifth century CE, magic increased in popularity within all cults in the Roman Empire, and early Christianity rapidly developed a distinct form of magic in coherence with its reality construction. In this process it absorbed magical traditions from Judaism as well as the surrounding Graeco-Roman world. The Oriental peoples, including the Jews, were especially addicted to the practice of wearing amulets.[29] With their absorption into the Roman Empire the use became equally common among the population in the West.[30] Plutarch's description well reflects the contemporary attitude towards amulets and magic:

> As people with chronic diseases, when they have despaired of ordinary remedies and customary regimens turn to expiations and amulets and dreams . . . [I]t is necessary to try those [accounts] that are more out of the way and not scorn them but literally to chant over ourselves the charms of the ancients and use every means to bring the truth to test.[31]

In the NT period amulets were probably regarded as among the magic arts and their use was strongly condemned (cf. Acts 19:17–20).[32] However, from the second century onwards popular Christianity showed an increasing interest in amulets and by the time of the

---

[29] See, for instance, B. Kern-Ulmer, "The Depiction of Magic in Rabbinic Texts: The Rabbinic and the Greek Concept of Magic," *JSJ* 27 (1996) 289–303; M. Bar-Ilan, "Between Magic and Religion: Sympathetic Magic in the World of the Sages of the Mishnah and Talmud," *Review of Rabbinic Judaism* 5 (2002) 383–399.

[30] Although there is no word in the Hebrew Bible denoting "amulet," objects of this kind seem to be implied at various places. Possibly, the golden ear-rings, out of which the molten calf was made, were amulets (Exod 32:2–3). The ornaments worn by women and condemned in Isa 3:16–26 were amulets of this nature (the Hebrew word used in v. 20, *lehashim*, is actually rendered "amulets" in many translations, e.g. RV, RSV, NRSV, NAS, ASV). Cf. Exod 13:16; Deut 6:8; 11:18; Prov 6:21; 2Macc 12:40.

[31] Plutarch, *Fac.* 920B (Cherniss, LCL).

[32] The incident recorded in Acts 19 took place in the town of Ephesus, infamous for its abundance of sorcery in ancient times. The practice of wearing written charms, the so-called Ἐφέσια γράμματα, in little leather bags is attested as early as the 4th century BCE. See C. Bonner, *Studies in Magical Amulets* (Ann Arbor 1950) 5. Aune's discussion of the magical use of the name of Jesus by some New Testament authors, and his references to Paul's use of amulet imagery in Gal 6:17 ("the marks of Jesus") and the name of Jesus functioning as a charm or amulet in Rev 14:7 is problematic (see Aune, "Magic in Early Christianity," 1545); the metaphorical language does not indicate a positive attitude to amulets as such on the part of these authors.

fourth century, when Christianity had won imperial favor, the use of amulets and devotional emblems had become so common that the official church through its bishops, synods and church fathers had to inveigh strongly against it.[33] The Council of Laodicea even issued a separate canon (36) prohibiting the manufacture and use of amulets: "They who are of the priesthood, or of the clergy, shall not . . . make what are called amulets, which are chains for their own souls. And those who wear such, we command to be cast out of the Church."[34] Another way of dealing with such practices of religious deviance was to "christianize" them. Several ancient Christian authors mention the custom of carrying portions of the Scripture as amulets.[35] However, the custom, especially persistent among the lower strata of society, seems to have been accepted by the official church rather reluctantly.[36] The fact that magical practices in general were associated with the lower strata of society is also reflected in the unpretentious common language of magical texts.

While the vast majority of amulets employed in the Graeco-Roman world has perished, archaeologists have discovered thousands of items that have survived.[37] Naturally, there is a wealth of extant amulets made of durable material, such as stone and metal.[38] However, these

---

[33] See the synods in Elvira (303 or 313 CE) can. 6; Ancyra (315 C.E.) can. 24; and Laodicea (c. 360 CE) can. 34–36. For the critical attitude of the church fathers, see Augustine, *Doctr. chr.* 2.24.45; Chrysostom, *Hom.* 7.7; see further discussion and references in M.W. Dickie, "The Fathers of the Church and the Evil Eye," *Byzantine Magic* (ed. H. Maguire; Washington D.C. 1995) 9–34.

[34] H.R. Percival (ed.), *The Seven Ecumenical Councils* (*The Nicene and Post-Nicene Fathers of the Christian Church* 2.14; eds. P. Schaff—H. Wace; repr. Grand Rapids 1979) 151.

[35] In Jewish tradition we notice a similar development, whereby the ancient pagan practice of wearing amulets was infused with new significance and a worthier motive in consistence with the dominant religion of Jahweh; it was namely common among Jews to wear small rolls of parchments (Heb. *tefillin*, Gr. *phylakterion*) in leather boxes, containing scriptural portions from the Law (the practice persists to this day). This was done according to Mosaic instruction (Exod 13:9, 16; Deut 6:8; 11:18).

[36] Apparently, both Chrysostom (*Hom.* 19.14; *Hom.* 43.4; *In Joh. tr.* 6.1) and Augustine (*Tract. Ev. Jo.* 7.12) accepted the practice, but they were careful to stress the importance of the inner faith of "heart" and "mind" in God's word, rather than the external efficacy of an amulet itself. Cf. R. Kaczynski, *Das Wort Gottes in Liturgie und Alltag der Gemeinden des Johannes Chrysostomus* (FThSt 94; Freiburg 1974).

[37] For an extensive, though somewhat dated, description of amulets in the Graeco-Roman world including many examples and a voluminous bibliography, see H. Leclercq, Art. "Amulettes", *DACL* 1:1784–1860.

[38] The most important survey of stone and metal amulets is C. Bonner, *Studies in Magical Amulets.*

necessarily held briefer inscriptions than another class of amulets written on small pieces of papyrus, of which a considerable number have survived in the dry heat of Egypt.[39] Some of these items contain biblical citations, prayers, or liturgical portions etc., and can therefore be provisionally defined as Jewish or Christian amulets.[40] A brief survey of the extant texts on these amulets reveals the fact that Psalms or extracts from Psalms, or Odes were very popular and in this regard LXX-Ps 90 holds an exceptional place.[41] The reason for the extensive use of this particular psalm is obvious from the contents, suggesting an apotropaic use.[42] The phenomenon of using verses from the Scripture in a magic context often derives from their liturgical prominence.[43] Therefore it is not surprising to find that the

---

[39] Many items are described in J. van Haelst, *Catalogue des papyrus littéraires juifs et chrétiens* (Université de Paris IV Paris-Sorbonne; Série "Papyrologie" 1: Paris 1976). Van Haelst listed 118 amulets in his index (item no. 967 and no. 1006 were not included in the index, but described as amulets). Information about more recent items can be accessed through the *Leuven Database of Ancient Books* (LDAB), at http://ldab.arts.kuleuven.ac.be, and the *Advanced Papyrological Information System* (APIS; A part of the *Columbia University Digital Library Projects*), at http://columbia.edu/cgibin/cul/resolve?ATK2059.

[40] It is tempting to assume that all amulets with biblical citations, etc., must be either Jewish or Christian, but in some cases it is difficult to prove that the wearer of an amulet was a follower of the religion indicated by the amulet, especially since the field of magic in this era was characterized by syncretism; the latter is especially evident in the magical papyri. See K. Preisendanz—A. Henrich (eds.), *Papyri Graecae Magicae: Die griechischen Zauberpapyri* (2 vols.; Stuttgart ²1973–1974]; and H.-D. Betz, *The Greek Magical Papyri in Translation Including the Demotic Spells* (Chicago—London ²1992); henceforth *PGM*; see also R.W. Daniel—F. Maltomini, *Supplementum Magicum* (2 vols.; ARWAW PapyCol 16.1–2; Opladen 1990–1992). The danger of misinterpretation is of course decreased in regard to items with exclusively Jewish or Christian features and of larger extent than single names or phrases.

[41] In a paper presented to *The 24th International Congress of Papyrology* (Helsinki, 2004), T.J. Kraus includes some 75 items (papyri and parchment MSS, medallions, rings, bracelets, wooden tablets, etc) that contain the psalm or parts of it ("Septuaginta-Psalm 90 in apotropäischer Verwendung: Vorüberlegungen für eine kritische Edition und [bisheriges] Datenmaterial"). For psalms on amulets in general, see P. Collart, "Psaumes et amulettes," *Aeg.* 14 (1934) 463–467. For a discussion of other passages, see E.A. Judge, "The Magical Use of Scripture," *Perspectives on Language and Text: Essays and Poems in Honor of Francis I. Andersen's Sixtieth Birthday* (ed. E.W. Conrad—E.G. Newing; Winona Lake 1987) 339–349; and A. Biondi, "Le citazione bibliche nei papiri magici cristiani greci," *StPapy* 20 (1981) 93–127.

[42] For the continuing apotropaic use of Ps 91 (masoretic) in Jewish tradition, cf. the passage in *yShab* VI.2, which says that it is permitted to recite Ps 3 and Ps 91:1–9 as a protection against approaching evil.

[43] Cf. J. Naveh—S. Shaked, *Magic Spells and Formulae* (Jerusalem 1993) 24.

Lord's prayer (Mt 6:9–13) is the most cited passage from the New Testament on extant amulets. Next in place comes Gospel *incipits*, often all four in a sequence.[44]

Without going into more detail concerning particular texts, it is important to note in regard to magical texts and amulets in general, that there is often a direct connection between the text and the particular function of the amulet, particularly in cases when they contain *historiolae*, i.e. mythic narratives, very often divine precedents, which would comprise the main point of reference for the mobilization and development of the particular magical action desired. In the Christian context the desired action most often involved healing and protection against evil forces and, thus, some amulets contain healing narratives, or texts about God's protection (cf. LXX-Ps 90).[45] Perhaps more surprising, we also find examples of *historiolae* in the context of love and fertility, and even in connection with cursing—if not on many extant amulets, at least amply in the magical texts from Christian Egypt.[46] Ernst von Dobschütz classified the ancient charms with their functions into three main categories, which are more or less applicable to amulets: *Defensive charms* (apotropaic, counter charms, curative, detective); *Productive charms* (fertility, weather charms, birth and capacity, love charms); and *Malevolent charms*

---

[44] The incipit represented the whole Gospel in question, which in turn was perceived as having a special power for protection, exorcism or healing. In *P.Rain.* 1, for example, the wearer of the amulet commands different types of fever to flee by appealing to the four Gospels of the Son (ὁρκίζω ὑμᾶς κατὰ τῶν τεσσάρων εὐαγγελίων τοῦ υἱοῦ . . .).

[45] For example, several amulets contain the passage in Matt 4:23–24, which records a summary statement of how Jesus went about in Galilee, preaching the Kingdom of God, curing all kinds of diseases including demon possession. Significantly, *P.Oxy.* VIII 1077 presents this text under a heading that expressly indicates its function, ιαματικον ευαγγελιον κατα Ματθαιον ("Curative Gospel according to Matthew").

[46] Sexual spells in magical texts of Christian character involve references to the Annunciation (London Hay 10376) and, in regard to desired fertility, to the remarkable pregnancy of Sarah, with citation of the divine promise in Gen 18:10 of an offspring (*P.Morgan Copt.* M662B 22). A sample of magical texts belonging to the category of malevolent magic include references to the curse mentioned in Zech 5:3 (*P.Berlin* inv. 10587; this item also refers to Gnostic traditions); to "the curses of the Law and Deuteronomy," (*P. Mich.* inv. 3565); the curse of Cain (London Or. 5986; *P.Lichačev*); the curse of Sodom and Gomorrah (Florence, Museo Arch., inv. 5645—this text is written on a human bone [!]; *P.Lichačev*). *P.Vindob.* G. 19929 is an amulet from the sixth century that contains an appeal to the Lord for vengeance (without *historiola*).

(cursing).[47] Perhaps we should here add a fourth category, that of *divination*.[48]

3. The Epistle of Jude on an Amulet?

Practically all of the biblical citations on the extant amulets indicate that Jewish and Christian amulets generally had either an apotropaic or a curative function, and, judging from the text of Jude, there is reason to believe that 𝔓⁷⁸ belongs to the former category of apotropaic amulets. A malevolent function of a Christian amulet, on the other hand, seems paradoxical, since it would contradict Christian doctrine in general, and Jesus' command to love one's enemies in particular. However, as mentioned above, there are examples of malevolent magic in a Christian context, and such a function of 𝔓⁷⁸ cannot a priori be excluded, especially if one considers the pronounced polemical character of Jude, which comes to expression in a fierce and violent judgment language, indirectly aimed at human adversaries.[49] If 𝔓⁷⁸ contained only a portion of Jude breaking off somewhere in the middle, e.g. vv. 1–13 (leaving out the final exhortations), the latter part would indeed form an effective verbal climax suitable for a malevolent purpose; apart from judgmental *historiolae* and a pejorative characterization of the antagonists, we find the repeated formulaic phrase, οὗτοί (or αὐτοί)/οὗτοί εἰσιν (vv. 8, 10, 12), marking the transition from "text" to interpretation, which in this case would mean the transition from *historiolae* to immediate application on to

---

[47] E.v. Dobschütz, "Charms and Amulets (Christian)," *Encyclopedia of Religion and Ethics* (eds. J. Hastings—J.A. Selbie; Edinburgh 1911) 3:416–421. An ancient classification of charms is found in Celsus, *Ap. Orig.* 6.39.

[48] For studies on the practice of fortune-telling in the ancient world, see e.g. T.C. Skeat, "An Early Medieval 'Book of Fate': The Sortes XII Patriarcharum. With a Note on 'Books of Fate' in General," *Mediaeval and Renaissance Studies* 3 (1954) 41–54. For divination in connection with NT MSS, see B.M. Metzger, "Greek Manuscripts of John's Gospel with Hermeneia'," *Text and Testimony: Essays on New Testament and Apocryphal Literature in Honour of A.F.J. Klijn* (eds. T. Baarda et al.; Kampen 1988) 162–169.

[49] Cf. T. Nicklas, "Zur historischen und theologischen Bedeutung der Erforschung neutestamentlicher Textgeschichte," *NTS* 48 (2002) 149, who says concerning 𝔓⁷⁸ and the choice of text for this amulet: "Soll die im Text angedrohte Strafe abgewendet werden? Geht es um einen Bann übelgesonnener Menschen oder wie auch immer gearteter dämonischer Kräfte?".

some contemporary adversaries.[50] In v. 11 we find the powerful per-
formative utterance of a "Woe!" against the evil enemies, οὐαὶ αὐτοῖς,
and, finally, the pronouncement of their eternal damnation in v. 13,
which would be a forceful climactic conclusion of such an amulet.

Interestingly, a Coptic papyrus from the 4th–5th century, *P.Lichačev*,
presents several parallels in this regard; the speaker in the text calls
upon God in the heavenly throne-room among the angels (Michael,
Gabriel, etc) urging him to bring judgment against people who have
committed violence against him (or someone else), and in doing so
he appeals to several of the Old Testament examples of God's judgment, as referred to in Jude. In the case of this text—the work of
a Coptic Christian—it is not unlikely that the influence actually goes
via the Epistle of Jude.[51]

However, there are still other features in the Epistles of Jude to
be considered, before we can make a final judgment as to the original function of our MS. One very prominent feature in contemporary magic in general was the appeal to Jewish or Christian divine
names and titles (e.g. "Iao," "Adonai," "Sabaoth," "Eloi," "God of
Abraham, Isaac, and Jacob," "Jesus the God of the Hebrews," and
all kinds of transcriptions of the *Tetragrammaton*, etc).[52] In particular,
the belief in the magical power of the name of Jesus is attested from

[50] The peculiar reading in v. 8, αυτοι for ουτοι, if not due to a simple scribal
error, may lend some support for this notion, since an original demonstrative pronoun might have rendered difficult an anaphoric reference to adversaries "outside"
the text, on the part of the scribe. Moreover, we recall the insertion of the superfluous
αδελφοι in v. 5, in this case perhaps to increase the exigency and immediateness.
The same address was probably present at least in v. 3 (and maybe in v. 17) in
𝔓78 instead of the normal address of Jude, ἀγαπητοί—again perhaps enhancing the
application in a context of magic, whether apotropaic or "malevolent," by down-
playing the exhortative features of the original letter and laying more stress on the
communal factor (perhaps the amulet was even used in public); the strength of
brotherly unity against evil. Consider also the passage in 1 Cor 5:3–5, where we
note the appeal to the name of the Lord Jesus, and the factor of unity in the curse-
like action, in this case turning an immoral person over to Satan. Cf. A. Deissmann,
Light from the Ancient East (transl. L.R.M. Strachan; New York 1927) 302–303.
[51] "... As you cursed Somohra and Komohra through the anger of your wrath,
[cf. Jd 7] you must curse the one who has committed this act of violence. You
must bring the vengeance of Enoch against them [cf. Jd 14–15]. As the blood of
Abel called out to Cain his brother [cf. Jd 11], the blood of this miserable man
will call out, until you bring judgment on his behalf..." Translation by M.W.
Meyer—R. Smith, *Ancient Christian Magic: Coptic Texts of Ritual Power* (Princeton 1999)
190–191. The text starts and ends with a staurogram.
[52] See further samples in *PGM*.

the earliest times of Christianity.[53] Significantly, in Jude we note an abundance of divine and angelic references, particularly in connection with Jesus.[54]

Possibly, two of the peculiar readings of 𝔓⁷⁸ may be explained as accentuated expressions of the divinity and glory of Jesus Christ, perhaps occasioned by a magical purpose:[55] In v. 4, the text as it stands in NA²⁷, τὸν μόνον δεσπότην καὶ κύριον ἡμῶν Ἰησοῦν Χριστόν, can be interpreted as two parallel references, to God and to Jesus.[56] However, it is also possible to interpret the whole phrase as a reference entirely to Jesus, and so the author of 2 Peter interpreted Jude 4, provided that Jude is prior.[57] This ambiguity may have led scribes to append θεόν (attested by the majority of witnesses) in order to clarify that the divine title, δεσπότης, refers to God.[58] However, 𝔓⁷⁸ most clearly attributes the title to Jesus by dropping the conjunction: και τον μονον δεσποτην κ̅υ̅ ημων ι̅η̅ν̅ χ̅ρ̅ν̅ αρνουμενοι.[59] Likewise, the rare reading, δοξαν, in v. 8, αυτοι . . . κυριειοτητα [singular] δε αθετουσιν δοξαν [singular] δε [βλασφημουσιν] may likewise be interpreted as a christological reference, "they set aside the majesty of the Lord [or simply "they set aside the Lord"], they blaspheme his glory."[60]

---

[53] See W. Heitmüller, *Im Namen Jesu: Eine sprach- und religionsgeschichtliche Untersuchung zum Neuen Testament, speziell zur altchristlichen Taufe* (FRLANT 2; Göttingen 1903). Cf. Aune, "Magic in Early Christianity," 1545–1549.

[54] Concerning the appeal to divine names in the context of Jewish, Christian and pagan magic, Aune, "Magic in Early Christianity," 1546, states: "The fundamental significance of the magical use of the names of divinities, supernatural beings or great men of the past is the supposition that such names share the being and participate in the power of their bearers; to possess a name is to possess power over the one who bears the name."

[55] Cf. M. Mees, "𝔓⁷⁸ ein neuer Textzeuge für den Judasbrief," *Orient Press* 1 (1970) 10.

[56] The absence of the article before κύριον does not resolve the issue since it is often omitted before κύριος.

[57] The passage in 2Peter 2:1b, describing the opponents, reads, καὶ τὸν ἀγοράσαντα αὐτοὺς δεσπότην ἀρνούμενοι, ἐπάγοντες ἑαυτοῖς ταχινὴν ἀπώλειαν.

[58] The title δεσπότης ("Master") attributed to God is widely attested in Judaism as well as in early Christian usage. In the New Testament we find this divine title ascribed to Christ only in Jude 4 and 2 Peter 2:1.

[59] Cf. the discussion in T.J. Kraus, *Sprache, Stil und historischer Ort des zweiten Petrusbriefes* (WUNT II.136; Tübingen 2001) 76–78.

[60] A few witnesses (ℵ Ψ 1845 1846) read the plural, κυριοτητας, probably referring to classes of angels (cf. Eph 1:20; Col 1:16) in analogy with δοξας in the latter part of the verse. The singular, δοξαν (𝔓⁷⁸ *pc*), probably reflects the Greek equivalent in LXX of the Hebrew *kabod*, originally used in reference to God, especially in the majesty of his historical acts of salvation and judgment.

Thus, in 𝔓⁷⁸ it is made clear right at the beginning that "the Lord" in the text refers to Jesus; hence, it was Jesus who acted mightily both in the history of Israel and in the history of the entire cosmos; he saved the people out of Egypt, but destroyed those who did not believe; he sent the fallen angels to be kept under darkness for judgment; and he punished Sodom and Gomorrah and the cities around them with eternal fire![61] References to divine acts of salvation were generally common in contemporary apotropaic magic, and in this regard the Exodus held a prominent place, being the great shining salvific event of the Hebrew Bible. More significantly, however, the specific reference in Jude 6 to an action by the Lord in the angelic realm definitely speaks in favor of an apotropaic function. In this connection I would like to draw the attention to another Greek papyrus amulet, *P. Fouad* inv. 203 (1), dated to the 1st or 2nd century. In my view, the fragmentary text mainly suggests an apotropaic function of the amulet. However, there is some ambiguity, which is perhaps reflected in the title of the article by Pierre Benoit, who edited the fragment, "Fragment d'une prière contre les spirits impurs?"[62]

> . . . the glorious name [cf. Deut 28:58] and you are impure [addressing the demons]. May he send [cf. LXX-Ps 19:2] his angel [probably Michael] who has led this people through the exodus, who revealed himself [cf. Jos 5:13–15] for Jesus [Joshua], son of Naoum [Nun], especially since he has plunged us [Benoit's conjecture, "you"] into the Abyss, into the place of destruction and covered you in Chaos [cf. 1 *En.* 10:5; Jd 6; *PGM* IV. 1247]. This is why you will not appear any more and not become present in order to commit evil against any living soul. Honor and praise to the Lord forever, to the One invoked, to [. . .], and for all who are near him and present.[63]

Here we find several interesting parallel features and conceptions in relation to Jude; first, the appeal to the divine name; secondly, the

---

[61] J. Fossum argues for the originality of the reading Ιησους in Jude 5 (not extant in our MS), and suggests that Jude 5–7 presents Jesus as the Angel of the Lord, since the acts described in vv. 5–7 were all attributed to the Angel of the Lord in pre-Christian tradition, and among later church fathers. The Angel of the Lord was said to share God's Name (Exod 23:21) and could even be designated by the Tetragrammaton or the Greek equivalent, κύριος. See J. Fossum, "Kyrios Jesus as the Angel of the Lord in Jude 5–7," *NTS* 33 (1987) 226–243.

[62] P. Benoit, "Fragment d'une prière contre les esprits impurs?," *RB* 59 (1951) 549–565.

[63] My translation after the Greek original and Benoit's reconstruction in French (ibid., 552–60).

reference to God's act of salvation in the Exodus event, here through an angelic agent, probably Michael; thirdly, the reference to his action against the impure spirits in throwing them into the Abyss (ἄβυσσος), again executed by an angelic agent in accordance with the tradition in 1 *En.* 10:4–6, 11–12 (here Raphael and Michael are mentioned).[64] In early Judaism and in the New Testament the Abyss is thought of as the place in which the rebellious angels, or spirits, are confined in darkness (*Jub.* 5; 1 *En.* 10; Jude 6; 2 Pet 2:4; Rev 9:1; 20:1, 3).[65] Hence, we see an example of how these same *historiolae* in question apparently filled an apotropaic function, whether the fragment is Jewish or Christian.[66] The main difference in relation to Jude is of course the direct confrontation of the unclean spirits in a vocative reference, which may suggest an exorcistic function of the text, but, on the other hand, the fact that the spirits are said to have been plunged into the Abyss and that they, therefore, are not to appear any more, indicates a primarily protective function.[67]

The usage of the same traditions is attested also in the incantatory texts of Qumran, particularly in 11Q11.[68] 11Q11 is a collection of at least three non-canonical incantation psalms followed by a version of Ps 91. E. Eshel has treated the incantation texts of this scroll extensively.[69] She highlights a number of interesting features of 11Q11 and the other incantation texts from Qumran, which have parallels in Greek and Aramaic magical papyri, such as the invocation of the name of the Lord, references to deeds of God on earth,

---

[64] The concept of the rebellious angels, or spirits, has its roots in Gen 6:1–4, a classical passage for the explanation of the origins of evil on earth. In turn, the story was elaborated first in the so-called 'Book of Watchers' of 1 Enoch (probably dated to the third century BCE), and then used frequently in Jewish-Christian literature of the period 200 BCE–300 CE; in the NT in 2 Peter 2:4, Jude 6, and perhaps 1 Pet 3:19–20 (cf. R. Strelan, "The Fallen Watchers and the Disciples in Mark," *JSP* 20 [1999] 73–92).

[65] See further J. Jeremias, "ἄβυσσος," *TDNT* 1:9.

[66] Cf. Benoit, "Fragment," 564–565.

[67] Cf. Benoit, "Fragment,", 564: "Il ne s'agit pas d'un 'exorcisme' au sens restreint du mot, car il n'est pas question de chaser des demons d'un corps humain qu'ils posséderaient."

[68] The script of this scroll is dated to the 1st century; see the edition in A.S. Van der Woude, "11QApocryphal Psalms," *11Q2–18, 11Q20–31* (eds. F. García Martínez—E.C.J. Tigchelaar—A. van der Woude; DJD 23; Oxford 1998) 181–205.

[69] E. Eshel, "Genres of Magical Texts in the Dead Sea Scrolls," *Die Dämonen. Demons* (eds. A. Lange—H. Lichtenberger—K.F.D. Römheld; Tübingen 2003) 394–415.

the direct address of the spirits, and, significantly, "the most popular threat being that they [the spirits] will be sealed in the abyss with iron chains."[70] Eshel also notes the call in 11Q11 for help by a powerful angel, with the epithet "the chief of the army of YHWH," who will bring the evil spirit to the Abyss, and she refers to the parallel in *P.Fouad* inv. 203.[71] Note, however, that in 11Q11 the angelic action is in the future, which confirms Eshel's judgment of this text as being primarily "exorcistic".[72]

A similar conception is reflected in the magical papyrus text *PGM* IV 1227–64 (*Bibl. Nat. suppl. gr.* 574; the so-called "Great Magical Papyrus of Paris"). In this extensive manual for exorcism from the 4th century, the practitioner, after the expulsion of the demon, is instructed to drape an amulet around the person, which contains magical words ending with "protect him, NN." Significantly, the incantation used for the exorcism proper concludes: "I deliver you into the black chaos in perdition" (*PGM* IV 1247), which surely reflects the threat of the demon returning unless properly confined.[73]

Hence, the desired magical action in appealing to the *historiola* in Jude 6 would arguably be to ensure that any threatening demons stay imprisoned, "kept in eternal chains under darkness." Unfortunately, this verse is no longer extant in 𝔓[78], so we cannot look for signs of any special treatment of the verse, but the apotropaic conception in question may have influenced the scribe in the very next verse,

---

[70] Eshel, "Genres," 403–404. In 11Q11 there is no specific reference to iron chains, but there is a similar threat that the angel will "shut the bronze gates through which no light penetrates" (ibid., 399).

[71] Eshel, "Genres," 405. Cf. also Kotansky, "Greek Magical Amulets," 295, who cites the text of a magical tablet from Beirut, "the Great Angelic Hierarchy" (Paris, Musée du Louvre inv. M.N.D. 274), from the 4th century CE, where the demons are addressed in a command to flee to a place under the springs and the Abyss, φύγετε... ὑποκάτω τῶν πηγῶν καὶ τῆς ἀβύσσου.

[72] Whereas Eshel, "Genres," 398, takes the "main body" of incantation texts to be "exorcistic," she classifies the concluding Ps 91 as an "apotropaic hymn". Hermann Lichtenberger, "Ps 91 und die Exorzismen in 11QpsApᵃ," *Die Dämonen. Demons* (eds. A. Lange—H. Lichtenberger—K.F.D. Römheld; Tübingen 2003) 420, who treats Ps 91 in the collection, points out that the concluding psalm is integrated with the other texts, not only in terms of content, but also by liturgical responsory phrases, and so concludes: "Durch die Einbeziehung in die Sammlung von Exorzismen wird Ps 91 selbst zu einem solchen Beschwörungstext." In my view, the manifest unity of the collection in spite of the diversity of its parts, does not exclude a combined exorcistic and apotropaic function.

[73] Cf. Matt 12:43–45; Luke 11:24–26; Rev 9:1–2; Josephus, *Ant.* 8:47.

recording the parallel judgment of the cities of Sodom and Gomorrah: Practically all witnesses read, δικην υπεχουσαι, "undergoing punishment" (or "judgment"), whereas our MS reads, δικην επεχουσαι, "staying in punishment."[74]

If we now return to the notion of angelic agents appealed to in Jewish-Christian magic, we find that Michael stands in a class for himself.[75] In the elaborate angelology that emerged in Judaism during the Hellenistic period, Michael is an archangel (1 *En.* 20:1–7; 71:3; 2 *En.* 22:6; cf. Jude 9), present along with Raphael, Gabriel and Phanuel before the throne of God (1 *En.* 9:1; 40; 54:6; 71:8–9, 13). He is often represented as the leader of the archangels (*Asc.Isa.* 3:16), and as patron angel of Israel (Dan 10:23; 12:1; 1 *En.* 20:5; 1QM 17:6–8). In the New Testament Michael is the leader of the angels who battles against Satan and his angels, and causes their fall from heaven. Michael's role in the angelic warfare against Satan and his demonic forces leads us on to the next "proof-text" in Jude 9, where Michael contends with Satan for the body of Moses, and here we find elements very suitable for apotropaic purposes; the kernel and climax of the story is the powerful utterance by Michael against the devil, ἐπιτιμήσαι σοι κύριος. The whole episode in Jude may be directly dependent on the *Assumption of Moses*, or, more likely, as Richard Bauckham has argued, a lost ending of the *Testament of Moses*.[76] Nevertheless, Michael's utterance is definitely an echo of Zech 3:2 where Satan is likewise rebuked by the Lord (or the angel of the Lord).[77]

Significantly, Naveh and Shaked state that this very passage is perhaps the most common used verse in Jewish magic texts.[78] Howard

---

[74] The verb in the sense of *staying* is intransitive (often accompanied by a time reference in the accusative; cf. Acts 19:22), and therefore δίκην is problematic since it cannot be an object of the verb. Perhaps it can be interpreted as an accusative of respect ("staying, so as to be punished with eternal fire"). See also Mees, "𝔓⁷⁸," 9.

[75] This fact can easily be deduced by looking in the index of personal names in any edition of contemporary magical texts.

[76] R. Bauckham, *Jude and the Relatives of Jesus in the Early Church* (Edinburgh 1990) 235–280.

[77] Many editors of the Hebrew Bible prefer the Syriac reading, "angel of Yahweh," for reasons of consistency within the verse and the vision scene as a whole. The rebuke formula in Zech 3:2 may in turn reverberate the primal "Cursed are you" of Gen 3:14.

[78] Naveh—Shaked, *Magic Spells*, 25. Cf. C.D. Isbell, *Corpus of Aramaic Incantation*

C. Kee has attempted to show that the Aramaic verb נער, lying behind ἐπιτιμώς in Zech 3:2 and other passages in the LXX, became a technical term used for exorcism in sectarian Judaism (see e.g. 1QSA 20:28) and the oldest layers of the gospel tradition (Mark 1:25 and 9:25 with par.) signifying "the word or command that brought the hostile powers under control."[79] Be that as it may, but there is no doubt that at least in Zech 3:2, and in Jude 9, the term occurs in a context of struggle between God and Satan.[80] Demonstrably, the powerful divine (or angelic) utterance was used frequently in Jewish incantations, and this may be another reason for the choice of Jude as text for our amulet, provided that the verse was once extant in 𝔓[78], as I have argued. The attested connection of the verb with exorcism, and the very distinct and direct address of Satan in this verse implicate that there is no sharp division between defensive and offensive magic.

4. Conclusion

In this examination of 𝔓[78], I have attempted to describe both the physical and textual features of the extant manuscript, and to reconstruct the codex of which it once was part. The reconstruction suggests that the codex once contained a larger portion of Jude, arguably vv. 1–13, and that it was produced, not reused, for the purpose of an amulet. Moreover, I have tried to answer the crucial question posed at the outset of the examination: Why would someone choose this text for an amulet to carry around on his or her body? The text itself may hint at an answer since there is often a clear connection between the text of an amulet and its particular function. Some examined features of the Epistle of Jude, for example the violent polemic against the adversaries, may suggest an amulet for a malevolent purpose, directed against other human beings. However,

---

Bowls (Missoula 1975) 195; C. Müller-Kessler, *Die Zauberschalentexte in der Hilprecht Sammlung, Jena* (Wiesbaden 2004) 69.

[79] H.C. Kee, "The Terminology of Mark's Exorcism Stories," *NTS 14* (1968) 232–246. Kee's overall attempt is deemed "unsuccessful" by Aune, "Magic in Early Christianity," 1530–1531, esp. note 106.

[80] Kee, Terminology, 239, finds that the verb is used in the same context of struggle between God and Satan in rabbinic literature, e.g. *Qid.* 81B.

an apotropaic usage is more likely, not only because such a function is more common for amulets in general, but also for the fact that the text in question seems very appropriate for such a purpose.

First, we find several divine and angelic references, particularly in connection with Jesus, such as were common in magic texts in general. Moreover, there are a number of references to particular divine acts of judgment and salvation, which evidently functioned as *historiolae* in apotropaic texts as attested elsewhere. For example, in Jude 6 it is said that the Lord sent the fallen angels to be kept under darkness for judgment. Apparently, this and similar notions play an important role in Jewish as well as Christian magic, both curative (exorcistic) and apotropaic. The reference to the bound angels in Jude is expressed as a past event (cf. *P.Fouad* inv. 203), rather than a direct threat such as occur in exorcistic texts (e.g. 11Q11). This points to an apotropaic function, i.e. a prophylactic measure because of the perceived threat of the unclean spirits escaping from their prison and returning to torment human beings. Another reference in Jude, very appropriate for the purpose, is the story of the dispute between the archangel Michael and the devil in Jude 9, where we find a powerful angelic command directed against the devil, echoing Zech 3:2, a text used very frequently in Jewish incantations.

In regard to the text of 𝔓⁷⁸, I have also considered a number of peculiar readings, some of which may have been occasioned by the specific purpose of the manuscript. This is difficult to say, but in any case the eccentric text in itself reflects the heavy influence by the context in which it was reproduced, and does strengthen the overall impression that we have to do it with an amulet. For this reason it might be argued that the manuscript, although valuable for the historian as a fingerprint of real existing people in antiquity and their reception and usage of the text, is of no value for the text-critic in the reconstruction of the text of Jude, and, therefore, should not have been included in the list of "New Testament papyri" in the first place.[81] However, the text-critical value of any extant

---

[81] Possibly, it was K. Aland's assumption that the codex once contained the whole continuous text of Jude that led to its inclusion in the 𝔓 list of so-called "New Testament papyri (see above). Cf. T.J. Kraus, "'Pergament oder Papyrus?' Anmerkungen zur Signifikanz des Beschreibstoffes bei der Behandlung von Manuskripten," *NTS* 49 (2003) 425–432, where the author deals with some inconsistencies of the Gregory-Aland list (where items designated "amulet," or "school exercise" are included and at the same time other items just so excluded).

manuscript can never be anything else than relative, in that it is more or less influenced by the context in which it was copied. Stuart R. Pickering discusses the value of non-continuous NT texts and says:

> ... it would clearly be fallacious to argue that they [school exercises or magical texts] can *never* transmit a passage according to the wording which one would expect from a continuous text ... The question of textual value goes beyond the merely verbal level. A manuscript is of text-critical value not only in the individual words which it contains, but in the evidence it provides for the scribal approaches which influenced the wording. In this respect, an alleged weakness of non-continuous texts—the likely extent of scribal interference—turns out to be one of their great strengths for New Testament text-critical purposes.[82]

This way of reasoning actually bridges the gap between the text and its transmission and use in a particular historical context. It points to the necessity to consider all the evidence for the New Testament text, not only continuous texts. Moreover, it underlines the importance of methodological integration and interaction between all the different disciplines with an interest in ancient manuscripts, such as archaeology, codicology, papyrology, palaeography, textual criticism, and, in extension, theology. It is my hope that this study will prove to be an example of such interaction.

---

[82] S.R. Pickering, "The Significance of Non-Continuous New Testament Textual Materials in Papyri," *Studies in the Early Text of the Gospels and Acts. The Papers of the First Birmingham Colloquium on the Textual Criticism of the New Testament* (ed. D.G.K. Taylor; Texts and Studies 3.1; Birmingham 1999) 125.

THEOLOGISCHE LINIEN IM
CODEX BODMER MISCELLANI?

Tobias Nicklas und Tommy Wasserman

> Manuscripts are part of material culture. They
> supply us with information far beyond the techni-
> cal and specialized questions of papyrologists, palae-
> ographers and textual critics.[1]

Eines der interessantesten archäologischen Zeugnisse des antiken Christentums ist ein zur Sammlung Bodmer gehöriger Codex, der einen in der neutestamentlichen Handschriftenliste Gregory-Alands als $\mathfrak{P}^{72}$ (*P.Bodm.* VII und VIII) bezeichneten Abschnitt enthält, den vielleicht ältesten erhaltenen Textzeugen des Judasbriefes und der beiden kanonischen Petrusbriefe. In Studien zu $\mathfrak{P}^{72}$ wurde allerdings leider meist zu wenig berücksichtigt, dass dieser neutestamentliche Textzeuge eigentlich Teil eines weit umfangreicheren Gesamtcodex (im Folgenden: *Codex Bodmer Miscellani*) ist, der eine Vielzahl von Problemen und Fragen aufwirft, die bis heute nicht ganz beantwortet sind.

1. Einführendes

Codex Bodmer Miscellani ist heute nur noch in einzelnen Teilen, deren Reihenfolge nicht ganz sicher ist, erhalten. Ursprünglich dürfte er aus etwa 190 beschriebenen Seiten von nahezu quadratischem Format bestanden haben (15,5–16 cm × 14–14,5 cm). Leider wurde der Codex nie als Ganzes publiziert—den einzelnen in ihm überliefer-ten Werken wurden je eigene Bezeichnungen beigefügt, die jeweils

---

[1] L.W. Hurtado, "The Earliest Evidence of an Emerging Christian Material and Visual Culture: The Codex, the *Nomina Sacra* and the Staurogram," *Text and Artifact in the Religions of Mediterranean Antiquity. Essays in Honour of Peter Richardson* (ed. S.G. Wilson—M. Desjardins; Studies in Christianity and Judaism/Études sur le christi-anisme et le judaïsme 9; Waterloo/Ont. 2000) 271–288, bes. 284.

zugehörigen Abschnitte separat ediert. Immerhin hat der Erstherausgeber von 𝔓⁷², M. Testuz, folgende These zum ursprünglichen Aufbau des Gesamtcodex vorgelegt:[2]

Mariae Geburt (*P.Bodm.* V)	Schreiber A	Serie I
3. Korintherbrief (*P.Bodm.* X)	Schreiber B	Serie I
11. Ode Salomos (*P.Bodm.* XI)	Schreiber B	Serie I
Judasbrief (*P.Bodm.* VII)	Schreiber B	Serie I
Melito, Pascha-Homilie		
(*P.Bodm.* XIII)	Schreiber A	Serie I
Hymnusfragment (*P.Bodm.* XII)	Schreiber A	Serie I
Apologie des Phileas (*P.Bodm.* XX)	Schreiber C	Serie II
Ps 33 und 34 LXX (*P.Bodm.* IX)	Schreiber D	Serie II
1 und 2 Petr (*P.Bodm.* VIII)	Schreiber B	Serie III

Testuzs Rekonstruktion wurde v.a. von E.G. Turner, der aber den Codex selbst nie zu Gesicht bekam, heftiger Kritik unterzogen, die hier nicht im Detail wiederholt zu werden braucht.[3] Spätere Untersuchungen durch W. Grunewald[4] und T. Wasserman[5] bestätigten in vielen Punkten die Analysen des Erstherausgebers. Offen ist u.E. die von Grunewald als sicher angenommene ursprüngliche Verbindung zwischen dem Judasbrief und der Paschahomilie des Melito von Sardes, da die Lage, auf der sich der Judasbrief findet, mit einer nicht paginierten Seite endet, auf der nur der Titel Μελιτωνος περι πασχα zu finden ist. Der Text der Paschahomilie, der nach Durchsicht der nunmehr veröffentlichten Fotos des Gesamtcodex u.E. nicht auf Schreiber A zurückgehen muss, beginnt erst mit einer neuen Lage. Zudem beginnt mit dem Anfang des Textes von *P.Bodm.* XIII eine neue Paginierung und sind die mit dem Text der Paschahomilie einsetzenden Seiten sowie das damit verbundene Fragment des Hymnus (*P.Bodm.* XII) etwas größer als die anderen (14,2 × 16 cm anstelle von 14,2 × 15,5 cm). Möglicherweise könnte also hier von einer eige-

---

[2] Nach M. Testuz, *Papyrus Bodmer VII-IX: VII: L'Épître de Jude. VIII: Les deux Épîtres de Pierre. IX: Les Psaumes 33 et 34* (Bibliotheca Bodmeriana; Cologny—Genf 1959) 8.

[3] Siehe E.G. Turner, *The Typology of the Early Codex* (Philadelphia 1977) 79–80. Jetzt auch ausführlich referiert bei T. Wasserman, "Papyrus 72 and the *Bodmer Miscellaneous Codex*," *NTS* 51 (2005) 137–154.

[4] Vgl. W. Grunewald—K. Junack, *Das Neue Testament auf Papyrus I: Die Katholischen Briefe I* (ANTF 6; Berlin—New York 1986).

[5] Wasserman, "Papyrus 72".

nen Sektion ausgegangen werden, die unabhängig von Serie I produziert und anschließend nach dem Judasbrief platziert wurde.[6] Für die folgenden Fragestellungen wichtiger ist aber folgendes Ergebnis: Anders als von Turner rekonstruiert sind tatsächlich auch die oben als Serie II und Serie III angegebenen Abschnitte mit den weiteren Abschnitten unverbunden. Dies lässt die Hypothese zu, dass der Gesamtcodex möglicherweise in mehreren Schritten aus Einzelsammlungen entstand. Wie viele Schritte dies gewesen sein können, ist vor allem abhängig von der Frage, ob der Schreiber von Serie III mit Schreiber B aus Serie I identifiziert werden kann. Während M. Testuz beide Abschnitte demselben Schreiber zuordnete, wurde diese Annahme von E.G. Turner, allerdings nur aufgrund der beiden Fotos, die in Testuzs Ausgabe zu finden sind, bestritten.[7] Ihm folgte v.a. K. Haines-Eitzen, die ebenfalls ohne Anschauung des gesamten Manuskripts mit einer Reihe von Argumenten die These Turners zu untermauern suchte.[8] Da aber gerade die Buchstaben auf der bei Testuz abgebildeten Seite der Petrinen offensichtlich in späterer Zeit nachgezogen wurden, lassen sich aufgrund dieses Fotos kaum sichere Urteile bilden—ein Manko, das die gesamte Diskussion um $\mathfrak{P}^{72}$ beeinflusste. Mit der Veröffentlichung von Faksimiles des gesamten Codex erweisen

---

[6] Siehe auch Wasserman, "Papyrus 72", 143.

[7] Vgl. E.G. Turner, *Typology*, 79–80. Vgl. auch schon J. Duplacy, "Bulletin de critique textuelle du NT," *RSR* 50 (1962) 253.

[8] Vgl. K. Haines-Eitzen, *Guardians of Letters. Literacy, Power, and the Transmission of Early Christian Literature* (Oxford 2000) 98–99. Ihr folgt E.J. Epp, "Issues in the Interrelation of New Testament Textual Criticism and Canon," *The Canon Debate* (ed. L.M. MacDonald—J.A. Sanders; Peabody 2002) 484–515, bes. 491. Beide allerdings hatten offensichtlich keinen Zugang zu den nun veröffentlichten Faksimiles.

(3) Zu den Punkten, die den Erstherausgeber Testuz, *Papyrus Bodmer VII–IX*, 32–33 (vorsichtiger G.D. Kilpatrick, "The Bodmer and Mississippi Collections of Biblical and Christian Texts," *GRBS* 4 [1963] 33–47, bes. 34), dazu veranlassten, die Herkunft des Schreibers von *P.Bodm.* VIII in der Region um Theben anzunehmen, gehört dessen mehrfache Verwechselung von γ und κ (daneben vgl. auch die Randnotiz ΠΗΕΙ [*P.Bodm.* VIII, S. 32, am rechten Rand von Z. 4–5]). Die Tatsache, dass dieses Phänomen nur in *P.Bodm.* VIII auftrete, nicht aber in *P.Bodm.* VII, spricht für Haines-Eitzen dafür, dass hier zwei unterschiedliche Schreiber am Werk seien. Dem ist allerdings Folgendes entgegenzuhalten: Zwar erwähnt Testuz dieses Phänomen in seiner kurzen Beschreibung von *P.Bodm.* VII nicht, es tritt aber wenigstens an einer Stelle des Judasbriefs auf (*P.Bodm.* VII, S. 2, Z. 9 [εγ anstelle von εκ]), der zudem deutlich kürzer als die beiden petrinischen Texte ist. Darüber hinaus ist zu berücksichtigen, dass die unterschiedlichen Texte möglicherweise auch auf verschiedene Vorlagen zurückgehen könnten, in denen sich das entsprechende Problem bereits—in unterschiedlicher Ausprägung—vorfand.

sich die Texte des 𝔓⁷² nun eindeutig als vom selben Schreiber stam-
mend.[9] Innerhalb von 𝔓⁷² aber lässt sich eine Entwicklung beobachten: Der Text des Judasbriefs ist bei Weitem nicht mit der gleichen
Sorgfalt ausgeführt wie der Beginn des 1. Petrusbriefs. Der Schreiber
scheint die Buchstaben hier in deutlich größerer Eile geschrieben zu
haben, als dies zumindest am Anfang des 1. Petrusbriefs noch der
Fall ist. Dies zeigt sich v.a. an der ungleichmäßigen Form der
Buchstaben, aber auch an Fehlern, die ihm z.b. schon in der Überschrift des Judasbriefs, in der das υ des Wortes Ιουδα oberhalb der
Zeile nachgetragen werden musste, unterliefen. Auch im Verlauf des
Textes der Petrinen schwindet erneut die Sorgfalt der Hand.
Offensichtlich erhöhte sich die Schreibgeschwindigkeit und nahm die
Konzentration des Schreibers ab. Allerdings wird deutlich—und in
diese Richtung sind u.E. die wichtigen Beobachtungen Haines-Eitzens
zu den Unterschieden zwischen *P.Bodm.* VII und VIII auszuwerten—,
dass derselbe Schreiber die Texte Jud einerseits und 1–2Petr andererseits offensichtlich unterschiedlich behandelte: durch den Eintrag
von Marginalien am Rand des Textes von 1–2Petr sowie durch die
Verwendung von Akzenten (kleine nach links offene Halbkreise, denen
eine kurze horizontale Linie folgt, über dem betreffenden Buchstaben).[10]

Serie I und Serie III sind also zwar codicologisch unverbunden,
gleichzeitig über den gemeinsamen Schreiber B eng miteinander zu
verknüpfen.

Dagegen nimmt Serie II (*P.Bodm.* XX und IX) offensichtlich eine
Sonderstellung innerhalb des Codex ein, was sich an den weder in
I noch III begegnenden Schreiberhänden, aber auch an den *Kolophonen*,
die sich am Ende einiger der Texte des Sammelcodex finden, zeigt:

P.Bodm. V (Geburt Mariens) bietet:[11]
ειρηνη τω γραψαντι και τω αναγινωσκοντι

---

[9] *Bibliotheca Bodmeriana. La collection des papyrus Bodmer 8–10: Abbildungen sämtlicher
originaler Manuskriptseiten* (München 2000). Leider hat diese Ausgabe weder Seitenzahlen
noch eine durchgehende Zählung der Tafeln. In dem mir zugänglichen Exemplar
fehlen zudem die im Inhaltsverzeichnis angekündigten Seiten zur Benutzung der
Ausgabe.
[10] Zu möglichen Folgerungen aus dieser Beobachtung vgl. T. Nicklas, „Der ‚lebendige Text' des Neuen Testaments. Der Judasbrief in 𝔓⁷² (P.Bodmer VII)," *ASE* 23
(2005) 69–88.
[11] Vgl. M. Testuz, *P.Bodmer V: Nativité de Marie* (Bibliotheca Bodmeriana; Cologny—
Genève 1958) 126.

Keine Kolophone finden sich am Ende der apokryphen Korrespondenz zwischen Ps-Paulus und den Korinthern (*P.Bodm.* X), der 11. Ode Salomos (*P.Bodm.* XI) und des Judasbriefs (*P.Bodm.* VII).

Nach dem Melito-Text (*P.Bodm.* XIII) steht dagegen:[12]

ιρηνη τω γραψαντι και τω αναγινωσκοντι και τοις αγαπωσι τον κ(υριο)ν εν αφελοτητι καρδιας

Von den beiden genannten deutlich unterschieden ist das Kolophon nach der *Apologie des Phileas* (*P.Bodm.* XX), dem außerdem ein Staurogramm folgt.[13]

ιρηνη τοις αγειοις πασει

Zwei den beiden ersten wiederum deutlich nähere Kolophone finden sich dann in *P.Bodm.* VIII, jeweils nach 1 und 2Petr, das zweite ganz am Ende des Sammelcodex—in beiden Fällen steht folgender Text:[14]

ειρηνη τω γραψαντι και τω αναγινωσκοντι

Die Gleichartigkeit der Kolophone am Ende der Texte zumindest zweier Schreiber lässt auf eine enge Verbindung zwischen ihnen schließen.[15] Deutlich unterschieden von den anderen aber ist das Kolophon am Ende von *P.Bodm.* XX. Dies spricht sowohl gegen die These Turners, dass der Codex als Gesamt in einem Zug produziert wurde,[16] als auch gegen den Vorschlag Grunewalds, dass Sektion II mit der Apologie den Nukleus der gesamten Kollektion gebildet habe.[17]

Dieser Hintergrund stützt einen Alternativvorschlag von Wasserman, der zeigt, dass die von Testuz vorgeschlagene Reihenfolge der Serien nicht die ursprüngliche gewesen sein muss.[18] So ergeben sich folgende Reihenfolgen als wahrscheinlich:

Serie I + Serie III (+ später hinten oder vorne angeschlossen: Serie II)

---

[12] Das Kolophon ist hier ans Ende der Seite gedrückt, die Schrift gegenüber dem Rest der Seite deutlich verkleinert.

[13] Hierzu V. Martin, *Papyrus Bodmer XX. Apologie de Philéas, evêque de Thmouis* (Bibliotheca Bodmeriana; Cologny—Genève 1964) 52, sowie Bildtafel 17 im Anhang. Es findet sich, gerahmt durch horizontale Linien oben und unten, auf der rechten Hälfte der Seite.

[14] Testuz, *P.Bodmer VII–IX*, 70. Die Buchstaben να von αναγινωσκοντι sind im zweiten Fall über der Zeile nachgetragen.

[15] Weiterführend hier auch Haines-Eitzen, *Guardians*, 101–102.

[16] Vgl. Turner, *Typology*, 80.

[17] Vgl. Grunewald—Junack, *Das Neue Testament*, 16–25.

[18] Deutlich ausführlicher die Argumentation bei Wasserman, "Papyrus 72", 140–148.

oder:

Serie III + Serie I (+ später hinten oder vorne angeschlossen:
Serie II).

2. Ein innerer Zusammenhang der Texte?

Die Zusammenstellung einer zumindest auf den ersten Blick derart
bunten Vielfalt von Texten hat bereits mehrfach den Versuch her-
ausgefordert, einen inneren Zusammenhang zwischen den Texten
bzw. eine theologische Motivation ihrer Zusammenstellung zu entdecken—und damit einen Schlüssel, der erlaubt, dem Sammler
bzw. der Gruppe von Sammlern dieser Texte historisch näher zu
kommen.

2.1 *Forschungsgeschichtliches*

Insgesamt sind drei Vorschläge zu unterscheiden:

(1) V. Martin, Herausgeber von *P.Bodm.* XX, der *Apologie des Phileas*,
sieht das alle Texte des vorliegenden Codex verbindende Element
in der einfachen Tatsache, dass es sich um theologische Literatur
mit der Tendenz, Aspekte christlicher Lehre in apologetischer Weise
zu verteidigen, handele.[19] Das Problem an dieser Sichtweise besteht
natürlich darin, dass ein großer Teil antiker christlicher Literatur
antihäretische Tendenzen verfolgt und sich so einordnen ließe.

(2) Einen sehr komplexen Vorschlag bietet W. Wiefel, der von einer
Entstehung des Codex in zwei Phasen ausgeht. Wiefel hält den seiner Meinung nach ursprünglichen Codex des 3. Jh.s, der aus den
Texten der hier angegebenen Serien I und III bestanden habe, für
eine Privatanthologie mit scharf antihäretischer bzw. antijüdischer
Tendenz (besonders wichtig: Jud und 1–2Petr).[20] Im 4. Jh. sei dann
durch die Hinzunahme der *Apologie des Phileas* sowie der beiden
damit verbundenen Psalmen[21] eine Sammlung zur erbaulichen

---

[19] Vgl. Martin, *Papyrus Bodmer XX*, 9.
[20] Vgl. W. Wiefel, "Kanongeschichtliche Erwägungen zu Papyrus Bodmer VII/VIII
(P[72])," *APF* 22 (1973) 289–303, bes. 298–300.
[21] Die Aufnahme von Ps 33 erklärt Wiefel, "Kanongeschichtliche Erwägungen,"
299, mit dessen intertextuellen Bezügen zu 1Petr.

Verlesung[22] an Festtagen—v.a. mit Beziehungen zum österlichen, aber auch winterlichen Festkreis—entstanden.[23] Unklar daran aber ist, welche Rolle dabei die *Apologie des Phileas* oder der 2. Petrusbrief einnehmen sollen; die Zuordnung zu verschiedenen Festen des Jahreskreises wirkt darüber hinaus etwas gekünstelt, vor allem wenn gleich mehrere Feste herangezogen werden müssen, um die Sammlung zu erklären.

(3) Eine sehr konkrete Verbindung schlägt K. Haines-Eitzen vor, die das gemeinsame Thema aller im Codex zu findenden Texte im Thema „Körper" bzw. „Körperlichkeit" entdeckt.[24] In allen Texten kämen in irgendeiner Weise Themen wie die Inkarnation, die Leiblichkeit der Auferstehung Jesu oder aber Probleme des (auch körperlichen) Leidens der Verfolgten zum Tragen. Tatsächlich ist hier ein Motiv angesprochen, das in vielen Texten in allerdings unterschiedlicher Weise auftaucht. Die Frage ist aber, ob es möglich ist, der Zusammenstellung der Einzeltexte wirklich gerecht zu werden.

2.2 *Beobachtungen am Text des Codex*

2.2.1 *Die Apologie des Phileas*

Sollte, wie T. Wasserman jüngst vermutet hat,[25] der ursprüngliche Codex mit der *Apologie des Phileas* eingesetzt haben, so wäre dessen erstes Wort απολογεια, „Apologie". Damit ist natürlich der apologetische Charakter des ersten Werkes betont, gleichzeitig ergibt sich vielleicht auch ein Leitmotiv durch die Gesamtheit der zusammengestellten Texte.[26]

Der Text der *Apologie des Phileas* ist durch insgesamt acht einander textlich sehr nahe stehende lateinische Handschriften (La) aus der Zeit zwischen dem 9. und dem 14. Jh. bezeugt. Die griechische Fassung des Werkes ist neben *P.Bodm.* XX (Bo) inzwischen auch durch *P.Chester Beatty* XV (Be) belegt.[27] Wie Bo wird Be ins 4. Jh. datiert, näherhin in eine Zeit etwa 50

---

[22] Wiefel, "Kanongeschichtliche Erwägungen," denkt hier offensichtlich an private Lektüre, wie 300 Anm. 4 nahelegt.

[23] Vgl. Wiefel, "Kanongeschichtliche Erwägungen," 300.

[24] Vgl. Haines-Eitzen, *Guardians*, 103–104.

[25] Vgl. Wasserman, "Papyrus 72", 143–145.

[26] Eine derartige Verbindung stellte bereits Martin, *Papyrus Bodmer XX*, 9–10, her.

[27] Edition: A. Pietersma (Hg.), *The Acts of Phileas Bishop of Thmuis (Including Fragments*

Jahre nach dem Tod des Phileas von Thmuis[28] zwischen 304 und 307 unserer Zeitrechnung. Vergleicht man die drei Hauptzeugen miteinander, so zeigt sich, dass Be und La häufig gegen Bo übereinstimmen.[29] Offensichtlich bietet Bo eine Textform, in der hagiographische und apologetische Interessen mehr im Mittelpunkt stehen, als dies in den beiden anderen der Fall ist, die offensichtlich einen mehr „liturgischen" Sitz im Leben besitzen dürften.[30] Dies zeigt sich schon in der bei Bo bezeugten Überschrift „Apologie", die sich so in den parallelen Versionen nicht findet, wo von „Akten" die Rede ist.[31] Der Begriff „Apologie" lässt sich hier möglicherweise nicht nur als „Verteidigung" vor Gericht, sondern als „Apologie des christlichen Glaubens" interpretieren.[32]

Der Text der Apologie ist zum großen Teil als Dialog zwischen Phileas und seinem Richter Culcianus gehalten. Die Szene spielt in Alexandrien, wohin Phileas als Gefangener von seiner Diözese Thmuis verbracht wurde. Der Text wird durch immer wiederkehrende Anordnungen, nun doch endlich zu opfern, gegliedert. Phileas betont, dass alleine dem Herrn geopfert werden dürfe.[33]

In dem sich nun entspinnenden Dialog betont Phileas zunächst die Auferstehung des Fleisches (nicht nur der Seele). Dies spräche tatsächlich für den von Haines-Eitzen geäußerten Vorschlag; das Thema bildet jedoch nur einen kleinen Abschnitt des gesamten Textes. Nach der dritten Aufforderung des Culcianus an Phileas, nun doch zu opfern, unterscheiden sich die Texte La/Be und Bo: Im Text des *P.Bodm.* XX wird von Phileas explizit die Göttlichkeit Jesu betont, ein Motiv, das in den anderen Zeugen zwar noch auftaucht, aber nach hinten rückt. Phileas begründet die Göttlichkeit Jesu mit dem Zeugnis seiner Taten, der Werke Gottes. Von hier aus stellt Culcianus die Frage, wie es möglich sei, dass Gott gekreuzigt wurde. In seiner

---

of the Greek Psalter): P.Chester Beatty XV (With a New Edition of P.Bodmer XX, and Halkin's Latin Acta) (Cahiers d'Orientalisme 7; Genève 1984). Eine kurze Einführung findet sich auch bei G.H.R. Horsley, *New Documents Illustrating Early Christianity. A Review of Greek Inscriptions and Papyri Published in 1977* (Sydney 1982) 185–191.

[28] Zu Phileas vgl. weiterführend E. Sauser, Art. "Phileas von Thmuis," *BBKL* 14 (1998) 1360–1361.

[29] So Pietersma, *Acts of Phileas*, 14–19.

[30] So auch Pietersma, *Acts of Phileas*, 22, der hier die Analysen Martins bestätigt.

[31] Allerdings fehlt die Überschrift in Be.

[32] So auch Martin, *Papyrus Bodmer XX*, 12–13, sowie H. Musurillo, *The Acts of the Christian Martyrs* (Oxford 1972) liv.

[33] An dieser Stelle fehlen in *P.Bodm.* XX zwei Seiten. Sie ist aber in beiden Parallelen belegt.

Antwort wiederum betont Phileas die Tatsächlichkeit des Leidens des göttlichen Jesus, das zu einem Vorbild für die Rettung der Christen geworden sei. Auch dieses Thema könnte noch im weitesten Sinne zum Thema „Fleischlichkeit" gezählt werden. Daneben aber werden weitere Fragen verhandelt: Ist es erlaubt zu schwören? War Paulus Gott—und wenn nein—wer war er dann? Wie lässt sich das Verhältnis zwischen Paulus und Plato beschreiben? usw.—Themen, die auch bei näherem Hinsehen nichts mit dem vorgeschlagenen gemeinsamen Leitmotiv zu tun haben.

2.2.2 *Ps 33 und 34 LXX*

Die codicologische Verbindung der beiden Septuaginta-Psalmen 33 und 34 mit der *Apologie des Phileas* ist unbestritten.[34] Ist es auch möglich, inhaltliche Verknüpfungen zwischen den beiden Texten und dem Rest des Manuskripts herzustellen?—Tatsächlich spielte der Psalter im frühen Christentum eine wichtige Rolle bei der theologischen Bewältigung des Christusereignisses, letztlich für die gesamte Aufgabe der Formulierung beginnender christlicher Theologie. Dies zeigen bereits die vielen Belege von Psalmenzitaten (mit einzelnen Schwerpunkten wie etwa Ps 22, 69 oder 110) im Neuen Testament. Daneben aber bot das Gebetbuch „Psalter"—wie im Judentum—für die verschiedensten christlichen Gruppierungen eine nahezu unerschöpfliche Quelle der Spiritualität.—Auch Ps 33 LXX, der Gottes Sorge für den Gerechten auch im Leid thematisiert, hat eine breite Rezeption im frühen Christentum erfahren. Unter den intertextuellen Bezügen, die sich zum Neuen Testament herstellen lassen (z.B. zu Mt 5,3; Lk 1,46; Joh 19,36; Hebr 12,14; 13,15; Jak 1,26; 2Tim 3,11)[35] ist für die vorliegende Fragestellung besonders interessant, dass er zwei Mal in 1Petr aufgegriffen ist:[36] Eine eher knappe, doch

---

[34] Interessanterweise findet sich das *Martyrium des Phileas* auch in Be in Verbindung mit griechischen Psalmen überliefert.

[35] Siehe L. Eriksson, *'Come, children, listen to me!': Psalm 34 in the Hebrew and in Early Christian Writings* (ConBOT 32; Stockholm 1991) 110. Die Formulierung "intertextuelle Bezüge" stellt offen, ob die Verbindungen auch immer vom Autor intendiert waren.

[36] Eine ausführliche Liste von Bezügen zwischen 1Petr und Ps 33 LXX bietet E.G. Selwyn, *The First Epistle of St. Peter* (London ²1947 [ND 1977]) 408–410.— Eine Verbindung zwischen Ps 33 LXX und 1Petr sieht auch W. Wiefel, "Kanongeschichtliche Erwägungen," 299.

deutliche Anspielung findet sich in 1Petr 2,3;[37] eindeutig ist 1Petr
3,10–12: Der paränetische Abschnitt 1Petr 3,8–12 setzt mit einer
Reihe von Forderungen an die Adressaten in Form eines Tugend-
katalogs ein, V. 9 erinnert zudem an die Bergpredigt.[38] Diese
Forderungen werden in den VV. 10–12 mit einem ausführlichen
Zitat von Ps. 33,13–17 LXX begründet.[39]—Warum aber steht Ps 33
nach der *Apologie des Phileas*? Ist ein Zusammenhang zwischen dem
vom Psalmisten ausgedrückten Leid und dem Martyrium des Phileas
herzustellen?[40] Dann würde auch Ps 34 LXX, das „Klagegebet eines
Einzelnen in der Situation feindlicher Bedrängnis"[41] eine Verbindung
ergeben, die durchaus nachvollziehbar wäre. Die erbauliche Lektüre
der Apologie und der nachfolgenden Psalmen würde tatsächlich Sinn
machen.[42]

Gleichzeitig aber stellt sich die Frage, ob dann die in der Apologie
entdeckte Thematik des „Körpers", die apologetischen Tendenzen
mit ihrer Betonung der Fleischlichkeit der Auferstehung für die
Zusammenstellung von Apologie und Psalmen wirklich entscheidend
sein können. Ist die Verbindung zwischen Ps 33 LXX und dem
(möglicherweise) erst deutlich später im Codex auftauchenden 1Petr
gewollt und bewusst gesetzt oder nur Zufall, der aus der Tatsache
erwächst, dass Ps 33 LXX im frühen Christentum häufig gelesen
wurde?[43] Für die Vermutung eines Zufalls spricht u.E. die Tatsache,
dass sowohl nach Ps 33 Ps 34, als auch nach 1Petr 2Petr folgt und
sich hier keine leicht erkennbaren Verbindungen herstellen lassen.
Darüber hinaus zeigt sich bei einer genauen Untersuchung der
Verbindungslinien zwischen 1Petr und Ps 33 im *Codex Bodmer Miscellani*,

---

[37] Hierzu weiterführend J.D. Quinn, "Notes on the Text of P72: 1Pet 2,3; 5,14;
and 5,9," *CBQ* 27 (1965) 240–249.

[38] Weiterführend z.B. N. Brox, *Der erste Petrusbrief* (EKK 21; Zürich—Neukirchen-
Vluyn 1986) 151.

[39] Zur Form des Zitats und der im Kontext nun völlig veränderten Tragweite
des Textes N. Brox, *1. Petrusbrief*, 154–155.

[40] W. Wiefel, "Kanongeschichtliche Erwägungen," 299, verneint dies.

[41] So E. Zenger, "Die Psalmen," *Stuttgarter Altes Testament* (ed. E. Zenger; Stuttgart
²2004) 1036–1219, bes. 1075.

[42] Dieser Gedanke ist eventuell noch plausibler, wenn man bedenkt, dass V. 1,
der Ps 33 LXX in den Kontext des Lebens Davids setzt, fehlt.

[43] Siehe auch die Tabelle bei Eriksson, *Come*, 131, wo Ps 33 LXX als einer der
Texte zu erkennen ist, die in der Beliebtheit bei frühchristlichen Autoren zwar keine
absolute Spitzenstellung einnahmen, aber doch häufiger als viele andere Psalmen
zitiert wurden.

dass keine Harmonisierungen in den entsprechenden Parallelen auf-
treten.[44] Ist es denkbar, dass sowohl Ps 33–34 als auch 1–2Petr nur
deswegen kopiert sind, weil sie innerhalb der jeweiligen Vorlagen in
einer Sammlung aufeinander folgten und gerade in dieser Reihenfolge
verfügbar waren?[45]

2.2.3 *Die Geburt Mariens*

Die „Geburt Mariens", heute besser bekannt als *Protevangelium Jakobi*,
das sicherlich bekannteste außerkanonische „Kindheitsevangelium"[46],
dürfte in ihrem Grundbestand auf das späte 2. Jh. zurückgehen.[47]
P.Bodm. V ist die älteste bekannte Handschrift des reich überlieferten Textes, er bietet diesen in einer etwas kürzeren Fassung als spätere Zeugen[48]—bereits 1980 waren É. de Strycker 140 griechische
Manuskripte bekannt,[49] darüber hinaus existieren syrische, georgi-
sche, lateinische, armenische, arabische, koptische, äthiopische und
slavische Versionen.[50] Literarisch setzt das Werk die beiden kanonischen Kindheitsgeschichten des Mt wie des Lk voraus, die es ab
Kapitel 11 recht frei zu einer geschlossenen Erzählung zusammenstellt. Dies wird mit einer Vorgeschichte (Kapitel 1–10) versehen, die
sich v.a. für die Gestalt Mariens interessiert, und mit einer Vielzahl
weiterer Elemente angereichert.[51] Ein Hintergrund der Entstehung

---

[44] Hierzu weiterführend Wasserman, "Papyrus 72", 147.

[45] Auch D. Trobisch, *Die Endredaktion des Neuen Testaments. Eine Untersuchung zur
Entstehung der christlichen Bibel* (NTOA 31; Freiburg/CH—Göttingen 1996) 49, schreibt
im Bezug auf *Codex Bodmer Miscellani*: "Es handelt sich hier wohl um eine einma-
lige Sammlung, bei deren Entstehung—ganz deutlich ist das bei den Psalmen zu
erkennen—*Schriften aus ihrem ursprünglichen Sammlungszusammenhang herausgerissen wurden*
[Herv. d. Vf.]."

[46] Zur Problematik dieser Bezeichnung, die dennoch mangels geeigneterer Begriffe
beibehalten sei, vgl. z.B. H.-J. Klauck, *Apokryphe Evangelien. Eine Einführung* (Stuttgart
2002) 88.

[47] Grundzüge des Textes scheinen schon Clemens v. Alexandrien bekannt gewe-
sen zu sein. Parallelen finden sich bereits bei Justin. Hierzu z.B. O. Cullmann,
"Kindheitsevangelien," *Neutestamentliche Apokryphen I: Evangelien* (ed. W. Schneemelcher;
Tübingen [6]1990) 330–372, bes. 335.

[48] Vgl. É. de Strycker, *La forme la plus ancienne du Protévangile de Jacques* (Subsidia
Hagiographica 33; Brüssel 1961) 34.

[49] Vgl. É. de Strycker, "Die griechischen Handschriften des Protevangeliums
Jacobi," *Griechische Kodikologie und Textüberlieferung* (ed. D. Harlfinger; Darmstadt 1980)
577–612.

[50] Vgl. Cullmann, "Kindheitsevangelien," 335–336.

[51] É. Cothenet, "Le Protévangile de Jacques: origine, genre et signification d'un
premier midrash chrétien sur la Nativité de Marie," *ANRW* II.25.6 (1988) 4252–4269,
bes. 4259–4263, spricht von einem "christlichen Midrasch".

von „Kindheitsevangelien" besteht sicherlich in der Frage nach dem
Leben Jesu in den Zeiten, von denen die kanonisch gewordenen
Evangelien[52] des Neuen Testaments (weitgehend) schweigen. Diesem
Informationsbedürfnis korrespondieren aber zumindest im Falle der
bekanntesten Kindheitsgeschichten Jesu immer auch handfeste theologische Interessen: Bereits in Mt 1–2 wie auch Lk 1–2 geht es vor
allem darum, christologische Glaubensinhalte der nachösterlichen Zeit
bereits in den Ursprung, die Kindheit Jesu von Nazaret, erzählerisch
hineinzuverlegen. Es geht also immer entscheidend auch um die
Frage: Wer ist Jesus von Nazaret? Auch im *Protevangelium* spielen christologische Themen sicherlich eine Rolle.

Die Vermutung, das *Protevangelium* könne eine doketische Christologie
vertreten, scheint sich nicht halten zu lassen.[53] Diese Annahme stützt
sich v.a. auf 19,2, wo davon die Rede ist, dass das Kind bei seiner
Geburt „erscheint" (φαίνω). Sinnvoller aber ist eine Interpretation
der Szene in dem Sinne, dass die Geburt Jesu als Epiphanie zu verstehen ist. Interessant ist vor diesem Hintergrund dann der folgende
Satz, der davon spricht, dass das Neugeborene daraufhin die Brust
seiner Mutter Maria nimmt—und sich damit in seiner „Menschlichkeit"
erweist. Dieser Gedanke scheint auch in der letzten christologischen
Aussage des Textes wieder auf, wo davon die Rede ist, dass dem
Simeon vom Heiligen Geist geoffenbart worden sei, „er werde den
Tod nicht schauen, bis er den Messias im Fleische sähe" (*ProtEv* 24,4,
natürlich in Anspielung auf Lk 2,25–26).—Da *P.Bodm.* V der mit
einigem Abstand älteste bekannte Textzeuge des *Protevangeliums* ist,
ist es kaum möglich, von textlichen Tendenzen dieses Zeugen zu
sprechen. Im Vergleich zu anderen Manuskripten bietet *P.Bodm.* V
einen deutlich kürzeren Text, was wohl darauf zurückzuführen ist,
dass hier eine frühere Redaktionsstufe des Werkes vorliegt. Immerhin

---

[52] Diese Redeweise schließt sich an die Bezeichnung "apokryph geworden" von
D. Lührmann, *Fragmente apokryph gewordener Evangelien in griechischer und lateinischer Sprache*
(MThSt 59; Marburg 2000); Id., *Die apokryph gewordenen Evangelien. Studien zu neuen
Texten und zu neuen Fragen* (NT.S 112; Leiden—Boston 2004) 4, an.

[53] Dieser Gedanke wird von A. De Santos Otero, *Los Evangelios Apócrifos* (Madrid
¹⁰1999) 123, und Klauck, *Apokryphe Evangelien*, 98, zwar angesprochen, aber letztlich
abgelehnt. Auch für A. Frey, "Protévangile de Jacques," *Écrits apocryphes chrétiens* I,
(ed. F. Bovon—P. Geoltrain; Paris 1997) 73–104, bes. 77, betont das Protevangelium
die wahre Menschlichkeit Jesu.—Zum Problem der Bezeichnung "Doketismus" allgemein vgl. weiterführend N. Brox, "„Doketismus"—eine Problemanzeige," *ZKG* 95
(1984) 301–314.

hingewiesen sei auf eine christologische Variante in 15,4, wo Josef in vielen Handschriften seine Antwort auf die Frage des Hohenpriesters, ob er sich an Maria vergangen habe, mit der Formel „So wahr der Herr, mein Gott, lebt" einleitet. *P.Bodm.* V, aber auch das Cesena-Palimpsest (9. Jh.), nennen hier Christus. Da nicht klar ist, zu welcher Zeit diese Lesart entstand, sagt sie über eine mögliche christologische Tendenz des Manuskriptes nichts aus.

So mag es in diesem Text *auch* um die Geburt Jesu im Fleisch gehen. Die Hauptintention des Werkes ist aber eindeutig mit dem Begriff „Marienlob"[54] zu umschreiben: Die Reinheit Mariens, ihre Herkunft, vor allem aber ihre Jungfräulichkeit ist das zentrale Thema des Textes.[55] Somit ist sicherlich die „Leiblichkeit" des Christus, möglicherweise auch der Leib der Gottesmutter als reines Gefäß ein Problem, das den Text interessiert. Wenn „Leib" aber entscheidend sein soll, warum wählt man nicht entscheidende Passagen aus oder markiert diese in irgendeiner Weise (z.B. durch Marginalien)?[56]

Möglicherweise könnte eine Verbindung zu den anderen Texten des Codex auch in den Parallelen zu sehen sein, die das *Protevangelium* an mehreren Stellen auf Jud und 1–2Petr bietet:[57] (*ProtEv* 9,2—Jud 11; *ProtEv* 15,4—1Petr 5,6; *ProtEv* 25,1—2Petr 3,15; *ProtEv* 3,2—2Petr 2,12; Jud 10; *ProtEv* 7,2—2 Petr 3,3).—Diese sind allerdings so vage, dass kaum nachweisbar ist, an welchen Stellen der bzw. die Autoren des *Protevangeliums* konkret Bezug auf diese Texte nehmen. Ob diese Parallelen reichen, um eine Zusammenstellung der Texte aus diesem Grunde wahrscheinlich zu machen, kann u.E. bezweifelt werden.[58]

---

[54] So H.-J. Klauck, *Apokryphe Evangelien*, 90.

[55] G. Schneider, *Evangeliae Infantiae Apocrypha. Apocryphe Kindheitsevangelien* (FC 18; Freiburg u.a. 1995) 27, schreibt: "Das *Hauptinteresse* des Protevangeliums gilt der Mutter Jesu. Sie ist von vornherein die Gottgeweihte. Gott selbst hat sie für ihre Aufgabe erwählt. Sie ist Jungfrau geblieben, auch nach der Geburt ihres Kindes." Vgl. auch H.R. Smid, *Protevangelium Jacobi. A Commentary* (Assen 1965) 14–20; É. Cothenet, "Protévangile," 4263–4266.

[56] Ein Beispiel, wie vorgegangen werden kann, wenn tatsächlich ein Thema die gesammelten Texte verbindet, bietet Crosby-Schøyen-Codex MS 193. Die hier gesammelten Materialien lassen sich alle mit Ostern verbinden (Melito, *Peri Pascha*; 2Makk 5,27—7,41; 1Petr, Jona und einige nicht zuzuordnende Fragmente). Das hier leitende Interesse aber sorgt auch dafür, dass nicht das gesamte 2Makk aufgeschrieben ist, sondern nur eine martyrologische Passage (so auch der Titel im entsprechenden Codex: "Die jüdischen Märtyrer, die unter König Antiochos lebten"), in der zugleich mehrfach von der Auferstehung der Toten die Rede ist.

[57] Siehe hierzu auch de Strycker, *Forme*, 427.

[58] So werden intertextuelle Verbindungen zu den Katholischen Briefen in dem Beitrag von W.S. Vorster, "The Protevangelium of James and Intertextuality," *Text*

2.2.4 *Die apokryphe Korrespondenz des Paulus mit den Korinthern (3Kor)*
Bei der apokryphen Korrespondenz des Apostels Paulus mit den
Korinthern steht tatsächlich ein konkret apologetisch-christologisches
Interesse im Mittelpunkt. Dieser pseudepigraphische Text setzt sich—
in Aufnahme theologischer Gedanken des historischen Paulus—mit
einer Reihe häretischer Ideen auseinander. V. Hovhanessian identifizierte darunter die Lehre, dass Gott weder allmächtig, noch der
Schöpfer der Welt sei, sowie die Zurückweisung alttestamentlicher
Prophetie und die Ablehnung der fleischlichen Geburt Jesu. Haupt-
thema allerdings war die Ablehnung der fleischlichen Auferstehung
von den Toten.[59] Der Text, wohl zwischen Mitte und Ende des 2.
Jh.s entstanden, lässt sich als Quelle polemischer Argumente der
(proto-) Orthodoxie gegen gnostische Gegner charakterisieren.[60]
    Da 3Kor in der syrischen und armenischen Kirche lange Zeit in
hohem Ansehen stand, ja offensichtlich als kanonisch anerkannt
wurde,[61] ist der Text im Vergleich zu vielen anderen apokryph gewordenen Schriften in einer großen Zahl von Handschriften bezeugt.
Deshalb können die Eigenheiten der Fassung von *P.Bodm.* X besser
erfasst werden als z.B. in der *Apologie des Phileas.*[62] So wird die
Bedeutung des „Fleisches" bzw. der Fleischlichkeit in der Textfassung
des *P.Bodm.* X im Vergleich zu anderen Handschriften zumindest in
2,5 besonders hervorgehoben, wo der Antwortbrief des ps-Paulus an
die Korinther mit der Überschrift „Paulus an die Korinther *über das
Fleisch* [Herv. durch Autor]" eingeleitet wird. Der Rest des Textes
ist deutlich kürzer als die armenische Parallele—der Text des *P.Bodm.*
konzentriert sich auf das Thema „fleischliche Auferstehung"—K.
Haines-Eitzen ist hier zuzustimmen: Dieser Text stellt ganz sicherlich das Thema des Leibes in den Mittelpunkt.

---

and Testimony. Essays on New Testament and Apocryphal Literature in Honour of A.F.J. Klijn
(ed. T. Baarda u.a.; Kampen 1988) 262–275, an keiner Stelle für erwähnenswert
befunden.
    [59] So V. Hovhanessian, *Third Corinthians. Reclaiming Paul for Christian Orthodoxy*
(Studies in Biblical Literature 18; New York u.a. 2000) 135.
    [60] So Hovhanessian, *Third Corinthians*, 136–137.
    [61] Zur Rezeptionsgeschichte vgl. Hovhanessian, *Third Corinthians*, 10–16.
    [62] Allerdings sollte mit großer Vorsicht von „Tendenzen" gesprochen werden, da
P.Bodm. X das einzige erhaltene griechische Manuskript des Textes darstellt, das
schon dadurch—und aufgrund seines Alters—eine Sonderstellung einnimmt.

2.2.5 *Die 11. Ode Salomos*

Spätestens an der 11. Ode Salomos[63] aber scheitert u.E. jeder Versuch, ein übergreifendes Thema oder eine gemeinsame theologische Richtung mit dem Rest des Manuskripts herzustellen. Taucht in V. 2 in der Rede von der „Beschneidung des Heiligen Geistes durch den Höchsten" das von K. Haines-Eitzen identifizierte Leitthema des „Leibes" auf?[64] Geht es um eine mögliche liturgische Verwendung der Oden?[65] Auch die Bemerkung von J.H. Charlesworth, dass die Oden Einblick in die Gebetspraxis des frühesten Christentums erlaubten und dabei eine besondere Betonung auf die Taufe gelegt werde,[66] lässt sich hier m.E. nicht auswerten. Für eine Verbindung der 11. Ode mit frühchristlicher Tauf- bzw. Initiationspraxis sprechen zwar die VV. 1–3, wo mehrfach die „Beschneidung" (u.a. durch den Heiligen Geist) thematisiert wird, 6–7, die das „redende" bzw. „lebendige Wasser" erwähnen, oder 10–11, wo von der Erneuerung des Sprechers durch das „Gewand des Herrn" die Rede ist. Von den erhaltenen Zeugen der 11. Ode bietet allein *P.Bodm.* XI in V. 22 schließlich die Lesart ευλογημενοι οι δρωντες των υδατων σου („gesegnet seien die Wärter deiner Wasser").[67] Doch eine Durchsicht des Textes zeigt, dass das

---

[63] Die *Oden Salomos*, eine Gruppe von 42 Schriften, die nicht mit den Psalmen Salomos verwechselt werden dürfen, wurden von einem oder einer Gruppe von Judenchristen an der Wende zwischen dem 1. und dem 2. Jh. unserer Zeitrechnung verfasst. *P.Bodm.* XI bietet den einzigen in griechischer Sprache erhaltenen Text der ansonsten in syrischer und koptischer Sprache überlieferten Oden. Weiterführend z.B. die Einleitung von M. Lattke, *Oden Salomos* (FC 19; Freiburg u.a. 1995) 7–90.

[64] Vgl. Haines-Eitzen, *Guardians*, 103.

[65] Zum liturgischen *Sitz im Leben* der Oden vgl. z.B. D.E. Aune, "The Odes of Solomon and Early Christian Prophecy," *NTS* 28 (1982) 435–460, bes. 436.—Die schräg von rechts nach links geneigten (z.T. Doppel-)Linien, die Abschnitte der 11. Ode im Text von *P.Bodm.* XI untergliedern, sind zu unsystematisch gesetzt, um sich als Einteilung in Strophen interpretieren zu lassen. Eher kann von einer Art stichischer Gliederung, einer Einteilung in „Verse" gesprochen werden, wie M. Lattke, *Die Oden Salomos in ihrer Bedeutung für Neues Testament und Gnosis I* (OBO 25,1; Göttingen 1979) 22, betont. Möglicherweise soll die poetische Form des Textes hier hervorgehoben werden. Für Fotos des Manuskripts vgl. neben den bereits genannten Ausgaben J.H. Charlesworth (Hg.), *The Odes of Solomon: Papyri and Leather Manuscripts of the Odes of Solomon* (Dickerson Series of Facsimiles of Manuscripts Important for Christian Origins; Duke University 1981) 8–12.

[66] Vgl. J.H. Charlesworth, "Odes of Solomon," *Old Testament Pseudepigrapha II* (ed. J.H. Charlesworth; New York 1985) 725–771, bes. 728: ". . . the Odes are a window through which we can occasionally glimpse the earliest Christians at worship; especially their apparent stress on baptism."

[67] So M. Testuz, *Papyrus Bodmer X–XII* (Cologny—Genève 1959) Anm. 3/67.

Motiv des „Wassers" hier wohl kaum im Taufkontext gebraucht wird.
M. Lattke bezeichnet Ode 11 daher als „Bildrede einer erlösten
Person in erzählender Form" und schreibt:[68]

> Da dieses Gedicht trotz seiner Doxologie (24) kein Hymnus ist und
> trotz der Thematik von „spiritual circumcision" (1–3a) bzw. „speaking
> waters" (6–8a) nicht auf das Ritual der Taufe anspielt..., kann man
> es nicht als eines der mit „Initiations-Hymnen" gleichgesetzten „Tauf-
> danklieder" bezeichnen, auch wenn einzelne „Gattungsmerkmale" der
> „Formensprache der Initiationslieder" hier vorkommen.... Wegen der
> reichen Bildersprache... handelt es sich um eine Bildrede, die das in
> seinem Geschlecht nicht bestimmbare „Ich" insgesamt in poetisch erzäh-
> lender Form vorträgt, ohne daß irgendwelche Adressaten zum Vorschein
> kämen.

Fraglich erscheint auch, wie und inwiefern Ode 11 als „Apologie"
verstanden werden könnte, ein Text, der einer Sammlung entstand,
deren Wurzeln in synkretistischen judenchristlichen Kreisen an der
Wende zwischen 1. und 2. Jh. liegen dürften.[69] Zwar begegnet in
der Fassung des *P.Bodm.* nie das Wort γνῶσις oder ἐπίγνωσις, während das in der syrischen Parallele zwei Mal vorkommende Wort
ܪܕܥܬܐ (V. 4 und 8a) häufig genau für diese Lexeme steht. Ob sich
der Text aber als Zeugnis christlicher Proto-Orthodoxie, als Text
mit Interesse am „Leib" oder an hoher Christologie einordnen lässt,
darf u.E. bezweifelt werden. Immerhin allerdings ist denkbar, dass
er Christen proto-orthodoxer Kreise Ägyptens keinen Grund für
Anstöße gegeben hat, so dass seine Aufnahme in eine Sammlung
von Texten eines Kreises aus proto-orthodoxem Milieu durchaus
nachvollziehbar ist.[70]

---

[68] M. Lattke, *Oden Salomos. Text, Übersetzung, Kommentar 1: Oden 1 und 3–14* (NTOA
41.1; Freiburg/CH—Göttingen 1999) 185.188.

[69] Lattke, *Oden Salomos* (1995), 34, schreibt von einem „gnostisch-synkretistische[n]
Christ[en]—oder eine[r] Gruppe von frühen Christen". Allerdings wäre es, wie J.H.
Charlesworth, "The Odes of Solomon—Not Gnostic," *Critical Reflections on the Odes
of Solomon 1: Literary Setting, Textual Studies, Gnosticism, the Dead Sea Scrolls and the Gospel
of John* (JSP.S 22; Sheffield 1998) 176–191, betont, irreführend, die Oden Salomos
als "gnostisch" im eigentlichen Sinne zu bezeichnen. Charlesworth schreibt (190):
"[I]t is safe to say that *the Odes of Solomon are not gnostic*. In prospect it appears probable that the *Odes* are a tributary to Gnosticism which flows from Jewish apoca-
lyptic mysticism... through such works as the *Hymn of the Pearl* and the *Gospel of
Thomas* to the full-blown Gnosticism of the second century."

[70] Die Rezeption der Oden Salomos in (proto-)orthodoxen Kreisen ist kaum
bekannt. Immerhin findet sich ein Zitat von Ode 19,6–7a in den *Divinae Institutiones*

2.2.6 Der Judasbrief

Mit dem pseudepigraphischen Judasbrief möchte eine christliche
Gruppierung ihre Glaubensidentität gegenüber häretischen Strö-
mungen—wohl in ihrer Mitte oder ihrer unmittelbaren Nähe—sichern.
Dabei nimmt der Text argumentativ v.a. auf die Tradition Bezug:
heilige Schriften Israels, aus denen aber zu diesem Zeitpunkt offensichtlich noch ein Text wie Henoch nicht bewusst ausgegrenzt ist,
und damit verbundene Auslegungstraditionen. Christologie und
Eschatologie sind eng miteinander verwoben. Der Herr wird mit seinen Engeln zum Gericht erscheinen, sich gegenüber der Gemeinde
barmherzig zeigen, die Gegner aber bestrafen. Wie die Ansichten
dieser Gegner konkret aussahen, ist in der Forschung bis heute zumindest im Detail umstritten. Dies liegt daran, dass die Häresie, die im
Judasbrief bekämpft wird, mit sehr allgemeinen Termini umschrie-
ben wird. Das wiederum macht diesen Text offen und anwendbar
für verschiedene Situationen.

Die apologetischen und theologischen Interessen des Briefes liegen
somit durchaus auf einer Linie mit denen, die sich zumindest in einigen anderen Texten des Manuskriptes gezeigt haben. Daneben bestehen enge Verbindungen zu 2Petr, die sogar darauf schließen lassen,
dass Letzterer von Jud literarisch abhängig sein dürfte.[71] Schließlich
zeigt die hier überlieferte Textform verglichen mit anderen Zeugen
möglicherweise bewusst gesetzte Tendenzen auf christologischer
Ebene:[72]

(1) Die sicherlich vom christologischen Standpunkt her interessan-
teste (und auch bekannteste) Variante im Text des Judasbriefes auf
P.Bodm. VII findet sich in V. 5:[73] Während die kritischen Ausgaben

---

des Laktanz (4,12,1–3). In der *Synopsis* des Athanasius von Alexandrien wie auch in
der *Stichometrie* des Nikephoros von Konstantinopel werden die Oden Salomos unter
den Antilegomena des Alten Testaments aufgeführt. Dagegen werden verschiedene
Oden Salomos in der gnostischen *Pistis Sophia* zitiert, was allerdings nicht bedeutet,
dass sie selbst als gnostisch zu bezeichnen wären. Weiterführend M. Lattke, *Oden
Salomos* (1995) 7–15.

[71] Hierzu ausführlich z.B. T.J. Kraus, *Sprache, Stil und historischer Ort des zweiten
Petrusbriefes* (WUNT II 136; Tübingen 2001) 368–376, sowie die dort zitierte Literatur.

[72] Hierzu weiterführend die ausführliche Analyse von Nicklas, "Der lebendige
Text".

[73] Dieser Vers gehört zu den textkritisch schwierigsten Stellen des gesamten Neuen
Testaments. Seine Probleme sollen hier nicht diskutiert werden. Weiterführend aber
z.B. C.D. Osburn, "The Text of Jude 5," *Bib.* 62 (1981) 107–115; B.M. Metzger,
A Textual Commentary on the Greek New Testament (Stuttgart ²1994) 657–658.

hier Ὑπομνῆσαι δὲ ὑμᾶς βούλομαι, εἰδότας *ὑμᾶς πάντα ὅτι ὁ κύριος ἅπαξ λαὸν ἐκ γῆς Αἰγύπτου σώσας τὸ δεύτερον τοὺς μὴ πιστεύσαντας ἀπώλεσεν* („Ich will euch aber, obwohl ihr alles wisst, daran erinnern, dass der Herr, nachdem er das Volk ein für alle Mal aus dem Land Ägypten befreit hatte, diejenigen, die nicht glaubten, beim zweiten Mal vernichtete . . .“), bietet *P.Bodm.* VII Υπομνησαι δε υμας βουλομαι ειδοτας *απαξ παντας οτι θ(εο)ς Χρ(ιστο)ς λαον εκ γης Αιγυπτου σωσας το δευτερον τους μη πιστευσαντας απωλεσεν* („Ich will euch aber, die ihr ein für alle Mal alles wisst, daran erinnern, dass der Gott Christus, nachdem er das Volk aus dem Land Ägypten befreit hatte, diejenigen, die nicht glaubten, beim zweiten Mal vernichtete . . .“). Für die Frage nach der christologischen Tendenz des Textes ist natürlich die Lesart „der Gott Christus" entscheidend, die sich nur in diesem Textzeugen findet.[74] Christus handelt hier nicht nur präexistenziell, er ist hier mit Gott gleichgesetzt, eine Lesart, die in ihrer Bedeutung als monarchianistisch, d.h. nicht mehr zwischen Vater und Sohn differenzierend, verstanden werden kann.[75] Das inhaltliche Gewicht dieser Variante sollte nicht unterschätzt werden: Wenn in V. 5 explizit Christus und Gott gleichgesetzt werden, so wirkt sich dies nicht nur auf den unmittelbaren Kontext der VV. 5–6 aus, die vom gleichen Subjekt abhängig sind, dann beeinflusst diese Variante die Bedeutung offeneren christologischen Aussagen im Rest des Briefes. Wenn im Folgenden vom κύριος die Rede ist, muss—zumindest für den Text von *P.Bodm.* V—nicht mehr gefragt werden, ob hier der präexistente Christus oder Gott der Vater gemeint ist: Beide sind ja als identisch angesehen.

(2)　Eine zweite, weniger auffällige Variante könnte man auch in V. 25 entdecken: Der Text von *P.Bodm.* V lautet hier: μονω θεω ημων αυτω δοξα κρατος τιμη δια Ιησου Χριστου του κυριου ημων αυτω δοξα και μεγαλωσυνη και νυν και εις τους παντας αιωνας αμην („unserem einzigen Gott—ihm sei Herrlichkeit, Macht und Ehre durch Jesus Christus unseren Herrn. Ihm sei Herrlichkeit und Erhabenheit jetzt und in alle Ewigkeit. Amen"). Anders als im Text der kritischen Ausgaben wird hier zwar nicht Christus mit Gott gleichgesetzt, ihm aber kommen gleiche bzw. ähnliche Epitheta zu wie Gott selbst.

---

[74] Siehe auch die Übersicht bei C. Landon, *A Text-Critical Study of the Epistle of Jude* (JSNT.S 135; Sheffield 1996) 70–77.

[75] Vgl. auch Landon, *Text-Critical Study*, 75.

Zwar ließe sich vor allem die so wichtige Lesart (1) auch auf andere Weise erklären, so z.B. als Schreibfehler für θεοῦ χριστός[76] oder als Kontamination der Lesarten Ἰησοῦς und ὁ θεός.[77] Vielleicht spricht ja auch die Doppelung des αὐτῷ δόξα dafür, dass hier irgendwann eine Parablepsis ins Spiel gekommen sein könnte. Da sich allerdings auch in den beiden Petrusbriefen Varianten mit ähnlicher Tendenz finden lassen, spricht u.E. doch einiges für eine bewusste Tendenz der Textgestaltung durch Schreiber B (oder seine entsprechende[n] Vorlage[n]).[78]

2.2.7 Melitos Paschahomilie

Melito (2. Hälfte des 2. Jh.s), laut Eusebius von Caesarea (h.e. 5,24,2–8) Bischof von Sardes/Lydien, verfasste seine Paschahomilie, die durch zwei griechische Papyri, einige koptische, z.T. fragmentarische Manuskripte sowie eine lateinische Übersetzung bezeugt ist, wohl zwischen 160 und 170 n.Chr. möglicherweise nach einer Jerusalemreise, in der er sich Gewissheit über den Kanon des Alten Testaments verschafft haben soll (so Hieronymus, vir. ill. 24).[79]

Der Text der Homilie lässt sich folgendermaßen gliedern: Nach einem hymnischen Prolog mit Hinweis auf die Lesung von Ex 12 (Kap. 1–10) wird die Lesung vom alttestamentlichen Pascha interpretiert (Kap. 11–45). Kapitel 46–65 thematisieren die Vorbereitung des christlichen Pascha im Alten Testament. Ziel der Homilie ist die Darstellung des neutestamentlichen Pascha, der Vollzug des Paschaopfers Christi (Kapitel 66–105).[80] Zwar nimmt das Pascha des Alten Testaments eine große Rolle ein, die zentrale Figur des Textes aber ist Christus.[81] Gottes Geschichte mit Israel wird als Typologie des

---

[76] So die Vermutung bei Metzger, *Textual Commentary*, 657.

[77] So z.B. A. Vögtle, *Der Judasbrief. Der zweite Petrusbrief* (EKK XXII; Zürich—Neukirchen-Vluyn 1994) Anm. 31/39.

[78] So auch Landon, *Text-Critical Study*, 75. Zur Charakterisierung von Tendenzen konkreter Schreiber vgl. außerdem weiterführend J.R. Royse, "Scribal Tendencies in the Transmission of the Text of the New Testament," in: *The Text of the New Testament in Contemporary Research. Essays on the* Status Quaestionis (ed. B.D. Ehrman—M.W. Holmes; StD 46; Grand Rapids 1995) 239–252, sowie die dort angegebene Literatur.

[79] Zu Melito vgl. z.B. M. Frenschkowski, Art. "Meliton von Sardes," *BBKL* V (1993) 1219–1223.

[80] Zur Gliederung vgl. H.R. Drobner, "Der Aufbau der Paschapredigt Melitos von Sardes," *ThGl* 80 (1990) 205–207.

[81] So auch D.F. Winslow, "The Polemical Christology of Melito of Sardis," *StPatr* 17,2 (1982) 765–776, bes. 765.

im Neuen Testament Geschilderten verstanden. Dabei wird—möglicherweise aufgrund von Kontroversen mit Markioniten oder gnostischen Gruppierungen[82]—zwar regelmäßig das Alte Testament zitiert, der Text aber weist z.B. in seiner Rede vom „Gottesmord" (Kap. 72–92) klar antijüdische Tendenzen auf.[83] Melito betont, dass der inkarnierte Christus identisch ist mit dem, der bereits im Alten Testament am Werk ist. Christus ist Gott und Vater aller Dinge. Dies zeigt sich auch daran, dass Melito Attribute und Aktivitäten Christi auf Gott anwenden kann und umgekehrt.[84] Bedeutsam aber scheint v.a. die apologetische Funktion der christologischen Aussagen Melitos. Einerseits wird—gegen mögliche gnostische Gegner?—die Realität des Leidens Christi im Fleisch betont, andererseits Christus— gegen markionistische Tendenzen?—als der Herr der Geschichte gezeichnet, der sich schon im Alten Testament als solcher geäußert hat.[85]

Für die Einbettung in das Gesamt des vorliegenden Codex aber ist nicht nur die Christologie Melitos oder seine Wertschätzung des Alten Testaments (wenn auch aus antijüdischer Perspektive) bedeutsam: Immerhin zeigt der Text auch intertextuelle Verbindungen zu Jud und 1–2Petr, so eine mögliche Parallele zwischen Kapitel 12 (ασπιλον αμνον και αμωμον) und 44 (τιμιως αμωμος αμνος) und 1Petr 1,19 (τιμιω αιματι ως αμνου αμωμου και ασπιλου χριστου). Kapitel 96 spricht von Christus als δεσποτης, ein Titel, der im Neuen Testament nur in Judas 4 und 2Petr 2,1 begegnet.[86] Immerhin existiert mit MS Crosby-Schøyen 193 ein weiteres Beispiel eines antiken Codex, in dem Melitos Pascha-Homilie und 1Petr miteinander verbunden wurden.[87] Aber: Genügt dieses zweite Beispiel und reichen die

---

[82] Vgl. z.B. S.G. Hall, *Melito of Sardis on Pascha* (Oxford 1979) xli.

[83] Hierzu weiterführend I. Angerstorfer, *Melito und das Judentum* (Regensburg 1985).

[84] So B.D. Ehrman, *The Orthodox Corruption of Scripture. The Effect of Early Christological Controversies on the Text of the New Testament* (New York—Oxford 1993) 87. Winslow, "Melito," 767 allerdings betont, dass diese Aussagen als „more incidental than . . . intentional" seien und Melito nicht als Modalist im klassischen Sinne verstanden werden dürfe.

[85] Winslow, "Melito," 771–772, allerdings macht deutlich, dass es Melito in der konkreten Situation seiner Predigt offensichtlich nicht um antignostische oder antimarkionitische Polemik ging. Sein Text aber konnte natürlich in dieser Richtung verwendet und ausgewertet werden.

[86] Siehe allerdings auch Lk 13,25 in 𝔓[75].

[87] Zu diesem Codex weiterführend die Edition von J.E. Goehring (Hg.), *The*

Verbindungen aus, um von einer bewussten Zusammenstellung dieser Texte zu sprechen?

Als verbindende Elemente zwischen beiden Codices könnten die etwa gleiche Größe, die Tatsache, dass sowohl 1Petr wie auch die Paschahomilie des Melito auf beiden Texten begegnen, sowie der gemeinsame Fundort angeführt werden. Allerdings zeigen sich auch Unterschiede: Dass beide Texte im Zusammenhang mit den *Dishna Papers* gefunden wurden, heißt zumindest, wenn J.M. Robinsons These zutrifft, dass diese Texte aus der Bibliothek einer pachomianischen Mönchsgemeinschaft entstammen,[88] noch nicht, dass sie auch im gleichen Kontext entstanden sein müssen. Immerhin scheint die Paschahomilie Melitos in Ägypten ein recht hohes Ansehen genossen zu haben, wie die Tatsache nahe legt, dass der Text inzwischen neun Mal in Ägypten belegt ist.[89] Wichtig aber ist auch, dass MS Crosby-Schøyen 193 die Texte in koptischer und nicht in griechischer Sprache wie *Bodmer Miscellani* überliefert sind. Vor allem aber zeigen sich bei genauerer Betrachtung gerade an dem einen Punkt der vorgeblichen Übereinstimmung deutliche Unterschiede:

(1) Der Text des 1Petr im MS Crosby-Schøyen 193 unterscheidet sich „teilweise ganz beträchtlich"[90] von dem in *Bodmer Miscellani*, was eindeutig nicht nur an der größeren Sorgfalt des Schreibers der ersteren Handschrift liegt.

Crosby-Schøyen-Codex MS 193 in the Schøyen Collection (CSCO 521 Subsidia 95; Louvain 1990).

[88] Weiterführend J.M. Robinson, "The Discovering and Marketing of Coptic Manuscripts: The Nag Hammadi Codices and the Bodmer Papyri," in: *The Roots of Egyptian Christianity* (ed. B.A. Pearson—J.E. Goehring; Studies in Antiquity and Christianity; Philadelphia 1986) 2–25; Id., "The First Christian Monastic Library," in: *Coptic Studies. Acts of the Third International Congress of Coptic Studies. Warsaw, 20–25 August, 1984* (ed. W. Godlewski; Warschau 1990) 371–378; Id., *The Pachomian Monastic Library at the Chester Beatty Library and the Bibliothèque Bodmer* (The Institute for Antiquity and Christianity. The Claremont Graduate School. Occasional Papers 19; Claremont 1990). Darüber hinaus vgl. auch B. Van Elderen, "Early Christian Libraries," in: *The Bible as Book. The Manuscript Tradition* (ed. J.L. Sharpe—K. Van Kampen; London 1998) 45–59, bes. 50–56.

[89] Weiterführend J.E. Goehring—W.W. Willis, "*On the Passover* by Melito of Sardis," *The Crosby-Schøyen-Codex MS 193 in the Schøyen Collection* (ed. J.E. Goehring; CSCO 521 Subsidia 95; Louvain 1990) 3–79, bes. 3.

[90] H.-G. Bethge, "1Petr in Crosby-Schøyen-Codex (Ms. 193 Schøyen Collection)," *ZNW* 84 (1993) 255–267, bes. 259. So auch W.H. Willis, "The Letter of Peter (1Peter). Coptic text, translation, notes and variant readings," *The Crosby-Schøyen-Codex MS 193 in the Schøyen Collection* (ed. J.E. Goehring; CSCO 521 Subsidia 95; Louvain 1990) 137–215, bes. 137.

(2) Offensichtlich war auch die Stellung des 2. Petrusbriefes in der Gruppe, in der MS Crosby-Schøyen 193 entstand, eine andere als die desselben Textes in *Bodmer Miscellani*: Dies wird durch die Überschrift sowie Subscriptio ⲡⲉⲡⲓⲥⲧⲟⲗⲏ ⲙ̄ⲡⲉⲧⲣⲟⲥ („der Brief des Petrus"—gemeint ist 1Petr) im ersteren Codex nahe gelegt: Ein zweiter, möglicherweise kanonischer Petrusbrief ist hier offensichtlich—anders als in *Bodmer Miscellani*—nicht bekannt oder anerkannt.[91]

2.2.8 *Das Hymnusfragment*
Othmar Perler schlug vor, das unidentifizierte Fragment eines Hymnus Melito zuzuschreiben—damit entstünde natürlich eine sehr enge Verbindung zur vorangehenden Schrift.[92] Vorsichtiger dagegen ist A. Stewart-Sykes, der aus der Tatsache, dass das Fragment in *Bodmer Miscellani* direkt auf Melito folgt und von derselben Schreiberhand stammt, nur schließt, dass zwischen beiden Texten früh ein Zusammenhang gesehen wurde.[93] Wie auch immer zu entscheiden ist: Dies führt u.E. zurück auf eine Spur, die sich bereits bei den beiden Psalmen aufgetan hat: Möglicherweise gehören der Melito-Text wie auch der nachfolgende Hymnus innerhalb des Codex enger zusammen, als dies für andere Texte gilt. Vielleicht wurden sie bereits aus einer Sammlung, die eventuell das Thema Ostern (und damit zusammenhängend Taufe) hatte, gemeinsam übernommen.

---

[91] Vgl. Bethge, "1Petr," 260. Zum 1. Petrusbrief in MS Crosby-Schøyen 193 vgl. Willis, The "Letter of Peter," 135–215.

[92] Vgl. O. Perler, *Ein Hymnus zur Ostervigil von Meliton?* (*Papyrus Bodmer XIII*) (Freiburg/CH 1960). Darüber hinaus stellt Perler (87) Verknüpfungen mit 1Petr her: „Gemeinsam ist ihm [1Petr] mit unserem Fragment und der ihm vorausgehenden Homilie Melitons das hymnische Element . . ., die Verbindung von Predigt und liturgischem Text, beide in ähnlichem Stil durch denselben Liturgen verfaßt, endlich die Gegenüberstellung jener, denen Christus infolge ihres Unglaubens zum Stein des Anstoßes wurde, und der von ihm zu seinem Volke Auserwählten, ‚damit sie seine Großtaten verkünden' (2,10). Diese und weitere Berührungen mit der Homilie offenbaren eine formal und inhaltlich bereits stark geprägte, gottesdienstliche Überlieferung."

[93] Vgl. A. Stewart-Sykes, *The Lamb's High Feast. Melito*, Peri Pascha *and the Quartodecoman Paschal Liturgy at Sardis* (VigChr.S 42; Leiden—Boston—Köln 1998) 180: "The fact that this fragment follows *Peri Pascha* in the manuscript, that it is in the same hand, and that it ends the collection, implies that it may have been connected with the *Peri Pascha* early in its history; Eusebius' source might likewise have believed this work to be part of *Peri Pascha*, but this belief implies neither Melito's authorship nor a Quartodeciman background." Weitergehende Folgerungen zur Einordnung des Hymnus, den das Fragment bezeugt, in eine quartodecimanische Liturgie finden sich ibid., 199–200.

2.2.9 *Die Petrinen*

Tatsächlich bestehen intertextuelle Verbindungen zwischen den beiden kanonischen Petrusbriefen und den bisher besprochenen Werken des Codex *Bodmer Miscellani*. Auch für einen flüchtigen Leser erkennbar sind in jedem Fall die Verknüpfungen zwischen 1Petr und Ps 33 wie auch die zwischen 2Petr und Jud. Die intertextuellen Verbindungen aller anderen Texte zu 1–2 Petr sind u.E. zu wenig deutlich, als dass sie wahrscheinlich machen könnten, dass diese deswegen bewusst mit 1–2 Petr zusammengestellt wurden.

Sicherlich lassen sich auch einige der Themen, die in den bisherigen Texten des Codex auftauchten, auch in 1Petr und 2Petr wiederfinden: So befinden sich die Empfänger des pseudepigraphischen 1. Petrusbriefes offensichtlich in einer äußert kritischen Situation, sind einem hohen Leidensdruck (möglicherweise im Rahmen von Verfolgungen) ausgesetzt, wie schon die 12malige Verwendung des Wortes πάσχειν signalisiert.[94] Eines der entscheidenden Themen des 1.Petrusbriefes ist die Taufe (1Petr 1,3.18.23; 3,21),[95] durch die die christliche Existenz erneuert wird. Dies zeigt sich im Gegenüber zur Welt. Sicherlich können in beiden Texten apologetische Tendenzen sichergestellt werden—aber in welchem an ein größeres Publikum gerichteten Brief des Neuen Testaments wäre dies nicht der Fall? Natürlich spielen in beiden Texten auch christologische Themen eine Rolle—aber in welchem Werk des Neuen Testament tun sie dies nicht?

Auf zweierlei Ebenen gibt die Überlieferung des 1. und 2. Petrusbriefs in *P.Bodm.* VIII aber doch die Chance, mögliche Interessen, die die Niederschrift der Texte bestimmten, wahrzunehmen:

(1) Interessant ist die Tatsache, dass an den Rand von *P.Bodm.* VIII anders als allen anderen Texten des Codex Marginalien eingetragen sind.

Diese lauten folgendermaßen:[96]

  (i) 1Petr 1,15 (S. 4, Z. 8)   Über die Heiligkeit
  (ii) 1Petr 1,22 (S. 5, Z. 15)   Über die Reinheit

---

[94] So auch U. Schnelle, *Einleitung in das Neue Testament* (Göttingen ³1999) 417.

[95] Zur Taufe im 1Petr vgl. z.B. F. Schröger, *Gemeinde im 1. Petrusbrief* (Passau 1981) 31–54.

[96] Listen finden sich neben der Erstedition auch bei Wiefel, "Kanongeschichtliche Erwägungen," 301 und Grunewald—Junack, *Das Neue Testament,* 21.

(iii)	1Petr 2,5 (S. 7, Z. 9)	Über die heilige Priesterschaft
(iv)	1Petr 2,9 (S. 8, Z. 5–8)	Über das auserwählte Geschlecht, die königliche Priesterschaft, den heiligen Stamm, das Eigentumsvolk
(v)	1Petr 3,18 (S. 15, Z. 6–8)	Über den Tod im Fleisch und das Lebendigmachen und die Eingeschlossenen
(vi)	1Petr 4,1 (S. 16, Z. 3–4)	Über das Leiden Christi im Fleisch
(vii)	1Petr 4,6 (S. 17, Z. 6)	Über das Fleisch
(viii)	1Petr 4,8 (S. 17, Z. 11)	Über die Liebe
(ix)	1Petr 4,19 (S. 19, Z. 10)	Über Gott den Schöpfer
(x)	2Petr 2,1 (S. 27, Z. 13f.)	Über die falschen Lehrer
(xi)	2Petr 2,14 (S. 30, Z. 12)	Über die Kinder des Fluchs
(xii)	2Petr 3,3 (S. 33, Z. 2)	Über die Spötter
(xiii)	2Petr 3,14 (S. 35, Z. 12f.)	Über den Frieden

Diese Marginalien sind keineswegs gleichmäßig über den Text von 1 und 2Petr verteilt. Folgen sie einem bestimmten Prinzip? In jedem Fall nehmen sie ein Schlagwort aus dem jeweiligen Text des Verses, an dessen Rand sie notiert sind, auf. Nur einige Male kann dabei ein Bezug zu einem längeren Abschnitt hergestellt werden.

So entsteht der Eindruck, dass hier nicht Zwischenüberschriften vorliegen, die als Gliederungssignale interpretiert werden wollen, sondern dass meist nur das bzw. ein Thema oder Begriff eines einzelnen Satzes oder Kurzabschnitts interessiert und hervorgehoben wird (so z.B. [i] nur in Bezug auf 1Petr 1,15–16; [ii] nur auf 1Petr 1,22; [iii] dagegen könnte sogar bis 2,10 bezogen werden, ab 2,9 begegnet aber schon [iv]; [v] nur in Bezug zu 1Petr 3,18; [vi] nur zu 1Petr 4,1 u.a.).

Tatsächlich tauchen hier mehrfach Fragen der „Fleischlichkeit" (etwa des Leidens Christi) (v, vi, vii) auf. Aber auch das Leben des von Gott erwählten Volkes gegenüber von Häretikern (i, viii, x, xi, xii) wie auch Dinge, die mit den bisherigen im Codex vermuteten Linien nichts zu tun haben, werden thematisiert.

(2)   Zumindest an zwei Stellen begegnen erneut „Singulärlesarten" von christologischer Relevanz. So bietet 1Petr 5,1 die Lesart θεου

für Χριστου[97] und wird in 2Petr 1,2 durch das Weglassen der Konjunktion καί zwischen den Wendungen τοῦ θεοῦ ἡμῶν und σωτῆρος Ἰησοῦ Χριστοῦ ein Text erzeugt, in dem von unserem Gott, dem Retter Jesus Christus, die Rede ist.[98] Da beide Lesarten dieselbe Tendenz wie die im Judasbrief festgestellten aufweisen, könnte man—mit einiger Vorsicht—Schreiber B die Tendenz zur Betonung einer hohen Christologie, in der Jesus Christus mit Gott gleichgesetzt wird, unterstellen.

3. Fazit

Innerhalb der im Codex *Bodmer Miscellani* gesammelten Schriften lässt sich u.E. weder ein allen Texten gemeinsames signifikantes Formelement, noch ein gemeinsamer Sitz im Leben oder ein dominantes, alle verbindendes Thema entdecken. Sicherlich wird in vielen Fällen eine hohe Christologie bezeugt, die Göttlichkeit Jesu (bei gleichzeitigem Festhalten an seiner Fleischlichkeit) betont. Viele der hier gesammelten Texte lassen sich als polemisch-apologetisch, mit antihäretischem Charakter beschreiben. Viele der hier gesammelten Themen hängen eng mit Fragen zusammen, die proto-orthodoxe Kreise in Auseinandersetzung mit aus ihrer Sicht „häretischen" Gruppierungen, z.B. verschiedenen Formen von Gnostikern, interessieren konnten. Zwar lassen sich die Texte nicht einmal auf diesen kleinen gemeinsamen Nenner bringen, lässt sich doch die 11. Ode Salomos nur schwer als „apologetisch" einordnen.

Vergleicht man das Gesamt von *Codex Bodmer Miscellani* mit anderen Sammelcodices—zum größten Teil aus demselben umfangreichen Fund—, so ergibt sich für ihn also eine Mittelstellung zwischen Codices, deren Texte ganz offensichtlich unter einem die Einzeltexte recht eng verknüpfenden leitenden Thema verzahnt sind, und solchen, bei denen keinerlei innerer Zusammenhang erkennbar ist.

Zu ersteren gehört z.B. der Mississippi Coptic Codex II + *P.Bodm.* XXII, der Materialien, die mit dem Propheten Jeremija verbunden sind,

---

[97] So auch S. Kubo, *P⁷² and the Codex Vaticanus* (StD 27; Salt Lake City 1965) 12.86.

[98] Hierzu siehe auch Ehrman, *Orthodox Corruption*, 85–86.

zusammenstellt (Jer 40,3–52,34; Klagelieder; Brief des Jeremija; Baruch), der sog. „Codex Visionum" (*P.Bodm.* XXIX-XXXVIII) oder der Crosby-Schøyen-Codex MS 193 mit Materialien, die alle mit Pascha/Ostern verbunden sind (Melito, *Peri Pascha*; 2Makk 5,27–7,41; 1Petr, Jona und einige nicht zuzuordnende Fragmente).[99] Demgegenüber besteht bei einigen anderen Sammelcodices keinerlei innerer Zusammenhang zwischen den einzelnen Texten, so z.B. im *Codex Miscellani* (P.Barcelonensis inv. 149–61 + *P.Duke* inv. L1 [ex P.Rob. inv. 201]) mit Ciceros *In Catilinam*, einem Psalmus Responsorius (beide Latein), einem griechischen liturgischen Fragment und Alcestis (Latein) oder in einem Codex (*P.Bodm.* XXVII + XLV–XLVII), der Thucydides mit Susanna, Daniel und moralischen Ermahnungen zusammenstellt.[100] Erst im Jahr 2003 ediert wurde zudem der Codex *P.Mich.* 3520 + 6868(a), der aufgrund seines Inhalts Kohelet, 1Joh und 2Petr in fayumischem Koptisch vom Herausgeber als *Biblical Miscellany* charakterisiert wird.[101]

Und auch ein weiterer Punkt sollte nicht vergessen werden: Wäre es dem bzw. den Sammler(n), die hinter *Bodmer Miscellani* standen, wirklich in erster Linie darum gegangen, Texte unter einem gemeinsamen, in einer konkreten Auseinandersetzung mit Gegnern brennenden Thema zusammenzustellen, stellt sich doch die Frage, warum sie nicht Texte aus den Evangelien oder auch dem *Corpus Paulinum* heranzogen.[102] Alle hier gesammelten Texte haben doch zumindest eines gemeinsam: Sie lassen sich als Schriften einordnen, die entweder nie kanonisiert wurden oder nur mit großen Hindernissen in den

---

[99] Zu möglichen Verbindungen zwischen Codex *Bodmer Miscellani* und diesem Codex siehe die Diskussion oben.

[100] Die Beispiele stammen alle aus dem selben Fund der sog. *Dishna Papers*, die dann u.a. als Bodmer Papyri bekannt wurden. Eine Übersicht bietet J.M. Robinson, "The Manuscript's History and Codicology", in: *The Crosby-Schøyen Codex MS 193 in the Schøyen Collections* (ed. J.E. Goehring; CSCO 521 Subsidia 85; Louvain 1990) XVIII–XLVII, bes. XXVIII–XXX.

[101] Vgl. H.-M. Schenke in Zusammenarbeit mit R. Kasser, *Papyrus Michigan 3520 und 6868(a). Ecclesiastes, Erster Johannesbrief und Zweiter Petrusbrief in fayumischem Dialekt* (TU 151; Berlin—New York 2003) 3.

[102] Natürlich müssen nicht alle Evangelien unseres heutigen Neuen Testaments oder auch nicht die paulinischen Briefe in allen christlichen Gemeinschaften der Antike den gleichen Rang eingenommen haben. Allerdings erschiene es doch eigenartig, wenn eine Sammlung von textlichen Belegen für eine konkrete Situation, die Argumente in einer apologetisch geführten Debatte erfordert, keinen einzigen dieser Texte enthielte.—Hier könnte auch erinnert werden, dass auch einige Texte von $\mathfrak{P}^{75}$ christologische Tendenzen aufweisen (vgl. M.C. Parsons, "A Christological Tendency in P[75]," *JBL* 105 [1986] 463–479), die vergleichbar mit denen sind, welche in *Bodmer Miscellani* zu finden sind. Sind von hier aus eventuell Verbindungslinien zwischen beiden Manuskripten zu ziehen?

Kanon christlicher Heiliger Schriften aufgenommen wurden, wo sie wiederum nie eine zentrale Rolle einnahmen. Wurden die Texte aus Gründen der Erbauung zusammengestellt? Vielleicht liegt der Sammlung einfach ein Interesse an christlich-jüdischer Literatur, die nicht allzu leicht zugänglich war, zugrunde. Der oder die Sammler(in)[103] oder Gruppe, in der der Codex entstand, ist dann gebildeten, sicherlich der entstehenden ägyptischen kirchlichen Proto-Orthodoxie nahe stehenden Kreisen zuzuordnen.[104] Diese(r) gebildete Sammler(in) oder (wahrscheinlicher) Kreis von gebildeten Christen muss in der Lage gewesen sein, an verschiedene Texte (eventuell durch Austausch) o.a. zu gelangen[105] und diese durch Schreiber, die mit wichtigen Konventionen antiker christlicher Buchproduktion (z.B. die Verwendung des Codexformats, des Staurogramms oder von *Nomina Sacra*) vertraut waren, zusammenstellen zu lassen.[106]

Ein wichtiger Punkt im Zusammenhang mit der in Codex *Bodmer Miscellani* bezeugten Sammlung ist vielleicht auch der Verweis auf die Begrenztheit der Möglichkeiten, an bestimmte Bücher zu kommen. Sicherlich verbreiteten sich, wie z.B. 𝔓[52] zeigt, christliche Schriften z.T. in überraschend schnellem Tempo.[107] Andererseits darf nicht damit gerechnet werden, dass in allen

---

[103] Das Feminin ist bewusst angefügt, da z.B. *P.Oxy.* LXIII 4365 auch mindestens eine Frau als Sammlerin von Büchern bezeugt.

[104] Eine genauere Zuordnung zu einer spezifischen Gruppe scheint uns kaum sicher möglich zu sein. Die meisten nachweisbaren monastischen Bewegungen sind erst nach dem 3. Jh. unserer Zeitrechnung belegbar, und die ersten Jh.e des christlichen Ägypten liegen zu sehr im Dunkeln, als dass die Quellenlage eine genauere Zuweisung des Mosaiksteinchens *Codex Bodmer Miscellani* erlauben würde. Vielleicht könnten zumindest vorsichtig Verbindungen zu Kreisen angenommen werden, die sich—eventuell im großen Kontext der Auseinandersetzung mit alexandrinischer Theologie (z.B. des Origenes)—für z.T. später apokryph gewordene Texte christlich asiatischer Herkunft interessierten. Solche Gruppierungen lassen sich auch anderweitig aufgrund der koptischen Überlieferung von Texten wie den *Paulusakten* oder der *Epistula Apostolorum* wahrscheinlich machen.

[105] Ein höchst interessantes Zeugnis, das Einblick in die Praxis antiker Buchleihe zum gegenseitigen Austausch bietet, ist *P.Oxy.* LXIII 4365 (4. Jh.n.Chr.), ein christlicher Privatbrief aus Oxyrhynchus, der—an eine Frau gerichtet—um die Ausleihe eines „Esdras" (4Esra?) bittet, nachdem der bzw. die Briefschreiber(in) eine „kleine Genesis" (wohl das Jubiläenbuch) ausgeliehen hat. Hierzu weiterführend mit ausführlicher Diskussion der Literatur T.J. Kraus, "Bücherleihe im 4. Jh.n.Chr. P.Oxy. LXIII 4365—ein Brief auf Papyrus und die gegenseitige Leihe von apokryph gewordener Literatur," *Biblos* 50 (2000) 285–296.

[106] So letztlich auch das Fazit von Haines-Eitzen, *Guardians*, 104, die von „private channels of text transmission" spricht.

[107] Vgl. hierzu etwa die Beispiele bei C.H. Roberts, *Manuscript, Society, and Belief in Early Christian Egypt* (SchL 1977; London 1979) 23–25.

Gemeinden bzw. Gemeinschaften große Zugriffsmöglichkeiten auf verschiedenste Texte antiker christlicher Literatur bestanden. Dies lässt sich z.B. anhand antiker Bibliothekskataloge aus Oberägypten genauer erweisen.[108] Hier zeigt sich zweierlei: Einerseits war offensichtlich selbst in spätantiken Bibliotheken mönchischer Gemeinschaften Ägyptens nicht einmal immer der gesamte „Kanon" heute biblischer Schriften vorhanden (so z.B. entsprechend *O.IFAO* 13315, der Katalog der Bibliothek des Klosters St. Elias vom Berg [wohl in der Diözese Kûs, etwa 50 km nördlich von Luksor; möglicherweise 5. Jh.]).[109] Andererseits werden immer wieder auch außerkanonische Texte erwähnt, die z.t. offensichtlich aus erbaulichen Gründen gelesen (z.B. *P.Vindob.* G 26015; 7.–8. Jh.),[110] z.T. möglicherweise in die Nähe später kanonischer Literatur gerückt wurden (z.B. die Erwähnung des Hirten des Hermas in *P.Ash.* Inv. 3; 4. Jh.).[111]

Konkretere Antworten zum Hintergrund der Entstehung des Codex *Bodmer Miscellani* sind u.E. nicht möglich bzw. sicher zu erbringen. Das Manuskript bleibt rätselhaft.

---

[108] Hierzu weiterführend die entsprechenden Zeugnisse bei C. Markschies, "Neue Forschungen zur Kanonisierung des Neuen Testaments," *Apocrypha* 12 (2001) 237–262, bes. 243–249. 262.

[109] Textedition und -erklärung: R.-G. Coquin, "Le catalogue de la bibliothèque du couvent de Saint Élie « du rocher »(Ostracon IFAO 13315)," *BIFAO* 75 (1975) 207–239. Tafel XXVIII und XXXIX.

[110] Veröffentlichung und Einführung bei H. Gerstinger, "Ein Bücherverzeichnis aus dem VII–VIII. Jh.n.Chr. im Pap. Graec.Vindob. 26015," *WSt* 50 (1932) 185–192.

[111] C.H. Roberts, "Two Oxford Papyri," *ZNW* 37 (1938) 184–188.

THE TEXT OF $\mathfrak{P}^{46}$: EVIDENCE OF THE EARLIEST "COMMENTARY" ON ROMANS?

MICHAEL W. HOLMES

The distinctive value of the Chester Beatty Papyrus II, more commonly known as $\mathfrak{P}^{46}$, as a witness to the archetype of the Pauline letter corpus has been recognized and acknowledged ever since it was first published.[1] The manuscript itself, as Zuntz observes, "is by no means a good manuscript," even though it was penned by a professional scribe and corrected (somewhat haphazardly) by an expert[2]: the mistakes, habits, and characteristics of its blundering and not always attentive scribe have been well documented.[3] Nonetheless, the *Vorlage* which lay before the scribe of $\mathfrak{P}^{46}$ preserved a text of perhaps unequaled quality; indeed, with surprising frequency it alone (or in combination with a very few others) among all extant witnesses preserves the true wording of the Pauline archetype.[4] Zuntz's characterization of $\mathfrak{P}^{46}$ as a "uniquely important manuscript" for the recovery of the text of the Pauline letters is well founded.[5]

The papyrus is, however, at least equally important for the light it sheds on the textual history of the Pauline corpus. For in addition to the many instances where it transmits the original wording, it transmits as well many secondary (or occasionally even tertiary) readings which find support in other witnesses. The presence of non-coincidental agreement in error between witnesses—what Paul Maas

---

[1] For bibliographic details consult J.K. Elliott, *A Bibliography of Greek New Testament Manuscripts* (SNTSMS 109; Cambridge ²2000) 29–30.

[2] G. Zuntz, *The Text of the Epistles. A Disquisition upon the* Corpus Paulinum (SchL 1946; London 1953) 18, 252–62.

[3] See Zuntz, *Text*, 17–23, 252–62; E.C. Colwell, "Scribal Habits in Early Papyri: A Study in the Corruption of the Text," *The Bible in Modern Scholarship* (ed. J.P. Hyatt; Nashville 1965) 370–389 (reprinted as "Method in Evaluating Scribal Habits: A Study of P⁴⁵, P⁶⁶, P⁷⁵," in: E.C. Colwell, *Studies in Methodology in Textual Criticism of the New Testament* [NTTS 9; Leiden—Grand Rapids 1969] 106–124); J.R. Royse, *Scribal Habits in Early Greek New Testament Papyri* (Ph.D. dissertation, Graduate Theological Union, Berkeley, CA 1981) 182–329.

[4] For examples see Zuntz, *Text*, 23–32, 42–43, 218.

[5] Zuntz, *Text*, 56.

termed a *Leitfehler*, or "significant error"[6]—is often more significant for analyzing the history of the transmission of a text than agreement in support of the original wording. The number and character of such readings in 𝔓⁴⁶ in conjunction with the age of the manuscript—which provides a firm *terminus ante quem* for the evidence it transmits—mean that 𝔓⁴⁶ holds a uniquely important place in the history of the transmission of the Pauline text.

In what follows I would like to focus both on a specific subgroup of "significant errors" found in 𝔓⁴⁶ and on a specific Pauline letter. That letter is Romans, which from a text-critical perspective is of particular interest for two reasons: first, the variation in its length (whether 14, 15, or 16 chapters) and second, the variation in the placement and number of the doxology and benedictions. With respect to its textual history Romans occupies a distinctive place within the Pauline corpus and thus offers special opportunities and challenges, and calls for special attention.

The specific subgroup of "significant errors" consists of readings that are supported by the bilingual manuscripts D F G, on the one hand, and one or more of the group composed of 𝔓⁴⁶, B, and 1739, on the other. The former trio are, of course, primary witnesses to the "Western" strand of the text of the Pauline letters; all three descend from a common ancestor. The other three are leading members of what Zuntz termed the "proto-Alexandrian" group of witnesses (𝔓⁴⁶ B 1739 sah boh Clem Orig).[7] Examples of this category of non-coincidental agreement in error include the following.[8]

13:1 [πᾶσα ψυχὴ ἐξουσίαις
ὑπερεχούσαις ὑποτασσέσθω]
πασα ψυχη εξουσιαις   01 A B D² Ψ
υπερεχουσαις υποτασσεσθω]

                                        6.33.104.1739.(1881) 𝔐 lat sy co
πασαις εξουσιαις   𝔓⁴⁶ᵛⁱᵈ F G it Irˡᵃᵗ Ambst
υπερεχουσαις υποτασσεσθε]

The editorial committee responsible for the United Bible Societies' *Greek New Testament* suggests that the variant is due to the adoption of "a less formal style, perhaps in order to avoid the Hebraic idiom

---

[6] See P. Maas, *Textual Criticism* (Oxford 1958) 42, with Zuntz, *Text*, 284.
[7] Zuntz, *Text*, 156.
[8] The text of the lemmas [enclosed in brackets] is that of UBS⁴/NA²⁷.

involved in πᾶσα ψυχή," (though one might wonder why the similar instance in 2:9 remains unchanged).⁹ Cranfield, closely paraphrasing Lietzmann, suggests an alternative view: "The variant . . . is an ancient but worthless reading, due no doubt to the accidental omission of ψυχή."¹⁰ Either explanation implies deliberate activity, whether it be a stylistic alteration or the conjectural restoration of sense to a text disrupted by an omission.

The variation in 13:5 is likewise deliberate:

> 13:5   [διὸ ἀνάγκη ὑποτάσσεσθαι, . . .]
> αναγκη υποτασσεσθαι]   01 A B Ψ 048.33.1739.1881 𝔐 (vg) sy co
> (και) υποτασσεσθε]   (𝔓⁴⁶) D F G it (Irˡᵃᵗ) Ambst

If the variant involved only the substitution of the imperative for the infinitive, itacism¹¹ would be a sufficient explanation, but in view of the substitution of και (in place of αναγκη) in 𝔓⁴⁶ and Irenaeus, and the parallel verb form in 13:1, some other cause—a deliberate one—must be found.

> 8:23   [. . . ἡμεῖς καὶ αὐτοὶ ἐν ἑαυτοῖς στενάζομεν
> υἱοθεσίαν ἀπεκδεχόμενοι . . .]
> υιοθεσιαν rell] omit   𝔓⁴⁶ᵛⁱᵈ D F G 614 t Ambst

8:23 offers another striking 𝔓⁴⁶/DFG agreement; Cranfield suggests that "the omission of υἱοθεσίαν . . . probably . . . reflects the presence of bewilderment in the face of the apparent inconsistency between the present tenses of vv. 14 and 16 and the future sense conveyed by ἀπεκδεχόμενοι. The omission of υἱοθεσίαν leaves τὴν ἀπολύτρωσιν τοῦ σώματος ἡμῶν as the quite straightforward object of ἀπεκδεχόμενοι."¹²

> 15:25   [νυνὶ δὲ πορεύομαι εἰς Ἰερουσαλὴμ διακονῶν τοῖς ἁγίοις.]
> διακονων]   01ᶜ A B C Ψ 33.1739.1881 𝔐

---

⁹ B.M. Metzger, *A Textual Commentary on the Greek New Testament* (Stuttgart—New York 1994) 467.

¹⁰ C.E.B. Cranfield, *A Critical and Exegetical Commentary on the Epistle to the Romans* (2 vols.; ICC; Edinburgh 1975–1979) 2.656 n. 1; H. Lietzmann, *An die Römer* (HNT 8; Tübingen ⁴1933) 112.

¹¹ For itacism see, e.g., F.T. Gignac, *A Grammar of the Greek Papyri of the Roman and Byzantine Period. Vol. I: Phonology* (Milan 1975) 191–193; E. Mayser, *Grammatik der griechischen Papyri aus der Ptolemäerzeit. Band I: Laut- und Wortlehre. 1. Teil: Einleitung und Lautlehre* (Berlin ²1970) § 14. Cf. also T.J. Kraus, "P.Vindob.G 39756 + Bodl. MS Gr. th. f. 4 [P]: Fragmente eines Codex der griechischen Petrus-Apokalypse," *BASP* 40 (2003) 45–61, here 53.

¹² Cranfield, *Romans*, 1.419 n. 1.

      διακονησων]   01*
      διακονησαι]   𝔓⁴⁶ D F G latt

In 15:25, the present participle is unexpected and ambiguous; both variants give the anticipated final sense.[13]

      15:20 [οὕτως δὲ φιλοτιμούμενον εὐαγγελίζεσθαι . . .]
        φιλοτιμούμενον]   01 A C D² Ψ 33.1739.1881 𝔐 syʰ
        φιλοτιμοῦμαι]   𝔓⁴⁶ B D* F G b syᵖ

15:20 offers another example of an altered participle, this time to a finite verb. Cranfield notes that the "rather more difficult" participle is "intrinsically better suited" to the context than the finite verb;[14] that very difficulty is sufficient cause to prompt the alteration.

      15:27 [εὐδόκησαν γὰρ καὶ ὀφειλέται εἰσὶν αὐτῶν]
        ευδοκησαν γαρ και οφειλεται]   01 A B C Ψ 33.1739.1881 𝔐
                                    vg sy co
        οφειλεται γαρ]   𝔓⁴⁶ (D—γαρ) F G it Ambst

The variant reading eliminates the awkward repetition of the opening words of v. 26 (ευδοκησαν γαρ). The placement of γαρ after οφειλεται reveals that the variant involves a deliberate change (probably for stylistic reasons), and not merely an accidental omission.

      15:31a [. . . ἐν τῇ Ἰουδαίᾳ καὶ ἡ διακονία μου ἡ εἰς Ἰερουσαλήμ . . .]
        διακονια]   𝔓⁴⁶ 01 A C D¹ Ψ 33.1739.1881 𝔐 sy co
        δωροφορια]   B D* F G it Ambst
                        – BDF §119(1): "δωροφορία (Hell.)" [= Hellenistic]
        εις]   𝔓⁴⁶ 01 A C D² Ψ 33.1611.1739.1881 𝔐
        εν]   B D* F G 1108.1505.1911.1952 *pc*

In this instance it is B, rather than 𝔓⁴⁶, that lines up with DFG. Here δωροφορια, "the bringing of a gift," looks very much like an explanatory gloss (one that specifies the precise nature of Paul's διακονια) that has worked its way into the text. That εις was replaced by εν in some witnesses is hardly a cause for surprise in view of the following reference to "the saints" (τοις αγιοις), who are obviously "in" Jerusalem. What is puzzling is the presence of the εν in B D F G, inasmuch as δωροφορια . . . εις would appear to be more natural than δωροφορια . . . εν.

---

[13] Cranfield, *Romans*, 2.771 n. 2.
[14] Cranfield, *Romans*, 2.763 n. 1.

15:13 [ὁ δὲ θεὸς τῆς ἐλπίδος πληρῶσαι ὑμᾶς πάσης χαρᾶς καὶ εἰρήνης . . .]
πληρωσαι υμας πασης χαρας και
ειρηνης]   𝔓⁴⁶ 01 A C D 1739 𝔐
πληροφορησαι υμας εν παση χαρα   B (F G—εν)
και ειρηνη]

Another instance of B lining up with FG (deserted, in this instance, by D). The variant involves not only the substitution of a less common verb (only 6 × in the NT, including Romans 14:5, and in the active voice only at 2 Tim 4:5), but also the recasting of the following clause from the genitive to the dative.[15]

6:12 [μὴ οὖν βασιλευέτω ἡ ἁμαρτία ἐν τῷ θνητῷ ὑμῶν σώματι εἰς τὸ ὑπακούειν
ταῖς ἐπιθυμίαις αὐτοῦ . . .]
(a) ταις επιθυμιαις αυτου]   𝔓⁹⁴ 01 A B C*
                                     6.81.1506.1739.1881 al lat
                                     syᵖ co (Or) Did
(b) αυτη]   𝔓⁴⁶ D F G pc b Ir^lat Tert
                                     Ambst
(c) αυτη εν ταις επιθυμιαις αυτου]   C K L P Ψ 1175.1241.2464
                                     𝔐 syʰ
(d) αυτην εν ταις επιθυμιαις αυτης] 049*² pc
(e) αυτου εν ταις επιθυμιαις αυτου] 33.1912 pc
                                     {υπακουειν] επακουειν F G}

In 6:12, the differing forms of the text reflect different interpretations of its meaning: in (a) the antecedent of αυτου is σωματι ("body"), while in (b) the antecedent of αυτη is αμαρτια ("sin"). Once again, the alteration cannot be accidental.

Also deliberate is the expansion in 16:17:

16:17 [. . . τοὺς τὰς διχοστασίας καὶ τὰ σκάνδαλα . . . ποιοῦντας, . . .]
ποιουντας]   01 A B C Ψ 33.1739.1881 𝔐 lat sy co
                                    Ambst
λεγοντας η ποιουντας]   D F G (a) m
η λεγοντας η ποιουντας]   𝔓⁴⁶

The variant in 9:26 may involve harmonization or adaptation to the following part of the verse (it is not an instance of harmonization to the LXX of Hosea 2:23 (2:25 LXX)):

[15] Cf. the similar verb shift in 15:29 (DFG only) and Col. 4:12 (where 𝔓⁴⁶ D²
𝔐 sy substitute the shorter verb for the longer verb read by 01 A B C D* F G
33 1739 al).

9:26 [καὶ ἔσται ἐν τῷ τόπῳ οὗ ἐρρέθη αὐτοῖς]
ερρεθη αυτοις] 01 A D Ψ 33.(1739).1881 𝔐 vg syʰ co
ερρεθη] B Irˡᵃᵗ ᵛⁱᵈ
(ε)αν κληθησονται] 𝔓⁴⁶ F G a b d* syᵖ

Whatever its origin or motive, it (like the others mentioned so far)
will not have been accidental.

15:22 [... ἐνεκοπτόμην τὰ πολλὰ τοῦ ἐλθεῖν ...]
τα πολλα] 01 A C Ψ 33.1739.1881 𝔐
πολλακις] 𝔓⁴⁶ B D F G 330.2400

15:22 offers a clearer case of harmonization, inasmuch as the variant πολλάκις probably reflects the wording of 1:13, ὅτι πολλάκις
προεθέμην ἐλθεῖν πρὸς ὑμᾶς.[16]

The next three examples indicate a clear link between 𝔓⁴⁶ and
DFG, but in such a way as to suggest that the 𝔓⁴⁶ reading is a
conflate one. These are:

11:1 [... μὴ ἀπώσατο ὁ θεὸς τὸν λαὸν αὐτοῦ ...]
(a) τον λαον αυτου] 01* B C 33.1739 rell vg
   syᵖ·ʰ sa bo
(b) τον λαον αυτου ον προεγνω] 01² A D [cf. 11:2]
(c) την κληρονομιαν αυτου ην προεγνω] 𝔓⁴⁶
(d) την κληρονομιαν αυτου] F G b Ambst Pel

Note how 𝔓⁴⁶ shares with FG the την κληρονομιαν, apparently an
assimilation to Ps 94:14b (93:14b LXX),[17] while it shares with 01²
A D the addition from 11:2; in all, an unusual alignment for the
earliest witness!

16:2 [προστάτις πολλῶν ἐγενήθη καὶ ἐμοῦ αὐτοῦ.]
προστατ. πολλων εγενηθη και εμου αυτου] (01, A) BCLP (Ψ pc)
   33ᵛⁱᵈ (1739.1881)
   𝔐 sy co
]και αλλων πολλων εγεν[𝔓⁴⁶
και εμου και αλλων πολλων προστατ. εγενετο] D¹
και εμου και αλλων προστατ. εγενετο] D* (F G)

In 16:2, the sequence και αλλων links 𝔓⁴⁶ with DFG, whereas the
sequence πολλων εγεν[ετο links it with the rest of the witnesses. A
similar situation obtains in 16:19b.

---

[16] Cf. Cranfield, *Romans*, 2.766.
[17] So Metzger, *Textual Commentary*, 464; Cranfield, *Romans*, 2.543 n. 1.

16:19b   [ἐφ᾽ ὑμῖν οὖν χαίρω, θέλω δὲ ὑμᾶς σοφοὺς εἶναι . . .]
       θελω δε]   01 A B C *rell*
       και θελω]   D* F G m
       και θελω δε] $\mathfrak{P}^{46}$

The examples presented above were selected because it is relatively certain that they are both (a) secondary rather than original, and (b) deliberate rather than accidental in origin. As such, they serve to raise and focus certain questions without the distraction of arguments about originality or cause of origin.

There are, of course, many additional examples that belong to this particular category of readings. These include:

(a) many minor instances of variation that are clearly secondary readings, but whose origins are probably but not demonstrably intentional.

(b) variation units where there is substantial uncertainty or disagreement as to which reading preserves the original text— indeed, many of the bracketed readings the UBS/NA text involve variants with "Western" + "proto-Alexandrian" support. Examples:

6:11   [λογίζεσθε ἑαυτοὺς [εἶναι] νεκροὺς μὲν . . . ζῶντας δὲ . . . ἐν Χριστῷ Ἰησοῦ]
       ειναι $\mathfrak{P}^{94vid}$ 01* B C 81.1506.1739.1881 *pc*
       ειναι *after* μεν   01² D¹ K L P Ψ 049 056 0142 0151 $\mathfrak{M}$ lat
       omit $\mathfrak{P}^{46vid}$ A D*ᶜ F G 33ᵛⁱᵈ *pc* Tert

3:2   [πρῶτον μὲν [γὰρ] ὅτι ἐπίστευθησαν . . .]
       πρωτον μεν γαρ οτι   01 A D² 33 $\mathfrak{M}$ syʰ co
       πρωτον μεν οτι   B D* G Ψ 81.365.1506.2464* *pc* latt syᵖ boᵐˢˢ
       πρωτον   γαρ οτι   1881 *pc*
       πρωτοι   γαρ   6.1739 Eus

4:22   [διὸ [καὶ] ἐλογίσθη αὐτῷ εἰς δικαιοσύνην]
       και   01 A C D¹ Ψ 6.33.81.1506.1739.1881 $\mathfrak{M}$ lat syʰ
       omit   B D* F G 365 *pc* b m syᵖ co

5:2   [. . . ἐσχήκαμεν [τῇ πίστει] εἰς τὴν χάριν ταύτην . . .]
       τη πιστει   01*² (A) C Ψ 33.81.365.1506.1739.1881 $\mathfrak{M}$ bo
       omit   B D F G 0220 sa Ambst

7:20   [εἰ δὲ ὃ οὐ θέλω [ἐγὼ] τοῦτο ποιῶ, . . .]
       εγω   01 A Ψ 6.33.81.1739.1881 $\mathfrak{M}$ bo Cl
       omit   B C D F G 104.1241.1506.2464 *pc* latt sa

10:20 [εὑρέθην [ἐν] τοῖς ἐμὲ ... ἐγενόμην τοῖς ἐμέ ...]

ευρεθην	01 A C D¹ Ψ 33.1739.1881 𝔐 Cl
ευρεθην εν	𝔓⁴⁶ B D* F G 1506ᵛⁱᵈ (it)
εγενομην	𝔓⁴⁶ 01 A C D¹ F G Ψ 33.1739.1881 𝔐 lat Cl
εγενομην εν	B D* 1506ᵛⁱᵈ

εν ... εν]	B D* 1506ᵛⁱᵈ
εν ... —]	𝔓⁴⁶ F G {***the text of UBS/NA!}
— ... —]	01 A C D¹ Ψ 33.1739.1881 𝔐 Cl

11:25 [... ἵνα μὴ ἦτε [παρ '] ἑαυτοῖς φρόνιμοι ...]

παρ'	01 C D 33.81.104.365.1881.2464 𝔐 b syʰ
εν	A B 630 pc
omit	𝔓⁴⁶ F G Ψ 6.1506.1739 pc lat Ambst

13:9 [... ἐν τῷ λόγῳ τούτῳ ἀνακεφαλαιοῦται [ἐν τῷ] ἀγαπήσεις ...]

εν τω	01 A D Ψ 048.33.1739.1881 𝔐 syʰ co Cl
omit	𝔓⁴⁶ᵛⁱᵈ B F G

(c) variants in which the 𝔓⁴⁶/DFG combination is joined by the Byzantine textual tradition.

Examples: (* signals a bracketed reading)

4:15 [ὁ γὰρ νόμος ὀργὴν κατεργάζεται· οὗ δὲ οὐκ ἔστιν νόμος οὐδὲ παράβασις.]

δε	01* A B C 81 104.945.1506 pc syʰᵐᵍ co
γαρ	01² D F G Ψ 365.1739.1881 𝔐 sy

In this instance, it is 1739 (which here probably preserves the text of Origen[18]) that provides the early "Alexandrian" witness that agrees with the reading of DFG (cf. 14:4 and 14:22 below).

---

[18] As J.N. Birdsall notes, the text of Romans in the exemplar from which 1739 ultimately descends "is largely derived from Origen's Commentary" (J.N. Birdsall, *A Study of MS. 1739 of the Pauline Epistles and Its Relationship to MSS. 6, 424, 1908 and M* [Ph.D. dissertation, University of Nottingham, 1959] 124). Origen's commentary (*tomoi*) was *not* extant for Romans 9 and 12:16–14:10: in these sections 1739 preserves the text of the "very ancient manuscript" (τὸ παλαιόν) from which the text of all the other Pauline letters in 1739 was copied (Zuntz, *Text*, 72). For the balance of Romans, 1739 is nearly always a witness to the lemmata and/ or the exegesis of Origen's commentary (cf. Zuntz, *Text*, 73, who lists instances where the marginal notes carefully distinguish between the reading of a lemma and the accompanying exegesis). But not always: as Birdsall observes, someone compiling a text from the lemmata and exegesis of a commentary would still need a continuous text "as a guide and a model," and in some instances the text of the guide (which almost certainly was the παλαιόν) has displaced the text of the commentary: "the outstanding instance of this is Rom. i.7 where ἐν Ῥώμῃ stands in the text in spite of the marginal note stating that neither lemma nor exegesis of Origen

9:11   [... μηδὲ πραξάντων τι ἀγαθὸν ἢ φαῦλον, ἵνα ...]

    φαυλον   01 A B 6.81.365.630.945.1506.1739.1881 *al* Or

    κακον   𝔓⁴⁶ D F G K L Ψ 049 056 0142 0151 𝔐

    cf. 2 Cor. 5:10   [... πρὸς ἃ ἔπραξεν, εἴτε ἀγαθὸν εἴτε φαῦλον.]

    φαυλον   01 C 048 0243 33.81.326.365.630.1739.(1881)
                     pc

    κακον   𝔓⁴⁶ B D F G K L P Ψ 049 056 075 0142
                     0150 0151 6.945 𝔐 Cl

9:27   [... τὸ ὑπόλειμμα σωθήσεται]

    υπολειμμα   01* A B 81.1360.1739ᶜ Eus

    καταλειμμα   𝔓⁴⁶ 01¹ D F G Ψ 6.33.104.1739*.1881 𝔐

    υποκαταλειμμα 1908

    [καταλειμμα is the reading of Isaiah 10:22 LXX.]

    εγκαταλειμμα 1506

*11:31   [... ἵνα καὶ αὐτοὶ [νῦν] ἐλεηθῶσιν ...]

    νυν   01 B D*·ᶜ 1506 *pc* bo

    υστερον   33.88.365 *pc* sa

    omit   𝔓⁴⁶ A D² F G Ψ 6.81.104.630.1739.1881 𝔐
                     latt

14:4   [δυνατεῖ γὰρ ὁ κύριος στῆσαι αὐτόν]

    κυριος   𝔓⁴⁶ 01 A B C P Ψ syᵖ co

    θεος   D F G 048.6.33.81.104.365.1506.1739.1881 𝔐
                     latt syʰ

Here too it is 1739 that provides the early Alexandrian witness, which in this case, however, is not Origen but the "very ancient manuscript" that was used where Origen's *tomoi* on Romans were not available.[19]

*14:12a   [ἆρα [οὖν] ἕκαστος ἡμῶν ...]

    αρα   B D* F G P* 6.630.1739.1881 *pc* lat

    αρα ουν   01 A C D² Ψ 0209.33 𝔐 syʰ

*14:12c   [... λόγον δώσει [τῷ θεῷ].]

    τω θεω   01 A C D L P Ψ 0209.33.81.104.1881 𝔐 lat sy co

    omit   B F G 6.630.1739.1881 *pc* r Polyc Cyp

---

attested these words" (Birdsall, *A Study of MS. 1739*, 77; differently Zuntz, *Text*, 76, who thinks that ἐν Ῥώμῃ is the result of corruption in the course of transmission). Consequently, while 1739 in general nearly always preserves (outside of those portions not extant) the text of Origen's commentary, in any specific instance we cannot be certain that it does, unless a marginal note is present to confirm the source of the reading.

[19] See Zuntz, *Text*, 72, and the previous note above.

*14:22   [σὺ πίστιν [ἣν] ἔχεις κατὰ σεαυτόν . . .]
       ην   01 A B C 048 *pc* r
       omit   D F G Ψ 6.81.104.1739.1881 𝔐 lat co

Again, it is 1739 (which here probably preserves the text of Origen) that provides the early "Alexandrian" witness.

15:14c   [πεπληρωμένοι πάσης τῆς γνώσεως, . . .]
       της   01 B P Ψ 6.1506.1739.1881 *pc* Cl
       omit   𝔓⁴⁶ A C D F G 33 𝔐

16:6   [ἀσπάσασθε Μαρίαν, . . .]
       Μαριαν   A B C P Ψ 104.365.1505.1739 *pc* co
       Μαριαμ   𝔓⁴⁶ 01 D F G 1881 𝔐

In a full examination, of course, all these would require discussion. But the examples already given in the first group above are sufficient to raise some intriguing and challenging questions.

The answer to one question raised by this set of readings is so foundational or axiomatic for any further discussion that it requires immediate attention. The question is this: are these readings that occur both in DFG and in Alexandrian witnesses such as 𝔓⁴⁶ and B the result of "Western" influence on the "proto-Alexandrian" textual tradition, or are they ancient readings that have survived in two unrelated textual traditions?

(1) The first view—that agreements between "Neutral" witnesses and "Western" witnesses represent "Western" intrusions into an otherwise pure tradition—was the view of Westcott and Hort.[20] This view is still very much alive and well today, as is clear from comments in the *Textual Commentary* published on behalf of the UBS/NA editorial committee. As one reads through the volume, one finds: 𝔓⁴⁶ (whose "proto-Alexandrian" character Zuntz indubitably established[21] occasionally characterized as a "Western" witness (see, e.g., the discussions of Rom 13:1 and 13:12); at Rom 11:1, the suggestion that the reading supported by 𝔓⁴⁶ "appears to be a Western assimilation" (cf. the discussion of Rom 3:7 and 4:19); at 14:21 a variant supported by 𝔓⁴⁶ᵛⁱᵈ B D F G 0209 33 Byz lat syʰ sa described

---

[20] Cf. B.F. Westcott—F.J.A. Hort, *The New Testament in the Original Greek.* [2,] *Introduction* [and] *Appendix*, (London—New York ²1896) 167, 228, 244, 257–9.

[21] Cf. Zuntz, *Text*, 156–7, 39–41, 61–84.

as "a Western expansion ... which gained wide circulation"; at
1 Cor 3:3, the suspicion that a reading supported by $\mathfrak{P}^{46}$ D F G 33
614 Byz a b sy Ir Cyp represents "the intrusion of a Western gloss";
at 2 Cor 2:17, the conclusion that a reading supported by $\mathfrak{P}^{46}$ D G
326 614 Lect sy$^{p.h}$ Marcion al "appears to be of Western origin".[22]
The implication of comments of this sort is clear: "Western" readings are a corrupting outside intrusion into a "proto-Alexandrian"
witness.

(2) Zuntz, on the other hand, answers unequivocally in the other
direction. In his opinion, the "outstanding feature" of the group of
witnesses he termed 'proto-Alexandrian,' and "foremost in $\mathfrak{P}^{46}$," is
the presence of

> 'Western' readings, or rather, those readings which have disappeared
> from the later 'Alexandrian' manuscripts (and often also from other
> Eastern witnesses) but recur in the West. The presence of these read-
> ings does not make the group 'Western' in any legitimate sense of the
> term; the 'Alexandrian' character of the 'proto-Alexandrian' witnesses
> is established by unequivocal facts. This element, common to the ear-
> liest Eastern and to the Western traditions, is a survival from a pre-
> 'Alexandrian' and pre-Western basis, the traces of which, most marked
> in P^{46}, gradually disappear from the later 'Alexandrian' tradition but
> often reappear in later Eastern witnesses, as well as in the West.[23]

In short, the evidence he collected yielded "one paramount conclusion: Western readings in non-Western witnesses are, generally, ancient
survivals. They are not, in the relevant witnesses, secondary intrusions into a previously pure form."[24]

In other words, any reading with both "Western" and Eastern
support, though not necessarily nor often original, must nonetheless
be very ancient, and thus may offer clues to the early history and
transmission of the text. The "Western" + "proto-Alexandrian" agreements in error listed above, these $Leitfehler$, "indicate some contact,
at a very early date, between the predecessors of both"; such readings date from "a pre-Western and pre-'Alexandrian' stage" in the
transmission of the text of Romans that "must lie far back, beyond

---

[22] Metzger, $Textual\ Commentary$, 464, 467, 469, 482, 508.

[23] Zuntz, $Text$, 156.

[24] Zuntz, $Text$, 142.

the emergence of separate Western and 'Alexandrian' texts."[25] These "agreements in error" preserve evidence of the handling and fate of the text in the earliest period of its transmission, and as such offer valuable clues illuminating the first century of its transmission—and 𝔓[46] is the most critical witness to this evidence.

If this is the case, then a question arises immediately: can anything be said about the origin or cause of this group of very early but also clearly secondary variant readings?

Zuntz, in discussing the unique reading of 𝔓[46] at Heb 10:1 (ουκ αυτην την εικονα] και την εικονα 𝔓[46]), suggests that the reading preserved by the papyrus

> "is a willful alteration, an alteration which could readily suggest itself to an attentive reader assessing the original text by the standards of educated Greek thought and mode of expression. . . . Such variant readings in 𝔓[46] . . . are not due to a scribe's slovenliness: they are conjectures, and indeed ingenious conjectures, witnessing to attentive study of the text and perfect command of the Greek language. Our scribe found them in his copy."[26]

That is, Zuntz is characterizing a certain kind of individual who is, he implies, responsible for at least some of these readings found in 𝔓[46].

Gilles Quispel, in a review essay surveying two investigations of Marcion's text, offers as a provisional conclusion a more developed sketch of the person he thinks is responsible for a pre-Marcionite, "pre-Western" text:

> It had been written down by an experienced Catholic *grammaticus*, who had, of course, his own *scriptorium*, and who made mistakes and scribal errors, like all scribes, but also opted for a better variant after having consulted another source: this scribe must have been familiar with all the methods of the classical techniques of edition, which flourished not only in Alexandria, but also in Rome.[27]

---

[25] Zuntz, *Text*, 96, 92.

[26] Zuntz, *Text*, 22–23.

[27] G. Quispel, "Marcion and the Text of the New Testament," *VigChr* 52 (1998) 359 (reviewing Ulrich Schmid, *Marcion und sein Apostolos: Rekonstruktion und historische Einordnung der marcionitischen Paulusbriefausgabe* [ANTF 25; Berlin and New York 1995] and J.J. Clabeaux, *A Lost Edition of the Letters of Paul: A Reassessment of the Text of the Pauline Corpus Attested by Marcion* [CBQMS 21; Washington, D.C. 1989]).

In general (leaving aside the purely hypothetical elements of Quispel's formulation), these suggestions correlate well with a suggestion I have made elsewhere regarding the origin of many of the substantive deliberate variant readings in the Gospel tradition: they are due to the activity of educated, thoughtful, usually conscientious but unscholarly *readers* (as distinguished from pure copyists as such).[28] Indeed, a description that the Alands give of some copyists applies more aptly, I think, to the early readers and users of manuscripts: at least some of them "felt themselves free to make corrections in the text, improving it by their own standards of correctness, whether grammatically, stylistically, or more substantively."[29]

As E.J. Kenney reminds us,

> a newly-copied text would normally be full of copying errors. A reader who took textual accuracy at all seriously had virtually to make his own edition of his book by correcting slips of the pen (and sometimes graver corruptions), where possible by comparison with other, putatively if not actually, more reliable copies . . . All users of books would have been habituated to do this from their schooldays.[30]

An observation regarding the surviving Latin classical manuscripts may be illuminating here. J.E. Zetzel reminds us that these

> manuscripts are those of amateur and wealthy book-lovers; and like modern readers, they wrote comments in the margins, made corrections of errors where they noticed them, and generally created a book that was of service to themselves. . . . it is pure wishful thinking to believe that our manuscripts descend only from those in which a scrupulous

---

[28] M.W. Holmes, "Codex Bezae as a Recension of the Gospels," *Codex Bezae: Studies from the Lunel Colloquium, June 1994* (ed. D.C. Parker—C.-B. Amphoux; NTTS 22; Leiden 1996) 123–160, here 142–152; E.J. Epp, "Anti-Judaic Tendencies in the D-Text of Acts," *The Book of Acts as Church History / Apostelgeschichte als Kirchengeschichte* (ed. T. Nicklas—M. Tilly; BZNW 120; Berlin—New York 2003) 111–146, here 135–138.

[29] K. and B. Aland, *The Text of the New Testament: An Introduction to the Critical Editions and to the Theory and Practice of Modern Textual Criticism* (Grand Rapids—Leiden ²1989) 69. A key phrase here is "their own standards": though from a much later date and time, the well known marginal comment in Codex Vaticanus at Heb 1:3 illustrates how different the same reading can appear to two different individuals: the original but incorrect φανερων was corrected by someone to φερων; subsequently a second person "uncorrected" the correction and added a marginal note that reads, "fool and knave, leave the old alone, don't alter it."

[30] E.J. Kenney, "Books and Readers in the Roman World," *The Cambridge History of Classical Literature*, II: *Latin Literature* (ed. E.J. Kenney—W.V. Clausen; Cambridge 1982) 18.

or cautious reader had made corrections. In general, there is no escaping the disturbing fact that, in antiquity, the preservation and the quality of a text were the result of the interests of its successive owners or readers, not of a scholarly editor. Whether or not we have a careful or a sloppy text, an interpolated version or an accurate representation of the author's original work, depends entirely on the individuals whose copies have been preserved.[31]

Zetzel's characterization of Latin classical manuscripts offers, I think, a useful analogy for thinking about New Testament manuscripts. Making due allowances for the fact that many NT MSS would have belonged to churches, we must not forget that they were copied and read by *individuals*,[32] who possessed widely varying levels of skill, taste, ability, and scruples. Moreover, many (if not most) of these individuals would have received a secular education and been at home within the larger Greco-Roman literary environment, an environment sketched above by Kenney. As Robert Grant notes, we have "a fairly clear picture of what the educated Greek or Roman was taught in school. . . . And the methods he learned did not slip from his memory if he became a Christian."[33] Porphory's own description of the method he utilized in preparing his anthology of oracles offers a glimpse of what this may have involved:

> I have added nothing, nor have I taken anything away from the meaning of the oracles (except where I have corrected a defective reading [λέξιν ἡμαρτημένην διώρθωσα], or made a change for the sake of greater clarity, or completed the meter when defective, or deleted anything irrelevant to the point), so that I have preserved untouched the meaning of what was spoken, carefully avoiding the impiety of such changes" (Eusebius, *Praeparatio evangelica* 4.7).

---

[31] J.E.G. Zetzel, *Latin Textual Criticism in Antiquity* (New York 1981) 238–239.

[32] Many of the NT MSS from Oxyrhynchus fit this pattern very closely. See E.J. Epp, "The Oxyrhynchus New Testament Papyri: 'Not Without Honor Except in Their Hometown'?," *JBL* 123 (2004) 5–55.

[33] R.M. Grant, *The Earliest Lives of Jesus* (New York 1961) 38; cf. H.Y. Gamble, *Books and Readers in the Early Church: A History of Early Christian Texts* (New Haven—London 1995) 6–10. On the level of literacy within the early Christian movement see Gamble, *Books*, 2–6, and T.J. Kraus, "(Il)literacy in Non-Literary Papyri from Graeco-Roman Egypt: Further Aspects of the Educational Ideal in Ancient Literary Sources and Modern Times," *Mn.* 53 (2000) 322–342; Id., "'Uneducated', 'Ignorant', or even 'Illiterate'? Aspects and Background for an Understanding of αγραμματοι and ιδιωται in Acts 4.13," *NTS* 45 (1999) 434–449.

Notice his emphasis on *meaning*: he is quite emphatic that he has not changed the meaning, while freely admitting he has changed details of the text itself. This correlates well, I would suggest, with what we find among the secondary "Western" + "proto-Alexandrian" readings examined earlier: in many instances, they leave the essential meaning unchanged, even as they offer variant forms of the actual wording of the text.

In many instances, but not all: some of the variants listed above seem to me to rise above the level of merely "readerly" comments. That is, some of the variants listed above testify to a considerably more active "clarification" or "explanation" of the text. They involve, in other words, that kind of activity to which we often apply the label of "commentary": bringing out (or even suggesting) the meaning of a text. Here are some (repeated from the first list above) which seem to rise to this higher level of intellectual engagement with the text:

15:31a [... ἐν τῇ Ἰουδαίᾳ καὶ ἡ διακονία μου ἡ εἰς Ἰερουσαλήμ ...]
      διακονια]   𝔓⁴⁶ 01 A C D¹ Ψ 33.1739.1881 𝔐 sy co
      δωροφορια]   B D* F G it Ambst

Here δωροφορια, "the bringing of a gift," looks very much like an explanatory gloss, one that specifies the precise nature of Paul's διακονια (namely, the delivering of the collection, cf. 15:28).

15:25 [νυνὶ δὲ πορεύομαι εἰς Ἰερουσαλὴμ διακονῶν τοῖς ἁγίοις.]
      διακονων]   01ᶜ A B C Ψ 33.1739.1881 𝔐
      διακονησων]   01*
      διακονησαι]   𝔓⁴⁶ D F G latt

In 15:25, the present participle is unexpected and grammatically ambiguous; the infinitive in 𝔓⁴⁶ D F G indicates clearly the anticipated final sense.

8:23 [... ἡμεῖς καὶ αὐτοὶ ἐν ἑαυτοῖς στενάζομεν υἱοθεσίαν
      ἀπεκδεχόμενοι ...]
      υιοθεσιαν *rell*] *omit*   𝔓⁴⁶ᵛⁱᵈ D F G 614 t Ambst

Cranfield, observing "the apparent inconsistency between the present tenses of vv. 14 and 16 and the future sense conveyed by ἀπεκδεχόμενοι," notes that the "omission of υἱοθεσίαν leaves τὴν ἀπολύτρωσιν τοῦ σώματος ἡμῶν as the quite straightforward object of ἀπεκδεχόμενοι."[34]

---

[34] Cranfield, *Romans*, 1.419 n. 1.

6:12 [μὴ οὖν βασιλευέτω ἡ ἁμαρτία ἐν τῷ θνητῷ ὑμῶν σώματι εἰς τὸ
ὑπακούειν ταῖς
ἐπιθυμίαις αὐτοῦ, . . .]
(a) ταις επιθυμιαις αυτου]   𝔓⁹⁴ 01 A B C* 6.81.1506.
                                  1739.1881 al lat syᵖ co
                                  (Or) Did
(b) αυτη]   𝔓⁴⁶ D F G pc b Ir^lat Tert
                                  Ambst
(c) αυτη εν ταις επιθυμιαις αυτου]   C K L P Ψ 1175.1241.
                                  2464 𝔐 syʰ
(d) αυτην εν ταις επιθυμιαις αυτης] 049*ᵛ² pc
(e) αυτου εν ταις επιθυμιαις αυτου] 33.1912 pc

In comparison to the standard text, in which the antecedent of αὐτοῦ
is σώματι ("body"), the antecedent of the αὐτή in 𝔓⁴⁶ DFG is ἁμαρτία
("sin"); in this form, verse 12 reinforces more clearly the main point
of the passage (cf. vv. 1, 2, 6, 7, 10, 11).

16:17 [. . . τοὺς τὰς διχοστασίας καὶ τὰ σκάνδαλα . . . ποιοῦντας, . . .
ποιουντας]   01 A B C Ψ 33.1739.1881 𝔐 lat sy co
                    Ambst
λεγοντας η ποιουντας]   D F G (a) m
η λεγοντας η ποιουντας]   𝔓⁴⁶

Here Paul exhorts the Roman congregation to "take note of" and
"avoid" those who cause (ποιουντας) dissensions and difficulties. The
text of 𝔓⁴⁶, with its repeated η (apparently lost from DFG when the
comment was incorporated into the text), has every appearance of
a marginal comment—"either speaking about or causing"—that both
affirms and expands somewhat Paul's injunction.

11:1 [. . . μὴ ἀπώσατο ὁ θεὸς τὸν λαὸν αὐτοῦ; . . .]
(a) τον λαον   αυτου]   01* B C 33.1739 rell
                                  vg syᵖ·ʰ sa bo
(b) τον λαον   αυτου ον προεγνω]   01² A D [cf. 11:2]
(c) την κληρονομιαν αυτου ην προεγνω]   𝔓⁴⁶
(d) την κληρονομιαν αυτου]   F G b Ambst Pel

The question in 11:1 (μὴ ἀπώσατο ὁ θεὸς τὸν λαὸν αὐτοῦ;) and the
answer in 11:2 (οὐκ ἀπώσατο ὁ θεὸς τὸν λαὸν αὐτοῦ) both echo the
wording of Ps 94:14a (93:14a LXX) ὅτι οὐκ ἀπώσεται κύριος τὸν λαὸν
αὐτοῦ, where in v. 14b τὴν κληρονομίαν is parallel to the τὸν λαόν
of 14a. The presence of variation in only one of the two instances
of τὸν λαόν in 11:1–2 suggests that we are not observing the result of
an effort to re-write the text (if that were the case, one would expect

that both instances would have been changed). Instead, someone seems to have written in the margin the parallel term from the Psalm, which effectively glosses the meaning of τὸν λαόν in its original context. A subsequent scribe then apparently (mis)read the comment as a correction to the text of 11:1.

These variant readings appear to involve a different level of intellectual engagement with the text than is typically associated with the process of reproducing a text. That is, they seemingly demonstrate a deliberate attempt to clarify, expand, and/or explain the meaning of the text—not simply to replicate its form. What now appear only as variant readings in the text originally were, I suggest, comments in the margins about the text[35]—the earliest "commentary" (in the sense of activity, rather than genre) on the text of Romans. In short, 𝔓⁴⁶ (and, in the case of 15:31b, its close ally, B)—or, to be more precise, the *Vorlage* from which the scribe of the manuscript worked—offers, as it were, a window through which we may catch a glimpse of an early reader of Romans actively and thoughtfully engaged with the content of the text being read. Thus the papyrus preserves not only evidence for the text itself, but also evidence bearing upon the transmission of that text, evidence that offers insight into the origins of some of the textual variants now found in Romans.

When did this activity take place? Occasionally, 𝔓⁴⁶/DFG agreements in error also occur in Marcion (e.g., Gal 3:14; 1 Cor 14:21). But these are not likely to be the work of Marcion; recent work has demonstrated that Marcion, rather than creating a text, passed along the wording of texts already in existence.[36] So the time frame is

---

[35] A manuscript with these comments in the margin no doubt would also have corrections to the text in the margins as well. We may envision, in other words, a text with two kinds of marginal notes: (1) a reader's short (mostly one or two word) "comments" or notes regarding the meaning of the text, and (2) the usual assortment of marginal corrections that one would find in any manuscript that had been subjected to the customary process of correction (διόρθωσις; on this point see M.W. Holmes, "Codex Bezae as a Recension," 142–50). A subsequent scribe (mis)understood the two different categories of marginal notes to be of the same sort or kind, and consequently treated the reader's comments as if they were textual variants. In this manner, probably, some of the earliest "commentary" entered the textual tradition of Romans.

[36] U. Schmid, *Marcion und sein Apostolos: Rekonstruktion und historische Einordnung der Marcionitischen Paulusbriefausgabe* (ANTF 25; Berlin and New York 1995); J.J. Clabeaux, *A Lost Edition of the Letters of Paul: A Reassessment of the Text of the Pauline Corpus Attested by Marcion* (CBQMS 21; Washington, D.C. 1989).

before Marcion. Was it before or after the formation of the Pauline corpus? If we knew more about the earliest stages of that process, perhaps an answer could be given.[37] At present, however, it seems possible to offer only a general time frame: sometime during the last decade or so of the first century or the first decades of the second. Wherever within this range they fall, these very early and clearly intentional readings discussed above stand as evidence for the earliest efforts yet known to "comment" on the text of Romans.

---

[37] For a survey of the *status quaestionis*, see S.E. Porter, "When and How was the Pauline Canon Compiled? An Assessment of Theories," *The Pauline Canon* (ed. S.E. Porter; Leiden—Boston 2004) 95–127.

THE STAUROGRAM IN EARLY CHRISTIAN MANUSCRIPTS: THE EARLIEST VISUAL REFERENCE TO THE CRUCIFIED JESUS?

Larry W. Hurtado

Among the several monograms used by early Christians to refer to Jesus, the so-called "staurogram" or "cross-monogram", which is comprised of the Greek majuscule forms of the letters *tau* and *rho*, the vertical line of the *rho* superimposed on the vertical stroke of the *tau*, is of particular historical significance.[1] The specific proposal that I shall support in the present essay is that the Christian use of this device in certain early manuscripts represents the earliest extant visual reference to the crucified Jesus, indeed, considerably prior to what is commonly thought to be the time (fourth or fifth century CE) when Christians began to portray the crucifixion of Jesus visually.[2] This has significant implications well beyond the area of codicology and palaeography, extending also into questions about early Christian beliefs and expressions of piety.[3] Before we examine this specific

---

[1] The most important previous studies are by K. Aland, "Bemerkungen zum Alter und Entstehung des Christogramms anhand von Beobachtungen bei P66 und P75," *Studien zur Überlieferung des Neuen Testaments und seines Textes* (Berlin 1967) 173–79; M. Black, "The Chi-Rho Sign—Christogram and/or Staurogram?" *Apostolic History and the Gospel: Essays Presented to F.F. Bruce* (eds. W.W. Gasque and R.P. Martin; Grand Rapids 1970) 319–27; and, more recently, Erika Dinkler-von Schubert, "CTAYPOC: Vom 'Wort vom Kreuz' (1 Kor. 1,18) zum Kreuz-Symbol," *Byzantine East, Latin West: Art-Historical Studies in Honor of Kurt Weitzmann* (eds. Doula Mouriki et al.; Princeton 1995) 29–39.

[2] I provide here further support for a point made earlier by E. Dinkler, *Signum Crucis* (Tübingen 1967) 177–78, about the historical importance of the *tau-rho* compendium, who in turn was seconding and amplifying observations by K. Aland, "Neue neutestamentliche Papyri II," *NTS* 10 (1963–64) 62–79, esp. 75–79; idem, "Neue neutestamentliche Papyri II," *NTS* 11 (1964–65) 1–21, esp. 1–3. I have discussed the matter more briefly in an earlier essay. See L.W. Hurtado, "The Earliest Evidence of an Emerging Christian Material and Visual Culture: The Codex, the *Nomina Sacra* and the Staurogram," *Text and Artifact in the Religions of Mediterranean Antiquity* (eds. S.G. Wilson—M. Desjardins; ESCJ 9; Waterloo, Ontario 2000) 271–88, esp. 279–82.

[3] J. van Haelst, *Catalogue des papyrus littéraires Juifs et Chrétiens* (Paris 1976) is an indispensable reference work for the use of papyrological data.

proposal, however, I address some introductory and background questions and set the staurogram into an appropriate historical context.

Several questions obviously present themselves. What is the historical relationship of these various Christian monograms to one
another? Were some or all of them created *de novo* by Christians, or
do they represent or include Christian appropriations of ligatures
already in use? In any case, what did these devices signify and how
did they function in Christian usage, especially in the earliest instances?
It is not possible here to deal comprehensively with these questions
with reference to all these monograms. Instead, I shall provide some
limited discussion of general matters and then focus more specifically
on questions about the *tau-rho* device.

EARLY CHRISTIAN MONOGRAMS

In addition to this *tau-rho* combination, early Christians also made
use of several other such devices to refer to Jesus Christ (see Illustration
1).[4] Perhaps most well known is the *chi-rho*, which certainly obtained
the most widespread and most long-lasting usage, down to the present time.[5] Less familiar, but also certainly found in ancient Christian
usage, were the *iota-chi* monogram (which with its six points can look
like a stylized star) and also the *iota-ēta*. In some later (post-
Constantinian) instances of Christian usage, we have two or more
of these devices used together, as is the case with the Christian
inscription from Armant (ancient Hermonthis, Egypt), at the bottom
of which there is a *tau-rho* and an *ankh* flanked on either side by a
chi-rho.[6] As to their derivation, with the possible exception of the *iota-
ēta* compendium, these are all pre-Christian devices and were appropriated by early Christians.[7] In each case, the Christian innovation

---

[4] See the discussion of "Abbreviations and Monograms" in J. Finegan, *The
Archaeology of the New Testament: The Life of Jesus and the Beginning of the Early Church*
(Princeton ²1992) 352–55.

[5] E.g., W. Wischmeyer, "Christogramm und Staurogramm in den lateinischen
Inschriften altkirchlicher Zeit," *Theologia Crucis—Signum Crucis: Festschrift für Erich
Dinkler zum 70. Geburtstag* (eds. C. Andresen—G. Klein; Tübingen 1979) 539–50.

[6] Finegan, *Archaeology*, 387–88, gives a photograph and discussion. The inscription was originally published in 1892, and is thought to have been made sometime
between the fourth and sixth centuries CE.

[7] In the following discussion of pre/non-Christian usage of these devices, I draw

was to ascribe new meanings and significance to these devices, so that in Christian usage they referred to Jesus and reflected early Christian piety.

Illustration 1

⚹ = ΧΡΙΣΤΟΣ
✗ = ΙΗΣΟΥΣ ΧΡΙΣΤΟΣ
Ⱨ = ΙΗ(ΣΟΥΣ)
⳨ = Used in early manuscripts: 𝔓66, 𝔓45, 𝔓75, ca. 200–250 CE

A "monogram" is an interweaving or combination of two (or sometimes more) alphabetic letters, the component-letters of resultant device typically referring to a person's name or title. But such letter-combinations (called "ligatures" and/or "compendia") can also serve other purposes, particularly as abbreviations of common words. For instance, in pre/non-Christian Greek papyri of the Roman period, the *chi-rho* is used as an abbreviation for several words (e.g., forms of χρονος), and in Greek inscriptions this ligature is found as an abbreviation for ἑκατονταρχια, ἑκατονταρχης, ἑκατονταχους, χιλιαρχης, and a few other terms.[8] As well as the more familiar form of the *chi-rho* device, one of the two letters superimposed over the other, there are also instances where the one component letter is written above the other.[9] To cite another early non-Christian instance of the familiar form of this particular ligature, Randolph Richards drew attention to a *chi-rho* in P.Mur. 164a (line 11), a text of Greek tachygraphic writing on parchment which, with the other manuscripts

upon the following studies: A. Blanchard, *Sigles et abbreviations dans les papyrus grecs: Recherches de paleographie* (ICSB.S 30; London 1974); K. McNamee, *Abbreviations in Greek Literary Papyri and Ostraca* (BASP.S 3; Chico 1981); M. Avi-Yonah, *Abbreviations in Greek Inscriptions (The Near East, 200 BC–AD 1100)* (repr. Chicago 1974; originally published as a supplement to *Quarterly of the Department of Antiquities in Palestine* 9 [1940]). E. Dinkler-von Schubert, "Wort vom Kreuz," 33–34, also surveys the pre/non-Christian usage of the *tau-rho* and the *chi-rho* devices. The most comprehensive survey of ancient monograms known to me is V. Gardthausen, *Das alte Monogramm* (Leipzig 1924), but unfortunately his discussion of earliest Christian monograms (esp. 73–79) is clearly incorrect in light of subsequently discovered evidence such as I discuss here.

[8] See, e.g., Don Pasquale Colella, "Les abbreviations ⳨ et ⚹ (XP)," *RB* 80 (1973) 547–558, who comments on the likely import of *chi-rho* marks on (non-Christian) amphorae.

[9] Examples cited by K. McNamee, *Abbreviations*, 118; A. Blanchard, *Sigles*, 26 (n. 36); and M. Avi-Yonah, *Abbreviations*, 112.

found in Wadi Murabba'at, is probably to be dated to the Jewish revolt of 132–35 CE.[10] In yet another instance, the device also appears in the margin of a *hypomnema* on Homer, *Iliad*, dated to the first century BCE, the *chi-rho* here a sign for χρηστον (marking passages "useful" for excerpting).[11]

The *tau-rho* combination, the focus of this discussion, appears in pre/non-Christian usage as an abbreviation for τρ(οπος), τρ(ιακας), and Τρ(οκονδας).[12] Among specific noteworthy instances, there is the use of this device on some coins of King Herod (37–4 BCE), the *tau-rho* intended to identify them with the third year of his reign.[13]

The *iota-chi* combination was an archaic form of the Greek letter *psi*, and was also sometimes used on Roman-era coins (probably as a numerical symbol). Moreover, there is an obvious similarity to six-pointed devices used for decoration ubiquitously in various cultures, and sometimes as stylized stars.[14]

The uses of the *iota-ēta* combination, however, in relevant surveys of the data with which I am acquainted are all Christian instances, comprising the first two letters of the name Ιησους and intended as an obvious reference to him.[15] But there are similar ligatures of other letters in non-Christian Greek documentary papyri, such as the combination of *mu* and *epsilon* (for μεγας, μερις, μετοχος, and other terms).[16] So, even if the specific *iota-ēta* combination may have been first employed as a monogram by Christians, the Christian use of other ligatures, for example the stylized six-pointed decorative device (*iota-*

---

[10] E. Randolph Richards, *The Secretary in the Letters of Paul* (Tübingen: J.C.B. Mohr [Paul Siebeck], 1991), 40–41. The full description of the manuscript is in P. Benoit *et al.*, *Les grottes de Murabba'ât* (DJD, 2; Oxford: Oxford University Press, 1961), 275–79.

[11] E. G. Turner, *Greek Manuscripts of the Ancient World* (2nd rev. ed.; London: Institute of Classical Studies, 1987), plate 58.

[12] K. McNamee, *Abbreviations*, 119; M. Avi-Yonah, *Abbreviations*, 105.

[13] B. Kanael, "The Coins of King Herod of the Third Year," *JQR* 62 (1951–52) 261–264; *idem*, "Ancient Jewish Coins and their Historical Importance," *Biblical Archaeologist* 26 (1963) 38–62, esp. 48. Use of devices involving a *tau-rho* ligature were also noted on items from Dura Europos, at least some instances likely craftsmen's marks. See R.N. Frye, J.F. Gillam, H. Inghold and C.B. Welles, "Inscriptions from Dura-Europos," *Yale Classical Studies* 14 (1955) 123–213, esp. 191–94.

[14] For instances and discussion, see M. Sulzberger, "Le Symbole de la Croix et les Monogrammes de Jésus chez les premier Chrétiens," *Byzantion* 2 (1925) 337–448, esp. 394–95, who also cites Gardthausen, *Das alte Monogramm*, 76–77.

[15] Avi-Yonah, *Abbreviations*, 72.

[16] Blanchard, *Sigles*, 4.

chi) to refer to Ιησους Χριστος, may have helped to suggest this device, and, in any case, the joining of various letters to form a ligature was familiar to readers of the time, especially in documentary texts and inscriptions.

As indicated already, in Christian usage, all of the monograms/ compendia in question served in one way or another as references to Jesus. Thus, the Christian appropriation of them all reflects the enormous place of Jesus in early Christian devotion, and these curious devices thereby became themselves expressions of this piety.[17] The *chi-rho*, for example (using the first two letters of Χριστος), was a direct reference to "Christ" and became one of the most familiar and widely-used emblems in Christian tradition.[18] The *iota-chi* seems to have functioned mainly as a combination of the initial letters of Ιησους Χριστος, and likewise served simply as a way of referring to him, as did the *iota-ēta*, which was formed from the first two letters of Ιησους.[19]

Moreover, it is important to note that all of these devices represent *visual* phenomena, and so, as reverential references to Jesus in early Christian usage, they have a certain iconographic function and significance, which should be recognized. The earliest Christian use of these devices, which takes us back at least to the late second century and quite possibly earlier, represents the emergence of what we may term a Christian "visual culture". I shall return to this point later. But in the case of the Christian use of *tau-rho* monogram, there are also interesting distinctives that now require further attention.

---

[17] See now, L.W. Hurtado, *Lord Jesus Christ: Devotion to Jesus in Earliest Christianity* (Grand Rapids 2003).

[18] Note, e.g., the use of the *chi-rho* in the Trisomus inscription in the Catacomb of Priscilla (Rome), a prayer to God, the last line of which reads "σοι δοξα εν [χρ]." For full text and discussion, see Finegan, *Archaeology*, 380. For other instances, see M. Burzachechi, "Sull' Uso Pre-Costantiniano del Monogramma Greco di Christo," *Rendiconti della Pontificia Accademia Romana di Archeologia, Series III* 28 (1955–56) 197–211.

[19] Finegan, *Archaeology*, 379–380, gives a photo and discussion of a painted sign in the Catacomb of Priscilla that appears to have a *iota-ēta* compendium, but in this instance the horizontal stroke extends through and beyond the letters, giving the appearance of three connected equilateral crosses.

The Staurogram: Origin

The first observation to make is that, whereas all of the other Christian letter-compendia that I have mentioned are true monograms, the component letters in each case directly referring to Jesus by name and/or a christological title, the *tau-rho* combination did not have any such function. Its component letters neither derive from, nor refer to, Jesus' name or any of the familiar christological titles. Indeed, in Christian usage, the two component letters in this device do not appear to refer to any words at all. So what suggested the Christian appropriation of this particular letter-compendium?[20] Furthermore, although the *tau-rho* seems to have had some later usage simply as a free-standing reverential cipher for the figure of Jesus, and/or perhaps simply as an emblem intended to signify Christian faith, what was its initial function and significance, and when might it first have appeared in Christian usage?

Let us first address the question of origins. Our most important evidence, and certainly the earliest, is provided by the instances of this device in some very early Christian manuscripts.[21] We may begin with Papyrus Bodmer II ($\mathfrak{P}^{66}$), the extant portion of a codex of the Gospel of John (chapters 1–14 relatively well preserved, the rest of John through chapter 21 in very fragmentary condition), and dated palaeographically to ca. 200 CE.[22] In this manuscript the noun σταυρος (three instances) and at least seven uses of forms of the verb σταυροω are written in abbreviated forms, and with the *tau* and *rho* of these words written as a compendium. In each case, the statement in which the noun or verb appears refers to Jesus' cross/crucifixion.[23]

---

[20] Cf. E. Dinkler-von Schubert, "Wort vom Kreuz," 32, who judged the question no closer to an answer. I acknowledge the difficulty involved in being entirely precise, as the following discussion will show. But I do not think that we are entirely without clues and a likely basic association of the device in earliest Christian use.

[21] K. Aland has the credit for first drawing scholarly attention to this evidence in two important articles (cited above in n. 2) in successive volumes of *NTS* in the early 1960s.

[22] V. Martin, *Papyrus Bodmer II: Evangile de Jean Chap. 1–14* (Cologny-Geneva 1956); idem, *Papyrus Bodmer II, Évangile de Jean, Supplément, Chaps. 14–21* (Cologny-Geneva 1958); V. Martin and J.W.B. Barns, *Papyrus Bodmer II, Supplement, Évangile de Jean chap. 14–2, Nouvelle edition augmentée et corrigée* (Cologny-Geneva 1962).

[23] K. Aland identified instances of σταυρος abbreviated and with the *tau-rho* in John 19:19, 25, 31, and abbreviated forms of σταυρος with this device in John 19:6

Likewise, in 𝔓⁷⁵, dated to about the same time and comprising portions of the Gospel of Luke (Papyrus Bodmer XIV) and the Gospel of John (Papyrus Bodmer XV), there are further instances of the *tau-rho* compendium used in abbreviated forms of the same two Greek words.²⁴ But the scribal practice in this manuscript was not so consistent. In all three cases where σταυρος appears in the extant portions of Luke (9:23; 14:27; 23:26) the word is written in an abbreviated form, and in two of these cases (9:23; 14:27) the *tau-rho* compendium is also used.²⁵ In the six extant occurrences of the verb σταυροω, however, the word is abbreviated twice (23:33; 24:7), and in the other four cases is written fully (23:21 [two], 23; 24:20). Only at Luke 24:7 in 𝔓⁷⁵ is there a verb-form extant with the *tau-rho* compendium.²⁶

These abbreviations of σταυρος and σταυροω (in each case with a horizontal stroke over the abbreviation) mean that the copyists in question were extending to them the special, and apparently distinctively Christian, abbreviation-practice now commonly referred to as "*nomina sacra*".²⁷ But, as Aland observed, on the basis of these two early, and roughly contemporary, manuscripts, it appears that the Christian practice of writing σταυρος as a *nomen sacrum* was somewhat more quickly and more firmly established than was the case for the verb σταυροω.²⁸

We should also note that in the Vienna fragment of 𝔓⁴⁵ (dated ca. 200–250 CE), at Matthew 26:2 (the sole place where either the

---

(three), 15 (two), 16, 18 ("Neue neutestamentliche Papyri II," *NTS* 10 [1963–64] 75, and further possible cases in 19:17, 20. Cf. instances identified by Martin and Barns in the 1962 augmented and corrected edition of chapters 14–21 of 𝔓⁶⁶: forms of σταυρος in 19:19, 25, plus another one restored as "des plus probables" in 19:18, and forms of σταυροω in 19:6 (two), 16, 18, plus a proposed restoration of another instance in 19:20. My own examination of the photos published in their 1962 edition enabled me to verify clear instances in abbreviated forms of σταυρος in 19:19, 25, and 31, and in forms of σταυροω in 19:6, 15, 16, and 18.

²⁴ V. Martin and R. Kasser *Papyrus Bodmer XIV, Evangile de Luc, chap. 3–24* (Cologny-Geneva 1961).

²⁵ The statements in Luke 9:23 and 14:27 have Jesus demanding his followers to "take up daily" and "bear" their own cross. But in each case, there is a clearly implied reference to his crucifixion.

²⁶ Martin and Kasser, *Papyrus Bodmer XIV*, 18; K. Aland, "Neue Neutestamentliche Papyri II," *NTS* 11 (1964–65) 2. The extant portions of John in 𝔓⁷⁵ (P. Bodmer XV) do not include any uses of σταυρος or σταυροω.

²⁷ For discussion and references to other key studies, see L.W. Hurtado, "The Origin of the *Nomina Sacra*: A Proposal," *JBL* 117 (1998) 655–73.

²⁸ Hurtado, "Origin," 2.

relevant noun or verb appears in the extant portions of the manuscript) the verb-form σταυρωθηναι ("to be crucified") is written in a contracted form and with the *tau-rho* compendium.[29] That is, we have three early third-century Christian manuscripts with this curious device, in all of which it is used in the same way, as part of a *nomina sacra* treatment of the Greek words for "cross" and "crucify".

It is unlikely that we happen to have the very first Christian usages of the *tau-rho*. We must suppose that this device had already been in Christian usage for some period of time for it to have been used independently by the copyists of these three manuscripts.[30] This obviously means that we should date the initial Christian appropriation of the *tau-rho* device at least as early as the final decades of the second century, and quite plausibly somewhat earlier. It is a very interesting question as to whether the earliest appropriation of the *tau-rho* was made by copyists of still earlier Christian manuscripts in references to Jesus' cross/crucifixion, or whether there was some previous and/or wider Christian usage of this ligature, i.e., beyond its use in Christian manuscripts. Unfortunately, I know of no clear evidence to settle the matter. 𝔓⁴⁵, 𝔓⁶⁶ and 𝔓⁷⁵ offer us the earliest extant Christian uses of the *tau-rho* device, and in all these cases it is used in references to Jesus' cross/crucifixion. But we can say with some confidence that these three early manuscripts are not likely the first such uses of the *tau-rho*. Instead, 𝔓⁴⁵, 𝔓⁶⁶ and 𝔓⁷⁵ offer us evidence of a Christian appropriation of the *tau-rho* device that (whatever and whenever its origin) was already becoming familiar in Christian circles at the time that these copyists worked.

---

[29] Gerstinger, "Ein Fragment des Chester Beatty-Evangelienkodex in der Papyrussammlung der Nationalbibliothek in Wien (Pap. Graec. Vinob. 31974)," *Aeg.* 13 (1936) 67–72, esp. 69; T.J. Kraus, "*Ad fontes*: Gewinn durch die Konsultation von Originalhandschriften am Beispiel von *P.Vindob.G* 31974," *Bib.* 82 (2001) 2–17 (with plate). The fragment (Matt. 25:41–26:39) forms part of Chester Beatty Papyrus I (van Haelst 371), 30 leaves of a codex originally comprising the four Gospels (in "Western" order) and Acts. See esp. T.C. Skeat, "A Codicological Analysis of the Chester Beatty Papyrus Codex of Gospels and Acts (P45)," *Hermathena* 155 (1991) 27–43, reprinted in *The Collected Biblical Writings of T.C. Skeat* (ed. J.K. Elliott; NovTSup 113; Leiden 2004) 141–57.

[30] Although these three manuscripts are dated to a roughly similar period, the differences in scribal hands and a number of other features indicate that 𝔓⁴⁵, 𝔓⁶⁶ and 𝔓⁷⁵ must derive from three distinguishable settings, which means that the copyists likely worked independently of one another.

In any case, this important manuscript evidence about the Christian appropriation of the *tau-rho* device rather clearly means that earlier (and still echoed) views, such as the influential analysis of early Christian Jesus-monograms by Sulzberger must be judged incorrect on a couple of important matters, and that any history of early Christian symbols must take account of this.[31] Most obviously, *contra* Sulzberger, the Christian *tau-rho* monogram did not first emerge in the post-Constantinian period, and is not to be understood as a derivation from a prior Christian usage of the *chi-rho*.[32] Instead, the evidence cited from $\mathfrak{P}^{45}$, $\mathfrak{P}^{66}$ and $\mathfrak{P}^{75}$ gives instances of the Christian use of the *tau-rho* considerably earlier than datable instances of the Christian usage of the *chi-rho*, and well before Constantine! Indeed, as K. Aland noted several decades ago, to go by this manuscript evidence, the earliest Jesus-monogram appears to be the *tau-rho*, not the *chi-rho*.[33] Moreover, and perhaps of equal significance, the instances

---

[31] M. Sulzberger, "Le Symbole de la Croix et les Monogrammes de Jésus chez les premiers Chrétiens," *Byzantion* 2 (1925) 337–448. A very similar schema of the evolutionary development of Christian monograms was set out earlier and briefer by L. Spence, "Cross," *Encyclopedia of Religion and Ethics* IV (1911) 324–30. Likewise in need of correction is the analysis by M.A. Frantz, "The Provenance of the Open Rho in the Christian Monograms," *American Journal of Archaeology* 33 (1929) 10–26, esp. 10–11.

[32] M. Sulzberger also made several other claims that have been influential but are shown to be incorrect by the manuscript evidence: that the earliest Christian symbol for Jesus' cross was the *chi*, not the *tau* (ibid., "Symbole", 366), that as a general rule "on ne trouve ni croix, ni monogrammes de Jésus, ni representations de la Passion avant le quatrième siècle" (ibid., 371), that possibly with rare exceptions there are no direct representations of Jesus' cross before Constantine (ibid., 386), that the *iota-chi* is the earliest-attested Jesus-monogram, and neither the *chi-rho* nor the *tau-rho* can be dated prior to the fourth century (ibid., 393). Granted, Sulzberger wrote before the Chester Beatty and Bodmer papyri were available to scholars, and he leaned heavily on inscriptional data. Based on Christian manuscripts then available, he observed that "Il est remarquable que, dans les papyrus chrétiens, on ne trouve ni croix ni monogramme avant le Ve siècle" (ibid., 446). But he cannot be excused entirely. Even on the basis of evidence available to him, he had reason to question his views. But, instead, he seems to have allowed what seemed to him an elegant theory to determine how to handle evidence, rather than shaping his theory to fit the evidence. To cite an important instance, in considering a Christian inscription from Egypt which ends with a *tau-rho* flanked by an *alpha* and an *omega*, he preferred to assume that these were added "après coup" (ibid., 376–77). $\mathfrak{P}^{45}$, $\mathfrak{P}^{66}$ and $\mathfrak{P}^{75}$ now clearly confirm that this was a serious mis-judgment. The influence of his weighty article is reflected in writings of many other historians of early Christian art, e.g., C.R. Morey, *Early Christian Art* (Princeton ²1953) 128.

[33] I restrict attention here to the use of these ligatures, and cannot engage the

of the *tau-rho* device in these manuscripts (i.e., in abbreviations of the Greek words for "cross" and "crucify" in New Testament passages referring to Jesus' death), the earliest Christian uses extant, show us that this compendium was used in this early period, not simply as a general symbol for Jesus, but more specifically to refer reverentially to Jesus' death.[34]

In an article on 𝔓[66] and 𝔓[75], Jean Savignac noted that evidence indicating the chronological priority of the *tau-rho* over the *chi-rho* rendered Sulzberger's view of the origin of the Christian use of these two ligatures invalid, but Savignac's own proposal seems to me no more persuasive. Based on the frequently-noted Armant Christian inscription from the fourth century CE (or later) which features a *tau-rho* and the hieroglyphic *ankh*-sign flanked by two *chi-rhos*, he suggested that the appropriation of the *tau-rho* derived from its visual similarity to the *ankh* (the hieroglyphic significance of the latter being "life"), which, he further proposed, had been adopted previously, perhaps in certain Valentinian circles in Egypt.[35] Savignac recognized that, in general, early Christians, especially those whose faith remained more influenced by Jewish monotheistic concerns, may have been loath to adopt a pagan religious symbol such as the *ankh*. But, claiming the appearance of an *ankh* on the final page of the copy of the *Gospel of Truth* in the Jung codex, and taking the widely-shared view that this text derives from Valentinian circles, Savignac offered this as a basis for thinking that Valentinians may have been more ready to adopt this ancient Egyptian symbol for "life", interpreting it as referring to the life given through Jesus. There are, however, major problems with Savignac's proposals.

First, his core thesis does not adequately respect the respective dates of the evidence. The earliest verifiable Christian uses of the

---

wider questions about other early Christian symbols, among which fish are prominent, including the anagram ΙΧΘΥΣ (= Ιησους Χριστος Θεου Υιος Σωτηρ), which probably goes back to the early third century or even earlier. On the latter, see, e.g., G.F. Snyder, *Ante Pacem: Archaeological Evidence of Church Life before Constantine* (Macon 1985), 24–26 (with further references), and esp. F.J. Dölger, *ΙΧΘΥΣ. Das Fisch-Symbol in frühchristlicher Zeit* (Münster 1928).

[34] K. Aland, "Neue Neutestamentliche Papyri II," *NTS* 10 (1963–64) 78.

[35] J. de Savignac, "Les Papyrus Bodmer XIV et XV," *Scriptorium* 17 (1963) 50–55, esp. 51. Much earlier, Gardthausen (*Das alte Monogramm*, 78–79) had proposed that the *chi-rho* was the earliest Christian monogram, and that a subsequent Christian use of the *tau-rho* derived from the *ankh*. Both of his proposals are now refuted by the evidence of early Christian manuscripts.

ankh symbol are considerably later than the uses of the *tau-rho* device in $\mathfrak{P}^{66}$, $\mathfrak{P}^{75}$ and $\mathfrak{P}^{45}$.[36] It is simply not sound historical method to derive the clearly-attested Christian use of the *tau-rho* from a supposedly prior Christian use of the *ankh*, when the evidence for the Christian use of the latter device is much later. It is always a better approach to develop a theory out of the evidence, taking the dates of evidence seriously. If there was any *causative* relationship between the Christian appropriation of the *ankh* and the *tau-rho*, the chronological data actually make it more likely that Savignac's proposal should be stood on its head: The appropriation of the *ankh* may well have resulted from its visual resemblance to the *tau-rho* device. In any case, the *sequential* relationship between the Christian appropriation of the *tau-rho* and the *ankh* is rather clearly the opposite to Savignac's theory.

There is a second problem in Savignac's proposal, and it is not confined to him. It is a mistake to presume that the Christian appropriation of the various Jesus-monograms must have involved one initial monogram from which subsequent Christian appropriation of the others then developed. It seems to me that this insufficiently-examined assumption contributed to the misjudgments of Sulzberger as well as Savignac, leading them to posit their respective developmental schemes, even although the evidence did not actually suggest either one.

Why should we suppose that there had to be one initial Jesus-monogram from which the others somehow developed?[37] It is at least

---

[36] K. Aland disputed whether an *ankh* could really be read on the last page of the Jung Codex ("Neue Neutestamentliche Papyri II," *NTS* 11, 2–3). But, whatever the valid reading of this particular manuscript, the *ankh* symbol indisputably appears elsewhere in the Nag Hammadi texts, particularly on the leather cover of Codex 2 and at the end of the text titled "The Prayer of the Apostle Paul". Moreover, other data such as the Armant inscription mentioned above rather clearly indicate Christian appropriation of the *ankh* by the fourth to sixth centuries CE, and this appropriation seems not to have been particularly connected to Valentinian circles. Although some of the Nag Hammadi *texts* may well have originated in Greek-speaking "gnostic" circles, the fourth-century Coptic *manuscripts* of the Nag Hammadi collection were likely prepared by monastic scribes who were certainly strongly ascetic, but not particularly "Valentinians". See, e.g., the discussion by J.M. Robinson (Gen. Ed.), *The Nag Hammadi Library* (Leiden ²1988), 10–22.

[37] Is the uncritical assumption of such a schema simply indicative of how Darwinian concepts of unilinear evolution have become so much a part of Western intellectual culture that we assume that the "historical" explanation of anything must have proceeded along these lines?

as reasonable to view the Christian uses of the various Jesus-monograms as reflecting quasi-independent appropriations of at least some
of the various pre/non-Christian compendia, each of the appropriations suggested to Christians by the perceived capability of the
respective devices to express Christian faith and piety.[38] As we have
noted already, all of the devices in question here were in pre/non-
Christian use already, and thus were readily available. All that was
needed for the appropriation of any one of them was for some
Christian to perceive it in a new light, seeing in it a reference to
Jesus. Of course, it is in principle possible that an initial Christian
appropriation of one of these compendia may have helped to stim-
ulate Christians to seize upon others as well. But this seems to me
no more than a possibility. In any case, even such a scenario does
not amount to the various Jesus-monograms evolving *out of* an initial one.

In summary of the import of the chronological data, the earliest
extant Christian uses of the *tau-rho* are notably prior to the attested
Christian usage of any of the other ligatures. This alone makes it
unlikely that the Christian appropriation of the *tau-rho* was directly
influenced by prior Christian use of any of these other devices.
Indeed, the chronological data suggest strongly that the *tau-rho* may
have been the first of the several ligatures that were appropriated
by early Christians to refer to Jesus. Likewise, the earliest Christian
use of the *tau-rho* was probably not derived from Christian use of
the *ankh*, for this is attested only considerably later.

Also, it is significant that, in distinction from the other ligatures,
the Christian *tau-rho* was not functionally a monogram. That is, unlike
the other ligatures in question, the *tau-rho* was not derived from, and
did not refer to, the name of Jesus or Christological titles. This is a
further reason for doubting that the Christian appropriation of the
tau-rho ligature was derived from a supposedly prior use of one of
the others. In earliest Christian usage, the *tau-rho* alone appears as

---

[38] By "quasi" independent, I mean that the appropriation of the various devices
as Jesus-monograms obviously happened among circles of Christians, who to a
greater or lesser extent shared features of faith and piety. Moreover, Christians
clearly made efforts to "network" with other Christian circles, both locally and trans-
locally. So, if any given ligature was first adopted in some circle of Christians, they
may well have known of the appropriation of one or more of the other ligatures
among their own or other circles of Christians.

part of the *nomina sacra* treatment of certain words (σταυρος and σταυροω), and simply functioned differently as an early Christian symbol. Indeed, an answer to the question of how the Christian use of the *tau-rho* originated is probably connected to its earliest function. So, to this question we now give further attention to this question.

THE STAUROGRAM: EARLIEST FUNCTION AND SIGNIFICANCE

The difference in derivation corresponds to a difference in function. To reiterate an important point, unlike the other compendia, the *tau-rho* did not function as a direct allusion to Jesus by name or title. In the earliest instances of the *tau-rho*, of course, the two letters are two of those that make up the Greek words for "cross" and "crucify". But this in itself is unlikely to explain either the reason for the Christian appropriation of the ligature or its original Christian symbolic meaning. The earliest manuscript evidence cited earlier shows that the writing of the Greek words in question as *nomina sacra* did not consistently involve the use of the *tau-rho* ligature, which strongly suggests that the two phenomena arose independently.

A more likely approach to the origin and original function/ significance of the *tau-rho* is readily available. We know that the Greek letter *tau* was invested with symbolic significance by Christians very early, specifically as a visual reference to the cross of Jesus. In the *Epistle of Barnabas* 9:7–9 (dated sometime 70–130 CE), commenting on the story of Abraham's rescue of Lot with a company of 318 servants (Gen. 14:14), the number represented by the use of the Greek letters ΤΙΗ, the author interprets the two letters *iota* and *ēta* (the first two letters of Ιησους), as referring to Jesus, and letter *tau* as a reference to (and prediction of) Jesus' cross.[39] We have other

---

[39] This rendering of the number in Gen. 14:14 is clearly instanced in, e.g., the Chester Beatty Genesis Manuscript (Chester Beatty Papyrus IV, Rahlfs 961, fourth century CE), and was almost certainly used also in the early fragment of Genesis, P.Yale 1 (P.Yale inv. 419, van Haelst 12, variously dated from early second to third century CE). Although there is a lacuna in this fragment at this spot, the space is scarcely adequate to have accommodated the number written out in words. The likelihood that the number was written as ΤΙΗ is one of the reasons that most papyrologists take P.Yale 1 to be an early Christian copy of Genesis. On this fragment, see esp. C.H. Roberts, "P.Yale 1 and the Early Christian Book," *Essays in Honor of C. Bradford Welles* (ed. A.E. Samuel; American Studies in Papyrology 1; New Haven

evidence confirming that the Greek letter *tau* was viewed by Christians in the second century CE as a visual symbol of the cross of Jesus. Indeed, Justin Martyr (*1 Apol.* 55) indicates that second-century Christians could see visual allusions to Jesus' cross in practically any object with even the remote shape of a T (e.g., a sailing mast with cross-beam, a plow or other tools with a cross-piece of any kind, the erect human form with arms extended, even the face with the nose extending!).[40] In another fascinating passage (*1 Apol.* 60), Justin cites a statement from Plato's *Timaeus*, ἐχίασεν αὐτὸν ἐν τῷ παντί ("He placed him crosswise in the universe"), which Justin appropriates as a reference to Jesus ("concerning the Son of God," *1 Apol.* 60:1). The verb, ἐχίασεν, suggests a *chi* shape, but Justin claims (*1 Apol.* 60:2–5) that Plato derived the idea from a misunderstanding of the account where Moses was directed by God to erect a brass object for the healing of the Israelites who had been bitten by serpents (Num. 21:8–9). Justin claims that Plato inaccurately understood the object that Moses made as *chi*-shaped, when in fact it was in the figure of a cross.[41] In light of his earlier comments about cross-shaped objects in *1 Apol.* 55, we can say that Justin almost certainly had something T-shaped object in mind here as well in claiming that Moses' brass object was "the figure of a cross".[42]

Closer to the probable date of the manuscripts in which the *tau-rho* device appears, there is another significant piece of evidence. Tertullian (*Contra Marcionem* 3:22), citing the passage in Ezekiel where God directs an angel to mark the foreheads of the elect, takes the "mark" as the Greek letter *tau*, and then comments as follows:

1966) 27–28; and the stimulating reflections by E. Dinkler, "Papyrus Yalensis 1 als ältester bekannter christlicher Genesistext: Zur Frühgeschichte des Kreuz-Symbols," *Im Zeichen des Kreuzes: Aufsätze von Erich Dinkler* (eds. O. Merk—M. Wolter; Berlin—New York 1992) 341–345. The way the number is written out in Greek, τριακο-σιους δεκα και οκτω, would have suggested to early Greek-speaking Christians the use of the three Greek letters in question.

[40] Somewhat later, Minucius Felix (*Octavius*, 29; ANF 4:191) echoes basically the same attitude. On the history and various types of cross-symbols, see, e.g., Erich Dinkler and Erika Dinkler-von Schubert, "Kreuz," *Lexicon der christlichen Ikonographie* (ed. E. Kirschbaum; Rome 1968), vol. 2 cols. 562–90.

[41] Justin says of Plato's putative reading of the Numbers account, "μηδὲ νοήσας τύπον εἶναι σταυροῦ ἀλλὰ χίασμα νοήσας, τὴν μετὰ τὸν πρῶτον θεὸν δύναμιν κε-χιάσθαι ἐν τῷ παντὶ εἶπε" (*1 Apol.* 60:5).

[42] The LXX has Moses fashion a brass serpent and place it "ἐπὶ σημείου". The Hebrew has Moses place a brass serpent on a "נֵס" ("pole").

Now the Greek letter *Tau* and our own [Latin] letter T is the very form of the cross, which He [God] predicted would be the sign on our foreheads in the true Catholic Jerusalem . . .[43]

So it seems most reasonable to see the Christian appropriation of the *tau-rho* ligature as connected to, and likely prompted by, this strong association of the Greek letter *tau* with Jesus' cross.

This certainly also fits with the fact that the earliest known Christian uses of the *tau-rho* device are in the special "*nomina sacra*" writing of the words for "cross" and "crucify".

But what is the significance of the superimposed letter *rho* in the Christian use of the *tau-rho* compendium? Many years ago, F.J. Dölger cited intriguing evidence indicating that the Greek letter *rho* (which = 100) could represent "good fortune" (by "isosephy" the letters in the expression "ἐπ' ἀγαθά" amount to 100).[44] Dölger also cited a statement by the Christian teacher and hymnist Ephraem the Syrian (ca. 306–73 CE) that is of interest. The statement comes in Ephraem's comments on the meaning of the Christian symbol apparently comprising a *tau-rho* with the *alpha* and *omega* placed under the left and right horizontal arms of the *tau*. Ephraem says that in this device we have represented the cross of Jesus (the *tau*, for which he says that Moses' outstretched hands are an OT type), the *alpha* and *omega* signifying that Jesus ("the crucified one") is the beginning and end, and, he continues, "The ρ signifies βοήθια [= "help"], the numerical value of which is 100".[45]

Dölger took Ephraem's statement to mean that he interpreted the *tau-rho* device by isosephy as signifying "Salvation is in the Cross"

---

[43] *Contra Marcionem* was written 207 CE. I cite here the translation of Tertullian in ANF 3 (pp. 340–341). The LXX of Ezek. 9:4, however, has the angel directed to place a σημειον upon the foreheads of the righteous. Tertullian seems to cite the reading that is reported by Origen to have featured in the translations of Theodotion and Aquila (Origen, *Selecta in Ezekiel*; Migne, 3.802), which is a more literal rendering of the Hebrew (תו).

[44] ε-5, π-80, α-1, γ-3, α-1, θ-9, α-1 = 100. F.J. Dölger, *Sol Salutis: Gebet und Gesang im christlichen Altertum* (Münster ³1972 [1925]) 73–74, citing Artemidorus of Ephesus ("Daldianus", late 2nd cent. CE), and an inscription from Pergamon from the time of Hadrian.

[45] β-2, o-70, η-8, θ-9, ι-10, α-1 = 100. I translate the Greek from the citation of Ephraem in Dölger, *Sol Salutis*, 74, n. 2). On Ephraem, see, e.g., K. McVey, "Ephraem the Syrian," *Encyclopedia of Early Christianity* (1988) 376–377 (with bibliography). McVey describes Ephraem as holding "a vision of the world as a vast system of symbols or mysteries" (ibid., 376).

or "the Cross is our help".[46] This seems to me a persuasive inference. Might this be also the original meaning and function of the *tau-rho* device? Is this how the scribes who first employed the *tau-rho* in the *nomina sacra* forms of σταυρος and σταυροω regard the device? Ephraem is, of course, considerably later than the time of the manuscripts that we are focusing on here, and so the question is whether his numerical interpretation manifests his own fascination with such things or reflects more broadly early Christian interpretation of the *tau-rho*.

To be sure, we have evidence that at least some Christians in the first and second centuries engaged in isosephy. Most familiar, of course, is the number of "the beast" in Revelation 13:17–18, which is "the number of his name".[47] We should also recall the interpretation of the 318 servants of Abraham noted previously in *Epistle of Barnabas* (9:7–9). In an earlier publication, I have offered support for C.H. Roberts' proposal that the *nomina sacra* writing of Jesus' name as IH may have derived from an association of the numerical value of these two Greek letters (18) with the same numerical value of the Hebrew word for life, חי.[48] But even if this particular proposal is not deemed persuasive to all, it is clear that some Christians from the earliest period were interested in using numerical symbolism to express their faith.[49] So, it is in principle a plausible possibility that the numerically-based meaning of the *rho* in the *tau-rho* device stated by Ephraem might go back much earlier, and might even have been the originating impulse for the Christian appropriation of the device.

But there are some reasons to hesitate. Precisely given the evidence of a readiness among Christian in the first few centuries to employ isosephy, it is curious that we have no hint that the *tau-rho* was interpreted in this way earlier than Ephraem. Moreover, there is to my knowledge no evidence that the number 100 featured in

---

[46] Dölger, *Sol Salutis*, 74.

[47] As is well known, there is some textual variation in manuscripts of Revelation, the best supported number being 666, but some witnesses reading 616 (𝔓[115] [= P.Oxy. LVI 4499] C and Irenaeus), and even 665 (the minuscule 2344).

[48] Hurtado, "Origin," 665–69.

[49] To cite another example, the number eight was appropriated by early Christians as a symbol for the resurrection and eschatological hopes. See esp. F.J. Dölger, "Die Achtzahl in der altchristlichen Symbolik," *Antike und Christentum* 4 (1934) 153–87; R. Staats, "Ogdoas als ein Symbol für die Auferstehung," *VigChr* 26 (1972) 29–52.

second-century Christian isosephy or that the word βοηθια was particularly prominent in Christian vocabulary of that period. Indeed, Ephraem's strong interest in finding mystical symbols of his faith everywhere in the world and nature suggests that the numerical interpretation of his *tau-rho* which he proposes may be his own contribution. Most significantly, Ephraem was commenting on the Christian use of a "free-standing" *tau-rho* device, that is, the *tau-rho* used on its own as a Christian symbol, such as we see in the Armant inscription cited previously.[50]

But I contend that this much later free-standing use of the *tau-rho* is significantly different from what we have in the earliest evidence of Christian use of the device, in which it appears within texts and as part of the marking off of words that refer to Jesus' cross/crucifixion. That is, in our earliest evidence of its Christian use, the *tau-rho* consistently appears *in a crucial context* as part of a *text* that has to do with Jesus' death. Used as a free-standing symbol, however, a device such as the *tau-rho* invites, perhaps requires, some imaginative interpretation such as Ephraem offered. But used in the way that we have the device employed in 𝔓[66], 𝔓[75] and 𝔓[45], the *tau-rho* takes its Christian meaning and function from the words of which it is a crucial part, and the sentences in which it is deployed.

This leads us to another intriguing possibility. The *tau-rho* device may have been appropriated by Christians originally, not (or not simply) on the basis of numerical symbolism, but because it could function as *a visual reference to the crucified Jesus*. This is not an original suggestion, but was proposed previously, notably by K. Aland and then supported strongly by E. Dinkler.[51] In this proposal, the *tau-rho* device was appropriated initially because it could serve as a stylized reference to (and representation of) Jesus on the cross. The *tau* is confirmed as an early symbol of the cross, and the loop of the superimposed *rho* in the *tau-rho* suggested the head of a crucified figure. This very simple pictogram reference to the crucifixion of Jesus fits with the simplicity and lack of decorative detail that

---

[50] Finegan, *Archaeology*, 387–88. Granted, the free-standing form of the *tau-rho* that Ephraem comments on includes the use of the *alpha* and *omega* symbols as well, but this is only a more elaborate version of the sort of free-standing use of the *tau-rho* we have reflected in the Armant inscription.

[51] Aland, "Bemerkungen"; Dinkler, *Signum Crucis*, 177–78.

characterizes earliest Christian art. As Robin Jensen notes in her recent excellent introduction to early Christian art, the simple nature of the visual expressions of faith in the earliest material "suggests that communication was valued above artistic quality or refinement and that the emphasis was on the meaning behind the images more than on their presentation."[52] Commendably, Jensen notes the instances of the *tau-rho* device in the early papyri to which I draw attention in this essay, characterizing the combined letters as forming "a kind of pictogram, the image of a man's head upon a cross," and observing that the device "seems to be an actual reference to the cross of crucifixion . . ."[53]

The wider importance of this view of the *tau-rho* is considerable. As Dinkler put it in his enthusiastic endorsement of Aland's study,

> Mit Recht macht Aland darauf aufmerksam, dass somit das Staurogramm älter ist als das Christogramm [*chi-rho*] . . . älter als jedes 'christliche' Bild, älter als die christianisierte oder auch schöpferisch-christliche Ikonographie, das Zeichen der Christen für *das* Heilsereignis, für das Kreuz Christi ist.[54]

That is, if this proposal is correct, the *tau-rho* represents a visual reference to Jesus' crucifixion about 150 to 200 years earlier than the late fourth or fifth-century depictions that are usually taken by art historians as the earliest.[55]

SIGNIFICANCE FOR SCHOLARSHIP

If in earliest Christian use the *tau-rho* is rightly referred to as a "staurogram", it is a noteworthy phenomenon to be reckoned with in charting the history of earliest Christian iconography.[56] As I noted

---

[52] R.M. Jensen, *Understanding Early Christian Art* (London—New York 2000) 24.

[53] Jensen, *Understanding*, 138.

[54] Dinkler, *Signum Crucis*, 178.

[55] Two Christian intaglio gems usually dated to the fourth century, and a fifth-century seal held in the Metropolitan Museum of Art in New York City are the frequently-cited items. For a discussion of these items and other relevant evidence, see now Jensen, *Understanding*, 131–41.

[56] A *tau-rho* written in red ink appears at the beginning of a single papyrus page containing Psalm 1:1 (Rahlfs 2116; van Haelst 84) dated initially (by A. Traversa) to the second century. Writing before the publication of the early manuscript data that I underscore here, and under the influence of Sulzberger's thesis, C.R. Morey, *Early Christian Art* (Princeton 1953), 128, rejected this dating because he was confident

in a previous publication, however, it is unfortunate that a good many historians of early Christian art are not aware of the staurogram (largely because early Christian manuscripts are not usually thought of as offering data for the study of art), and so do not take account of its import.[57] But the staurogram is both important and rather unusual. In its earliest extant occurrences, it is a *scribal* device but entirely with a *visual* function, and so an *iconographic* phenomenon, a visual/material expression of early Christian faith/piety. Whether the *tau-rho* was adopted originally as a pictogram of the crucified Jesus (as I tend to think), or was interpreted more along the lines of Ephraem's numerical symbolism, either way it was a *visual* reference to the cross of Jesus.

Moreover, this has ramifications far beyond papyrology or the history of early Christian art. On what has been the dominant assumption that visual references to Jesus' crucifixion do not pre-date the fourth century CE, some scholars have drawn far-reaching conclusions about the nature of Christian faith/piety in the pre-Constantinian period.[58] For instance, in a study of earliest archaeological evidence of Christianity with many other positive features, Graydon Snyder emphatically denied that there was any evidence of a visual reference to Jesus' crucifixion prior to the fourth century.[59] On this basis, he then made the further dubious claim that there was "no place in the third century [or earlier] for a crucified Christ, or a symbol

---

that the Christian use of the *tau-rho* did not pre-date Constantine. Morey was right to suspect the second-century date of the manuscript, but his reason was wrong! Cf., e.g., Roberts, "P. Yale 1," 27–28.

[57] Hurtado, "Earliest Evidence," 281–82. I cite there as an example of otherwise valuable histories of early Christian art that omit any reference to the staurogram, R. Milburn, *Early Christian Art and Architecture* (Berkeley 1988), but this omission is in fact typical of the *genre*.

[58] In an essay written before he became aware of the manuscript evidence of the Christian use of the staurogram, E. Dinkler, "Comments on the History of the Symbol of the Cross," *Journal for Theology and Church* 1 (1965) 124–46 (German original 1951), once referred to the "absolute dogma that the symbol of the cross makes its first appearance in the age of Constantine" (ibid., 132), and claimed an absence of archaeological evidence of cross-marks made by Christians from the first two centuries (ibid., 134), reflecting, of course, the influential judgment by Sulzberger (cited above).

[59] Snyder, *Ante Pacem*, 26–29 (I have not yet had access to the revised edition of this work which appeared in 2003, but from reviews it appears that it does not rectify the inadequately informed view of the matter expressed in first edition).

of divine death."[60] But Snyder showed no awareness of the staurogram, and so his estimate of cross-symbolism in the pre-Constantinian period is simply wrong.[61] We can also say, therefore, that his sweeping characterization of pre-Constantinian Christian piety/faith is equally questionable. In the earliest instances of Christian usage, the staurogram (again, whether taken as a pictogram or a numerical symbol) obviously makes reference to the crucifixion/cross of Jesus, and so (along with the abundant textual evidence) reflects an importance given to Jesus' crucifixion in Christian faith/piety, from at least as early as the late second century.

---

[60] Snyder, *Ante Pacem*, 29.

[61] I intend no particular condemnation of Snyder, for a failure to take account of the staurogram (and of the phenomena of early Christian manuscripts generally) is, sadly, rather widely demonstrated in contemporary studies of Christian origins. In a book currently in preparation, I aim to help students and scholars recognize the importance of the data offered: L.W. Hurtado, *The Earliest Christian Artifacts: Manuscripts and Christian Origins* (Grand Rapids, forthcoming 2006).

MANUSCRIPTS WITH THE *LORD'S PRAYER—*
THEY ARE MORE THAN SIMPLY WITNESSES
TO THAT TEXT ITSELF*

Thomas J. Kraus

1. Some Preliminary Notes on the Purpose of this Essay

In the "Glossary of Technical Terms" of his classic compilation of the texts of the Christian eastern liturgies F.E. Brightman describes the usage of the *Lord's Prayer* as follows: *"Occurs in all liturgies, except* Ap. const., *as the conclusion of the central action and summing up of the great prayer . . . and the transition to the communion; with a proem and a conclusion."*[1]

It is hardly surprising this text was so popular with early Christianity as it is the "prayer taught by Jesus to his disciples, and the principal prayer used by all Christians in common worship"[2] and "seit den Anfängen der chr. Gemeinden . . . sowohl Grundtext der

---

* Abbreviations of papyrological editions (manuscripts), series, corpora, and proceedings of international congresses correspond to: John F. Oates, Roger S. Bagnall, Sarah J. Clackson, Alexandra A. O'Brien, Joshua D. Sosin, Terry G. Wilfong, and Klaas A. Worp, *Checklist of Editions of Greek, Latin, Demotic and Coptic Papyri, Ostraca and Tablets* (Web Edition; http://scriptorium.lib.duke.edu/papyrus/texts/clist.html; last updated December 2004; last access 02/12/2005). The recent printed edition is *Checklist of Greek and Latin Papyri, Ostraca and Tablets* (ed. J.F. Oates et al.; BASP Suppl. 9; Atlanta ⁵2001).

[1] F.E. Brightman, *Liturgies Eastern and Western. Vol. I: Eastern Liturgies* (Oxford 1896), 581. Furthermore see C.A. Swainson, *The Greek liturgies, chiefly from original authorities. With an appendix containing the Coptic ordinary canon of the mass from two manuscripts in the British Museum* (London, 1884; repr. Hildesheim, 1971); P.D. Day, *Eastern Christian Liturgies: The Armenian, Coptic, Ethiopian and Syrian Rites. Eucharistic rites with introductory notes and rubrical instruction* (Shannon 1972), and the detailed bibliography about "Early Christian Texts (to c. 325 CE)" by M. Harding, "A Bibliography," in: J.H. Charlesworth (ed.), *The Lord's Prayer and Other Prayer Texts of the Greco-Roman Era* (Valley Forge/PA 1994), 101–257, here 229–39.

[2] "Lord's Prayer," *Encyclopædia Britannica*, 2005 (Encyclopædia Britannica Premium Service; http://www.britannica.com/eb/article?tocId=9048957; last access 03/05/2005). Or see, for instance, the entry in a printed version of this encyclopedia ("Lord's Prayer," *Encyclopædia Britannica* 14 [1973] 311), in which the *Lord's Prayer* is characterized as "perhaps from the beginning meant as that unifying bond it has become in Christendom" being "at the centre of the Mass and all services."

Verkündigung u. Katechese als auch des gelebten Glaubens"[3] ("since the beginning of Christian communities . . . both the basic text for proclamation and catechesis as well as the lived faith"). This understanding is proved by the *Didache*, the earliest surviving Christian manual, as the *Lord's Prayer* is naturally given as a feature that distinguishes believers and hypocrites (*Did.* 8:2) and should be said "three times a day" (τρὶς τῆς ἡμέρας; *Did.* 8:3).[4]

Scholars of the New Testament interested in its textual attestation would expect that the parallel and at the same time differing versions of this central Christian text, the *Lord's Prayer*, should be attested by numerous manuscripts originating from the very early days of manuscript attestation. However, after flicking through the official and updated lists of Greek manuscripts of the New Testament[5] their expectations are disappointed.[6] Of course, the major codices preserved the *Lord's Prayer* for posterity, be it in its shorter (Luke 11:2–4) or its longer (Matthew 6:9–13) version. But only one papyrus of the Lukan version, *P.Bodm.* XIV ($\mathfrak{P}^{75}$), and none for the Matthean might come as a slight surprise. By relying exclusively on the lists of Greek

---

[3] G. Bitter/G. Hunze, "Art. Vaterunser. II. Historisch-theologisch" in: *LThK* 10 (2001) 548–9, here 548.

[4] Cf. the commentaries by A. Milavec, *The Didache: Faith Hope, and Life of the Earliest Christian Communities, 50–70* CE (Mahwa/NJ 2003), 308–350 (explicitly about the *Lord's Prayer*), and his short *The Didache: Text, Translation, Analysis, and Commentary* (Collegeville/MN 2003), here 65–66. As Milavec understands διδαχή as "training" he can infer that the whole writing is a kind of training program for converts attracted by Jesus and the way of life of the tried and tested members of his movement.

[5] See the internet pages of the "Institut für neutestamentliche Textforschung (INTF)" in Münster (http://www.uni-muenster.de/ NTTextforschung, click on "Aktuelles"; last access 02/07/2005), which continues its *Kurzgefaßte Liste der griechischen Handschriften des Neuen Testaments* (ed. K. Aland et al.; ANTT 1; Berlin-New York ²1994). Though lacking a printed version of an updated list of the Greek manuscripts of the New Testament, still helpful are the lists in NA²⁷ and GNT⁵ in addition to the forthcoming publications of the Institute in Münster, above all the series *ANTT* (Arbeiten zur neutestamentlichen Textforschung) and detailed critical edition *ECM* (*editio critica maior*).

[6] Even modern approaches dealing with the Lord's Prayer and its 'textual tradition' (e.g., J. Delobel, "The Lord's Prayer in the Textual Tradition. A Critique of Recent Theories and Their View on Marcion's Role," in: *The New Testament in Early Christianity. La reception des écrits néotestamentaires dans le christianisme primitif* [ed. J.-M. Severin et al.; BEThL 86; Leuven 1989], 293–309) or 'the text in tradition' (e.g., K.W. Stevenson, *The Lord's Prayer. A Text in Tradition* [Minneapolis 2004]) are made without any mention of the manuscripts referred to here.

manuscripts or the apparatuses of the critical editions of the New Testament, the reader gets the impression that there are no other extant manuscripts to the textual passage under discussion than those mentioned there.[7]

The reverse, however, is true: with the help of the fine tool of the *Leuven Database of Ancient Books* (see below) maintained and updated by W. Clarysse, a considerable number of objects with (parts of) the *Lord's Prayer*—on papyrus, parchment, wood, and as a potsherd—can be found as confirmation of a rich process of applying and, thus, preserving this text of fundamental significance.[8] Nevertheless, those objects were eventually not incorporated into the list of the Greek manuscripts of the New Testament, even if E. von Dobschütz recognized their importance and attempted to install two new categories ("Ostraka" and "Talismane") in vain.[9] Remnants of von Dobschütz's work can be seen in the items under list entries [0152] and [0153]. Unfortunately, a number of papyri[10] in the official list were later on identified as amulets ($\mathfrak{P}^{50}$; $\mathfrak{P}^{78}$—see T. Wasserman's study in this volume), a lectionary ($\mathfrak{P}^2$; $\mathfrak{P}^3$; $\mathfrak{P}^{44}$), an excerpt ($\mathfrak{P}^{43}$; $\mathfrak{P}^{62}$), a writing exercise ($\mathfrak{P}^{10}$), a manuscript with a song ($\mathfrak{P}^{42}$), an occasional note of a verse ($\mathfrak{P}^{12}$), a single sheet of miniature format ($\mathfrak{P}^{105}$; used as an amulet?) or texts with commentary (i.e., ἑρμηνεία: $\mathfrak{P}^{55}$; $\mathfrak{P}^{59}$; $\mathfrak{P}^{60}$; $\mathfrak{P}^{63}$; $\mathfrak{P}^{80}$), all of them classifications that led to the exclusion of other manuscripts, above all potential amulets.[11] Becoming fully aware of

---

[7] It is not the purpose of this paper to discuss the *Lord's Prayer* as regards content or the relationship of the three versions (Matthew 6:9–13; Luke 11:2–4; *Didache* 8:2) and origin and age of the doxology. For these issues refer to the literature given by Harding, "A Bibliography" (see note 1), 186–201, and the most recent commentary by Milavec, *The Didache: Faith* (see note 4), above all 305–380.

[8] Not to forget the indispensable catalogue by J. van Haelst, *Catalogue des papyrus littéraires juifs et chrétiens* (Université de Paris IV Paris-Sorbonne. Série Papyrologie 1; Paris 1976) and the items listed by G.H.R. Horsley, "88. The Lord's Prayer in a Necropolis," *NDIEC* 3 (1983) 103–5; C.A. La'da/A. Papathomas, "A Greek Papyrus Amulet from the Duke Collection with Biblical Excerpts: Septuagint Psalm 90, the Heading of Psalm 91 and the Lord's Prayer with a Doxology," *BASP* 41 (2004; forthcoming) Appendix III.

[9] Cf. E. von Dobschütz *Eberhard Nestle's Einführung in das Griechische Neue Testament* (Göttingen: ⁴1923) 86 and 97; Id., "Zur Liste der Neutestamentlichen Handschriften II," *ZNW* 25 (1926) 300; "III," *ZNW* 27 (1928) 218–9; "IV," *ZNW* 32 (1933) 188.

[10] Here 'papyrus' is used for the writing material and not for the materials relevant for the field of papyrology. Cf. T.J. Kraus, "'Pergament oder Papyrus?': Anmerkungen zur Signifikanz des Beschreibstoffes bei der Behandlung von Manuskripten," *NTS* 49 (2003) 425–32.

[11] Cf. K. Aland/B. Aland, *The Text of the New Testament* (transl. E.F. Rhodes;

that shortcoming K. Aland tried to do something about it by introducing a new category for them in his repertory of Greek Christian papyri called "Varia."[12] Even if this effort is to be praised, again a low opinion of manuscripts classified that way is implied, primarily hold against so-called amulets. From a retrospective view these amulets are still sometimes looked down upon as manifestations of primitive magic, and so the persisting notion survives that magic and (normative or orthodox) religion form a distinctive dichotomy. To the contrary, forms of magic must be investigated within the wider limits of religion as they depict a characteristic facet of it and form an integral part of religion.[13]

In addition to this first premise, the approach to the sample manuscripts of the *Lord's Prayer* performed here rests on a second one. As traditional textual criticism of the New Testament primarily and often only focuses on the reconstruction of a text closest to the hypothetical original, textual critics are hardly interested in the paleographical and codicological data provided by manuscripts and the other preserved non-biblical texts on them, but concentrate on the shape and quality of the text given.[14] Although that remains a legitimate objective and "[E]stablishing the earliest text-forms provides

---

Grand Rapids ²1989), 85. Generally on this issue see T.J. Kraus, "'Pergament oder Papyrus?'" (see note 10), 425–32. Additionally, some further list entries remain doubtful such as 𝔓⁷ (from a patristic context?), 𝔓²⁵ (affinity with the Diatessaron) and 𝔓⁷⁶ (with ερμηνεία).

[12] Cf. *Repertorium der griechischen christlichen Papyri I: Biblische Papyri* (ed. K. Aland; PTS 18; Berlin-New York 1976), 10–11.

[13] Succinctly, J.N. Bremmer, "The Birth of the Term 'Magic'," *ZPE* 126 (1999) 1–12, above all 9–12, now corrected and updated in idem./J.R. Veenstra (eds.), *The Metamorphosis of Magic from Late Antiquity to the Early Modern Period* (Groningen Studies in Cultural Change 1; Leuven-Paris-Dudley/MA 2002) 1–11, above all 276–71, and H.D. Betz, "Magic and Mystery in the Greek Magical Papyri," in: *Magika Hiera. Ancient Greek Magic & Religion* (ed. C.A. Faraone/D. Obbink; New York-Oxford 1991), 244–59.

[14] Cf. B.M. Metzger, *The Text of the New Testament. Its Transmission, Corruption, and Restoration* (New York-Oxford ³1992), v: "The textual critic seeks to ascertain from the divergent copies which form of the text should be regarded as most nearly conforming to the original. In some cases the evidence will be found to be so evenly divided that it is extremely difficult to decide between two variant readings. In other instances, however, the critic can arrive at a decision based on more or less compelling reasons for preferring one reading and rejecting another." Even if Metzger's handbook—as most of the others of that kind—provides basic information on the material and making of manuscripts, an obvious emphasis is put on the readings, i.e. the text itself.

one dimension" of textual criticism, "the real-life contexts of variant readings"[15] run the risk of falling into oblivion. Manuscripts reveal quite a lot of "the sociocultural and intellectual character of the communities where manuscripts resided and which left its mark on those manuscripts."[16] My own objective is similar to Eldon J. Epp's, because manuscripts are "Fingerabdrücke einer vergangenen Zeit, die sich im jeweiligen Material, in der spezifischen Schrift bzw. Beschriftung und der Rechtschreibung eines Manuskripts verfestigt haben"[17] ("fingerprints of a bygone time that had become fixed in individual material, a specific layout and performance of the writing, and the orthography of a manuscript"), or to be more precise, fingerprints of real people. Therefore, it is obvious that manuscripts of the *Lord's Prayer*, too, even if they are ruled out by the traditional textual criticism of the New Testament, deserve to be examined without bias and in their own right. So, equal and additional to other witnesses of Christian texts—for instance, any other archaeological finds as well as allusions and quotes in the writings of the early Christian writers—they help to initiate fresh investigations so that we may reach new insights into the lives of the early Christians and those living together with them in that long gone world.

On the basis of these two premises I intend to present a list of various extant manuscripts of the *Lord's Prayer*, each entry accompanied by a brief description. Then follows a brief survey of their materials and basic purposes. Finally and with the help of one specific sample item, the benefit to be gained from examination of individual

[15] E.J. Epp, "The Oxyrhynchus New Testament Papyri: 'Not Without Honor Except in Their Hometown'?," *JBL* 123 (2004) 5–55, here 9.

[16] Epp, "The Oxyrhynchus New Testament Papyri" (see note 15), 10. Basically, such a widened understanding of textual criticism forms the basis for some of E.J. Epp's other recent studies: "The New Testament Papyri at Oxyrhynchus in Their Social and Intellectual Context," *Sayings of Jesus: Canonical and Non-Canonical. Essays in Honour of Tjitze Baarda* (ed. W.L. Petersen/J.S. Vos/H.J. de Jonge; NovTSup 89; Leiden 1997) 47–68; "The Codex and Literacy in Early Christianity and at Oxyrhynchus: Issues Raised by Harry Y. Gamble's *Books and Readers in the Early Church*" *Critical Review of Books in Religion* 11 (1997) 15–37; "The Jews and the Jewish Community in Oxyrhynchus: Socio-Religious Context for the New Testament Papyri" (in this volume).

[17] T.J. Kraus, "*Ad fontes*: Gewinn durch die Konsultation von Originalhandschriften am Beispiel von *P.Vindob.G* 31974," *Biblica* 82 (2001) 1–17, here 1. Similarly Id., "P.Vindob.G 2325: Das sogenannte Fayûm-Evangelium—Neuedition und kritische Rückschlüsse," *Zeitschrift für antikes Christentum* 5 (2001) 197–212, here 198; Id., "'Pergament oder Papyrus?'" (see note 10), 432.

manuscript is to be demonstrated. As every list entry could easily serve to achieve that goal and due to space restrictions, the scope of this essay especially concentrates on those manuscripts where images are produced in order to offer a brief overview of significant conclusions that eventually focus on *P.Princ.* II 107 = *Suppl.Mag.* I 29 as a model text to demonstrate in detail what a manuscript like that can tell us today. This way, in some specific cases my descriptions and observations can be comprehended with the help of the images supplied.

2. Manuscripts with the Lord's Prayer (without a Gregory-Aland number)

2.1 *A compilation in list form*

The list entries are sorted according to date and first identified with the help of their (a) *LDAB* number (*Leuven Databank of Ancient Books*; http://ldab.arts.kuleuven.ac.be; last access 02/07/2005), (b) their *APIS* number (*Advanced Papyrological Information System*; http://www.columbia.edu/cu/lweb/projects/digital/apis; last access 02/07/05), (c) their entry number in van Haelst's catalogue (see note 8) and (d) the inventory name or number they have in their home collection. Additionally, the lists provided by Horsley (see note 8) and La'da/Papathomas (see note 8) proved to be invaluable for the process of compiling the list.[18] In order to guarantee an accessible orientation entries are structured as follows: plates, literature, text, purpose, and description.

---

[18] Horsley accumulated 13 manuscripts (his inscription *IGA* V 357 not counted): (1), (3) [of course, only *P.Oslo.inv.* 1644], (4), (6), (8), (9), (12), (13), (14), (15), (16), (17) and inconsistently *P.Oxy.* III 407, which only has a doxology and no traces of the *Lord's Prayer*. La'da/Papathomas list 17 entries: (1), (2), (3) [*P.Oslo.inv.* 1644], (5), (6), (7), (8), (9), (11), (12), (13), (14), (15), (16), (18), (19) and, of course, (10) *P.Duk.inv.* 778. They exclude (4), "since it originates from Megara in Greece" (their note 17). Analogous to the search result of the *LDAB* they include *P.Oxy.* VIII 1151, an amulet against fever with John 1:1–3, Matthew 4:23 and an allusion to John 5:2, but not with any quotation from the *Lord's Prayer* (cf. my comments on *P.Princ.* II 107).

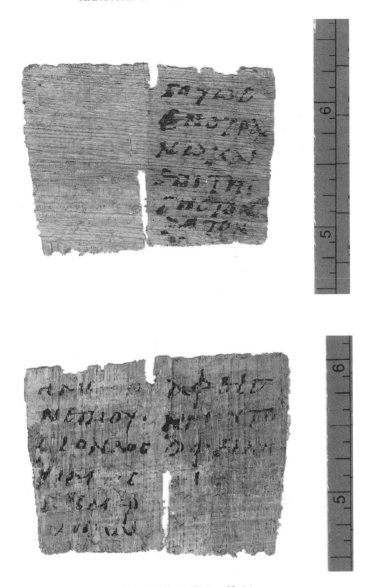

Figs. 1 & 2: P.Ant. II 54
Courtesy of the Egypt Exploration Society © (Nikolaos Gonis, The
Oxyrhynchus Papyri Project, Papyrology Rooms, Sackler Library, Oxford).

(1) *P.Ant.* II 54 (fig. 1 & 2)

LDAB 5425, van Haelst 347, Aland, *Repertorium I* (see note 12), Var 29 (additional studies in which the papyrus is mentioned); R. Cribiore, *Writing, Teachers, and Students in Graeco-Roman Egypt* (ASP 36; Atlanta 1996), 273 no. 387; Oxford, Sackler Library.

Plates: Editio princeps, plate IV (verso); B. Legras, *Lire en Égypte d'Alexandre à l'Islam* (Antiqua 6; Paris 2002), 93 (verso).— *Literature*: E. Bammel, "Ein neuer Vater-Unser-Text," *ZNW* 52 (1961) 280–281; Id., "A New Text of the Lord's Prayer," *ET* 73 (1961/62) 54; K. Treu, *APF* 19 (1969) 180; C.L. Roberts, *Manuscripts, Society and Belief in Early Christian Egypt* (The Schweich Lectures of the British Academy 1977; Oxford 1979), 82; L. Koenen, "Manichäische Mission und Kölster in Ägypten," in: *Das römisch-byzantinische Ägypten. Akten des internationalen Symposiums 26.–30. September 1978 in Trier* (Aegyptiaca Treverensia 2; Mainz 1983), 93 note 6; G.H.R. Horsley, "Reconstructing a biblical codex: the prehistory of MPER *n.s.* XVII. 10 (*P.Vindob.G* 29831), in: *PapCongr.* XXI (1997) 473–481, here 490; *The Text of the Earliest New Testament Greek Manuscripts. New and Complete Transcriptions with Photographs* (ed. P.W. Comfort/D.P. Barrett; Wheaton/IL 2001), 678–679; Legras, *Lire en Égypte*, 93.—*Text*: Matthew 6:10–12.— *Purpose*: amulet?; "toy book for a child" (*ed. pr.*)?; miniature codex?; "miniature notebook" (Cribiore)?—*Description*: III CE, Antinoopolis. Papyrus bifolium (5.2 × 4 cm) in a rather crude and sloping hand; in order to establish the complete *Lord's Prayer* three preceding pages would have preceded so that then the codex would have consisted of two double leaves; maybe slits on top and bottom indicate the binding by a thread (see figs. 1 & 2, and *P.Ryl.* I 28); recto with one blank page (then p. 6); on p. 5 (verso) the text abruptly stops in the middle of the word ὀφειλη | μ[ατα; Horsley's suggestion that the piece might be a bifolium originally "from a papyrus codex or a free-standing double leaf" then reused as an amulet provides problems as far as the scribe's hand is taken into account (as Roberts correctly pointed out). Be that as it may, it remains a mystery that the scribe ended in the middle of a word on p. 5 (as p. 6 was blank). Nevertheless, the bifolium does belong to the category of miniature formats as designated by E.G. Turner (*The Typology of the Early Codex* [University of Pennsylvania 1977], 22, 29–30 ["Breadth Less Than 10 cm"])[19] and may be a "miniature notebook" (Cribiore) based on paleographical observations (inconsistency of letter formation in a specific way; according to Cribiore "[e]volving hand"; compare with the other notebooks listed, cf. Cribiore, *Writing*, nos. 379–412).

(2) *P.Erl.Diosp.* 1
University of Erlangen-Nuremberg, Inv. 27–32.
Plates: P.Erl.Diosp., plates I–XII (Matthew 6:9 on plate XII).—*Literature: P.Erl.* 105–110 (W. Schubart); *P.Erl.Diosp.* (F. Mitthof), especially pp. 25, 32, 58; reviews by M. Schentuleit, *Enchoria* 28 (2002/03), 203–4; R.S. Bagnall, *Bryn Mawr Classical Review* 2003.06.23 (http://ccat.sas.upenn.edu/bmcr/2003/2003–06–23.html; last access 02/11/2005); T. Kruse, *HZ* 278 (2004) 156–8.—*Text*: accounts in form of a single-quire codex (24 pages) with beginning of Matthew 6:9.—*Purpose*: Administrative and documentary.—*Description*: 313/314 CE, Diospolis Parva. Single-quire papyrus codex (page size 12.5 × 24 cm) published by W. Schubart in 1942 under six numbers (*P.Erl.* 105–110), who recognized that these belong together; republished by F. Mitthof in 2002, who reconstructed the shape of the codex; six incomplete sheets with writing on both sides (24 pages); pagination (thus, originally 26 sheets with additional cover and 103 pages); top and bottom margins preserved; accounts "not written into the book in any systematic form or in a single direction" (Bagnall); two columns on each page; diverse transactions in money by different people noted down by a single scribe; on page 52 (Inv. 29, recto, page on the right, upside down to the text of the account): πάτερ ἡμῶν ὁ ἐν τοῖς [οὐρανοῖς] (no more room left there except for an addition like the potential οὐρανοῖς); on the one hand it is surprising that the first few

---

[19] Of course, Turner's list needs to be updated. Unfortunately, due to other tasks and projects I am still not in the position to complete my own list of more than sixty entries of Greek miniature codices according to Turner's definition. Nevertheless, such a list then requires an introductory methodological reflection and must be supplemented by the Coptic manuscripts belonging to that category.

words of the *Lord's Prayer* (written over the pagination ρημ
there) are to be found in such a context—something that
makes *P.Erl.Diosp.* 1 a unique case—written with characteristics of a calligraphic hand, maybe by the same hand as
the accounts (cf. Mitthof; Bagnall), even if those are performed in a cursive business hand; on the other there are
some individuals (even the accounts of a bishop, a presbyter
and priests; according to Bagnall "the earliest securely datable documentary references to these Christian offices in the
papyri") mentioned whose names are or might be those of
Christians (cf. Mitthof, pp. 17 note 72 and 20–21); above
all, the name Ἠλίας is used several times for one of the
assistants; but why should an employee write down something like the *Lord's Prayer* in his employer's account book?
Possibly, this is an occasional note not necessarily to be
linked with a magical background (as Mitthof, p. 58, does).
Nevertheless, the *Lord's Prayer* might have been written into
the document by a different scribe, after this had already
been out of use for some time (cf. Mitthof; Kruse).

(3) *P.Schøyen* I 16
LDAB 2994, van Haelst 345, Aland, *Repertorium I* (see note
12), Var 27, Rahlfs 2115; *P.Oslo inv.* 1644 + Schøyen Collection MS 244/4.
Plates: P.Schøyen I 16 (*ed. pr.*), plate XI.—*Text*: Cross; Matthew
6:9–13 (without ἀπὸ τοῦ πονηροῦ) followed by doxology and
potential apostolic valediction formula (somewhat similar to
2 Cor 13:3); ornamental line; LXX-Psalm 90:1–4 (*P.Oslo.inv.*
1644) + LXX-Psalm 90:4–13 (Schøyen Collection MS
244/4)—*Purpose*: amulet.—*Literature*: L. Amundsen, "Christian
Papyri from the Oslo Collection," *SO* 24 (1945) 121–147,
here 141–147; K. Treu, *APF* 19 (1969) 195; joined together
and edited anew by R. Pintaudi, "Amuleto cristiano: LXX,
Ps. 90.4–13," in: *Greek Papyri I* (= *P.Schøyen* I; ed. Id.;
Manuscripts in the Schøyen Collection 4; Oslo 2004), no.
16 and plate XI.[20]—*Description*: late IV CE, Oxyrhynchus?

---

[20] I am indebted to Anastasia Maravela-Solbakk, Oslo, and Rosario Pintaudi, Florence, for their helping hand, especially to the latter for sending his forthcoming manuscript and images of the papyrus fragments.

(acquired in Egypt together with documents from Oxyrhynchus). Two papyrus fragments (11.7 × 3.9 cm; 13 × 7.7 cm) rejoined with another one in the Schøyen Collection (9 × 9.7 cm); lacuna of about 1.5 cm between the two Oslo fragments, which preserved some of the left margin; breadth of the original leaf about 30 cm, width about 35 cm; "unskilled writer" of "the early Byzantine type" (Amundsen, 142); mixture between literary and cursive letter forms; letters quite large and upright with few ligatures; no traces of folding; verso blank; text of the *Lord's Prayer* ends abruptly with ῥῦσε ἡμᾶς (read ῥῦσαι) and immediately is completed by εἰς τίους αἰῶνας τῶν αἰώνων before the apostolic valediction formula follows. For papyri preserving the *Lord's Prayer* together with LXX-Psalm 90 see the notes under (c) to *P.Princ.* II 107 = *Suppl.Mag.* I 29 below.

(4) *O.Athens inv.* 12227 = *Pap.Graec.Mag.* II O4
LDAB 5594; van Haelst 348; Athens, National Archaeological Museum 12227. With others subsumed to Gregory-Aland 0152 for 'talismans.'
Plates:[21] R. Knopf, "Eine Thonscherbe mit dem Texte des Vaterunser," *MDAIA* 25 (1900) 314 (photo) and 315 (drawing); O. Kern, *Inscriptiones Graecae* (Tabulae in usum scholarum 7; Bonn 1913), plate 50; M. Guarducci, *Epigrafia Greca IV: Epigrafi sacre pagane e cristiane* (Roma 1978, first reprint 1995), 337 Fig. 97.—*Literature*: Knopf, "Eine Thonscherbe," 313–24; Id., *ZNW* 2 (1901) 228–33; E. Nestle, "Zum Vaterunser von Megara," *ZNW* 2 (1901) 347–9 and U. Wilcken, "Bibliographische Notizen und Mitteilungen," *APF* 2 (1903) 161–80, here 166; C. Schmidt, *APF* 2 (1903) 383 no. 8; A. Deissmann, *Licht vom Osten. Das Neue Testament und die neuentdeckten Texte der hellenistisch-römischen Welt* (Tübingen ⁴1923), 43 note 2 and *Light from the Ancient East: The New Testament Illustrated by Recently Discovered Texts of the Graeco-Roman World* (New York 1927), 56 note 3; E. Peterson, *ΕΙΣ ΘΕΟΣ. Epigraphische,*

---

[21] Due to intensive restoration and renovation works of the National Archaeological Museum in Athens the clay tablet is still packed so that I was not able to obtain a photo. However, the Deputy Director, Rosa Proskynitopoulou, advised me to inquire again later after the reopening of the museum.

formgeschichtliche und religionsgeschichtliche Untersuchungen (FRLANT 41; Göttingen 1926), 53–5; Guarducci, *Epigrafia Greca IV*, 336–8; Epp, "The Oxyrhynchus New Testament Papyri" (see note 15), 38 note 113.—*Text*: Matthew 6:11–13.—*Purpose*: (apotropaic) house benediction (Knopf; Schmidt).—*Description*: IV CE, Megara (Greece). Fragment of a reddish brown clay tablet (12 × 13.5 cm, originally 18.5 × 22.5 cm), broken on top and left; inscribed when soft and then fired to fix it (Deissmann, who himself saw the tablet in Athens and possessed a plaster cast); thus, probably specifically produced to carry the *Lord's Prayer* for being used as a house benediction in order to protect a house, its inhabitants and visitors; the text on the fragmentary tablet starts with ἐ]πιούσιον and ends with πονηροῦ; in the middle of the last line κ]ύριε (cf. *P.Bad.* IV 60; *BGU* III 954; *P.Duk.inv.* 778), followed by a form of the *crux monogrammatica* (Knopf, 318; Guarducci, 338) better known now as *staurogram* consisting of a ligature of the Greek letters *tau* and *rho* with the corpus of the letter above the horizontal line of the first (see Guarducci, 551–2, and, above all, L. Hurtado, "The Staurogram in Early Christian Manuscripts: The Earliest Visual Reference to the Crucified Jesus?" in this volume); insecure orthography; upright and single letters.

(5) *P.Oxy.* LX 4010
LDAB 5717.
Plates: POxy: Oxyrhynchus Online (http://www.csad.ox. ac.uk/POxy/papyri/vol60/pages/4010.htm; last access 02/09/2005)—*Literature*: C. Römer, *APF* 43 (1997) 126 no. 20; S.R. Pickering, "A New Papyrus Text of the Lord's Prayer," *New Testament Textual Research Update* 2 (1994) 111–18, about *P.Oxy.* LX 4010 111–12; A.H. Cadwallader, "An Embolism in the Lord's Prayer," *New Testament Textual Research Update* 4 (1996) 81–86 (with his own reconstruction); Epp, "The Oxyrhynchus New Testament Papyri" (see note 15), 36–8.—*Text*: Introductory prayer; 2 Cor 1:3?; *Liturgia Marci?*; Matthew 6:9–13.—*Purpose*: amulet? (but see the physical size of the leaf and lacking signs of folding); liturgical text— *Description*: IV CE, Oxyrhynchus. Papyrus fragment (11.5 × 15 cm) with ample margin on the left and at bottom of c. 3 cm; writing with the fibres; verso blank; handsome hand

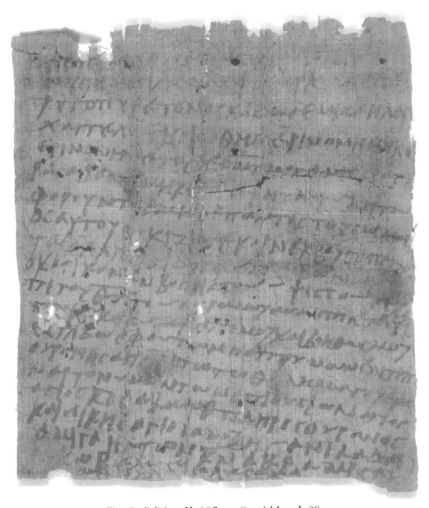

Fig. 3: P.Princ. II 107 = *Suppl.Mag.* I 29
Princeton University Library. Princeton Papyrus 107.
Manuscripts Division. Department of Rare Books and Special Collections.
Princeton University Library.

of "the Severe Style, written upright with a thickish pen
and some attempt at differential shading", performed by a
"competent penman" (K. Treu, *P.Oxy.* LX, p. 5); no lectionary signs except the suprascript stroke of the *nomina sacra*
θ(εό)ς and οὐ(ρα)νοῖς; tendency to separate words by leaving blank spaces; hardly legible in the first few lines; preliminary prayer similar to *Liturgia Marci* (Brightman, *Liturgies
Eastern and Western* (see note 1), 135 l. 31); the *Lord's Prayer*
without γενηθήτω τὸ θέλημά σου in l. 13, but with duplica-
tion of Matthew 6:13 at the end. According to Cadwallader
the trace of a letter (α?) is to be seen at the left margin, so
that the complete leaf had had a second column and, thus,
was part of a scroll. Even if the observation on the photograph Cadwallader refers to might be doubtful, he convincingly argues for a liturgical use of the leaf (for instance,
layout; language and quotations; insertion of the *Lord's Prayer*;
repetition of 'Deliver us'; cf. *P.Oslo inv.* 1644 with the *Lord's
Prayer* ending that way before the doxology starts).

(6) *P.Princ.* II 107 = *Suppl.Mag.* I 29 (fig. 3)
    See below.

(7) *P.Col.* XI 293
    LDAB 2953; APIS (columbia.apis.p1812); Columbia University
    inv. 571.
    Plates: Editio princeps, plate 1; APIS (columbia.apis.p1812).—
    Literature: C. Römer, *APF* 45 (1999) 140 no. 3; P. Mirecki,
    "Review of: Teeter, Timothy M., *Columbia Papyri XI*," *BASP*
    38 (2001) 135–45, here 135–8—*Text:* Matthew 6:4–6.—
    Purpose: codex leaf reused as an amulet? (Teeter); random
    fragment of a damaged book? (Mirecki).—*Description:* V CE,
    provenance unknown. Parchment fragment (7.1 × 6.2 cm)
    of a codex leaf, badly damaged; according to the *ed. pr.* (T.
    Teeter) perhaps reused as an amulet (*P.Col.* XI, p. 3: "if it
    was torn out to be kept as a charm or used for recitation,
    whoever did so was careless and lost the portion of the
    prayer") or "a random fragment of a damaged book, per-
    haps a deliberately destroyed book" (Mirecki, 136); margins
    of over 2 cm (recto: right; verso: left); broken on top and
    bottom; written in a formal biblical hand (cf. *P.Oxy.* VI 848;
    Codex Alexandrinus); no lectionary signs but scribe left blank

spaces and, thus, separated sections; is ἀν(θρώπ)οις a *nomen sacrum* (without suprascript stroke due to fading), whereas πάτερ and οὐρανοῖς are written in full (Mirecki, 137: "I suggest that the practical purpose is related to this scribe's demonstrated tendency to draw attention to logical divisions within the text without lectionary signs.")? For suggestions how to reconstruct the original size of the page see Teeter, *P.Col.* XI, pp. 3–4.

(8) *P.Köln* IV 171
LDAB 5971; Papyrus Collection in Cologne Inv. 3302.
Plates: Editio princeps, Tafel Ic; online: Papyrus Collection in Cologne (http://www.uni-koeln.de/phil-fak/ifa/NRWakademie/papyrologie/Karte/IV_171.html; last access 02/09/2005).—*Literature*: Cf. the comments by C. Römer, in: *P.Köln* IV, 31–34; K. Treu, *APF* 30 (1984) 123 no. 348a.—*Text*: recto—ll. 1–6 Matthew 6:12–13, l. 7 doxology, l. 8 ἀμήν (thrice), l. 9 ἅγιος (thrice); verso—blank.—*Purpose*: amulet—*Description*: V CE, provenance unknown. Dark papyrus fragment (8.5 × 5.5 cm) with writing on 9 lines with the fibres on the recto; verso blank; no margins left; untrained hand (irregular slope of the letters to the right or left; cursive μ and η; cf. *PSI* XII 1265; *P.Med.inv.* 6907); *nomina sacra* Ἰη(σο)ῦ and Χρ(ιστο)ῦ; doxological formula according to the *euchologion* of Serapion of Thmuis (furthermore, see Mart.Pol. 20,2; Const.Apost. 8,40,2; *P.Würz.* I 3; *P.Berol.* 13918); ἀμήν ≡ ἀμήν ≡ ἀμήν in order to intensify the effect of the previous prayer (Pistis Sophia 2,18; 11,28; 125,1; *P.Bon.* I 9; *P.Ross.Georg.* I 24 = *Pap.Graec.Mag.* II, P16; *P.Ross.Georg.* I 24 = *Pap.Graec.Mag.* II, P15a); ἅγιος ≡ ἅγιος ≡ ἅγιος—on the *trisagion* see the comments under d) on *P.Princ.* II 107 = *Suppl.Mag.* I 29 below; the *Liturgy of St. Basil* (Byzantine Rite) contains both this form of the *trisagion* and the thrice repeated ἀμήν (Brightman, *Liturgies Eastern and Western* [see note 1], 403 and 407); slanting lines at the bottom indicate that text ends here, i.e. Isa 6:3 is not cited completely.

(9) *P.Iand.* I 6 = *Pap.Graec.Mag.* II, P17 = *P.Giss.Lit.* 5,4
LDAB 6107, van Haelst 917, Aland, *Repertorium* I (12), Var 30; Papyrus Collection at the University Library, Gießen, *P.Iand.inv.* 14.

Plates: *P.Iand.* I, Tafel IV (E. Schäfer); *P.Giss.Lit.*, Tafel XI
(P.A. Kuhlmann); online: Papyrussammlung an der Universitätsbibliothek Gießen (http://digibib.ub.uni-giessen.de/cgi-
bin/populo/pap.pl?t_allegro=x&f_SIG=P.%20Iand.%20inv.%
2014; last access 02/09/2005).—*Literature*: See editions mentioned above; C. Wessely, "Les plus anciens monuments du
christianisme écrits sur papyrus II, *PO* 18,3 (1924; repr.
Turnhout 1985) 415–7; R.W. Daniel, *ZPE* 50 (1983) 149
note 14; M. Naldini, *ASP* 7 (1970) 384; M. Meyer, "Protective
spell using the Lord's Prayer and the Exorcism of Solomon,"
in: *Ancient Christian Magic. Coptic Texts of Ritual Power* (ed.
M.W. Meyer/R. Smith; Princeton 1999 [San Francisco
1994]), 45–6 no. 21 (English translation).—*Text*: introduction
'Gospel of Matthew' and parts of verses from Matthew and
Luke; Matthew 6:9–13 (without the sixth request) and doxology (short form); Ἐξορζισμὸς Σαλομῶνος against demons,
all kinds of diseases, and wild animals with citations from
different biblical texts, above all LXX-Psalm 90:5, 6, 13
(allusions?).—*Purpose*: amulet (textual character; orthography;
hand; foldings)—*Description*: V/VI CE, provenance unknown
(acquired in Hermopolis Magna). Papyrus fragment (30 ×
15.5 cm) with 18 legible lines on the recto; verso blank;
seven times folded lengthwise, five times widthwise; quite
large letter by a clumsy untrained hand squeezing the letters together to the end of the lines; awkward and irregular orthography; text starts with a cross and ends with ἀμήν
written in number symbols (for 99; *isopsephistic*; 9 = well-
being and luck; about the importance of the number nine
in magical context see Peterson, *ΕΙΣ ΘΕΟΣ*. [see list entry
(4)] 232ff.; nevertheless, the number nine in its abbreviated
form as (ἔτους) θ was avoided to date documents of the 3rd
and 4th century, because the letter *theta* was regarded as a
symbol for death the so-called *theta nigrum*; cf. A.U. Stylow
and J.D. Thomas, "Zur Vermeidung von Theta in Datierungen nach kaiserlichen Regierungsjahren und in verwand-
ten Zusammenhängen," *Chiron* 10 [1980] 537–51); deranged
sequence of the texts (e.g., the *Lord's Prayer* can only be read
in its usual sequence if read as follows: l. 1, l. 7b/8a, l. 14b,
l. 17a, then l. 2, l. 8b/9a, l. 13c/14a, l. 17b/18a, and l. 3).
For more details, see P.A. Kuhlmann, *P.Giss.Lit.*, pp. 170–83.

(10) *P.Duk.inv.* 778 (= formerly *P.Rob.inv.* 41)

Plates: online: Duke Papyrus Archive (http://scriptorium.lib. duke. edu/papyrus/records/778.html; last access 02/11/ 2005).—*Literature*: Short description (Catalogue record) given online; *P.Bingen* 16 (P. Arzt-Grabner/M. Ernst), p. 84; *editio princeps*: La'da/Papathomas, "A Greek Papyrus Amulet from the Duke Collection" (see note 8).—*Text*: Crosses; LXX-Psalm 90; heading of LXX-Psalm 91; Matthew 6:9–13 with doxology (*Liturgia Marci*); crosses.—*Purpose*: amulet.— *Description*: VI CE (second half), provenance unknown. Complete papyrus sheet of mediocre quality (26.8 × 11.5 cm), pieced together from diverse fragments; folded eight times vertically and once horizontally to form a handy and transportable packet for the owner; writing runs along the fibres on both sides (*transversa charta*) in black ink; on the recto small top, bottom, and right margins; left margin of 0.5 cm; verso with upper margin of 0.5 cm and lower of 17.5 cm; thus, the recto written first, as more than half of the verso was left blank (also see the crosses at the beginning of the recto and directly underneath the writing on the verso); recto with fourteen lines: the complete LXX-Psalm 90 (ll. 1–13) and the heading of LXX-Psalm 91 (l. 14) ending with ἄλλους (reference to other Psalm on the manuscript the scribe was copying or used in the sense of 'and so on'); faint traces of ink at the end might have been crosses or *staurograms* in order to frame the text (according to *ed. pr.*); verso with 11 lines: the *Lord's Prayer* (ll. 15–20) ending with the vocative κ[ύρι]ε as *nomen sacrum* with suprascript stroke (cf. *P.Bad.* IV 60; *O.Athens inv.* 12227; *BGU* III 954) and a common doxology (ll. 21–25: *Liturgia Marci* = Brightman, *Liturgies Eastern and Western* [see note 1], 115 ll. 20–21), then completed by three large crosses (l. 26); for other amulets with the *Lord's Prayer* followed by a doxology see *BGU* III 954 and *P.Bad.* IV 60 (also compare *P.Iand.* I 6); "rather careless and quick Byzantine literary hand" (*ed. pr.*); letters quite upright and in most instances separated from each other (cf. hands of *P.Warr.* 10; *P.Grenf.* II 84 = *MPER N.S.* XV 117; *MPER N.S.* XVII 49); texts on both sides of the sheet quite faulty and with variants; the *Lord's Prayer* is missing "as we forgive our

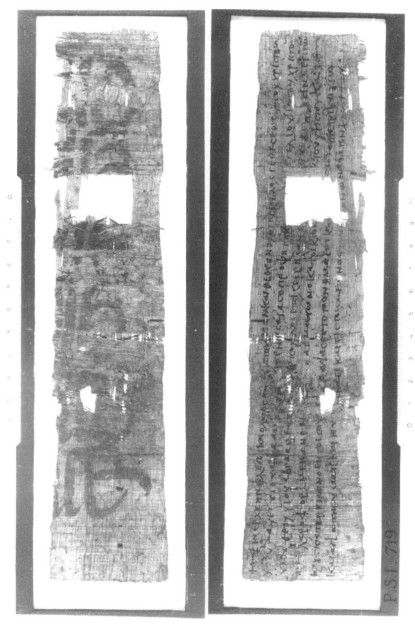

Fig. 4 & 5: PSI VI 719 = *Pap.Graec.Mag.* II P19
Courtesy of Biblioteca Medicea Laurenziana, Florence

debtors" in ll. 18–19; probably the text on the verso ends ἀμήν written in number symbols (*isosephistic* as *P.Iand.* I 6; see the comments given there; see also the threefold ἀμήν on *P.Köln* IV 171); unique attestation of these four texts on one papyrus.

(11) *P.Köln* VIII 336
LDAB 6282; Papyrus Collection in Cologne Inv. 3583.
Plates: Editio princeps, plate IVc; online: Papyrus Collection in Cologne (http://www.uni-koeln.de/phil-fak/ifa/NR Wakademie/ papyrologie/Karte/VIII_336.html; last access 02/10/2005).—*Literature*: C. Römer, *APF* 45 (1999) 140 no. 4.—*Text*: Matthew 6:11–13.—*Purpose*: single leaf; amulet?—*Description*: VI CE, provenance unknown. (12 × 4 cm). Fragment of a single, free-standing leaf of papyrus (12 × 4 cm; originally about double size) with writing along the fibres on the recto only; large, round and irregular letters of a clumsy hand; bottom margin of about 1 cm; rests of the end of the *Lord's Prayer* without any doxology; lines might have been unequally long (see the potentially shorter l. 3); faulty orthography; irregular highpoints and colon; a magical usage of this papyrus is not backed by any folds or textual indications (cf. *P.Princ.* II 107 = *Suppl.Mag.* I 29 or *P.Köln* IV 171); but folds could have caused the actual fragmentary condition of the papyrus; end ενχ[—according to the editor (M. Gronewald)—perhaps ἐν Χ[ριστῷ with instrumental ἐν.

(12) *PSI* VI 719 = *Pap.Graec.Mag.* II P19 (fig. 4+5)
LDAB 2767, van Haelst 423, Aland, *Repertorium I* (see note 12), Var 31; Rahlfs 2075; Biblioteca Medicea Laurenziana *Plates*: M. Naldini, *Documenti dell'antichità cristiana. Papiri e pergamene greco-egizie della Raccolta Fiorentina* (Firenze 1965), no. 40, tavola XXIV; R. Pintaudi, "Per la datazione di PSI VI 719," *AnalPap* 2 (1990) 28 (both sides).—*Literature*: U. Wilcken, *APF* 1 (1901) 429; Wessely, "Les plus anciens monuments" (see list entry (9)), 413; Naldini, *Documenti*, 32–3; Pintaudi, "Per la datazione," 27–28 (protocol).—*Text*: Cross; John 1:1; Matthew 1:1; John 1:23; Mark 1:1; Luke 1:1; LXX-Psalm 90:1; Matthew 6:9 with doxology;

crosses; protocol (reverse side).—*Purpose*: amulet.—*Description*:
VI CE, Oxyrhynchus? Papyrus fragment of a single sheet
(25 × 5.5 cm) with one column of six very long lines (on
average 69 letters along the fibres); at least two vertical
folds (on the left of the recto; confirmed by Rosario Pintaudi,
Biblioteca Medicea Laurenziania); non-calligraphic hand;
after the initial cross the texts starts with Χριστὲ σῶτερ, of
which only χῶρ is visible (the *rho* looks like a *staurogram*; cf.
O.Athens inv. 12227 = *Pap.Graec.Mag.* II O4); text ends with
ἀμήν and Χ(ριστός)? and three crosses; no other *nomina
sacra* used; between LXX-Psalm 90:1 and the *Lord's Prayer*
(Matthew 6:9) and following the latter and preceding the
doxology twice καὶ τὰ ἑξῆς; diaeresis over ι and υ and *spir-
itus asper*; reverse side with rests of a protocol[22] (top, bottom and right margin preserved) in a perpendicular
Byzantine hand (similar to that of *PSI* I 65; cf. R. Pintaudi,
"Una nota a PSI I 65," ZPE 56 [1984] 137–8) that helps
to date the papyrus to the sixth century (Pintaudi, "Per la
datazione").

(13) *BGU* III 954 = *W.Chr.* 133 = *Pap.Graec.Mag.* II P9
LDAB 6231, van Haelst 720, Aland, *Repertorium I* (see note
12), Var 28; burnt on arrival in the port of Hamburg.
Plates:—*Literature*: U. Wilcken, "Heidnisches und Christliches
aus Ägypten," *APF* 1 (1901) 396–436, here 431–6 (*editio
princeps*); G. Milligan, *Selections from the Greek Papyri* (Cambridge
1910), pp. 132–4 (no. 55); T. Schermann, *Ägyptische
Abendmahlsliturgien des ersten Jahrtausends* (SGKA 6; Paderborn
1912), 206; Wessely, "Les plus anciens monuments" (see
list entry (9)), 420–2.—*Text*: Cross; invocation; prayer against
demons and diseases; cf. Matthew 4:23 (ll. 11–12); Matthew
6:9–13 (ll. 15–24) followed by a short doxology; allusion
to Nicaean symbolum.—*Purpose*: amulet.—*Description*:—VI
CE, Herakleopolis Magna. According to Wilcken's report
(p. 431) a tightly pressed bundle of papyrus (folded into a
square packet of about 2 × 1 cm) wound around with a

---

[22] Cf. Aland, *Repertorium I* (see note 12), Var. 31 and van Haelst 423, who incorrectly report that the reverse side is blank, probably relying on G. Vitelli (*ed. pr.* of
PSI VI 719), *Pap.Graec.Mag.* II P19 and M. Naldini, who remained silent on the
protocol.

brown string and in the process of unwrapping broken into many tiny pieces: thus, a fragment of a folio with 30 lines in one column; careful hand of the ὀξύρυγχος τύπος with rounded letters slightly sloping to the right (ε, θ, ο, σ in an oval shape); *nomina sacra* θ(έ)ε, σ(ωτῆρ)ο[ς], κ(υρίο)υ and κ(ύρι)ε (cf. *P.Bad.* IV 60; *O.Athens inv.* 12227; *P.Duk.inv.* 778); the *Lord's Prayer* is introduced by τὴν εὔ αγγελικὴν εὐχήν with ευ written above the line ("the Gospel prayer"); vocative κ(ύρι)ε inserted before "deliver us . . ."

(14) *MPER N.S.* XV 184
LDAB 6398, van Haelst 1206; Vienna, Papyrussammlung Nationalbibliothek, L91 (*P.Vindob.L* 91).
Plates: E.A. Lowe, *Codices Latini Antiquiores X* (Oxford 1963), no. 1533; R. Seider, *Paläographie der lateinischen Papyri II.2* (Stuttgart 1981), no. 47; *MPER N.S.* XV 184, plate 82; K. Treu, *APF* 34 (1988) 77 no. 1206; J. Henner, "Der Unterricht im christlichen Ägypten," in: *Christliches mit Feder und Faden. Christliches in Texten, Textilien und Alltagsgegenständen aus Ägypten* (ed. J. Henner/H. Förster/U. Horak; Nilus 3; Vienna 1999), no. 43; J. Gascou, "Sur la date du *pater noster* de Vienne: *P.Rain.Unterricht* 184," in *P.Thomas*, 20 Fig. I (protocol).—*Literature*: Lowe, *CLA X*, no. 1533; Seider, *Paläographie der lateinischen Papyri II.2*, 123 no. 47; A. Martin, "*P. Vindob. L.* 91, un fragment du Pater latin," *Latomus* 42 (1983) 412–418 (identification); K. Treu, *APF* 34 (1988) 77 no. 1206; Henner, "Der Unterricht," 53 no. 43; J. Gascou, "Sur la date," 19–23; T. Nicklas, "Zur historischen und theologischen Bedeutung der Erforschung neutestamentlicher Textgeschichte," *NTS* 48 (2002) 151–2.—*Text*: Matthew 6:11–12 (Latin text, alternately in Latin and Greek letters); rest of protocol on verso.—*Purpose*: amulet (Seider), more likely writing exercise/school text—*Description*: late VI

Fig. 6: Louvre MND 5528
Réunion des Musées Nationaux (RMN)—Agence photographique, Paris.

to mid VII CE, Hermopolites? Papyrus fragment (17.5 ×
7.5 cm) with 10 lines of writing along the fibres in black
ink; right margin complete; verso protocol in brown ink;
scribe with some training, whereas the Greek letters appear
somewhat less careful and dynamic; orthographic faults;
reasons for partly transcribing a Latin text in Greek letters?
Cf. *P.Bad.* IV 60 (the Greek *Lord's Prayer* in Coptic letters).

(15) *Louvre MND* 5528 (fig. 6)
LDAB 6594, van Haelst 349, Cribiore, *Writing* (see list
entry (1)), 252–3 no. 322; Département des Antiquités
Grecques et Romaines—Musée du Louvre, Paris, MND
552B.
Plates: Editio princeps = A. Passoni Dell'Acqua, "Frammenti
inediti del Vangelo secondo Matteo," *Aegyptus* 60 (1980)
plates 4–5 (between pp. 112 and 113).—*Literature*: S. de
Ricci, "Fouilles de M. Gayet," *REG* 15 (1902) 452–3;
Passoni Dell'Acqua, "Frammenti," 96–119, here 107–9; K.
Treu, *APF* 30 (1984) 123 no. 349.—*Text*: Chrism and
beginning of Matthew 6:9; incomplete words on reverse
side.—*Purpose*: amulet (Passoni dell'Acqua; Treu), writing
exercise (Treu) or notebook (Cribiore).—*Description*: VII CE
(?), Antinoopolis. Fragment of a wooden tablet (15.5 × 1.8
cm); surface not waxed (with Treu against van Haelst);
possible text of the *Lord's Prayer* continued on the rest of
the tablet broken off; πατήρ (read πάτερ) in full and not
as *nomen sacrum*; hand "'[r]apid.' in 'Alexandrian Majuscule,'
not completely even and with faulty alignment" (Cribiore,
p. 253); ελχα τωϗη βοηθ on the reverse side might indicate
an invocation or request for help (τῷ βοηθῷ) as often found
in magical context, what leads Passoni Dell'Acqua to the
assumption that the tablet might be an amulet, whereas
Cribiore takes the holes in the tablet as clues for suggesting a notebook as its purpose. Personally, I favor the latter alternative due to the writing on both sides of the tablet
and a probable use in a school context as *P.Bad.* IV 60,
although the first remains possible.

(16) *P.Bad.* IV 60 (fig. 7 & 8)
LDAB 6662, van Haelst 346; University of Heidelberg,
Egyptian Collection, Inv. 761. In contrast to the indication

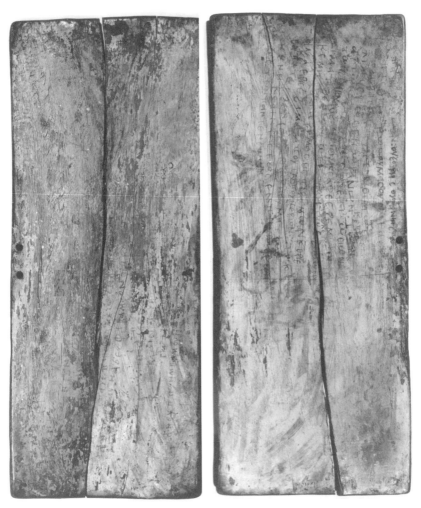

Figs. 7 & 8:—P.Bad. IV 60
Holztafel Heidelberg Inv.-Nr. 761—Courtesy of the University of Heidelberg—
Ägyptologisches Institut (Dina Faltings, curator)

of LDAB ("unknown; not in Heidelberg, Aegyptische Sammlung 425 = 761") this wooden tablet actually is there.[23] *Plates:—Literature: P.Bad.* IV 60 (*ed. pr.:* F. Bilabel); *Vom Nil zum Neckar. Kunstschätze Ägyptens aus pharaonischer und koptischer Zeit an der Universität Heidelberg* (ed. E. Feucht et al.; 1986), 214 no. 647.—*Text:* Matthew 6:9–13 with doxology (palimpsest); names with epithets on reverse side.— *Purpose:* school text.—*Description:* VIII CE, Qarara (found in a tomb in 1914). Wooden tablet (42 × 16 cm) horizontally cracked in two pieces; 2 round holes for strings; whitened with molding; recto: twelve lines of writing in the left half of the tablet separated from the right by a line drawn vertically; palimpsest as remnants of letters wiped out are still visible; upright and single letters of an irregular hand; thus, probably a school text written from dictation and as required corrected or wiped out (according to *Vom Nil zum Necker*) and not amulet (F. Bilabel; LDAB); text of the *Lord's Prayer* written in Coptic letters (cf. *MPER N.S.* XV 184) ends with the vocative κ(ύρι)ε added as a *nomen sacrum* with suprascript stroke above the line (cf. *O.Athens inv.* 12227; *BGU* III 954; *P.Duk.inv.* 778); the Coptic alphabet used in order to preserve the text in its original wording, however to transmit it to Egyptians who did not know any Greek; verso: names, partly supplemented by epithets.

(17) *Chicago MS 125*

Van Haelst 386; University of Chicago Library, Department of Special Collections, MS 125.

Plates:—Literature: E.J. Goodspeed, "New Manuscript Acquisitions for Chicago," *University of Chicago Magazine* 12 (1930) 141; E. von Dobschütz, *ZNW* 32 (1933) 188; S. de Ricci/W.J. Wilson, *Census of Medieval and Renaissance Manuscripts in the United States and Canada I* (New York 1935), 568; K.W. Clark, *A Descriptive Catalogue of Greek New Testament Manuscripts in America* (Chicago 1937), 226–7.—*Text:* Mark 1:1–8; Luke 1:1–7; John 1:1–17; Matthew 6:9–13; Nicaean Creed; LXX-Psalm 68; some miniatures (Matthew, Mark

---

[23] Many thanks to Dina Faltings, Curator of the Collection of the Egyptian Institute, Ruprecht-Karls-University Heidelberg, for her pleasant help with finding out more about this wood tablet as well as for sending copies and photos.

etc.); diverse magic operations in Arabic on the verso.—
Purpose: magical roll and/or amulet.—*Description:* XIII CE,
Egypt? Parchment roll in Greek and Arabic, fairly long
(175.6 cm) and quite narrow (9.2 cm);[24] 114 lines parallel
to the narrow side; verso with magical practices in Arabic
for an Arabian Christian called Suleyman ibn Sara; miniatures of Matthew, Mark, Luke, Jesus Christ, John, the
Trinity, the Virgin and David.

The following two papyri are put separately, as they have received
a Gregory-Aland number, are recognized by traditional textual criticism and without doubt preserve continuous texts.[25] Be that as it
may, they nevertheless form a supplement to the list made up above
as they may help us to scrutinize the other manuscripts for similarities and differences, for instance in the text of the *Lord's Prayer* itself,
its phrasing and orthography, a scribe's hand or the layout of the
manuscripts.

(18) *P.Oxy.* IX 1169
      LDAB 2958, van Haelst 344; Gregory-Aland 0170; Prince-
      ton, Theological Seminary, Speer Library, Pap. 11. Gregory-
      Aland 0170.
      Plates:—*Literature:* Clark, *A Descriptive Catalogue* (see list entry
      (17)), 177–8.—*Text:* Matthew 6:5–6, 8–9, 13–15, 17.—
      Purpose: leaf from a codex.—*Description:* V–VI CE, Oxy-
      rhynchus. Fragmentary outer leaf from a parchment codex
      (14.1 × 8 cm; originally 20 × 25 cm) with two columns (6
      and 12 lines on the recto; 11 and 5 lines on the verso;
      originally 27 lines in each column); upper part apparently
      cut off, lower portion worm-eaten and decayed; text divided
      into paragraphs (like Codex Alexandrinus); upright, rather
      large and careful hand (explicit contrasts of light and heavy
      strokes); same type as *P.Oxy.* V 848; continuous text from
      the Gospel of Matthew, interrupted by lacunae; of the
      Lord's Prayer only the first line—π(άτ)ερ ἡμῶν ὁ ἐν τοῖς
      οὐ(ρα)νοῖς—and some rests of Matthew 6:13 are preserved.

---

[24] I am grateful to Jay Satterfield, Head of Reader Services of the Special
Collections Research Center at the University of Chicago Library, for supplying
descriptive details about that parchment roll (email from 01/07/2004).
[25] Cf. S.E. Porter, "Textual Criticism in the Light of Diverse Textual Evidence
for the Greek New Testament: An Expanded Proposal" (in this volume).

(19) The Freer Gospels Codex = Freer Codex III
LDAB 2985, van Haelst 331+597; Washington, Smithsonian
Institution Library, Freer Gallery of Art, 06.274. Gregory-
Aland 032.
Plates: H.A. Sanders, *Facsimile of the Washington Manuscript
of the Four Gospels in the Freer Collection* (Ann Arbor 1912);
W.H.P. Hatch *The Principal Uncial Manuscripts of the New
Testament* (Chicago 1936), plate 21; 17; G. Cavallo, *Ricerche
sulla maiuscola biblica* (Studi e testi di papirologia 2; Firenze
1967), plate 108; G. Cavallo/H. Maehler, *Greek Bookhands
of the Early Byzantine Period AD 300–800* (BICS.S 47; London
1987), plate 15a.—*Literature*: H.A. Sanders, *The New Testament
Manuscripts in the Freer Collection* (New York 1918) 1–247;
Cavallo, *Ricerche*, 118–9 (papaeography: "La maiuscola di
tipo ogivale inclinato"). *Text*: The four Gospels (Matthew;
John 1–14:25, 16:7–21; Luke; Mark 1–15:12, 38–16:20
(occidental order of the Gospels as in *Codex Bezae*).—*Purpose*:
codex.—*Description*: IV/V CE, Giza or White Monastery?
Parchment codex of 187 surviving leaves with 30 lines per
page; for a more detailed description consult the references
given.

To complete the picture it should not be concealed, as already indicated by the clay tablet (that is listed among other inscriptions by
Guarducci, *Epigrafia Greca IV* [see list entry (4)]) and the two wooden
tablets, that there are inscriptions with the *Lord's Prayer* as well. Among
other inscriptions on the wall of a funeral chapel in el-Bagawat is
IGA V 357. Following the mention of the Trinity Matthew 6:13 is
cited or an allusion to it is made. Correctly, G.H.R. Horsley remarks:
"Quite what is the significance of the quotation within a context also
mentioning the Trinity is unclear, unless πειρασμός is intended here
as an allusion to post-mortem judgement."[26] A second example is
IGLS V 2546 from Al-Moufaggar, Syria, with the *Lord's Prayer* on a
fragment, possibly from a former tombstone, framing a cross surrounded by a circle. The *Lord's Prayer* is followed by a fragmentary
doxology and a request for help for a certain Silvanus. A second
similar request is inscribed within the circle horizontally in the lower
half, this time for a certain Helenis. Further remarks and work on

---

[26] Horsley, "The Lord's Prayer" (see note 8), 103.

inscriptions is to be left to epigraphers or to a more extensive study of the *Lord's Prayer*, including all kinds of related artifacts.

2.2   *Some summarizing remarks on the manuscripts of the* Lord's Prayer

To start with what I hope has become obvious is that each manuscript deserves a fresh assessment before judgments are made, conclusions drawn, and further research is done. Many list entries reveal that their purposes as manuscripts have to be determined first in order to make a sound assessment. Let's take the miniature bifolium *P.Ant.* II 54—list entry (1), potentially the oldest witness of the *Lord's Prayer*: even if it cannot be ruled out that this item was used as an amulet, it appears to be unlikely that it was produced for that purpose. Paleography supports the notion that this papyrus was once a miniature notebook or a small codex. The case might be similar with *P.Col.* XI 293—list entry (7)—which could have served as a codex leaf or was torn out of a damaged book and then never used as an amulet.

All in all, we have items with exclusively the *Lord's Prayer* and nothing else on them, those where this is followed by a doxology, and those with a compilation of texts (see below). Papyrus, parchment, wooden tablets, and a clay tablet are the materials employed. What is more significant is that, even if subsumed under the purpose 'amulet,' the eight manuscripts clearly discernible from the others as amulets—(3), (6), (8), (9), (10), (12), (13) and (17)—deserve and desperately need an assessment on their own so that their individual features will come to light and so something of the people behind them becomes visible. Others discussed as potential amulets—(5), (7), (11), (14) and (15)—might have served another purpose: (5) seems to be a liturgical text; as mentioned above, (7) could have been torn out of a damaged book; (11) might have been a single leaf or an amulet; (14) shows a close relationship with school education and was probably a school text or writing exercise; the same might be said for (15), above all if its physical condition is taken into account. Then, especially (14) and (15) fit into the same context as (16)—what else could a waxed wooden tablet like that with traces of other texts have been used for?

Two striking objects are the clay tablet (4) and the account book (2), whereas the latter is the only documentary text with a quotation from the *Lord's Prayer* and needs deeper reflection about its origin. In contrast to some of the other entries in the list, the clay tablet in Athens was actually designed for its purpose of carrying solely the *Lord's Prayer* on one side and nothing else. Therefore serving as a house blessing or even being attached to a wall like a plaque might have been the plausible purpose of this extraordinary object.

It is a pity that (13)—the bundle of papyrus unrolled by Wilcken— is not extant anymore. This could have helped to complete the picture, especially if traces of its original condition as a bundle would have been visible.

3. More than Simply a Witness to the Text of the *Lord's Prayer: An Assessment of P.Princ. II 107 = Suppl.Mag. I 29 as a Model*

Even a plain but detailed list helps to accumulate observations and to draw conclusions from them, as was done above (cf. 2.2), which is more than simply looking at the text of the *Lord's Prayer* itself. So, its purposes and the material is was written on or into demonstrate that this central prayer was not only regarded as a living text but at the same time employed exactly like that. However, there is even more to a manuscript than what has already been pointed out with the help of the descriptions above.

List entry (6) has not been dealt with up to now, as a closer look at this papyrus may serve as a role model of how to delve into a more profound discussion of specific features of early Christianity with the help of one single papyrus. Not only the diverse texts preserved, but also the physical condition of that artifact help to draw attention to the manuscript itself—either originally in its collection or with the help of quality photographs—and ensures further research and conclusions based on critically edited and described manuscripts. Thus, *P.Princ.* II 107 = *Suppl.Mag.* I 29 is singled out to achieve these goals.

I intend to publish a collection of all available and published artifacts with verses or all of Septuagint Psalm 90. In order to illustrate how such a collective edition might eventually look, the fact that *P.Princ.* II 107 = *Suppl.Mag.* I 29 is one of those items with parts of the psalm under discussion (among other texts) turns this papyrus into the ideal role model here.

Before I present the papyrus in detail, I must put forward one final preliminary and essential maxim for working with manuscripts like those here: by isolating a specific feature or text from its larger context the interpreter runs the risk of misinterpretation as the interplay of texts on the one hand and the inseparable symbiosis of text and material or way of writing on the other are totally ignored. That is why the presentation of *P.Princ.* II 107 = *Suppl.Mag.* I 29 might appear to be even pedantically keen on details. At the same time, this presentation is intended to value this archeological object as what it is: a physical object and a preserver of texts, or to paraphrase the whole, a concrete artifact of individuals.

P.Princ. II 107 = *Suppl.Mag.* I 29

Date:	V/VI (Daniel/Maltomini) [IV/V (Kase)]
Provenance:	unknown
Material:	papyrus
Contents:	Invocation of the Archangel Michael; LXX-Psalm 90:1–2; Matthew 6:9–11; *Liturgia Marci* (*trisagion*, doxology); set of names.
Use:	amulet against fever
Brief description:	See fig. 3.

Incomplete single sheet (13 × 15.5 cm) with upper margin of about 1 cm, left margin of about 0.5 cm and no lower margin left, where the text is squeezed in till right above the edge; on the recto writing against the fibres: ll. 1–9 invocation of the Archangel Michael (mentioning of fever in l. 3); ll. 10–13 LXX-Psalm 90:1–2; ll. 13–15 parts of the *Lord's Prayer*; ll. 15–17 *Liturgia Marci* (*trisagion*, doxology); ll. 17–20 set of names; verso blank; folded six times from right to left and then in half (according to A. Hanson referred to by Daniel/Maltomini).

"The hand is a fluent cursive" (according to APIS), tendentiously bilinear, forming inconsistent letters that slightly slope to the right. The more to the bottom of the sheet the more the lines are sloping down to the right. Even if there are quite some spelling problems and the whole sheet makes an impression of irregularity, the scribe was not inexperienced (e.g., he forms usual ligatures, such as αι of καί in l. 17). The writing process appears to have been hastened somewhat in ll. 11–12 and then slowed down again (more single letters as in the previous lines), before the scribe successfully endeavors to squeeze in the ending above the broken bottom of the sheet.

In the *editio princeps* the papyrus was denominated as 'gnostic' but various features prove that it is a common Christian charm, even if it contains quite conspicuous features.

Editio princeps:	E.H. Kase (*P.Princ.* II [1936] = *Princ.Stud.Pap.* I); reedited by R.W. Daniel/F. Maltomini (*Suppl.Mag.* I [1992]).
Plate(s):	*Suppl.Mag.* I, Tafel V. See fig. 3 of this study.
Repertory/Catalogue:	LDAB 5835; van Haelst 967; APIS princeton.apis.p5.
Bibliography:	K. Preisendanz, "Zur Überlieferung der griechischen Zauberpapyri," in: *Miscellanea critica. Festschrift zum 150-jährigen Bestehen des Verlages B.G. Teubner* I (Leipzig 1964), 203–217, hier 214; Kotansky, "*PGM* LXXXIII. 1–20" (see note 27), 300 (translation and short commentary following Kase's *ed. pr.*). For ll. 15–17 *Liturgia Marci* Brightman, *Liturgies Eastern and Western* (see note 1), 132 ll. 8–9.
Ref. to other Mss:	See below ('Comments . . . and additional remarks').
Location:	Princeton University Library, Inv. AM 8963
Text:	Transcription according to *Suppl.Mag.* I 29 (collated with the photo)

```
1  †   προς . . . . . . ρε . . ọ . γωβα . ⲥ . μω . .
        νουⲥηα . ειεγε . . . . ọⲥαρκ . . . αυⲥε.
        ῥυγοπύρετον, ὁρκίζω ⲥε, Μιχαηλ, ἀρ-
        χάγγελε γῆⲥ, καθημερινὸν ἢ νυκτ-
5       ερινὸν ἢ τεταρτέον· τὸν παντοκράτο-
        ρα Ⲥαβαωθ, μηκέτι ἅψῃ τῇ ψυχῇ τοῦ
        φοροῦντοⲥ μηδὲ παντὸⲥ τοῦ ⲥώματ-
        οⲥ αὐτοῦ· ὁρκίζω ⲥε καὶ νεκρούⲥ,
                               ἀπαλλάξ<ατε>
        Ταιόλληⲥ Ἰⲥιδόρου π . βων . . . . .
```

10 ὁ κατικῶν ἐν βοηθίᾳ τοῦ ὑψίστου ἐ`ν´ cκέ-
πι τοῦ θ(εο)ῦ τοῦ οὐρανοῦ αὐλ[ι]cτήcετε. ἐρῖ
τοῦ θ(εο)ῦ καὶ καταφυγή μου καὶ βοηθώc μου,
ἐλπίδω ἐφ᾽ αὐτών. πατὴρ υμῶν <ὁ> ἐν τῆc
οὐρανῆc, ἁγιαcθήτω τὼ θέλημά cου, τὼ-
15 ν ἄρτον ὑμῶν τὼν ἐπιούcιων. ἄγιοc
ἄγιοc κ(ύριο)c Cαβαωθ, πλήριc οὐρανὸc
καὶ γῆ κηc ἁγία<c> co<υ> δόξηc. ανιααδαιι-
α, Μιγαηλ, τὼν κ(ύριο)ν Αβραμ, Icακ,
Ιακωβ, Ελωει, Ελε, Cαβα-
20 ωθ, Ωηλ.

ll. 10–13 Psalm 90:1–2; ll. 13–15 ex Matthew 6:9–11; ll. 15–17 *trisagion*
(*Liturgia Marci*).
l. 3 ῥιγοπύρετον; l. 5 τεταρταῖον; l. 9 Ἰcιδώρου; l. 10 κατοικῶν ἐν βοηθείᾳ;
ll. 10–11 cκέπη; l. 11 θ͞ω Pap. θ͞υ; αὐλιcθήcεται; ἐρεῖ; l. 12 Pap. θ͞υ; βοηθόc;
l. 13 ἐλπίζω ἐπ᾽ αὐτόν; πάτερ ημῶν; ll. 13–14 τοῖc οὐρανοῖc; l. 14 τὸ; ll. 14–15
τὸν; l. 15 ημῶν τὸν ἐπιούcιον; l. 16 Pap. κ͞c; πλήρηc; l. 17 τῆc Pap. κῆc;
Kase read καὶ δίκηc ἄγιοc ὁ δόξηc; l. 18 Μιχαηλ; τὸν; Pap. κ͞υ.

Translation (from *Suppl.Mag.* I 29):[27]

"† - - - (lines 3 ff.) fever with shivering—I
adjure you, Michaêl, archangel |[4] of the
earth—quotidian or nocturnal or quartan;
by the almighty Sabaôth no longer fasten to
the soul of the wearer (of this amulet) nor
to his whole body. |[8] I adjure you and the
dead, deliver Taiolles, daughter of Isidoros,
- - -. "He who dwells in the help of the
Highest will reside in the shelter of the God
of heaven. He will say |[12] to God < > and
my refuge < > and my helper, I put my
trust in him." "Our father who art in heaven,
hallowed < > thy will, < > our daily
bread." "Holy |[16] holy Lord Sabaôth: heaven
and earth are full of your holy glory."

[27] Compare the English translation by R. Kotansky ("*PGM* LXXXIII. 1–20," in:
The Greek Magical Papyri in Translation Including the Demotic Spells [ed. H.D. Betz;
Chicago-London ²1992], 300), who, for instance, renders l. 17 as "holy is the one
of glory" according to Kase's transcription in the *editio princeps* (see the apparatus
given above).

Aniaadaïa, Michaêl, the Lord of Abraham,
Isaac and Jacob, Elôei, Ele, Sabaôth |²⁰ Ôel."

Comments (partly following *Suppl.Mag.* I, 80–82, however often
modified, rearranged, and enlarged):

(a) Invocation of the Archangel Michael (ll. 1–9; fever in l. 3)

1–2 Incomplete words and phrases.

3–5 The syntax is hardly comprehensible.

3–4 Μιχαηλ, ἀρχάγγελε γῆc: Direct address to the Archangel Michael
(vocative), who thus becomes the subject of the invocation; for
a context in which the Archangel Michael observes and con-
trols the earth see *PGM* IV 2768–70 καὶ Ὠρίων καὶ ὁ ἐπάνω
καθήμενος Μιχαηλ· ἑπτὰ ὑδάτων κρατεῖς καὶ γῆς ("and Orion
and Michael, who sits on high you have the power over the
seven waters and the earth"; whereas *P.Heid.* VII 411,2–3 provides a totally different context with οἰκονομίαν τοῦ ἀρχ[α]γγέλου
Μιχαηλ κα̣ι̣ [.] . [..]θερισε[| αὐτὴν τὴν γῆν ["administration (of
the church) of the Archangel Michael and . . . now . . . the same
site"]). The Archangel Michael is quite often mentioned in
documents dating from the sixth and seventh century (cf. *P.Bad.*
II 30; *P.Cair.Masp.* I 67111; *PSI* I 63; VIII 953; *P.Sorb.* II 69;
Stud.Pal. III 103; 268; VIII 1304; X 75; 177); *London Oriental
Manuscript* 5525 (A.M. Kropp, *Ausgewählte koptische Zaubertexte*
[Brussels 1930–31], Vol. I: 15–21; Vol. II: 199–207); *P.Berol.inv.*
8322 (W. Beltz, "Die koptischen Zauberpapyri der Papyrus-
Sammlung der Staatlichen Museen zu Berlin," *APF* 29 [1983]
59–86, here 72–4; Kropp, *Ausgewählte koptische Zauberpapyri*, Vol.
II: 16–9); *Moen* 3 (H. Satzingern/P.J. Sijpesteijn, "Koptisches
Zauberpergament Moen III," *Le Muséon* 101 [101] 51–63). The
Old and the New Testament know the term ἀρχάγγελος only
from Jude 9, when Michael argues with the διάβολος over
Moses' body (cf. Deut 34:5–6; Philo, *Mos.* 2.291), and 1 Thess,
where the Coming of the Lord is announced by "the voice of
the Archangel and the trumpet of God." Further, compare
Rev 12:7 telling that Michael (Archangel) and his angels fight
the dragon in heaven (see Dan 12:1, where Michael [the prince]
is called ὁ ἄγγελος in contrast to Dan [Th] 12:1). Moreover,
cf. the many Jewish sources and Herm.Sim. 8.3.3, Apoc.Paul

14, 43, and Gos.Bart. 4.29 referred to by D.E. Aune, *Revelation 6–16* (WBC 52B; Nashville 1998), 693–5, in his excursus on "Michael the Archangel."

4–5 καθημερινὸν ἢ νυκτερινὸν ἢ τεταρτέον (read τεταρταῖον): Cf. *P.Erl.* 15.4–6 (= *Suppl.Mag.* I 14.4–6). For καθημερινός cf. *Suppl.Mag.* I 4.5–6; 9.11; 10.9; 21.17; 34 A 10–11; 35.13; II 82 fr. B5 [?] (further, see *Repertorio bibliográfico de la lexicografía griga (RBLG)* (ed. J.R. Somolinos; Diccionario Griego Español. Anejo III; Madrid 1988), s.v.), for νυκτερινός cf. *Suppl.Mag.* I 18.13; 29.4–5; II 82 fr. B5 (further, see *RBLG*, s.v.), and for τεταρταῖος cf. *Suppl.Mag.* I 3.5; 10.8–9; 18.10–11; 19.19–20, 27; 21.15 (further, see *RBLG*, s.v.).

5–6 τὸν παντοκράτορα Cαβαωθ: For this accusative ("by the almighty Sabaoth") cf. the literature provided by Daniel/Maltomini, p. 80. The LXX often has παντοκράτωρ where the Masoretic Text has צבאות. Moreover, of the eight places where παντοκράτωρ is to be found in the New Testament, seven are in the Book of Revelation (1:8; 4:8; 11:17; 15:3; 16:7; 19:6; 21:22; but 2 Cor 6:18). Although any interpretation has to take into account that this term "is a favorite designation for God found frequently in early Jewish sources, and occasionally in pagan sources" (D.E. Aune, *Revelation 1–5* [WBC 52; Dallas 1997], 58; see his discussion of the term and his many references to *Pap.Graec.Mag.*, the Apostolic Fathers, and the Jewish Greek literature, to mention the most important fields of its usage), it is noteworthy that this Greek word and its Hebrew equivalent transcribed in Greek letters are to be found in such a close proximity (for other constellations of titles together with other divine designations in Christian magical papyri, above all in invocations cf. *Pap.Graec.Mag.* II P1; P8; P9; P13a; P21 etc.; Kropp, *Ausgewählte koptische Zaubertexte* [see above a)], Vol. II: 176, 178, 180).

6 μηκέτι ἅψῃ: Similarly used in an amulet cited by H. Leclerq, "Art. Salomon," *DACL* 15.1 (1950) 588–602, here 597–8 and discussed by L. Robert, "Amulettes grecques," *Journal des Savants* [Paris 1981], 3–44, here 19, where evils are mentioned (among others, fever) and are beseeched not to touch its owner. In the context of diseases ἅπτομαι is quite often used (for example, Sophocles, *Trach.* 1010; Thucydides 2.48; Galen 15.702K; *SIG*³ 1170.23 (Dittenberger). Cf. Colossians 2:21 μὴ ἅψῃ, 1 John

5:18 ὁ πονηρὸς οὐχ ἅπτεται αὐτοῦ or LXX-Psalm 104:15 μὴ ἅπτεσθε τῶν χριστῶν μου.

6–8 τοῦ φοροῦντος---αὐτοῦ: Generalizing masculine formula (patient is Taiolles, daughter of Isidoros).

8 νεκροὺς: An invocation of the dead appears to be out of place in a Christian context, above all if paralleled with one to the Archangel Michael. Nevertheless, the Greek magical papyri often reveal that there is a mixture of different religious ideas at work (see below my comments to l. 18). Although they are not mentioned explicitly, the saints as deceased must be taken into consideration here as well, because there definitely were relationships between Christianity and cults of the dead in those days. Cf. F. Pfister, "Art. Ahnenkult," *RAC* 1 (1950) 190–2; P. Brown, *The Cult of the Saints. Its Rise and Function in Latin Christianity* (HLHR N.S. 2; Chicago 1981), 5; in general see *The Cult of Saints in Late Antiquity and the Middle Ages: Essays on the Contribution of Peter Brown* (ed. J.D. Howard-Johnston; Oxford 1999).

9 Ταϊόλλης: The name is used in *P.Oxy.* VII 1031,7 = *W.Chr.* 343,7: παρὰ Αὐρηλίου Βιαίου Βιαίου μητρὸς Ταϊόλλης (cf. F. Preisigke, *Namenbuch enthaltend alle griechischen, lateinischen, ägyptischen, hebräischen, arabischen und sonstigen semitischen und nichtsemitischen Menschennamen* etc. [Heidelberg 1922; repr. Amsterdam 1967] and search with the *Duke Databank of Documentary Papyri* (*DDBDP*; http://scriptorium.lib.duke.edu/papyrus/texts/DDBDP. html; last access 02/12/2005).

π βων . . . : Daniel/Maltomini "suspect mention of the evil(s) from which Taiolles was to be delivered (*ed. pr.* γρϲβωνωῃ . . .).

Additional Christian amulets against fever *P.Oxy.* VI 924 (= *Pap.Graec. Mag.* II P5a; Wessely, "Les plus anciens monuments" [see list entry (9)], 401–2); *P.Oxy.* VIII 1151 (= *Pap.Graec.Mag.* II P5b; Wessely, "Les plus anciens monuments" [see list entry (9)], 417–20); *P.Prag.* I 6 (= *Suppl.Mag.* I 25); *Suppl.Mag.* I 34 (= *P.Köln inv.* 851); *P.Coll.Youtie* 91; *P.Turner* 49; *P.Batav.* (= *P.Lugd.Bat.* XIX) 20. For the last and a survey of amulets against fever see G.H.R. Horsley, "93. Credal formula in a Christian amulet against fever," *NDIEC* 3 (1983) 114–9. It is not certain whether *P.Erl.* 15 (improved re-edition by F. Maltomini, *SCO* 32 [1982] 235–8; reprinted as *Suppl.Mag.* I 14 [bibl.]) is Christian or not. Further *P.Princ.* III 159 (= *Suppl.Mag.* I 11; APIS [princeton.apis.p62]; see B.M. Metzger, "A Magical Amulet for Curing

Fever," in: *Studies in the History and Text of the New Testament in Honor of K.W. Clark* [edd. B.L. Daniels/M.J. Suggs; Salt Lake City 1967], 89–94, repr. in Id., *Historical and Literary Studies: Pagan, Jewish and Christian* [Leiden 1968], 104–10); *P.Mich.inv.* 6666 (= *SB* XVI 13019 = *Suppl.Mag.* I 3; APIS michigan.apis.2920); *P.Berol.inv.* 8324 (Beltz, "Die koptischen Zauberpapyri" [see above a)], 74); a parchment amulet from the Moen collection (P.J. Sijpesteijn, "Amulet against Fever," *CEg* 57 [1982] 377–81); *P.Heid.Inv.Kopt.* 544 and 564 (H. Quecke, "Zwei koptische Amulette der Papyrussammlung der Universität Heidelberg," *Le Muséon* 76 [1963] 255–65).

(b) LXX-Psalm 90:1–2 (ll. 10–13):

12 τοῦ θ(εο)ῦ für τῷ θ(ε)ῷ (genitive for dative): Quite a number of manuscripts and recensions have τῷ θεῷ in contrast to τῷ κυρίῳ (cf. the apparatus of Psalm 90:2 in A. Rahlfs, *Psalmi cum Odis. Septuaginta. Vetus Testamentum Graecum Auctoritate Academiae Litterarum Gottingensis editum* X; Göttingen ³1979 [1931]), e.g. *P.Vindob.G* 348,6. Cf. R.W. Daniel, "A Christian Amulet on Papyrus." *VC* 37 (1983) 400–404, here 403.

After τοῦ θ(εο)ῦ omission of ἀντιλήμπτωρ μου εἶ; after καταφυγή μου omission of ὁ θεός μου.

καὶ βοηθός μου: βοηθός μου without καί is an addition often found in manuscripts, for instance, *P.Vindob.G* 348.7 (cf. Daniel, "A Christian Amulet," 403) and *P.Laur.* IV 141.3. Furthermore, a few manuscripts belonging to the Lucian recension and Theodoret (cf. the apparatus of Psalm 90:2 in Rahlfs, *Psalmi cum Odis*) have this addition that might be motivated by the parallel phrasing in LXX-Psalm 17:3: ὁ θεός μου βοηθός μου, καὶ ἐλπιῶ ἐπ' αὐτόν.

13 ἐλπίδω: the same spelling for LXX-Psalm 90 in *P.Oxy.* XVI 1928,2. Cf. F.T. Gignac, *A Grammar of the Greek Papyri of the Roman and Byzantine Periods. I: Phonology* (Milan 1976), 76. In contrast to the Masoretic text, the Septuagint focuses on 'hope' as a central term (verses 2b, 4b, 9a, 14a with ἐλπίζω or ἐλπίς) and turns this psalm into 'a psalm of hope.'

Among the psalms popular among early Christians to be applied to magical and specifically apotropaic purposes, Psalm 90 of the Septuagint ranks first (together with Psalm 120) if in addition to papyri and inscriptions in the common sense medallions, rings, armbands, *intaglios* and the like are considered as well. In a first assessment I counted more than seventy-five objects with verses of this psalm or even its complete text (those mentioned in the list above included; cf. T.J. Kraus, "Psalm 90 der Septuaginta in apotropäischer Verwendung— erste Anmerkungen und Datenmaterial," in: *PapCongr.* XXIV [Helsinki 2004], forthcoming). However, there are more to be added to the list, as only after dealing with the armbands in detail (Kraus, "Fragmente eines Amuelt-Armbands" [see note 28]) more than eighty-five objects are now accumulated to form a database for a further evaluation of the usage of this psalm.

(c) Matthew 6:9–11 (the *Lord's Prayer*; ll. 13–15)

13–15 The *Lord's Prayer* is lacking τὸ ὄνομά cου· ἐλθάτω ἡ βαcιλεία cου· γενηθήτω, then ὡc ἐν οὐρανῷ καὶ ἐπὶ γῆc and δὸc ἡμῖν cήμερον κτλ.

Above all, the omission of τὸ ο;νομά cου alters the meaning of the first and second request completely, as then it is the father's "will" that should be "hallowed." It is questionable whether the scribe deliberately aimed at this sense and such a short form.

For a parallel attestation of LXX-Psalm 90 and the *Lord's Prayer* see *P.Duk.inv.* 778; *P.Iand.* I 6 (= *Pap.Graec.Mag.* II P17 = *P.Giss.Lit.* 5,4); *P. Schøyen* I 16 (= *P.Oslo. inv.* 1644 + Schøyen Collection MS 244/4); *PSI* VI 719. On the *Lord's Prayer* on amulets cf. Amundsen, "Christian Papyri" (see list entry (3)), 142–4; Horsley (see note 8), 103–105; C. Römer, *P.Köln* IV, p. 32.

(d) *Liturgia Marci* (*trisagion*, doxology; ll. 15–17)

15–17 ἅγιοc . . . δόξηc: The writer omitted the third ἅγιοc and articles before οὐρανόc and γῆ. This is a reminiscence of Isa 6:3. However the third ἅγιοc qualifying "your glory" identifies this formula as part of the *Liturgia Marci*. Cf. Brightman, *Liturgies Eastern and Western* (see note 1), 132.8–9: Ἅγιος ἅγιος ἅγιος Κύριος σαβὼθ πλήρης ὁ οὐρανὸς καὶ ἡ γῆ τῆς ἁγίας σου δόξης. Analogously *P.Vindob.G* 19887 with the *trisagion* repeated three times always preceded by a cross with the first two— the papyrus is broken off in the middle of the third—having ε (read ἡ) γῆ τῆς ἁγίας σου δόξης. Thus, this papyrus, too, represents the *Liturgia Marci* and not plainly the *sanctus* or

Isa 6:3 (according to Wessely, "Les plus anciens monuments" [see list entry (9)], 437, and van Haelst 1009). Cf. *Bodl. MS. Gr. liturg. c. 3* (P), d. 4 (P) [= *Papyrus Dêr-Balizeh*; van Haelst 737] with the *trisagion* lacking the qualification of the earth by means of ἅγιος (leaf II, recto, ll. 11–12). This has an equivalent in the *Constitutiones Apostolorum*—Syrian Rite (Brightman, *Liturgies Eastern and Western* [see note 1], 18.32–19.1).

For the *trisagion* see *Suppl.Mag.* I 25; 32; 36 and the literature given there; a general overview with several items and a distinction between the two essential forms is given by L. Koenen, "Ein christlicher Prosahymnus des 4. Jhdt.s," *Antidoron Martino David oblatum miscellanea papyrologica* (ed. E. Boswinckel; *P.Ludg.Bat.* XVII; Leiden 1968), 31–52; Aune, *Revelation 1–5* (see above, note to ll. 5–6), 302–6; D.G. Martinez, *P.Michigan XIX: Baptized for our Sakes: A Leather Trisagion from Egypt (P.Mich. 799)* (Beiträge zur Altertumskunde 120; Stuttgart-Leipzig 1999), 6–20. For further examples, see F. Maltomini, "Crito all' Eufrate—P.Heid.G.1101: amuleto cristiano," *ZPE* 49 (1982) 149–70, here 158. Furthermore, the two forms of the *trisagion* were often used for inscriptions on armbands, rings, medallions and lintels to mention the most common objects.[28]

(e) Set of names (ll. 17–20)

17–18 αvιααδαιια: A letter combination not to be reconstructed in a justifiable and reasonable way, as so many of them are "unparalleled, because the ancient texts for the most part lack word division, and because much is meaningless gibberish that cannot be explained in Egyptian, Hebrew and other languages" (Daniel/Maltomini, *Suppl.Mag.* II, p. 325;

---

[28] For lintels see, for instance, *IGLS* II 317; V 2176, 2528, 2529, 2543, 2606; W.K. Prentice, *Syria: Publications of the Princeton University Archaeological Expeditions to Syria in 1904–5 and 1909. Division III: Greek and Latin Inscriptions. Section B: Northern Syria* (Leyden, 1908–22), nos. 856, 859; for armbands see T.J. Kraus, "Fragmente eines Amulett-Armbands im British Museum (London) mit Septuaginta-Psalm 90 und der Huldigung der Magier," *JbAC* (2005; forthcoming); a medallion was published by M.C. Ross, *Catalogue of the Byzantine and Early Medieval Antiquities in the Dumbarton Oaks Collection I: Metalworks, Ceramics, Glass, Glyptics, Painting* (Washington D.C. 1962), no. 60; a ring in the Walters Art Gallery, Baltimore (no. 4515), is discussed by G. Vikan, "Two Byzantine Amuletic Armbands and the Group to which They Belong," *The Journal of the Walters Art Gallery* 49/50 (1991/92) 33–51, here 43 note 43 (= Id., *Sacred Images and Sacred Power in Byzantium* [Variorum Collected Studies Series; Aldershot-Burlington 2003], Art. XI).

see their list of such magical words, pp. 325–35, but also the diverse vowel combinations, pp. 336–7). Of course, some of these magical words might consist of meaningful elements, which however are hardly discernible from the rest of the words. Neither in *Pap.Graec.Mag.* (or other editions and/or translations of magical papyri) nor with the help of the *Duke Databank of Documentary Papyri* (*DDBDP*) could I find any parallel attestation of this or a similar sequence of letters.

18 Considering the background of the papyrus the singular τὸν κ(ύριο)ν appears more likely than the plural τῶν κ(υρίω)ν; θεός might have been expected instead of κύριος in such a formula, whereas L. Robert ("Amulettes grecques," 16–17) cites exactly such an amulet with the singular κύριος. Basic information is provided by M. Rist, "The God of Abraham, Isaac, and Jacob: A Liturgical and Magical Formula," *JBL* 57 (1938) 289–303.

19 Ελωει, Ελε: Cf. *Pap.Graec.Mag.* IV 3019–3020 ελε· | ελω·; Maltomini/Daniel refer to a clue provided by A. Vivian that Ελε might be written for the *status constructus* plural of אל and Ελωει the status constructus plural of אלהים. This might be seen in Mark 15:34, when Jesus cried out ελωι ελωι λεμα σαβαχθανι—written as a transliteration of the Aramaic Psalm 22:2 (but compare Matthew 27:46)—and, thus, this employs a direct address (vocative) in that way. Definitely, this is a working hypothesis, as the great magical papyrus in Paris additionally has other transcriptions of God's names, such as ιαβα (for יהוה) and ιαη (maybe ΙΑΩ for יהוה as in 4Q120 = 4QLXXLev^b). Cf. *London Orientral Manuscript* 5525 (Kropp, *Ausgewählte koptische Zaubertexte* [see above a)], Vol. I: 15–21; Vol. 2: 199–207) with an invocation of a series of divine names (among them Ιαω, Σαβάθ and Ελωει) followed by the names of angels (ll. 38–41) and a Christian amulet published by S. Eitrem/A. Fridrichsen, "Ein christliches Amulett auf Papyrus," *FVSK* 1921,1, 1–31, with the invocation of Ἰαώ, Σαβώθ Ἀδωναί Ἐλωέ Σαλαμάν (l. 1) similar to the sequence of *P.Oxy.* VIII 1152 (ll. 1–3 ωρωρ φωρ Ελωει | Αδωναει Ιαω Σα|βαωθ Μιχαηλ Ιεσου κτλ.). Generally speaking the pronunciation of יהוה was heavily discussed by the early Christian writers. Ephiphanius, for instance, mentions Ἰάβε to be understood as ὃς ἦν καὶ ἔστι καὶ ἀει ὤν (*adv. haer.* 1,3,40), whereas Theodoret claims that only the Samaritans pronounced God's

name as Ἰάβε (*in exod. quaest.* 15). Origen regularly refers to this issue of how the *tetragrammaton* is to be understood (for example, *in ps.* 2,4; *cels.* 6,32), pronounced and written (as do others, too, such as Irenaeus, *adv. haer.* 1,4,1 and Tertullian, *adv. Valent.* 14). Of course, today a vast number of archaeological artifacts give evidence of the practice of applying, for instance, ΙΑΩ in magical formulae and similar contexts. See R.A. Kraft, "4. Format Features in the Earliest Jewish Greek Literary Papyri and Related Materials (click on 'magic') and/or 5. Selected Issues and Features of Early Greek Scriptural MSS (click on 'magic')," as part of: Id., *Files and Information on Early Jewish and Early Christian Copies of Greek Jewish Scriptures* (http://ccat.sas.upenn.edu/rs/rak/earlylxx/jew-ishpap.html; last access 02/20/05), where Kraft offers a helpful selection of intaglios and symbols from E.R. Goodenough *Jewish Symbols in the Greco-Roman Period* (Bollingen Series 37; New York 1953–68), especially Vol. III, with the Greek transliteration ΙΑΩ followed or preceded by another divine name or abbreviated form (like the probably paleo-Hebrew ℨℨ); F. Dunand, *Papyrus Grecs Bibliques (Papyus F. Inv. 366). Volumina de la Genèse et du Deutéronome* (RAPH 27; Le Caire 1966), 46–52. This was not only a serious proposal but it can be proved by several items, for instance, the silver tablet *P.Köln* VIII 338.13–19 (*Inv. T3*) + plate V and its editors' comments (D. Jordan/R.D. Kotansky, above all pp. 62–9). Nevertheless, it may not be overlooked that the divine names here could have served as means of protection of the wearer of the amulet or of strengthening him, as is the case with *P.Mich.inv.* 3023a and 3472 (*ed. pr.* of both by P.A. Mirecki, in: *Ancient Christian Magic* [see list entry 9] 250–1 nos. 124 and 125.

19–20 The last few letters were squeezed above the lower edge by the scribe in order to finish the text within the limits of the papyrus given.

20 Ωηλ: Cf. Berliner Koptische Urkunden III 387.31ⲱⲏⲗ.

(f) *P.Princ.* II 107 = *Suppl.Mag.* I 29: a 'Gnostic' amulet?

According to E.H. Kase's *editio princeps* from 1936, *P.Princ.* II 107 is a Gnostic amulet (p. 102). This classification was probably based on the last few lines (above all ll. 19–20) containing elements known from *voces magicae* and the odd compilation of diverse texts on this sheet of papyrus (for Gnostic amulets still see, among others, E.A. Wallis Budge, *Amulets and Superstitions* [London 1930; repr. New York 1978], 200–11; *Ancient Christian Magic* [see list entry (9)], 59–76, 129–346). Many followed Kase's judgment or simply copied it (Cf. van Haelst [see note 8] 967; A. Samuel, "How Many Gnostics?," *BASP* 22 [1985] 297–322, here 317; Kotansky, "*PGM* LXXXIII. 1–20" [see note 27], 300; APIS princeton.apis.p5). However, usual and traditional Christian texts for such a φυλακτήριον—LXX-Psalm 90, the *Lord's Prayer* and a liturgical text (*Liturgia Marci* with *trisagion* and doxology)—are strung together introduced by a cross and characterized by the ordinary *nomina sacra* (as contractions for θεός and κύριος), so that "this is a conventionally Christian charm" (Daniel/Maltomini, *Suppl.Mag.* I, p. 78).

Neither the invocation of the Archangel Michael combined with a request to stop the fever of the wearer nor the last few lines with possible *voces magicae* (here Ελωει, Ελε, Cαβαωθ, Ωηλ) cause any trouble. They do not turn this charm into anything other than a Christian one, as the first feature is to be seen quite often (see the examples of other, even Christian, fever amulets above) and the latter might serve as an emphasis on the previous quotations and invocation. Cf. R. Kotansky, "Incantations and Prayers for Salvation on Inscribed Greek Amulets," in: *Magika Hiera* (see note), 107–37, referring to a "gold *lamella* from Tyre employing a Christian Trinitarian formula to cure ophthalmia [i.e., eye disease; author's note]" (117, and ongoing). "[T]his phylactery can in every sense be understood as an inscribed Christian prayer; the believer prays both for deliverance from a current medical condition and for the prevention of a relapse of the disease", even if there are *voces magicae* present. So, this similar case shows that *P.Princ.* II 107 = *Suppl.Mag.* I 29 can be characterized as a Christian charm, no matter if the scribe, Ταιόλλης, or the 'I-speaker' (see l. 3 ὁρκίζω) were actually Christians. Whether it is appropriate to designate this amulet as "syncretistic rather than distinctively Christian" (Kotansky, "*PGM* LXXXIII. 1–20 [see note 27], 300) remains doubtful and depends on the view of 'syncretism' and 'orthodoxy' an interpreter holds—if such classifications do not turn out to be completely inapplicable to the people forming the background of such items. Moreover, the scribe here compiles conventional Christian texts for such a purpose and it cannot be decided whether he "was ignorant of their content and meaning" (Kotansky, 300) or not.

ECHO AND QUOTATION OF THE NEW TESTAMENT
IN PAPYRUS LETTERS TO THE END
OF THE FOURTH CENTURY

Malcolm Choat

The approach has wide implications, and touches on many areas of the study of the New Testament and the ancient world in general. Classicists, of course, have dealt with citations and quotations as a way to access lost authors for hundreds of years,[1] and those interested in citation of the New Testament could well learn methodologically from scholars struggling to retrieve the text of lost works from the offerings of other ancient writers.

Scriptural citations, quotations, and echoes of the New Testament in private[2] letters have been examined in several places, but never at length.[3] They have been used to test the Christian authorship of private letters, contextualise an individual or community's attitude or attachment to a particular part of scripture, and (so far only sparingly) to help establish the text of the New Testament itself. Above and beyond these issues we deal with a testimony to the living Greek of the Imperial and Late Imperial Roman world, investigation of which, outside a scriptural context, and in a documentary environment, assists in charting the influence of the New Testament on quotidian language, and the influence of contemporary language on the New Testament.

---

[1] See G.W. Most (ed.), *Collecting Fragments* (Göttingen, 1997), where A.C. Dionisotti's "On Fragments in Classical Scholarship" (pp. 1–33) provides an entertaining history of the collection and assessment of classical fragments.

[2] Given that dictation of letters, and having them read to the addressee, was common, the class 'private letter' seems somewhat anachronistic; it appears here more out of convention than any personal sense that it is appropriate.

[3] See B.F. Harris, "Biblical Echoes and Reminiscences in Christian Papyri", *Proceedings of the XIVth International Congress of Papyrologists, Oxford, 24–31 July 1974* (London, 1975), pp. 155–60; M. Naldini, *Il cristianesimo in Egitto. Lettere private nei papiri dei secoli ii–iv. Nuova edizione ampliata e aggiornata* (Florence, 1998), pp. 54–55; G. Tibiletti, *Le lettere private nei papiri greci del III⁰ IV secolo d.C. Tra paganesimo e cristianesimo* (Milan, 1979), pp. 115–6; G.H.R. Horsley, *New Documents Illustrating Early Christianity*, vol. 2 (Sydney, 1982), pp. 154–58.

The latter question is beyond the scope of this discussion, which limits itself to providing a list of citations and echoes of the New Testament in documentary papyri from Egypt to the end of the fourth century, and making some comments on their context and utility to scholars.

DEFINITIONS AND METHODOLOGY

While Greek in the primary focus in relation to the New Testament's most immediate context, a number of interesting Coptic examples can be securely dated to the fourth century. They are taken account of here not only because no previous examination of this issue has done so, but also on account of the interesting questions thus made possible, given the critical role Christian scriptures played in the rise of Coptic as is standardly supposed.

Harris sets up a tripartite division into 'citations', 'verbal echoes', and 'biblical reminiscences'. Tibiletti speaks of 'citazione', Naldini only of 'reminiscenze'. Horsley maintains Harris' classifications in an updated listing of occurrences.

Harris could locate only one instance in which scripture was explicitly cited, reserving the term (although he does not say so) for when an identifiable quotation follows. Naldini avoids the term 'citation', but it is not inappropriate in certain circumstances. I here reserve it for instances in which a biblical author or work is specifically cited, or, more generally, where 'the scriptures' are invoked. 'Quotation' is used here for those instances when it is demonstrable that the writer is actually quoting scripture, although without identifying it as such. Harris' 'echoes' and 'reminiscences' might be intended to catch the distinction between conscious and unconscious use of biblical language. I have attempted here to divide by whether the context is at all related to the purported biblical locus (including coming in a religious context); or if the only relationship to the New Testament is a word found therein but rarely elsewhere.

For the purposes of this treatment, I have largely culled the suggestions of editors and commentators to form the analytic base. A more exhaustive search would undoubtedly uncover further examples of reminiscence and echo, but such would not have substantially changed the points made here. Of the echoes previously identified, I am not convinced that *SB* V 7872 is actually a private letter, so

I here ignore it. I also do not include (in line with this study's para-
meters) the petition *P.Ryl.* IV 617 (c. 318) where the appeal in line
5–6 to the emperors, Lords 'of us, those in this world' (ἡμᾶς τοὺς ἐν
τῷ κόσμ[ῳ τούτῳ]) might be compared to 1 John 4:17 (καὶ ἡμεῖς ἐσμεν
ἐν τῷ κόσμῳ τούτῳ).

At the outset, it might be noted that while echoes or reminiscences identified by editors and commentators are mainly to the text
of the New Testament, actual citations are as commonly made of
the OT as the New Testament.[4] This suggests that editors, more
familiar perhaps with the text of the New Testament, have been
more prone to seeing echoes and reminiscences of such; and that
the strong and intense study of the New Testament in the explicit
light of the papyri (as our best witness of the contemporary *koine*)
has produced a tendency to see the language of the New Testament
where it may not necessarily exist.

Even where an explicit invocation of scripture is made[5] such provides no guarantee of 'correct' reporting of the New Testament text.
[το]ῦ μακαρίου ἀποστό[λ]ου λέγοντες (*l.*-τος) at *P.Lond.* VI 1915.14 is
followed by a general reflection of apostolic advice culled from a
number of sources. Allowing for a moment an OT citation to intrude
into this discussion, ⲕⲁⲧⲁ ⲑⲉ ⲉⲧⲥϧⲉⲓ ⲏ̄ⲛ̄ⲓ̈ⲥⲁⲏ̄ⲥ̄ ('according to what
is written in Isaiah') in *P.Lond.Copt.* I 1123 this is followed by a quote
which does not form part of the canonical book: 'they have known
me, those who did not know him'. In the latter case the allusion is
certainly to some other (lost?) work associated with Isaiah, but where
our New Testament quotations are identifiable, the writers seem to
have the canonical works in mind.

We must not assume, of course, that actual 'copying' from text is
taking place. With ancient standards of memory, even the most
perfect citation will not guarantee that the writer copied it from a

---

[4] For citations of the OT see *P.Lond.* III 981.4ff (καθὼς γέγραπται ἐν τῇ γραφῇ
ὅτι μακάριοί εἰσιν οἱ ἔχοντες σπέρμα ἐν Σίων, Isaiah 31.9); *P.Lond.* VI 1928.12ff (καὶ
ὁ προφήτης βοᾷ ἐν θλίψ(ε)ι ἐπεκαλεσάμην καὶ εἰσήκουσεν μου, Combination of Ps.
127:5 & Jon. 2:3); see also *P.Lond.Copt.* I 1123.38–40 (Late IV), discussed above in
the text, and *P.Lond. Copt.* II 191.20–22 (IV/V), where, although syntax and grammar are not entirely similar to Ps. 50(49): 15, ⲛ̄ⲑⲏ ⲉⲧϣⲁⲩ ϫⲁⲥ ('as is said') implies
a citation (cf. H.-M. Schenke, "Mittelägyptische 'Nachlese' II", *ZÄS* 119 (1992)
43–60, at 56). For a quotation, *SB* I 2266.7–10 (ἐν γὰρ [πο]λλῇ λαλιᾷ οὐκ ἐκφεύξοντ[αι]
ἡ ἁμαρτίη (*l.* αἱ ἁμαρτίαι or ⟨τ⟩ὴ⟨ν⟩ ἁμαρτίη⟨ν⟩?), Prov. 10:19.
[5] See Table I and the discussion below.

nearby codex. Not is it necessary to class deviations from the New Testament text[6] as 'mistakes', per se. They could bear witness to a text now lost. We should also bear in mind that ancient ideas of citation and quotation may not always have included our standards of literal quotation and correct attribution; citation as a concept can be more than the exact relationship to the text we expect in using the term. One may also, of course (although such is not done here[7]), choose to discuss citation practice within a theoretical construct that does not consider the exact textual relationship to be a meaningful datum.

The citation made in *P.Lond.* VI 1915.3–5 gives it a status in this discussion it might otherwise not have, for it is not the intention here to discuss the quite natural appearance of Christian sentiments, which ultimately nearly all have their origin in the New Testament. At *SB* I 2266.12–14 (mid IV), the writer uses words which (somewhat unsurprisingly) appear in the New Testament in asking for 'a share in the forgiveness of sins', ἵνα δυνηθηθῶμεν μέρος τὸν (l.τῶν) <ἁμ>αρτιῶν καθαρίσεως; he is not citing the New Testament in any sense, although he is of course reflecting an important Christian concept.

If we may thus measure the impact of the New Testament on language in the ensuing centuries as a text read from, listened to, and talked about, we must allow sufficient latitude in the model to discuss intervening stages of Christian discourse. At *P.Lond.* VI 1920.9 (c. 330–340) the words fit, but the biblical context is not strictly relevant; we may reasonably wonder whether the ascetic discourse of the angelic life is not closer to the writer's mind.

In this context, a reminiscence should not be characterised as such if it consists merely of using particular words. Ἀγαπητὸς ἄδελφος is a direct echo of Pauline language, an expression traceable directly back to scripture though community usage from the time of the Apostles. But it is precisely for this reason that it should not count as a 'scriptural echo' here. Its status as a validating greeting means it is in far more frequent use than many of the words and phrases listed below: while it would be difficult for a Christian to use the phrase and not know its spiritual locus in the records of the early Church, it is unlikely. Likewise I would not count the phrase θεοῦ

---

[6] In this context I mean this phrase to designate the modern critical text.

[7] I should emphasise that this is done on grounds of space rather than any inherent suspicion of such theories.

ἄνθρωπος, which becomes virtually a monastic title, as an echo in the sense in which I want to discuss them here.

CITATIONS AS TESTIMONY TO THE TEXT OF THE NEW TESTAMENT

As a testimony to the text of the New Testament, citations and quotations in private letters have a much-neglected value. Those which are acceptably close to our critical texts deserve as to be treated at least at the same level as citations in early Christian literature, especially as there is no chance of the citation being helpfully 'corrected' by a Medieval scribe in the case of the papyri. This is rightly stressed by Stuart Pickering; although focussing on citations in non-scriptural Christian literary papyri, he shows that a citation of Matt. 10:42 in *P.Abinn.* 19.8–12 (346–351) preserves evidence for a variant reading to the gospel of Matthew at this point, with which the text of the letter harmonises nicely.[8] Where 'Dorotheos the Oxyrhynchite' in *P.Lond.* VI 1927.45–46 cites Eph. 5:16, NA[26] records no variations in the MSS. The quote dovetails with the preceding comment on time (*kairos*), and is skilfully applied. Many other places in the letter would qualify as echoes and reminiscences, were not our attention drawn to the quote by κηρύττει ὁ τρισμακάριος ἀπόστολ[ο]ς. But can Dorotheos' letter be taken as testimony that a manuscript existed which read the active participle used by Dorotheos instead of the middle, which appears (as far as can be judged by the editions) in all the MSS?

Mistakes in case endings in this letter are orthographic—the phonetic interchange -ε / -αι causes most—rather than being true morphological errors in form. Some MSS of Eph. have the quoted text beginning with καιρόν[9] but none have the active participle. Dorotheos' prose would arguably flow better had he adopted the middle; the change in voice is not caused by the need to fit into the syntax of a sentence, as it is in other examples. The variation may be conscious, with the voice of the participle encoding the belief that

---

[8] The editors of the text had suggested a conflation of Mark 9:41 and 42; see S.R. Pickering, "The Significance of Non-Continuous New Testament Textual Materials in Papyri", in D.G.K. Taylor (ed.), *Studies in the Early Text of the Gospels and Acts* (Birmingham, 1999), pp. 121–141.

[9] So H.I. Bell, *P.Lond.* VI 1927.40f.n., although there is no sign of this in the app.crit. to NA[26]. Or did the writer have in mind Col. 4:5: τὸν καιρὸν ἐξαγραζόμενοι?

Paphnuthios and his fellow anchorites are redeeming the current age. Whether that or a mistake, unsupported as it is, Dorotheos' citation should not qualify for the apparatus to an edition, but it should be mentioned in such an investigation of the papyrological evidence for Ephesians as is expected in the *Papyrologische Kommentare zum Neuen Testament* series directed by Peter Arzt-Grabner.[10]

The writer of *P.Lond.* VI 1921 quotes the New Testament as we have it in Coptic at 2Tim. 2.4 and 2.6 almost exactly (*l.* 11); the citation of 2 Tim may be held to extend to the sentence before the quote is explicitly signalled, where ⲘⲘⲁⲧⲁ·ⲉⲓ ⲛ̄ⲧⲉ ⲡ\ⲉ/ⲭ̄ⲥ̄ ('soldiers of Christ') clearly echoes 2 Tim 2.3, and gives context to the following quotation. The 'best texts' are also followed closely at line 17, where the quote extends to quoting Paul's introductory clause where the apostle cites Isaiah 28.16. Indeed, as the Introductory clause as quoted is further away from the Biblical text than the Isaian quote which follows, one might consider this a quote of the Old rather than the New Testament. This proposition is difficult to test further, as no Sahidic text of this exact section of Isaiah is extant,[11] but the acephalous writer of the Coptic letter at least follows the OT quote as transmitted in MSS of Romans closely, only making a relative into a verbal form at one point and shifting from a converted to a simple future verb at another. Showing that orthographical skill and knowledge of the biblical text are not necessarily always found alongside one another, Daniel's quotation of Hebr. 12:6 at *P.Nag Hamm.* Copt. 4.17 also follows Thompson's[12] text almost exactly.

In the case of these Coptic examples, we might also raise the possibility that the composers are making their own translations from the Greek New Testament; although there seems little prospect of testing this, such was probably more common than is supposed.[13]

These examples are all testimony to the stability of the New Testament text, and the ability of the MSS tradition to transmit it.

---

[10] See already P. Artz-Grabner, *Philemon* (Papyrologische Kommentare zum Neuen Testament 1; Göttingen, 2003).

[11] See K. Schüssler, *Biblia coptica = Die koptischen Bibeltexte* (Wiesbaden, 1995), Gesamtregister (Bd. 1 L. 4, p. 156).

[12] H. Thompson, *The Coptic Version of the Acts of the Apostles and the Pauline Epistles in the Sahidic Dialect*, (Cambridge, 1932).

[13] Suggested by J. Timbie with regard to Shenoute: "Non-canonical Scriptural Citation in Shenoute", paper read at the 8th International Congress of Coptic Studies, Paris, 1.6.2004.

In the case of the Coptic, they show that these writers knew texts very similar or identical to our first record of the text, parts of which survive in MSS copied near the time these letters were written. Given that we have no testimony to the New Testament text in these places as early as these letters, they, more so even than the Greek, deserve to be considered in the new edition of the Coptic New Testament for which the groundwork is now being laid.[14]

ECHO OR CITATION AS AN INDICATOR OF CHRISTIANITY

Harris rates the citation of scripture only below the appearance of 'Christian titles and symbols' as a 'criteria for Christian attribution'.[15] In the case of the secure citations and quotations of scripture, this undoubtedly holds true. But all these cases are marked as Christian by other elements, and would have been characterised as 'securely Christian' letters if the quote had not been made. As we step from citations and quotations to echoes and reminiscences to attribute private letters to a Christian milieu, problems become apparent. The lexica themselves may prove an insecure guide, as there is no guarantee that a word used only in Scripture (or only rarely outside) *as far as we know* will have *never* been used outside a Christian context in the Roman Imperial East.

In a number of instances, even isolated words or phrases, used in contexts which have little or no relation to the New Testament passage in which the words appear, can still have a powerful predicative value as regards determining the milieu. At *P.Lond.* VI 1915.9, 'blessed hope' seems a good candidate for a product of general discourse, but it does not appear elsewhere in Greek letters on papyrus; even if an intermediary (textual or oral) is proposed, the ultimate source is still likely to have been Tit. 2:13.[16] At *P.Abinn.* 7.19, only διαβλεπόμεθα links Apa Mios' text to such loci as Rom. 7:5; Luke 6:42 and Gos.Thom. 26; but outside of Mios' letter, only the writer of *P.Cair.Zen.* IV 59639, in the third century b.c.e. uses the word in a papyrus letter. Ἐλπίζω εἰς θεόν at *P.Iand.* II 11.2 seems innocuous, but the phrase is unknown until the fourth century, in and after

---

[14] See esp. the work of Schüssler cited above.
[15] Harris 1975, p. 156.
[16] Made more likely by the fact that the composer has already invoked 'the blessed apostle'.

which it is used in a number of certainly Christian letters. This is no 'citation', but as an echo, it deserves to be counted as an important indicator of the letter's milieu. The ὁδὸς εὐθεῖα of *P.Oxy.* XII 1494 also seems relevant here, as the expression does not reoccur elsewhere in the papyri.

At times, however, the search for biblical parallels produces improbable results. The first editor of *P.Mich.* VIII 482 could not fail to notice that ll. 15–17:

> καὶ ὅπου ἐὰν [λά]βῃς μοι ἀκολουθήσω σοι καὶ [ὡ]ς φειλῶ σοι ὁ θεὸς ἐμὲ φειλήσι.

> 'wherever you take me I will follow you, and as I love you God will love me'.

'recall the famous sentiment of Ruth 1:16'.[17] But he took it no further. Naldini saw this 'reminiscence', as well as one to Matt. 8:19 (ἀκολουθήσω σοι ὅπου ἐὰν ἀπέρχῃ) and John 16:27 (αὐτὸς ὁ πατὴρ φιλεῖ ὑμᾶς, ὅτι ὑμεῖς ἐμεπεφιλήκατε). Leaving aside the inverted 'order of love' when compared to e.g. 1 John. 3:11ff. and especially 4:19: ὑμεῖς ἀγαπῶμεν, ὅτι αὐτὸς πρῶτος ἠγάπησεν ἡμας, the writer's 'Matthean reminiscence' makes more sense in a military context. ἀκολουθέω can bear a 'military' sense of 'to follow as ally' (cf. *DGE* I, 119), and such might explain the otherwise odd greeting sent to the horse Bassus.[18] One might also note that—very unusually for private letters—*P.Mich.* VIII 482 is dated,[19] rare outside civic or military usage.

The latter context is unavoidably present in *C.Epist.Lat.* 169,[20] when Julius Dominus, military tribune, tells the *benificiarius* Aurelius Archelaus that his friend Theon 'has left his people and property and affairs and followed me' (*reliquit · enim su[o]s [e]t rem suam et actum et me secutus est*). Grenfell and Hunt missed the 'allusion' to the words of Peter in Matt. 19:27 = Mark 10:28 = Luke 18:28, but a number of subsequent scholars did not, and the second century letter was enrolled for a short time among the ranks of 'the earliest Christian letters'. But the suggestion survived neither Deissmann's disapproval,[21] nor

---

[17] LXX: ὅπου ἐὰν πορευθῇς πορεύσομαι . . . καὶ ὁ θεός σου θεός μου.

[18] Both E. Wipszycka ("Remarques sur les lettres privées chrétiennes des IIe–IVe siècles [a propos d'un livre de M. Naldini]", *Journal of Juristic Papyrology* 18 [1974] 203–221, at 212) and Harris (1975, p. 158) reject this echo.

[19] To 23.6.133, a date which might also be thought to count against a Christian attribution.

[20] First published as *P.Oxy.* I 32.

[21] 'If Archelaus were a Christian it is extremely unlikely, I think, that he would have profaned St. Peter's words by applying them to the relations of ordinary human

the reflections of subsequent scholars. Cotton invokes the common cultural background of Dominus and Paul as an explanation,[22] but even that may be unnecessary, as it is difficult to see how Dominus could have expressed himself without 'echoing' the New Testament here.

Vocabulary common to the New Testament and the world from which it proceeded, is, unsurprisingly, not difficult to locate, and it is sometimes the case that even the seemingly most distinctive 'Christian words' need not suggest a Christian context. At *P.Oxy.* XLII 3057, εἰρηνεύειν, ἀφορμή,[23] ὁμόνοια and φιλαλληλία (the last two in combination at 15–16) all recall Christian language.[24] But although common enough in Christian usage, they are not found in the New Testament, and both the latter terms had a existence in mathematical and philosophical writers.[25] Furthermore, in this letter, φιλανθρωπία, ἀμείψασθαι and χαρισάμενος μοι—which do occur in the New Testament—are used in a manner unlike that context, applied by the composer Ammonios to man, rather than God.[26] In this case, however, the letter is still considered by some as a genuine candidate for 'one of the oldest extracanonical Christian letters'.[27]

Single words, no matter how distinctive, have difficulty being counted in the categories under discussion here. So when *P.Oxy.* XLVI 3313 catches the eye with its opening—χαρ[ᾶς ἡμ]ᾶς ἐπλήρωσας εὐαγγελισαμένη τὸν γ[άμον] τοῦ κρατίστου Σαραπίωνος ('You filled us with joy when you announced the good news of the wedding of the excellent Sarapion')—we need look no further than the language of social relations between the educated.[28] And is the (incorrectly

friendship', *Light from the Ancient East*, 4th ed., trans. L.R.M. Strachan (Grand Rapids/MI, 1927), p. 199.

[22] H.M. Cotton, *Documentary Letters of Recommendation in Latin from the Roman Empire* (Königstein, 1981) pp. 15–17.

[23] Cf. C.J. Hemer, "Ammonius to Apollonius, Greeting", *Buried History* 12 (1976) 84–91, at 85–88.

[24] In addition to the comment in the edition see P.J. Parsons, "The Earliest Christian Letter", in R. Pintaudi, (ed.), *Miscellanea Papyrologia* (Florence, 1980), p. 289.

[25] See G.R. Stanton, "The Proposed Earliest Christian Letter on Papyrus and the Origin of the Term Philallelia", *ZPE* 54 (1984) 49–63; S.R. Llewelyn, *New Documents Illustrating Early Christianity*, vol. 6 (Sydney, 1992), p. 174.

[26] E.A. Judge, *Rank and Status in the World of the Caesars* (Canterbury 1982), p. 23.

[27] I. Ramelli, "Una delle più antiche lettere cristiane extracanoniche?", *Aegyptus* 80 (2000 [2002]), 169–88; cf. O. Montevecchi, "τὴν ἐπιστολὴν κεχιασμένην: P. Oxy. XLII 3057", *Aegyptus* 80 (2000 [2002]), 189–94. I do not regard these latest two contributions as having settled this issue.

[28] G.H.R. Horsley, *New Documents Illustrating Early Christianity*, vol. 3 (Sydney, 1983), pp. 10–15; Judge, 1982, pp. 24–26.

impersonal) use of the verb δυνατεῖν, rare outside the letters of Paul,[29] in *P.Oxy.* LV 3819.9ff., a sufficient indication of Christian authorship of this monotheistic but ultimately 'religiously neutral' letter?[30]

Context should not tell against a Christian attribution if scriptural allusion is to have force as an 'indicator of Christianity'. In ειτου δε εδημαζω αυτα, (*l.* ἰδοὺ δὲ ἐτοιμάζω αὐτά?) a suspicious mind might see a biblical reminiscence to Isaiah 54.11, ἰδοὺ ἐγὼ ἐτοιμάζω σοὶ ἄνθρακα τὸν λίθον. But *P.Fouad* I 82 (for the quote see l. 10), although using monotheistic phraseology, also reports a transaction involving a priestess of Triphis; in light of this, use of a scriptural phrase might seem less likely.

Even within a certainly Christian letter, we must be careful what is allowed to count as a New Testament echo if the catgory is going to have meaning. In *P.Lond.* III 981.8–11, where a deacon tells a famous monk or bishop that his fame has encircled 'the entire world' is he really thinking of Rom. 1:8?[31] He is undoubtedly familiar with this text, but I do not believe this should qualify as a fully fledged 'echo'. The 'cup of water' in *P.Abinn.* 19 forms part of a certain quotation of Matt. 10:42. But does the 'cup of water', which no one will give the writer of *P.Oxy.* XLVI 3314 as he lies sick in Babylon, suggest his Christianity? The fact that these are the only two 'cups of water' referred to in the papyri using these words does not guarantee that Judas (whose name also raises questions about his religion) is a Christian, as there seem few other ways of expressing what the writer needs to say. Arguments from the silence of the papyrus record have a notoriously short shelf-life, nor are they always methodologically sound.

Language of 'God willing' need not always be traced back to (e.g) 1 Cor. 12:18; 15:38 (see e.g. Naldini on *BGU* I 27.11;[32] the text is not likely to be Christian). 'If God wishes' is simply too common a sentiment: there is no suggestion that, e.g. *P.Bas.* 18 (?, 30 BCE–100 CE) is a Christian text, despite 9–10: ἐὰν ὁ θεὸς θέλῃ εὐθέως ἥξω{ι}

---

[29] Only in Philodemus according to LSJ and BDAG; Lampe does not record the word. Cf. *P.Oxy.* LV 3819.9–11n, where the suggestion of a Christian reminiscence is made.

[30] An idea promoted by the editor, J. Rea (Intro. and at 9–11n); see however J. Chapa, *Letters of Condolence in the Greek Papyri* (Florence, 1998), p. 126 and his discussion of ll. 9–11 on pp. 128–9.

[31] See Harris 1975, p. 157.

[32] Naldini 1998, no. 2.

πρὸς σε; nor *P.David* 14 or *P.Mich.* III 218.[33] ἐὰν ὁ θεὸς θέλῃ is the most common formulation across social groups, and ὡς θέλει ὁ Σοκνεβτῦ{νις} ὁ κύριος θεὸς καταβήσομαι ἐλευθέρως (*P.Tebt.* II 284 (Tebtynis, I ce)) starkly indicates the danger of such an approach. Christians use these words, but their antecedent is the common vocabulary of divine wish, rather than the words of Paul.

Likewise with regard to the phrase '(for) God knows' (οἶδεν (γὰρ) ὁ θεός); its usage cannot be said categorically to constitute necessarily echo of 2 Cor. 11–12 when found in Christian letters,[34] as earlier clearly non-Christian employment shows the phrase to be formulaic.[35]

In every case of citation or clear quotation, the composer's Christianity is proved by other elements (in particular *nomina sacra*, Pauline 'in the Lord' (ἐν κυρίῳ) phraseology, and Christian titles); so too in many cases of 'echoes'. But given the commonalities of religious language observable in the papyri, we should be careful about using scriptural echoes or reminiscence in cases where Christian attribution is otherwise doubtful. The suggested New Testament echoes in *P.Herm.* 6,[36] for example, can be set against 'echoes' of Plato and Euripides.[37] Here, prosopography and a reading of the archive from which the piece comes suggests a Christian context is likely, but most papyrus letters are isolated and cannot be contextualised in anything except the history and language of the period.

The scriptural citation in the Manichaean letters shows (if any more proof were thought needed) the important place of the gospels in the articulation of religiosity among Manichaeans. However, the identification of securely Manichaean letters, which would in isolation have been identified as Christian, raises some problems with the use of scripture to identify a letter as 'Christian' in a restricted sense. I tend to the view that we need to include Manichaean evidence, even

---

[33] Despite arguments to the contrary, the 'archive of Paniskos' makes most sense against the background of worship of Sarapis or a similar Graeco-Egyptian god.

[34] E.g. *P.Stras.* I 35 (?, IV/V); *P.Ben.Mus.* 5 (Fayum, IV).

[35] *SB* XIV 11644 (?, I/II); see also *P.Stras.* VII 652.73 (?, c. 136–141): οἱ θεοὶ ἴσασι. Cf. A.M. Nobbs, "Formulas of Belief in Greek Papyrus Letters of the Third and Fourth Centuries", in T.W. Hillard, R.A. Kearsley, et al. (eds.), *Ancient History in a Modern University* (North Ryde, 1998), vol. 2, pp. 233–37, at pp. 235–36.

[36] R.S. Bagnall, *Egypt in Late Antiquity* (Princeton 1993), p. 272 n. 78.

[37] A. Moscadi, "Le lettere dell'archivio di Teofane", *Aegyptus* 50 (1970), 88–154, at 97, 141–6; E. Wipszycka, "La christianisation de l'Égypte aux iv⁰–vi⁰ siècles. Aspects sociaux et ethniques", *Études sur le christianisme dans l'Égypte de l'antiquité tardive*, (Rome, 1996), pp. 63–105, at p. 85.

if only in a Christianising context such as this, in our totality of evidence for late-antique Christianity. As the editor of the recently discovered *Epistles* of Mani comments, 'What is found in these *Epistles*
fragments is an authentic Christian voice'.[38] We should be led in the
first instance by how people self-identified, and there are numerous
indications that many Manichaeans thought of themselves as 'the
true Christians'. Even within this framework, however, we can begin
to delimit the phraseology of various traditions.

A number of the Coptic letters from Kellis show a phraseology,
that, when viewed before their discovery, was thought to distinctively
represent Christianity. The distinctive (and until very recently unparalleled) prayer formula in *P.Harr.* I 107 contains a conflation of multiple elements with their origins in the New Testament:

πρὸ μὲν πάντων εὔχω-	Before all things I pray
5 μαι τῷ πατρὶ θεῶι τῆς ἀλη-	to the Father God of truth
θείας καὶ τῷ παρακλήτῳ	and to the paraclete
πνεύματι ὃς σὲ διαφυλά-	Spirit that they may protect
ξωσιν καιτά τε θυχὴν κα⟨ὶ⟩	you in soul and
σῶμα καὶ πνεῦμα, τῷ μὲν	body and spirit; for your
10 σώματι ὑιγίαν, τῷ δὲ πνεύ-	body, health, for your spirit,
ματι εὐθυμία, τῇ δὲ ψυ-	joy, for your soul,
χῇ ζωὴν αἰώνιον.	eternal life.

4–5 *l.* εὔχομαι   7 *l.* ὡς· ς corr. from τ   8 *l.* κατά   10 ὑιγιαν pap. *l.* ὑγίειαν
11 *l.* εὐθυμίαν

The suggestion that the text might emanate from an 'unorthodox
circle'[39] was countered by contributions showing how nearly every
part of the prayer had firm New Testament antecedents.[40] As indeed
it does: John 14:26 and 1 Thess. 5:23 are only two of the verses
which could be noted. But Ghedini, who withdrew his suggestion in
the face of early reaction, was on the right track. Virtually the same

---

[38] I. Gardner, in the introduction to *Kellis Literary Texts*, volume 2 (Oxford,
forthcoming).

[39] G. Ghedini, "Note a tre lettere cristiane in P.Har." *Aegyptus* 17 (1937) 98–100;
id., "La lettera P.Har. 107", *Aegyptus* 20 (1940) 209–11.

[40] H. Crouzel, "La lettre du P. Harr. 107 et la théologie d'Origene", *Aegyptus* 49
(1969) 138–143; A. Emmett, "The concept of Spirit in papyrus letters of the third
and fourth century: Problems posed by P.Harr. 107", *Prudentia* Suppl. (1985) 73–79;
J. O'Callaghan, "Sobre la interpretación de P.Harr. 107", *Aegyptus* 52 (1972) 152–57.

pattern (allowing for slight variations) is clearly visible in letters from Kellis, in the Dakhleh Oasis, with a frequency and near identity which show that not only must Besas, the inexperienced[41] writer of *P.Harr.* I 107, must be a Manichaean, but that the prayer forms a unit and must derive its immediate context from a letter of Mani or a Manichaean liturgical text.[42]

Almost certainly a quotation of a letter of Mani is *P.Kell.* V Copt. 19.9–10: ⲕⲁⲧ[ⲁ] ⲧϩⲉ ⲉⲧⲉ ϩⲁ ⲡ̄ⲡⲁⲣⲁⲕⲗⲏⲧⲟⲥ ϫⲟⲥ ϫⲉ ⲡ̄ⲙⲁⲑⲏⲧⲏⲥ ⲛ̄ⲧ̄ⲇⲓⲕⲁⲓⲟⲥⲩⲛⲏ ϣ[ⲁⲩ] ϭⲛⲧϥ̄ ⲉⲣⲉ ⲧ̄ϩⲉⲣⲧⲉ ⲙ̄ⲡⲉϥⲥⲁϩ ϩⲓϫⲱϥ ⲉϥⲟⲩⲏⲩ ⲙ̄ⲙⲁϥ ⲛ̄ⲧϩⲉ ⲛⲉⲣϥ̄ϩⲁⲣⲁϩ, 'just as the Paraclete[43] has said: "The disciple of righteousness is found with the fear of his teacher upon him (even) while he is far from him." Like guardians (?).'[44] The source, unidentified to this point,[45] must be Manichaean scripture.

Such is probably not true in the case of the echo identified in *P.Oxy.* XXXI 2603.28–29: εἴ τι αὐτοῖς ποιεῖς ἐμο[ι] ἐποίησας; on Naldini's advice 'evidente reminiscenza di Matt. 25.40': ἐφ' ὅσον ἐποιήσατε ἑνὶ τούτων τῶν ἀδελφῶν μου τῶν ἐλαχίστων, ἐμοὶ ἐποιήσατε. The characteristic greetings to 'the elect and the Catechumens', which so many of the Kellis Manichaean letters feature, suggest a similar context here.[46] Such of course does not rule out that the writer here echoes Matthew; but *P.Oxy.* LI 3646—καὶ ὃς ἂν ποιήσας τῷ προφήτῃ, ἐμοὶ ποιεῖς—where the context for the 'prophet' is certainly the Egyptian priesthood, might give us pause for thought in equating this immediately with the biblical locus.

---

41 Although his slowly-formed letters need not mean he is a 'boy' (so ed.pr.).

42 I. Gardner, A. Nobbs and M.Choat, "P.Harr. 107: Is this another Greek Manichaean letter", *ZPE* 131 (2000) 118–124.

43 I.e. Mani himself, see *P.Kell.* V Copt. 19.9n.

44 Trans. eds., who signal by their placement of the quotation marks an opinion that does not belong in the quote, but it certainly belongs with this clause and not the following.

45 Not unexpected, seeing as nearly the whole of Mani's Gospel has perished; for what remains see I. Gardner and S. Lieu, *Manichaean Texts from the Roman Empire* (Cambridge, 2004), pp. 156–59.

46 For the suggestion of a Manichaean context, see S. Lieu, *Manichaeism in Mesopotamia and the Roman East* (Leiden 1994), p. 98 n. 316; I. Gardner, "Personal Letters from the Manichaean Community at Kellis", in L. Cirillo and A. van Tongerloo (edd.), *Atti del Terzo Congresso Internationale di Studi 'Manicheismo e Oriente Cristiano antico'* (Leuven, 1997), pp. 77–94, at p. 87. If so, this might open up another line of investigation on the 'mirror' imagery used by the writer, which (although related lines of thought can be seen in Christian and Hellenic writing, see the ed.pr., J.H. Harrop, *JEA* 48 (1962) 132–40; Naldini 1998, p. 215) has eluded exact identification of its source.

In the context of these quotations it seems worthy noting (even if I do not wish to draw any direct conclusion) that while ἀνεφάνη at *P.Oxy.* VI 939.3 echoes Tit. 2:11 and 3:4 (cf. Luke 19:11) it is here the γνῶσις of the master God which appears, rather than the Salvation (*soteria*) of the letter to Titus.

CONTEXT AND IMPLICATIONS

That identifiable echoes of the New Testament do not appear until the late third century, and the practice of explicit citation not until the post-Constantinian age confirms the general picture we see in the documentary papyri, of an infrequent Christian presence in the third century, growing exponentially in the fourth.

There seems little point in speculating whether any particular echo is directly inspired by the New Testament. Those phrases which are not in wide use may be suspected to have been inspired by scriptural usage, but again there is no guarantee the biblical passage is the direct source; a sermon, reading of other literature or hearing the phrase in another way surely usually stand between this usage of the words and the holy text; other times the New Testament is probably not even the indirect source; coincidence, or another source entirely (i.e. language itself, devoid of specific textual inspiration) is likely to be closer to the truth.

Of the people whose quotes conform most closely to the text of the New Testament, we may note that two (*P.Lond.* VI 1920, 1921) write to the monastic leader Paieous,[47] and one to the anchorite Paphnouthios (*P.Lond.* VI 1927); all three may well have been monks

---

[47] The editors believed it likely that *P.Lond.* VI 1921 was sent *by* rather than *to* the Apa Paieous to whom the rest of the archive is directed, but I believe they were in error. The first line is imperfect (ΠЄΤϹ[ϩЄΙ c. 7] ΠΑ[Ι]ΗΟΥ), but *contra* the editors ('ΠΑ[Ι]ΗΟΥ comes at the end, where we naturally look for the name of the writer', *P.Lond.* VI, p. 94) the normal formula is [sender] ΠЄΤϹϩΑΙ Ν-/Є- [addressee]; an epithet such as ΠΠΙϢΤ ΠΜЄΡΙΤ ('beloved father') might fill the gap, with the sender's name having been lost above. On the verso, where the eds. took Π/ ΠΑЄΙ-ΗΟΥϹ ΔΙΚΑΙΟΥ/ for ΠΑΡΑ (παρά), i.e. 'from Paieous son of Dikaious', one might restore instead [Α]Π, i.e. ἀπόδος, 'to Paieous'; and since *P.Lond.* VI 1913.2 shows that Paieous' father's name was Hor, Dikaios will not be his patronymic, but either the sender's name, or a title for Paieous (*contra* the statement of the eds. that '[Paieous] is not likely to have called himself "the just"' (*P. Lond.* VI 1921, Intro.), see the common use of *dikaios* as an epithet for monks: Antony is so described by Evagrius, *apud* Socrates, *H.E.* 4.23.43, and ascetics are called οἱ *dikaioi* in the *de virginitate* (spuriously) attributed to Athanasius (*PG* 28.251–282, at 277).

themselves, although we are not permitted to conclude that only on the basis of their knowledge of scripture. Almost certainly a monk is Apa Shoi, *presbyteros* of the 'Mountain' (ⲧⲟⲟⲩ) of *Pnomt* who writes to the well-known (in our time, and surely in his) *apotaktikos* and *anachoretes*[48] Apa Johannes.[49] The latter is arguably also the addressee of *P.Ryl.Copt.* 292 and 311.[50] A village priest in the Fayum, Apa Mios,[51] quotes scripture to the commander of the local garrison.[52] Daniel quotes the epistle to the Hebrews to Aphrodisias, who himself associates with Sansnos, a monastic leader;[53] it is not unlikely that at least Aphrodisias is a monk like, too, probably Kapiton, who reports the loss of his ἱμάτιον to the monk Nepheros in *P. Neph.* 11.[54] The other citer of the New Testament (although it precedes only echoes) also writes to Paieous (P.Lond. 6.1915).

Neither the fact that someone cites scripture or uses Coptic confirms they are a monk, and some or all of Herieous (*P.Lond.* VI 1915), Hatres of 'Eagle Island' (*P.Lond.* VI 1920),[55] 'Dorotheos the Oxyrhynchite' (*P.Lond.* VI 1927), and the nameless writers of *P.Lond.* VI 1921, *P.Ryl.Copt.* 292, and *P.Ryl.Copt.* 311 may not have been monks. This notwithstanding, the wider monastic and clerical context is clear. Were people more likely to quote scripture to monks? Or did the context, usually a request for temporal or spiritual assistance, provide a context in which such quotations came more naturally?

In the case of the Nepheros archive, the concentration of reminiscences of 1 Tim. detected by the editors, suggested to them a reflection of the community of Hathor's articulation of its theory of

---

[48] On these monastic titles see M. Choat, "The Development and Usage of Terms for 'Monk' in Late Antique Egypt", *JbAC* 45 (2002) 5–23; E. Wipszycka, "'Αναχωρητής, ἐριμίτης, ἔγκλειστος, ἀποτακτικός. Sur la Terminologie Monastique en Égypte", *JJP* 31 (2001) 147–68.

[49] His archive is primarily preserved by *P.Herm.* 7–10 and *P.Ryl.Copt.* 268–276; cf. P. van Minnen, "The Roots of Egyptian Christianity", *APF* 40 (1994) 71–85.

[50] Both have lost their beginnings and addresses, but the tone and the fact they were purchased with the archive and are similar in date, suggest a connection.

[51] *P.Abinn.* 19 has lost the lines recording its sender, but phraseology and tone strongly indicate it belongs with *P.Abinn.* 6–8, sent by the priest.

[52] Another indication that he was probably himself a Christian (see T.D. Barnes "The Career of Abinnaeus", *Phoenix* 39 (1985) 368–74, at 373–74, *contra* the feelings of the editors at *P.Abinn.*, Intro., 33).

[53] *P.NagHamm.* Gr. 68, 72, 75, 76, 77, 78, and Copt. 5 are addressed to a Sansnos, probably the same man, and seemingly a monastic leader.

[54] Cf. *P. Neph.*, p. 71, nn. 12–13. Cf. the same term in *P.Neph.* 12.4, by a self-identified μοναχός.

[55] *P.Lond.* VI 1920.1: ϩⲁⲧⲣⲉ ⲡⲣⲏⲛ̄ⲧⲏⲟⲩ ⲙ̄ⲡⲁϩⲟⲛ: in a monastic context the last word invites resolution as a proper name, but I can find no island associated with Pachomius which would make sense of 'the Island of Pachom'.

leadership through this biblical book.[56] Announcing oneself to be 'faithful and worthy of full acceptance' (*P.Neph.* 11.6–7) deserves to be classified as a quotation, and the concept of the *presbyteros* as 'worthy of all honour' (*P.Neph.* 7[57]) finds a clear reflection in 1 Tim. Phrases such as 'soldiers of Christ' and 'Man of God'[58] are too widely used in the monastic discourse to have much value in this connection, but taking into account also the quotations from 2 Tim. in *P.Lond.* VI 1921, from the same monastic community at an early stage,[59] one might see a formative ideological and perhaps liturgical role for these Pauline letters in particular in the development of this Melitian monastic community. Less convincingly, but admittedly not definitely,[60] the editors posit a particular reflection of James 5:14–15 in the Melitian community's theology of healing,[61] to which passages in the letters to Nepheros are supposed to refer.[62] Yet the healing traditions of the Church should be seen as arising from a more varied background than this one biblical passage, and it is not certain it is even the direct catalyst here.[63]

The outsider, of course, is the Manichaean use of Matthew (*P.Kell.* V Copt. 32),[64] and this provides valuable evidence for the important role of the New Testament in the lives of Manichaeans. It also reveals the process of exegesis of the New Testament text within the Manichaean community. The writer of *P.Kell.* V Copt. 32 follows his first citation of Matthew by noting that the treasuries / storehouses 'are the sun and the moon', one of the few places in these Manichaean letters that distinct Manichaean theology is evident.[65]

---

[56] *P.Neph.*, p. 70, n. 3.

[57] Cf. the sixth century *P.Oxy.* XVI 1841, where the phrase, abbreviated π(άσης) τιμ(ῆς) ἀξ(ίοις) seems a formulaic accompaniment to the names and titles (*komes*), and other epithets of the addressees.

[58] *P.Neph.* 4, 11; see below.

[59] See H. Hauben, "Aurêlios Pageus, alias Apa Paiêous, et le monastère mélitien d'Hathor", *AncSoc* 32 (2002) 337–52.

[60] 'Es bleibt also am Ende unklar', *P.Neph.*, p. 24.

[61] 'Die Fürbitten des Priesters Nepheros und Jak 5,14–15', in *P. Neph.*, Intro., pp. 21–24; cf. the discussion at *P.Neph.* 10, pp. 65–69.

[62] Esp. *P.Neph.* 1.10–13, 10.7–9, see *P.Neph.*, p. 22.

[63] See R.-J. Barrett-Lennard *Christian Healing After the New Testament* (New York, 1994) pp. 53–4, 74–5; see also A.M. Nobbs, Review of *P.Neph.*, *JEA* 67 (1991) 229. Not the least among the important other antecedents are Jesus' own healings, on which see J.P. Meier, *A Marginal Jew. Rethinking the Historical Jesus* (2 Vols; New York, 1991, 1994), Vol II, Chapter 21, pp. 679–772.

[64] The context seems secular in *P.Princ.* II 102, but is difficult to assess without the quotation itself surviving.

[65] See the remarks of I. Gardner, *P.Kell.* V. Copt., Intro., 80. On the sun and

We may think of such citers and quoters of scripture as 'educated',[66] but I am not convinced we need to posit such as a necessary conclusion in all our cases of citation. And the 'education' sometimes is only in a catechetical sense: handwriting, orthography and grammar does not always reflect a wider application of the term. We see perhaps in some of these letters the effects of catechetical education. While our literary sources for a Christian education are fulsome, evidence for catechetical schools that we know existed from other sources[67] is difficult to find. Most school exercises we have are exercises in writing, grammar, and mathematics.[68] We meet catechumens 'being instructed in Genesis' and 'in the beginning of the Gospel' in letters between Church leaders[69] but it is difficult to locate them 'on the ground' in the towns of Egypt, at least as far as the educational record is concerned. Texts marked for reading may have served in catechetical situations as well as in more classrooms as scripture took over from classical models as models for copying and reading.[70] But in these private letters we see, whether intentionally, or in the case of some echoes, probably otherwise, the language of the New Testament, both as a text to be quoted, and as a source which had already contributed distinctive words and phrases to the common language of the day.

---

moon, cf. Alexander of Lycopolis' summary of Manichaean doctrine, at Garnder and Lieu 2004, pp. 180–81; and *PsBk* II 223, as cited at *ibid.*, p. 178.

[66] Cf. Tibiletti 1979, p. 116: 'persone presumibilmente di una certa cultura'. Cf. *P.Kell.* V, p. 208: the style and content [of *P.Kell.* V Copt. 32] suggest a well educated member of the [Manichaean] elect'.

[67] In an Egyptian context, see esp. the *Canons of Pseudo-Hippolytus*, composed in a Lower Egyptian town in the late 340's; Ed. R.-G. Coquin, *Les Canons d'Hippolyte* (Paris, 1966) (on whom the assessment given here of place and date depend, see pp. 54–63), trans. ed. P. Bradshaw, trans. C. Bebawi, *The Canons of Hippolytus* (Bramcote, Nottingham, 1987). This work, though written in Greek (Coquin, *Les Canons*, pp. 32–3), survives only in Arabic, and is based ultimately of course on the *Apostolic Tradition* of Hippolytus (ed. B. Botte, *La Tradition Apostolique de saint Hippolyte. Essai de reconstitution* (Münster, 1972); *idem, La Tradition Apostolique d'après les anciens versions* (2nd ed. Paris, 1968).

[68] It is a frequent, and in my opinion grave, error to cite such schools-exercises alongside literary references to what is primarily catechetical instruction.

[69] *PSI* IX 1041; *P.Oxy.* XXXVI 2785 (both Oxyrhynchus, early IV). On these 'letters of recommendation', see T.M. Teeter, "Letters of Recommendation or Letters of Peace?", *Akten des 21. Internationalen Papyrologenkongresses* (Stuttgart—Leipzig, 1997) pp. 954–60; K. Treu, "Christliche Empfehlungs-Schemabriefe auf Papyrus": *Zetesis. Bijdragen . . . E. de Strycker* (Antwerp/Ultrecht, 1973), pp. 629–36.

[70] E.g. *P.Laur.* IV 140 (?, III/IV); *P.Lond.Lit.* 207 (Fayum, III/IV), both texts of the Psalms.

Table I: Citations

Papyrus	Identifying clause	Content	Biblical Reference	New Testament Text(s)
P.Lond. VI 1915.14	[το]ῦ μακαρίου ἀποστό[λ]ου λέγοντες (l.-τος)	τοὺς ἀσθενοῦντας μὴ παρορᾶν [ο]ὐ μόνον [ε]ἰν τῇ πίστ(ε)ι ἀλλὰ καὶ ἐ[ν] ταῖς κο(σ)μικαῖς π[ρ]άξεσι.	Reminiscence of eg. Rom. 14:1; Acts 20:35; Ja. 5:14; 1 Thess. 5:14	
P.Lond. VI 1927.45–46	κηρύττει ὁ τρισμακά-ριός ἀπόστολ[ο]ς	τὸν καιρ[ὸ]ν γὰρ ἐξαγ̣ο̣ρά̣ζ̣[ο]ντες, ὅτι αἱ ἡμέραι πονηραί εἰσιν	Eph. 5:16	ἐξαγοραζόμενοι τὸν καιρόν, ὅτι αἱ ἡμέραι πονηραί εἰσιν
P.Lond. VI 1921.11	ⲕⲁⲧⲁ ⲑⲉ ⲛ̄[ⲧ]ⲁ ⲡ̄ϫⲁⲉⲓⲥ ϫⲟⲟⲥ ϩ̄ⲛ ⲡⲉⲡ̄ⲁ̄ⲛ̄ (l. ⲡ̄ⲛ̄ⲁ̄?) ϫⲉ ... ⲁⲩⲱ ϫⲉ	ⲙⲁⲣⲉⲗⲁⲁⲩ ⲉ̣ϫ̣ⲟ ⲛ̄ⲙⲁⲧⲉⲓ ⲧⲁϩⲣ ϩⲛ̄ ⲛⲉϩⲃⲏⲟⲩ\ⲉ/ ⲛ̄ⲧ[ⲉ] ⲡⲃⲓⲟⲥ ⲁⲩⲱ ϫⲉ ⲡⲟⲩⲁⲉⲓⲉ ⲉⲧϩⲁⲥⲉ ⲡⲉϥϩⲁ-[ϥ]ϫⲓ ϩ̄ⲏ̄ⲡⲉϥ ⲕⲁⲣⲡⲟⲥ ⲛ̄ϣⲁⲣⲡ̄	2 Tim. 2:4, 2:6	ⲙⲉⲣⲉⲗⲁⲁⲩ ⲉϫϥⲟ ⲛ̄ⲙⲁⲧⲟⲓ ⲧⲁϩϥ̄ ϩⲛ̄ ⲛⲉϩⲃⲏⲩⲉ ⲙ̄ⲡⲃⲓⲟⲥ (2:4) ... ⲡⲟⲩⲟⲉⲓⲉ ⲉⲧϩⲟⲥⲉ ⲡ̄ⲧⲟϥ ⲉϥⲁϫⲓ ⲉⲃⲟⲗ ϩ̄ⲙ̄ ⲡ̄ⲕⲁⲣⲡⲟⲥ ⲛ̄ϣⲟⲣⲡ̄ (2:6)
P.Lond. VI 1921.17	ⲧⲉⲕⲣⲁⲫⲏ ⲅⲁⲣ ϫⲱ ⲙ̄ⲙⲁⲥ ϫⲉ	ⲟⲩⲁⲛ ⲛⲓⲙ ⲉ̣ⲧ̄[ⲡⲓ]ⲥ̣ⲧⲉⲩ ⲁ̄ⲣⲁϥ ⲥⲉⲛⲁϫⲓϣⲓⲡⲉ ⲉ̄ⲛ	Rom. 10:11	ϣⲁⲣⲉ ⲧⲉⲅⲣⲁⲫⲏ ⲅⲁⲣ ϫⲟⲟⲥ ϫⲉ ⲟⲩⲟⲛ ⲛⲓⲙ ⲉⲧⲡⲓⲥⲧⲉⲩⲉ ⲉⲣⲟϥ ⲛ̄ϥⲛⲁϫⲓϣⲓⲡⲉ ⲁ̄ⲛ

P.Nag Hamm. Copt. 4.17	εϥϭΗ2 ΓΑΡ ΧΕ	[ΠΕΤΕ]ΡΕ ΠΧΟΕΙС ΝΕ ΜΜΟϤ ϢΑϤΠΑΙΔΕΥΕ ΜΜΟ[ϥ] ϢΑϤ[ΜΑС]ΤΙΓΟΥ ΝϢΗΡΕ ΝΙΜ ΕΤϤΝΑϢΟΟΠΟΥ ΕΡΟϤ	Hebr. 12:6	ΠΕΤΕΡΕ ΠΧΟΕΙС ΓΑΡ ΝΕ ΜΜΟϤ ϢΑϤΠΑΙΔΕΥΕ ΜΜΟϤ. ϢΑϤΜΑСΤΙΓΟΥ ΔΕ ΝϢΗΡΕ ΝΙΜ ΕΤϤΝΑϢΟΠΟΥ ΕΡΟϤ.
P.Princ. II 102	μνημόνευε ὑπομύμνη- ὑποσχέσε[ως τοῦ] μακαρ[ίου Πα]ύλου καθώς	Lost	—	—
P.Ryl.Copt. 269.13 (late IV)	]ΠΕΝ[Τ]ΑΠΑΥΛΟС [ΧΩ ΜΜΟС ΧΕ?]	]2ΩϤ Ν[.] . ΑΙΑΑΤ . . . [71]] . ΝΑ[Τ]2ΗΥ ΜΠΕ . . . [72] restore perhaps [εῖο ΓΑΡ Ν̄ΡΠΡϤΕ 2Ν]2ΩϤ Ν[Ι]Μ ΑΙΑΑΤ||2Ν2ΑΛ ΝΟΥΟΝ ΝΙΜ ΧΕ Ε]ΙΝΑ[Τ]2ΗΥ ΜΠΕ||2ΟΥΟ	1 Cor. 9:19[73]	ΕΙΟ ΓΑΡ Ν̄ΡΠΡϤΕ 2Ν 2ΩΒ ΝΙΜ ΑΙΑΑΤ 2Ν2ΑΛ ΝΟΥΟΝ ΝΙΜ ΧΕ ΕΙΕΤ2ΗΥ ΜΠΕ2ΟΥΟ
P.Ryl.Copt. 292.5 (IV/V)	ΠΕΤΟΥΟΧ Ν̄ΓΑΡ ΕϢϢΝΕ ΝΗΕϤΧΙ ΠСΑΕΙΝ ΕΡΟϤ	ΚΑΤΑ Θε[74]		ΝΕΤΤΗΚ ΑΝ ΝΕΤΡΧΡΙΑ ΜΠСΑΕΙΝ, ΑΛΛΑ ΝΕΤΜΟΚ2 ΝΕ

---

[71] Half a line is lost between each of the line-fragments here.

[72] Or perhaps ΝΕ]ΝΝΑ[Τ]2ΗΥ.

[73] The editor (Crum) suggested an allusion to 1 Cor. 13:3 on the basis of Ν̄ΤΝΑΤ2ΗΥ, but felt the verse contextually inappropriate; the restoration proposed here fits the context better.

[74] ΚΑΤΑ Θε follows the quotation, and it seems likely that 'according to what the Lord has said/what is written' *vel sim.* may have stood in the lacuna at the beginning of the next line.

Table II: Quotation or Clear Allusion

Papyrus	Content	Biblical Reference	Biblical Text
P.Abinn. 19.8–10 (346–351)	[πο]:[ή]ριον ὑδα[δα]τος ἐνὶ τῶν [μικ]ρῶν [τ]ούτων οὐκ ἀπολ᾽ λ⟨ε⟩ῖ τὸν [μ]ισθὸν ἑαυτοῦ	Matt. 10:42 (cf. Matt. 18:6, 9:41 and 9:42)	καὶ ὃς ἂν ποτίσῃ ἕνα τῶν μικρῶν τούτων ποτήριον ψυχροῦ μόνον εἰς ὄνομα μαθητοῦ, ἀμὴν λέγω ὑμῖν, οὐ μὴ ἀπολέσῃ τὸν μισθὸν αὐτοῦ. [ποτήριον ὕδατος θυχρου D and others] (Matt.)
P.Lond. VI 1920.9 (c. 330–340)	ειογω ψεnλγ επετπ̄2ο n̄θε n̄π2ο n̄2εnλγγελοc	Acts 6:15?	λγnλγ επεq2ο n̄θε n̄φο n̄ογλγγελοc
P.Kell. V Copt. 32.10–12; 42–45 (c. 350–380; Manichaean)	λc]6λλωογ λnε2ωр ετ21 ετε nλρε 2λλε 6n̄ nλῑτ᾽ ογλε nλρε λнcтнc [x]λxτ᾽ λрλγ λxιογε (10–12); прωnε cλγnε εn xε εω πε πnο ετερε πλнcтнc nλει λxλxτ᾽ λπнῑ (42–45)	Matt. 6:20, cf. 19; conflation of Matt. 24:42–43	cωογ2 xε nнтn̄ ε2ογn n̄2пλ2ο 2n̄ тпε. пнλ ετε nερε xοολεc мꞮ 2οολε тλко n̄2нтq. λγω пнλ ετε nερε nρεqxιογε 6ωтꞁ ероq n̄cεxιογε (6:20; ωοxꞁ ероq 19); n̄τετncοογn λn xε εω πχοειc nнγ 2n̄ λω n̄2ооγ.

			ⲧⲉⲧⲛⲉⲓⲙⲉ ⲇⲉ ⲉⲡⲁⲓ. ϫⲉ ⲉⲛⲉϥⲥⲟⲟⲩⲛ ⲛ̄ϭⲓ ⲡϫⲟⲉⲓⲥ ⲙ̄ⲡⲏⲓ ϫⲉ ⲉⲣⲉ ⲡⲣⲉϥϫⲓⲟⲩⲉ ⲛⲏⲩ ⲛ̄ⲁϣ ⲛ̄ⲟⲩⲣϣⲉ. ⲛⲉϥⲛⲁⲣⲟⲉⲓⲥ ⲡⲉ ⲛ̄ϥ̄ⲧⲙ̄ⲕⲁⲁⲩ ⲉϭⲱⲧϩ̄ ⲙ̄ⲡⲉϥⲏⲓ (24:42–43).
P.Ryl.Copt. 311.1–2 (IV/V)	ⲓⲏⲥⲟⲩⲥ ϣⲛ²ⲏⲧϥ ϩⲁⲛⲃⲗⲗⲉⲉⲩ	Matt. 20:30–34 and parallels; cf. e.g. Matt. 9:27–30[75]	ⲁϥϣⲛ ²ⲏⲧϥ ⲛ̄ϭⲓ ⲓⲏⲥⲟⲩⲥ (Matt. 20:34)
P.Neph. 11.6–7 (c. 360)	πιστὸν ἡγησάμην καὶ πάσης ἀποδοχῆς ἄξιον (6–7)	1 Tim. 1:15; 4:9; 6:1	πιστὸς ὁ λόγος καὶ πάσης ἀποδοχῆς ἄξιος (1:15; 4:9); τοὺς ἰδίους δεσπότα πάσης τιμῆς ἀξίους ἡγείσθωσαν (6:1)

[75] Healing of the blind is of course a recurring topos; I select Matt. 20:34 as the 'quote' here because of the inclusion of ϣⲛ²ⲏⲧϥ in this biblical verse.

Table III: Word or Phrase in Religious Context[76]

Papyrus	Content	Biblical Reference	Biblical Text
P.Gron. 17.14–15 (III/IV)	ὡς δὲ ἐγένετο, θ(εὸ)ς μετὰ σοῦ.	Rom. 15:33, Luke 1:28 (cf. 2 Thess. 3:16; 2 Cor 13:11; Phil. 4:9)	ὁ δ ' θεὸς τῆς εἰρήνης μετὰ πάντων ὑμῶν (Rom. 15:33, similarly but with ἔσται μεθ' ὑμῶν at Phil. 4:9, 2 Cor. 13:11); ὁ κύριος μετὰ πάντων ὑμῶν (2 Thess. 3:16); ὁ κύριος μετὰ σοῦ (Luke 1:28)
P.Oxy. XII 1592.3–6 (III/IV)	καὶ πάνυ ἐμεγαλύνθην καὶ ἠγαλλ(ε)ίασα ὅτ[ε]ι τοιοῦτός μου π(ατ)ὴρ τὴν μνήμην ποιεῖται	Lk 1:46–47	μεγαλύνει ἡ ψυχή μου τὸν κύριον, καὶ ἠγαλλίασεν τὸ πνεῦμά μου ἐπὶ τῷ θεῷ τῷ σωτῆρί μου.
P.Lond. VI 1915.9 (c. 330–340)	τῆς μακαράας (*l.* -ίας) ἐλπίδος	Tit. 2:13?	τὴν μακαρίαν ἐλπίδα
SB I 2266.3–4 (mid IV)	πιστεύομεν γὰρ τὴν πολιτί[αν σ]ου ἐν{ν} οὐρανῷ	Phil. 3:20	ὑμῶν γὰρ τὸ πολίτευμα ἐν οὐρανοῖς ὑπάρχει
SB I 2266.12–14 (mid IV)	ἵνα δυνηθῶμεν μέρος τὸν (*l.* τῶν) <αφμ>αρτιῶν καθαριθσεο"	Heb. 1:3, 2 Pet. 1:9	καθαρισμὸν τῶν ἁμαρτιῶν (Heb); τοῦ καθαρισμοῦ τῶν πάλαι αὐτοῦ ἁμαρτιῶν (2 Pet)
P.Neph. 7.6 (c. 360)	οὔτε σὲ τὸν πάσης τιμῆς ἄξιον δυσοπ(ε)ῖτε (*l.* -ται)	1 Tim. 6:1, 5:17	τοὺς ἰδίους δεσπότας πάσης τιμῆς ἀξίους ἡγείσθωσαν (6.1);

P.Neph. 11.13–14 (c. 360)	πάντας τοὺς στρατιώτας τοῦ Χριστοῦ	2 Tim. 2:3	οἱ καλῶς προεστῶτες πρεσβύτεροι διπλῆς τιμῆς ἀξιούσθωσαν (5:17); ὡς καλὸς στρατιώτης Χριστοῦ Ἰησοῦ (2:3)
P.Nag. Hamm. Gr. 68.11	οὕτω γὰρ πρέπει τῇ ἐν Χριστῷ σου ἀγάπῃ	Eph. 5:4	καθὼς πρέπει ἁγίοις
P.Iand. II 11.2 (III/IV BL)	ἐλπίδω (l. -ζω) γὰρ εἰς θεόν	2 Cor. 1:10 Acts 24:15? (cf. 1 Pet. 3:5).	εἰς ὃν (sc. θεόν) ἠλπίκαμεν (2 Cor.); ἐλπίδα ἔχον εἰς τὸν θεόν (Acts); ἐλπίζουσαι εἰς θεόν (1 Pet)
P.Lond. III 981.8–11 (IV)	ἡ γὰρ εὐφημία σου, πάτερ, περικύκλωσεν τὸν κ[όσ]μον ὅλον ὡς ἀγαθὸν πατέρα	Rom. 1:8?	ἡ πίστις ὑμῶν καταγγέλεται ἐν ὅλῳ τῷ κόσμῳ
P.Oxy. VI 939.3–4 (IV)	ἡ πρὸς σὲ [τοῦ δεσπό]του θεοῦ γνῶσις ἀνεφάνη ἅπασιν ἡμῖν	Tit. 2:11, 3:4	Ἐπεφάνη γὰρ ἡ χάρις τοῦ θεοῦ σωτήριος πᾶσιν ἀνθρώποις (2:11); ἡ φιλανθρωπία ἐπεφάνη τοῦ σωτῆρος ἡμῶν θεου (3:4)

[76] By which I mean those where praise is being made of another Christian in terms drawn from the New Testament, or when religious sentiments are being expressed. In those cases where allusion is made to a range of biblical texts, especially where they occur in opening or closing formulae, I refrain from quoting the biblical texts, and group them at the end of the table.

Table III (cont.)

Papyrus	Content	Biblical Reference	Biblical Text
P.Oxy. VI 939.7 (IV)	ὅτι ἡμῖν ἵλεως ἐγένετο	Hebr. 8:12 (citing Jer. 31:34)	ὅτι ἵλές ἔσομαι
P.Oxy. XII 1494.4–9 (IV)	μά[λ]λειστα (l. μάλιστα) μὲν δεήσει καὶ ὑμᾶς εὔχεσθαι περ{ε}ὶ ἡμῶν, εἵν' οὕτως ἐπακούσῃ ὁ θεαὸς (l. θεὸς) τῶν εὐχῶν ὑμῶν καὶ γένηται ἡμ{ε}ῖν ὁδὸς εὐθεῖα	Hos. 14:10, Isa. 40:3=Matt. 3:3, Acts 13:10	ὁδὸς εὐθεῖα
P.Herm. 8.18 (late IV)	θεοῦ ἄνθρωπε	1 Tim. 6-11	Σὺ δέ, ὦ ἄνθρωπε θεοῦ
P.Herm. 9.16–20 (late IV)	ἀσπάζομαι τοὺς ἀγαπητοὺς καὶ τοὺς φιλοῦντας τὸν λόγον τοῦ θεθ̣ο̅ τοῦ κυρί[ο]υ μου. ἐν ἐλα ἰᾶιοἶν̣	Luke 11:28, Tit. 3:15	Μενοῦν μακάριοι οἱ ἀκούοντες τὸν λόγον τοῦ θεοῦ καὶ φυλάσσοντες (Luke); Ἀσπασαι τοὺς φιλοῦντας ἡμᾶς ἐν πίστει. ἡ χάρις μετὰ πάντων ὑμῶν (Tit.)
P.Lond. VI 1915.3–5 (c. 330–340)	τοῖ[ς ἐν . . . .]ηφθονει συμφορᾷ παραπεσοῦσιν βοη[θεῖ]ν π[α]ρ[α]—γγέλ(λ)εται ἡμῖν ὁ θεῖος λόγος πᾶσι, μάλιστα τοῖς ἀδελφοῖς ἡμῶν.	Gal. 6:10, I Tim. 5:8	
P.Harr. I 107.4–12 (III/IV?)	πρὸ μὲν πάντων εὔχομαι τῷ πατρὶ θεῷ τῆς ἀληθείας καὶ τῷ παρακλ-	Epistle of Mani or Manichaean liturgy (see	

	ἥτῳ πνεύματι ὃς σὲ διαφυλάξωσιν κα{ι}τά τε θυχὴν κα⟨ὶ⟩ σῶμα καὶ πνεῦμα, τῷ μὲν σῶματι ὑγίαν, τῷ δὲ πνεύματι εὐθυμία, τῇ δὲ ψυχῇ ζωὴν αἰώνιον.	above)?; John 14:26, 1 Thess. 5:23
P.Neph. 4.30 (c. 360)	ἐρρῶσθαί [σε εὔχομαι,] ἄνθρωπε [θεοῦ.]	1 Tim. 6:11
P.Oxy. VIII 1161.1–7 (IV)	[c ?] . . ασ καὶ τῷ ἀγαθ[ῷ ἡμῶ]ν σωτῆρι καὶ τῷ οἱ[ι]ῷ[(l. υἱῷ) αὐτοῦ τῷ ἠγαπημένῳ ὅπος οὗτοι πάντες β[ο]ηθήσοσιν ἡμῶν τῷ σῶματι, τῇ ψυχῇ, τῷ πν(εύματ)ι.	Mark 1:11, Eph. 1:6, 1 Thess. 5:23
P.Iand. II 14.3–4 (IV)	πρὸ μ[ὲν] πάντων [εὔ]χομαι τῷ ἐν ὑψίσ[τ]ῳ θεῷ περὶ [τῆς] ὁλοκλ-ηρίας σου	Luke 2:14, Job 16–19
P.Ben.Mus. 5.33–35 (IV)	ἡ χάρις του κ(υριο)υ ἡμῶν Ἰη (σοῦ) Χ(ριστο)ῦ μετὰ πν(ευμάτο)ς	Paul, Gal. 6:18, Phil 4:23; Phlm 25.
SB XIV 11532.11 (IV)	ἡ χάρις τοῦ κ(υρίο)υ ἡμῶν Ἰη(σοῦ) [Χρ(ιστοῦ)] μετὰ πάντων ὑμῶν	Gal. 6–18, Phil. 4:23, 1 Thess. 5:28 etc
P.Oxy. LVI 3862.12 (IV/V)	ἐλπίδα{ν} ζῶσαν	1 Peter 1:3

ἐλπίδα ζῶσαν

Table IV: Word or Phrase not in Religious Context

Papyrus	Content	Biblical Reference	Biblical Text
P.Gron. 17.20 (III/IV)	οὕτω γὰρ καὶ **πρέπει**	Eph. 5:4 (cf. Tit. 2:1; 1 Tim. 2:10)	καθὼς **πρέπει** ἁγίοις
P.Abinn. 7.19 (346–351)	ἄρτι γὰρ **διαβλεπόμεθα** πέμθε (*l.* πέμθαι) αὐτά	Matt. 7:5; Luke 6:42; Gos Thom 26:1	καὶ τότε **διαβλέσθεις**
P.Abinn. 36.15 (346–351)	{ε}ἵνα καυτῆ εὑρε[θῆ κα]τὰ χαίρα (*l.* χέρα) αὐτῆς ὀλίγον **λεπτάριον**	Luke 21:2?	εἶδεν δέ τινα χήραν πενιχρὰν βάλλουσαν ἐκεῖ **λεπτὰ** δύο
P.Oxy. XLVI 3314.10–11 (IV)	καὶ μέχρις **ποτηρίον ὕδατ[ο]ς** οὐκ εἴχομεν τὸν ἐπιδιδοῦντά μοι θυχροῦ	Mark 9:41, Matt. 10:42?	καὶ ὃς ἂν ποτίσῃ ἕνα τῶν μικρῶν τούτων **ποτήριον** [**ποτήριον ὕδατος** θυχροῦ D and others]

THE APOCRYPHAL ACTS OF THE APOSTLES ON PAPYRUS: REVISITING THE QUESTION OF READERSHIP AND AUDIENCE

KIM HAINES-EITZEN

Several years ago, a scholar explained to me that Chaim Potok's novel *The Chosen* was a book for the "sisterhood." I must have given a puzzled look because afterwards he apologized for his statement. And yet, such a comment—which implied somehow that the "popular" nature of *The Chosen* made it accessible for women readers— shares much with certain assumptions made about early Christian novels. The core of the Apocryphal Acts literature—consisting of the Acts of Paul, Peter, John, Andrew, and Thomas—betrays a fascination with travel, miracles stories, erotic language in the service of an ascetic message, and prominent female characters. These features— and, in particular, the female characters: Thecla, Candida, Rufina, Eubula, Mygdonia, Drusiana, Maximilla—have been precisely the elements drawn upon in modern arguments, especially in the last twenty years, about the authors and audiences for these works.

To be sure, we have evidence to suggest that women served a variety of roles in the production, reproduction, dissemination, and consumption of ancient literature.[1] Recall, for example, the fourth-century letter from Oxyrhynchus in which the writer requests a copy of a book from an anonymous woman: "To my dearest lady sister, greetings in the Lord. Lend the Ezra, since I lent you the little Genesis" (*P.Oxy.* LXIII 4365).[2] Alongside of such documentary evidence

---

[1] Currently, I am completing a book-length study entitled *Women and Books in Early Christianity*, which aims to collect and assess the intersections between early Christian women, the rise of asceticism, and the production, reproduction, dissemination, and use of early Christian literature.—I would like to thank Tobias Nicklas and Thomas J. Kraus, in particular, for their suggestions on this article; thanks go also to the audience in the "Papyrology and Early Christian Background" group at the SBL where I first presented these ideas.

[2] Recently, there has been increased interest in this particular papyrus: see, e.g., T.J. Kraus, "Bücherleihe im 4. Jh. n. Chr.: *P.Oxy.* LXIII 4365—ein Brief auf Papyrus und die gegenseitige Leihe von apokryph gewordener Literatur," *Biblos* 50 (2001)

we might profitably read Jerome's letters in which he offers a glimpse into the roles of wealthy women as owners of libraries and, therefore, involved in the dissemination (through borrowing and lending for copying) a variety of Christian texts.[3] If we know that women were involved (at least to some extent) in the mechanics of book distribution, we also know of their participation in the actual copying of early Christian literature; our best known literary references to these are Eusebius' account of Origen's female calligraphers (*h.e.* 6.23) and, somewhat later, the references to women copyists in monastic settings (*Life of Melania* 26; *Vita Caesarius* 1.58).[4] To these practices, we can also now add Roger Bagnall and Raffaella Cribiore's recent study of papyrus letters written by women from 300 BCE–800 CE, which collects and evaluates the documentary evidence for women letter-writers in ancient Egypt.[5] As we shall see, the subject of the present essay, as well as its central argument, is corroborated by Bagnall and Cribiore's study. But the rather general claim that women were involved in the various activities associated with the production and reproduction of early Christian books, for here I am prin-

---

285–296; E.J. Epp, "The Oxyrhynchus New Testament Papyri: 'Not Without Honor Except in their Hometown'?," *JBL* 123 (2004) 5–55, esp. 21–23; K. Haines-Eitzen, *Guardians of Letters: Literacy, Power, and the Transmitters of Early Christian Literature* (Oxford—New York 2000) esp. 77–79; D. Hagedorn, "Die 'kleine Genesis' in *P.Oxy.* XLIII 4365," *ZPE* 116 (1997) 147–148.

[3] See, for example, Jerome's letter to Desiderius (*Ep.* 47) in which Jerome tells him he can borrow copies of Jerome's writings from Marcella (3). See also his letter to Pammachius (*Ep.* 49, 4). With respect to women as book-owners in the Middle Ages, see the provocative study by S.G. Bell, "Medieval Women Book Owners: Arbiters of Lay Piety and Ambassadors of Culture," *Signs* 7 (1982) 742–768; more broadly on the issue of education levels among the women friends of Jerome (and Chrysostom) see E. Clark, "Friendship Between the Sexes: Classical Theory and Christian Practice," in her *Jerome, Chrysostom, and Friends: Essays and Translations* (New York—Toronto 1979) 35–106, esp. 70–78.

[4] See Haines-Eitzen, *Guardians of Letters*, 41–52, for an assessment of the evidence for female scribes in antiquity and early Christianity.

[5] R.S. Bagnall and R. Cribiore, *Women's Letters from Ancient Egypt, 300 BC–AD 800* (Ann Arbor forthcoming); I am grateful to Roger Bagnall and Raffaella Cribiore for sending me a manuscript of their work prior to publication. On the subject of women's authorship in antiquity, see also more generally J. McIntoch Snyder, *The Woman and the Lyre: Women Writers in Classical Greece and Rome* (Carbondale—Edwardsville 1989); M.R. Lefkowitz, "Did Ancient Women Write Novels?" and R.S. Kraemer, "Women's Authorship of Jewish and Christian Literature in the Greco-Roman Period," both in A.-J. Levine, ed., *"Women Like This": New Perspectives on Jewish Women in the Greco-Roman World* (Atlanta 1991) 199–220 and 221–242, respectively.

cipially interested in the specific claims made about the apocryphal acts literature and their appeal to ancient women readers.

The use of prominent and even subversive women in the apocryphal Acts led Stephen Davies in 1980 to claim "that many of the apocryphal Acts were written by women" and had "an audience which was predominantly female";[6] Virginia Burrus took up this issue in her Master's Thesis, published in 1987, writing that "the stories [probably] reflect the experience of some second-century women who were converted to Christianity and chastity";[7] more recently, Jan Bremmer has argued that women were both the intended and the actual readers of the "AAA";[8] and most recently, Stephen Davis has continued in the tradition of the Apocryphal Acts—here specifically the Acts of Paul and Thecla—as literature about and for women.[9] The claim that the Apocryphal Acts are "women's literature"—or that they are "literature by, about, and for women"—is often elided with the idea that they were "popular literature," a notion that derives at least in part from a scholarly denigration of this literature and one that shares much in common, of course, with proposals made about the ancient (classical) "novels" more generally. These texts were written—so this position goes—to entertain the popular masses; they are certainly not written for ancient elite intellectuals (one sees here the imposition of modern "scholarly" ideals upon the ancient world).

But the argument that the AAA and the classical novels were written for a "popular audience" has been challenged on a number of fronts: first, the extent to which we should plausibly imagine "popular" reading at all, given limited literacy in antiquity. Since William Harris's influential book *Ancient Literacy*[10] there has been a virtual

---

[6] S.L. Davies, *The Revolt of the Widows: The Social World of the Apocryphal Acts* (Carbondale—Edwardsville 1980) 95–96.

[7] V. Burrus, *Chastity as Autonomy: Women in the Stories of Apocryphal Acts* (Studies in Women and Religion 23; Lewiston/Queenston 1987) 108.

[8] J.N. Bremmer, "The Novel and the Apocryphal Acts: Place, Time and Readership," *Groningen Colloquia on the Novel* 9 (1998) 157–180, esp. 176.

[9] S.J. Davis, *The Cult of St. Thecla: A Tradition of Women's Piety in Late Antiquity* (Oxford Early Christian Studies; Oxford 2001) 12–14. While Davis acknowledges that the notion of a female audience/readership (and he uses both terms without distinction), he does seem to side with the testimony of Tertullian to conclude that the *Acts of Paul and Thecla* "did in fact have an early audience among women" (12).

[10] W. Harris, *Ancient Literacy* (Cambridge—London 1989).

explosion of literature on levels of literacy in antiquity, the intersections of orality and literacy, and the uses of texts.[11] While there
is little consensus on the issue of levels of literacy, at the very least
we have become more cautious and more nuanced in our estimates
of how many people could read, how many people could write, and
how these skills intersected with economic status. Second, some scholars have pointed out that the tropes, allusions, and rhetoric of the
novels suggest a rather educated elite (implied) audience for whom
through the novels aristocratic men negotiated relationships among
themselves and vied for status. The most compelling proponents of
such views are Simon Goldhill and Kate Cooper, who approach the
novels and the Apocryphal Acts, respectively, in differing ways;
Goldhill sees in the language of eros in the Greek novels the idea
that how "representations of women" served constructions of male
desire; Cooper claims that the "Christian rhetoric of virginity," written by and for men, transformed religious identity in late antiquity.[12]

But if we can plausibly argue that our ancient novels were written by male authors, can we go any further on the issue of the con-
sumers or readers of these texts? In the case of the classical novels
several authors—Sarah Stephens and Ewen Bowie most prominently—
have taken the approach of studying the material (papyrological)
remains of these novels to see what they might yield about audience
or readership. Stephens, for example, has collected the fragments of
ancient Greek novels on papyrus; she counts some 42 papyrus fragments of ancient "novels" in comparison with the more that 1000
fragments of Homer, 120 of Demonsthenes, 77 of Thucydides.[13]
Although what numbers of remaining papyri can really tell us about

---

[11] See, e.g., the articles collected in *Literacy in the Roman World*, *JRA.S* 3 (1991);
R. Thomas, *Literacy and Orality in Ancient Greece* (Cambridge 1992); J. Watson, ed.,
Speaking Volumes: Orality and Literacy in the Greek and Roman World (Leiden 2001);
A. Millard, *Reading and Writing in the Time of Jesus* (New York 2000).

[12] S. Goldhill, *Foucault's Virginity: Ancient Erotic Fiction and the History of Sexuality*
(Cambridge: 1995); K. Cooper, *The Virgin and the Bride: Idealized Womanhood in Late
Antiquity* (Cambridge—London 1996).

[13] S.A. Stephens, "Who Read Ancient Novels?" and E. Bowie, "The Readership
of Greek Novels in the Ancient World," both in J. Tatum, ed., *The Search for the
Ancient Novel* (Baltimore—London 1994) 405–418 and 436–459, respectively; more
recently, in their collection of the papyrological remains of ancient Greek novels
S.A. Stephens and J.J. Winkler address issues of authorship and readership briefly
(*Ancient Greek Novels, The Fragments: Introduction, Text, Translation, and Commentary* [Princeton
1995], esp. 9–11).

readership is debatable, this comparison is quite striking and suggests at least some re-evaluation of the notion of "popular" (i.e.,
widespread) readership for ancient Greek novels. But Stephens goes
further in her analysis of the papyri of Greek novels to argue that
the features they exhibit are "indistinguishable" from those that
appear in "rolls and codices of Sappho, Thucydides, Demosthenes,
and Plato."[14] Moreover, in her study of the papyrological fragments
of the Greek novels, Stephens notes that the "novel fragments are
written in practiced hands ranging from workmanlike to elegant;
books contain wide margins and employ the formats in vogue for
the prose writing of oratory, philosophy, or history."[15] Stephens claims
that the form of the papyrus remains of ancient novels "tends to
undermine a common misconception about them, namely, that they
were targeted for a clientele qualitatively different from that for other
ancient books."[16] In other words, the very "indistinguishability" of
these papyri suggests perhaps that the readership may well have also
been indistinguishable—in other words, the same—as that for philosophical, historical, and poetic works more generally.

This brings me to the question at the center of this essay: can the
earliest papyri of the Apocryphal Acts of the Apostles shed light on
who read them? Such a question depends first on the notion that
the physical form of a book can tell us something about the readers of the book—an idea that has found some of its most compelling
treatment in the work of Roger Chartier.[17] For the ancient world,
we might recall (in addition to Stephen's work) Eric Turner's typology of "scholars' texts"—papyri whose features suggested that they
were made for use by scholars. Turner stressed the following features: 1) "the presence or absence in the texts as we have them of
indications of informed revision, especially of revision involving

---

[14] Stephens, "Who Read Ancient Novels?," 413.
[15] Stephens, *Ancient Greek Novels*, 9–10.
[16] Stephens, *Ancient Greek Novels*, 10.
[17] See especially his treatment of reading practices in *The Order of Books* (Trans.
L.G. Cochrane; Stanford 1994) esp. 1–23; and his engagement with the work of
D.F. McKenzie in *On the Edge of the Cliff: History, Languages, and Practices* (Trans. Lydia
G. Cochrane) (Baltimore—London 1997) 81–89; and his assessment of the notion
of "popular literature" in *Forms and Meanings: Texts, Performances, and Audiences From
Codex to Computer* (Philadelphia 1995). Some of the themes from Chartier's work are
also picked up in James J. O'Donnell, *Avatars of the Word: From Papyrus to Cyberspace*
(Cambridge—London 1998).

collation with a second, perhaps named, exemplary; 2) the addition
of critical signs, additions which . . . show that the text was revised
in connection with a scholarly commentary."[18] Working with the earliest Christian papyri, C.H. Roberts (and others) tried to determine
which papyri might have been used for public liturgical readings.
He pointed, for example, to the size of a codex, large handwriting,
breathing marks, "reading aids," and critical markings as indicators
of public reading.[19]

For the remainder of this essay, I would like to experiment with
the earliest papyrological remains of the Apocryphal Acts to see what,
if anything, we can learn from their physical form. This exploration
is necessarily preliminary and the conclusions I draw tentative. First,
the question of numbers: we currently have approximately 12 Greek
fragments of the Apocryphal Acts of the Apostles: for the Acts of
Peter, 1; for the Acts of Andrew, 1; for the Acts of John, 1; for the
Acts of Paul, 9.[20] The Acts of Thomas was probably originally written in Syriac, so for my limited purposes here, it will not be included.[21]

---

[18] *Greek Papyri: An Introduction* (Princeton 1968) 92; and his "Scribes and Scholars
of Oxyrhynchus," *MPER* 5 (1955) 141–149.

[19] *Manuscript, Society and Belief in Early Christian Egypt* (London 1979).

[20] These figures must remain preliminary, since some still unidentified papyri may
well be remains of apocryphal acts materials. My figures were collected in large
part from the edition of *Clavis Apocryphorum Novi Testmanti* by M. Geerard (Corpus
Christianorum; Turnhout 1992). The 12 consist of *P.Oxy.* VI 849 (Acts of Peter);
P.Oxy. VI 851 (Acts of Andrew); *P.Oxy.* VI 850 (Acts of John); *P.Hamb.bil.* 1 (= van
Haelst 605); *P.Oxy.* XIII 1602; *P.Oxy.* I 6; *P.Mich.inv.* 1317. 3788, and *P.Berol.inv.*
13893 (vgl. van Haelst 607 and 608); *P.Ant.* I 13; *P.Fackelmann* 3; *P.Bodm.* X (all for
the *Acts of Paul*).

[21] There continues to be a debate about the original language of the *Acts of
Thomas*. Han J.W. Drijvers agreed with a widely held view that "the ATh came
into being at the beginning of the 3rd century in East Syria, and were originally
composed in Syriac" ("The Acts of Thomas," in E. Hennecke and W. Schneemelcher,
ed., *The New Testament Apocrypha*. Vol. 2 [Cambridge 1992] 323). On the other hand,
A.F.J. Klijn has more recently argued (in his translation of the Syriac text) that the
Greek text "represents and earlier tradition of the contents" of the Acts of Thomas
(*The Acts of Thomas: Introduction, Text and Commentary* [Leiden: Brill, 2nd rev. ed., 2003]
8–9). Elsewhere, Klijn writes of his decision to focus in his edition on the Syriac
text: he wanted to emphasize the "Syriac origin of the ATh," but he had to make
continual reference to the Greek manuscripts because their texts are "much better
than the various Syriac texts"; thus, he concludes: "The Greek text shows that his
work was written in an environment in which at least the Syriac language was well
known. It appears that sometimes the Greek cannot be understood without the help
of the Syriac version. We have to conclude that the work was written in a bilingual environment" ("The Acts of Thomas Revisited," in J.N. Bremmer, ed., *The*

We should not, of course, limit ourselves to Greek papyri for a comprehensive discussion of the "popularity" of these texts; for we know that they were translated into Latin, Syriac, Coptic, Armenian, Georgian, Ethiopic, and Arabic. Moreover, we know—particularly since Stephen Davis's recent book *The Cult of St. Thecla*[22]—that material remains and literary allusions can shed light on the popularity of the stories, the pilgrimages and cult centers they inspired, and their use by patristic writers. But here I am particularly interested in what papyrological remains can tell us about ancient readers and readers of the Christian 'novels' in particular.

The estimate of 12 papyrus (and parchment) fragments, all of which derive from pre-6th century codices, stands in marked contrast to canonical New Testament more generally for which we have upwards of one hundred papyri dated from the second through sixth or seventh centuries, but I am considering here four apocryphal Acts in comparison to the 27 books that eventually become canonized. The Acts of Paul is indeed attested most widely, leading C.H. Roberts to claim, in 1950, that the Acts of Paul "together with the Shepherd [of Hermas] it must rank as the most popular work of Christian literature outside the canon."[23] However, it is worthwhile noting that the Acts of Paul is perhaps the lengthiest of the apocryphal acts and originally circulated, it appears, in various parts: the Acts of Paul and Thecla, the Acts of Paul, the Correspondence of Paul and the Corinthians, and the Martyrdom of Paul.[24] Furthermore, extant numbers of papyri—particularly when we do not have a big pool to begin with—are not particularly compelling evidence for the popularity of a text, much less for the gender of the readership.

Let me now give you some examples from the thirteen papyri, beginning with the earliest fragment.

Apocryphal Acts of Thomas [Studies on the Apocryphal Acts of the Apostles 6; Leuven 2001] 1–10, esp. 4).

[22] *The Cult of St. Thecla: A Tradition of Women's Piety in Late Antiquity* (Oxford 2001).

[23] C.H. Roberts, ed., *The Antinoopolis Papyri* I (London 1950) 27.

[24] The textual unity of all of the apocryphal acts is a subject of enormous complexity and still requires much research, although there is a wide-ranging bibliography on this subject. For brief introductions to the problems associated with each of the texts, see the edition of Hennecke-Schneemelcher, *New Testament Apocrypha*. Vol. 2.

P. Bodmer X: The Apocryphal Correspondence of Paul and the Corinthians[25]

The apocryphal correspondence of Paul and the Corinthians (also called III Corinthians) is part of the larger Acts of Paul, but appears to have circulated on its own in antiquity and may well have had an independent origin.[26] The third-century dating makes it the earliest of the Acts of Paul fragments and at 14.2 cm × 15.5 cm it is one of the largest fragments. The handwriting here is clearly legible and careful, but not particularly elegant or calligraphic. The margins are only approximately even and there is some variation in the lines themselves. Of all the papyri of apocryphal Acts, this one is the least elegant, and yet the scribe does appear to be practiced and professional. This particular fragment derives from a composite third-fourth century codex, which appears to contain the work of multiple scribes who copied different texts (and possibly placed into different codices originally) that were later bound into a single codex.[27]

P.Oxy. 849: Acts of Peter Fragment

This fragment has been dated to the early fourth century; it is written on vellum not papyrus; and the size of the fragment is 9.8 × 9 cm—a small, nearly square codex. The handwriting does not in any

---

[25] I have not yet seen the very recent re-edition of this codex (*Bibliotheca Bodmeriana. La collection des papyrus Bodmer 8–10: Abbildungen sämtlicher originaler Manuskriptseiten* [Munich 2000]). The standard edition is that by Michel Testuz, *Papyrus Bodmer X–XII* (Cologny-Genève 1959).

[26] The most recent study of III Corinthians is that of V. Hovhanessian, (*Third Corinthians: Reclaiming Paul for Christian Orthodoxy* [New York 2000]) who argues "that manuscript evidence, Patristic references, and the content, style and theology of the two documents point to III Cor having an origin independent of AP" (48). See also A.F.J. Klijn, "The Apocryphal Correspondence between Paul and the Corinthians," *VigChr* 17 (1963) 2–23; W. Rordorf, "Hérésie et Orthodoxie selon la Correspondance apocryphe entre les Corinthiens et l'Apôtre Paul," *Cahiers de la Revue de Théologie et de Philosophie* 17 (1993) 21–63. Because we remain uncertain about the textual relationships of 3 Corinthians, I have included it in this preliminary study.

[27] The new reassessment of this interesting codex, based on a new photographic edition, will likely correct the views of Eric Turner (*Typology of the Early Codex* [Philadelphia 1977] 79–81, Testuz, and myself (*Guardians of Letters*, 96–104) regarding the precise hands and codices involved in this composite. I am grateful to Tobias Nicklas for sending me a copy of his and Tommy Wasserman's forthcoming essay on this subject (see "Theologische Linien im *Codex Bodmer Miscellani?*" in this volume).

way look unusual for a fourth-century book-hand; it is medium-sized, carefully and professionally written, and regular.[28] The scribe has used the familiar *nomina sacra* and though there are some rather glaring grammatical errors, on the whole it is a good copy. Although this is not a lavish deluxe codex, there is nothing to suggest that this was poorly made—or made with limited means.

P.Oxy. 850: *Acts of John*

This fragment is also dated to fourth century; it is a papyrus codex, the fragment of which measures somewhat larger than the first fragment: 12.1 × 10.7 cm. Any words we use to describe handwriting, are necessarily subjective, but on the whole the handwriting here is less calligraphic and less regular than that for P.Oxy. 849. The editors describe the hand as "a good-sized, irregular and rather inelegant uncial of the fourth century."[29] The lines are not as even, there is more of a tendency towards ligatures, but it certainly remains within the range of professional bookhands for the fourth century. This scribe also employs punctuation marks—middle and low points—and occasional breathings. And again we find the use of the *nomina sacra* we would expect.

P. Fackelmann 3: *Acts of Paul and Thecla*

Published and edited by M. Gronewald in 1978, dated to the early fourth century, this fragment of a papyrus codex measures approximately 4 × 6 cm.[30] The editor suggested that originally there would have been 30 lines to a page and each line would have had 20–25 letters, so that it would have been larger than the others fragments we have seen, possibly 9 cm wide and 18 cm long. It is hard to

---

[28] See the plate provided in *P.Oxy.* VI. The editors describe the hand as follows: "The handwriting is a medium-sized upright uncial of a common third to fourth century type. Had the material used been papyrus, we should have been more disposed to assign it to the late third than to the fourth century, but since vellum was not commonly used in Egypt until the fourth century, it is safer to attribute the fragment to the period from Diocletian to Constantine" (p. 7).

[29] *P.Oxy.* VI, p. 12.

[30] M. Gronewald, "Einige Fackelmann Papyri," *ZPE* 28 (1978) 274–276.

glean much of anything from such a tiny fragment, but at the very least we can make out a fairly regular book-hand, a type quite familiar to us from other late third and early fourth century Christian papyri. There is nothing here to suggest a hand that is distinguishable from other papyri of Christian literature from this period.

P. ANTINOOPOLIS I.13: ACTS OF PAUL AND THECLA

This parchment fragment was first published and edited by C.H. Roberts in 1950; it can also be dated to the fourth century; and its dimensions (7.2 × 8.7) put it well within the category of a miniature codex. Each column of writing measures 4 × 4.8 cm and the outer margin is 2.4 cm. Given its small size, the codex probably only contained the *Acts of Paul and Thecla*. It is also deluxe codex; Roberts' description is as follows: "Both the material, which is thin and translucent to an unusual degree, and the script, in its regularity and delicacy reminiscent of the great Biblical codices, are of exceptional quality."[31] The handwriting is for the most part bilinear in Turner's terms;[32] certainly, it is the work of a highly trained and professional book scribe. Such a copy could only have been produced with a certain kind of infrastructure—either a monastic setting with highly trained scribes or a wealthy individual who could afford such a copy. Even Roberts argued that this particular fragment suggested that the *Acts of Paul* must not have been only popular "only among the poorer strata of the population."[33]

What can we say from this sampling? As we should expect, they are all codices; the codex form does not really tell us about readership. No one of these papyri (and vellum) fragments shows evidence that it was poorly or unprofessionally made. If the quality of the papyrus or the quality of its script is an indicator of cost and hence suggestive of the economic and educational level of its funders, readers, and/or users, these copies appear to be prepared by and/or for

---

[31] *P.Ant.* I, p. 26.
[32] E. Turner, *Greek Manuscripts of the Ancient World* (ed. P.J. Parsons; Princeton ²1987) 3–5.
[33] *P.Ant.* I, p. 27.

those who had sufficient economic means and education. At the very least, the physical form of these books suggests nothing of a qualitatively different kind of audience (or scribes, producers, users) for this literature. If anything, the features of this admittedly small sampling show fewer signs of unprofessional productions: we can think, for example, of the papyrus copy of 1 and 2 Peter and Jude (P72) contained in the same codex as the Correspondence of Paul and the Corinthians but produced by a very different—and, as I have argued elsewhere, less professional or perhaps unprofessional—scribe.[34]

With so few fragments of the apocryphal Acts, and still fewer for the sections of the Acts that feature women (which lead to the arguments about popular/female audiences) it is hard to come to any more of a conclusion than a negative one: it is highly problematic to continue to argue for the popular readership—or the popular/female readership—of the Apocryphal Acts of the Apostles. These fragments do not testify to a qualitatively different kind of audience and, if anything, can be used to bolster the claim that reading in antiquity remained predominantly a leisure of the elite few. If, indeed, the form of ancient books can tell us something about their readers—a subject we still have much to learn about—then these apocryphal Acts were read not by the "popular" masses or necessarily by "women" but rather by those members of the upper-echelons who likewise enjoyed poetry, history, and perhaps philosophy.

One of the most interesting features of these papyri is their size. Although only 3 of the 5 collected here are what can properly be called miniatures, the size of a codex may well tell us something about its use. Consider, for example, the evidence we have for pilgrims carrying "pocket codices" on their travels to holy places: Eugenia reads from the "book of Thecla" as she journeys; Egeria records how the *Acts of Thecla* are read out at Thecla's martyrium in Seleucia; John Chrysostom and Isidore of Peluseum both refer to the wearing of miniature books.[35] In the preliminary list of 62 known Greek

---

[34] *Guardians of Letters*, 67.

[35] *Life of Eugenia* 2; Egeria, *Itinerarium* 23.5–6; John Chrysostom, *Hom.Mt.* 72.2; Isidore of Pelusium, *Ep.* 150.2; Stephen Davis collects these references (and others) to the use of miniature codices particularly by women in order in support of his claims for the female audience of the *Acts of Paul and Thecla* (*Cult of Saint Thecla*, 143–146). On miniature codices see also H.Y. Gamble, *Books and Readers in the Early Church: A History of Early Christian Texts* (New Haven and London 1995) 235–236.

miniature codices compiled by Thomas J. Kraus, what is most striking, however, is not the preponderance of apocryphal literature, but
rather the frequency with which the book of Psalms appears in miniature form: some 10 miniatures out of the 62 contains passages from
the Psalms, by contrast with 4 from the Gospel of John, 2 from the
Acts of Paul and Thecla, 2 from the *Acts of Peter*, and so forth.[36] That
the Psalms were often used for private reading in early Christian
elite circles seems apparent from the letters of Jerome and others;
hence, we should not be too quick to associate our "pocket codices"
exclusively with pilgrimages. All of the codices examined above would
have lent themselves well to private reading in contrast to the large
fourth-century (and beyond) Christian codices that may well have
been used in public (i.e., Church) settings.

By way of conclusion, it is worth reflecting on the larger issue of
constructions of "popular culture" so often elided with "women's culture." Roger Chartier has outlined some of the assumptions behind
"the dominant and classical understanding of popular culture in
Europe and perhaps in America": "first, that popular culture can be
defined in contrast to what it is not; second, that it is possible to
characterize as popular the public of particular cultural productions;
and third, that cultural artifacts can be considered socially pure, as
popular in and of themselves."[37] This serves as a useful reminder
that any construal of an ancient popular culture—or popular readership—in some sense assumes a comparative model. For the ancient
world, the term "popular culture" or the construction of a "popular readership" carries with it an implicit assumption about what
constitutes sophisticated, elite, educated, and dominant. Likewise, our
suggestion that certain literature was written by or for a "female
readership" makes implicit assumptions about the literature itself as
well as about women's reading practices and preferences.

---

[36] I am very grateful to Thomas J. Kraus for sending me his current list of Greek
miniature codices. There remains much work to be done on this collection, including a proper typology of miniatures as well as a socio-historical assessment of their
contents and use in early Christianity. Given the frequency with which the Psalms
appear in miniature, Stephen Davis highlights (somewhat misleadingly) the apocryphal texts (in which category he includes the *Didache* and the *Shepherd of Hermas*)
in miniature to support his claims for the use (by women) of miniature codices (*The
Cult of Saint Thecla*, 145).
[37] *Forms and Meanings*, 88.

TEXTUAL CRITICISM IN THE LIGHT OF DIVERSE TEXTUAL EVIDENCE FOR THE GREEK NEW TESTAMENT: AN EXPANDED PROPOSAL[1]

STANLEY E. PORTER

1. INTRODUCTION

It is a commonplace today to recognize that the textual situation of early Christianity early-on became increasingly more complex. Regardless of what one thinks regarding the nature of the 'original texts,' Christianity soon became a writing and then a copying religion.[2] Over the first few centuries, as the shape of what would become the New Testament canon began to emerge, the fact that a number of texts, because of their content and/or origins, became recognized as serving the life of the Church in a special and particular way meant that other texts were seen not to serve this function.[3] As

---

[1] I wish to thank my colleagues, Dr. Thomas Kraus and Professor Dr. Tobias Nicklas, for their helpful suggestions regarding this paper, many of which are incorporated below.

[2] The question of the origins of Christianity can be raised at this point. For my perspective on this topic, see S.E. Porter and B.W.R. Pearson, "Why the Split? Christians and Jews by the Fourth Century," *JGRChJ* 1 (2000), pp. 82–119 (Sheffield: Sheffield Phoenix Press, 2004), which would help to explain the early development of Christianity's own textual tradition, including the use of the codex. For recent discussion of the issue of the codex, see G. Stanton, 'Early Christian Preference for the Codex', in *The Earliest Gospels: The Origins and Transmission of the Earliest Christian Gospels—The Contribution of the Chester Beatty Gospel Codex P⁴⁵* (JSNTSup 258; London: T. & T. Clark International, 2004), pp. 40–49; *idem, Jesus and Gospel* (Cambridge: Cambridge University Press, 2004), pp. 165–91.

[3] There have been many histories of the development of the canon. Several of those include: B.F. Westcott, *A General Survey of the History of the Canon of the New Testament* (London: Macmillan, 7th edn, 1896 [1855]); C.R. Gregory, *Canon and Text of the New Testament* (Edinburgh: T. & T. Clark, 1907); A. Souter, *The Text and Canon of the New Testament* (rev. C.S.C. Williams; London: Duckworth, rev. edn, 1954 [1913]); H. von Campenhausen, *The Formation of the Christian Bible* (trans. J.A. Baker; Philadelphia: Fortress Press, 1972 [1968]); B.M. Metzger, *The Canon of the New Testament* (Oxford: Clarendon Press, 1987); F.F. Bruce, *The Canon of Scripture* (Glasgow: Chapter House, 1988); L.M. McDonald, *The Formation of the Christian Biblical Canon* (Peabody, MA: Hendrickson, 1995); and L.M. McDonald and J.A. Sanders (eds.), *The Canon Debate* (Peabody, MA: Hendrickson, 2002); H.V. Lips, *Der neutestamentliche Kanon: Seine Geschichte und Bedeutung* (ZGB; Zürich: TVZ, 2004); among others.

a result, these latter documents were not finally included in what came to be recognized as the canon. Consequently, there are a number of texts that were used and transmitted within the early Christian world, some of which were later recognized as canonical and others that were not. Those that became canonical have clearly been given priority in the life of the Church, while those that did not have often been overlooked in such matters as historical reconstruction, theology and even textual criticism of the New Testament itself. In terms of establishing the texts of early Christianity, the area that I am concerned with specifically in this essay for this volume, those manuscripts that contain the canonical texts are given pride of place in textual criticism, while the others do not find a comfortable place in which they can be used. Currently, there are estimated to be over 5000 New Testament Greek manuscripts alone, of varying sizes and lengths, ages and textual types, uses and configurations, that are used in New Testament textual criticism.[4] This does not take into account the various other types of Greek documents, besides versions, that might also be related in some way to these documents. Such a large and varied number and type of manuscripts reflects significant complexity. The issue of how the variety of available manuscripts might be used in establishing the text of the Greek New Testament is what I wish to address in this essay.

2. Some Factors in New Testament Textual Criticism

The reality of the variety and sheer number of manuscripts available for establishing the text of the New Testament necessitates the development of some principles of textual criticism. New Testament textual criticism has developed such principles, focused upon manuscripts that, to use the words of Epp regarding the papyri in particular, though applicable to the parchments as well, 'are continuous-text MSS, that is, MSS containing (originally) at least one NT writing in continuous fashion from beginning to end . . .'[5] This sounds like

---

[4] Various New Testament scholars have arrived at this estimate. See, e.g., K. Aland and B. Aland, *The Text of the New Testament* (trans. E.F. Rhodes; Grand Rapids: Eerdmans, 2nd edn, 1989), p. 74.

[5] E.J. Epp, 'The Papyrus Manuscripts of the New Testament', in *The Text of the New Testament in Contemporary Research: Essays on the Status Quaestionis* (ed. B.D. Ehrman and M.W. Holmes; SD 46; Grand Rapids: Eerdmans, 1995), pp. 3–21, here p. 5.

a clear basic defining characteristic of what constitutes a New Testament manuscript, but nothing could be further from the truth.

In an essay first written in 1998, and then finally published in 2003, I commented upon the current state of New Testament textual criticism.[6] One of the factors that I noted was that New Testament manuscripts are assigned numbers according to what is sometimes referred to as the Gregory-Aland numbering system. Instead of New Testament manuscripts being known by their accession numbers within various papyrological collections,[7] the Gregory-Aland system ensures that a relatively standardized system of classification is used to categorize New Testament manuscripts according to whether they are papyri, uncials, minuscules, or lectionaries.[8] This system was begun by Gregory, and continued by Dobschütz and Aland, as a means of both overcoming a relatively confusing system of enumeration

---

[6] See S.E. Porter, "Why so many Holes in the Papyrological Evidence for the Greek New Testament?, in *The Bible as Book: The Transmission of the Greek Text* (ed. S. McKendrick and O. O'Sullivan; London: British Library & Oak Knoll Press, 2003), pp. 167–86, which I readily draw on in this section.

[7] I believe that it is unfortunate that this has become a neglected factor in textual criticism for many. In my comments below, I will refer to the manuscripts often in terms of their larger published context, which makes it clear that knowing the manuscripts as artifacts in their own right rather than simply as part of the Gregory-Aland scheme has benefit.

[8] One notes (as the Alands do, *Text of the New Testament*, p. 74) that this referential classificatory system has internal inconsistencies, since the first, papyri, refers to a specific writing surface, while the second and third refer to the type of writing (the first of which is in fact also used on the papyri), and the last to the use of the document (not content, as the Alands state, p. 74), which may be written in either majuscule or minuscule. I also prefer the term 'majuscule' to that of 'uncial', since 'uncial' refers to a particular type of Latin writing hand, whereas 'majuscule' (like 'minuscule') to the type of Greek hand. See D.C. Parker, "The Majuscule Manuscripts of the New Testament," in *Text of the New Testament* (ed. Ehrman and Holmes), pp. 22–42, here p. 22. This terminology is further confused by the fact that the term 'papyrus' is often used within papyrological studies to refer to any ephemeral writing surface, whether it is actually made of the papyrus reed or other substances, such as animal skins. See R. Bagnall, *Reading Papyri, Writing Ancient History* (London: Routledge, 1995), pp. 9–10. This is a mistake that F. Bovon makes ('*Fragment Oxyrhynchus 840*, Fragment of a Lost Gospel, Witness of an Early Christian Controversy over Purity', *JBL* 119 [2000], pp. 705–28, here p. 706). Bovon's proposal that this document should no longer be labeled P.Oxy. is misguided, when the Oxyrhynchus publications include numerous papyri and parchments. Some of the text-critical problems and inconsistencies of distinguishing by the material on which manuscripts are written are pointed out by T.J. Kraus, '"Pergament oder Papyrus?": Anmerkungen zur Signifikanz des Beschreibstoffes bei der Behandlung von Manuskripten', *NTS* 49 (2003), pp. 425–32.

in the nineteenth century and bringing order to New Testament paleography as increasingly more manuscripts were discovered and entered into discussion.[9] The Gregory-Aland system clearly has a number of advantages. These include the fact that the common system brings together under one enumeration various manuscripts now found in various collections (e.g. 𝔓45, the so-called Chester Beatty codex is found in Dublin, with one page in Vienna; 𝔓33 and 𝔓58, and 𝔓64 and 𝔓67 and quite possibly 𝔓4, are respectively parts of the same manuscript; etc.), and it provides a rough and ready classification system to differentiate the types of manuscripts.

There are also a number of disadvantages, however. One of the most obvious disadvantages is that this system has a way of restricting the data that are included in New Testament textual criticism. This restriction occurs in at least two ways. One is the external one, in that privilege is given to those manuscripts that are given Gregory-Aland numbers—they are the ones considered within New Testament textual criticism as providing the basis for establishing the text of the New Testament, while those that are not given numbers are often, if not inevitably, neglected and not taken fully into consideration if at all. A number of examples will be offered in the next section of this paper to show that texts not given Gregory-Aland numbers, and hence not included in the catalogue of New Testament papyri, have not been included in New Testament text-critical discussion, even if they might have some bearing on the issue of the development of the text of the New Testament. For example, some of the Apocryphal Gospel papyri are assigned fairly early dates,[10] putting them among the earliest papyri that reflect the text of the New Testament (e.g. P.Egerton 2/P.Lond.Christ. 1 is assigned a date sometimes as early as the second century or, more recently, around 200).[11] They have not been assigned Gregory-Aland numbers, and

---

[9] For a history of the development of the system, see Aland and Aland, *Text of the New Testament*, pp. 72–75. The book that inaugurated the list is C.R. Gregory, *Die Griechischen Handschriften des Neuen Testaments* (Leipzig: Hinrichs, 1908).

[10] For a comparative chart that compares manuscript numbers for the New Testament and apocryphal gospel fragments, see D. Lührmann with E. Schlarb, *Fragmente apokryph gewordener Evangelien in griechischer und lateinischer Sprache* (Marburg: Elwert, 2000), pp. 22–23.

[11] Cf. M. Gronewald, P.Köln VI 255 (Opladen: Westdeutscher Verlag, 1987), pp. 136–45, here p. 137, who concludes with a date of around 200.

hence are not regularly referred to in textual criticism.[12] In fact, they are referred to simply as the apocryphal Gospels by many scholars, lumping together a number of disparate texts that range over several centuries.[13] The effect of the numbering system is that some are adamant that these apocryphal papyri have no place in New Testament textual criticism since they are clearly later composite texts that draw upon the various canonical Gospels and other New Testament texts, including even Paul's writings.[14] As an apparent reaction, there are others who wish to assert their priority, so much so that they are seen to be even earlier than the canonical texts.[15] As a result, their potential significance, on an individual basis, for chronicling the emergence of different variants, or helping to arbitrate variants in the Synoptic Gospels, has not been appreciated.

Another restriction is the internal one, by means of which certain New Testament manuscripts are privileged over others. Even though many of the majuscule manuscripts are older than many of the papyri,[16] the papyri are given notional or theoretical priority by virtue of their classification—even if not de facto priority. Epp notes that modern critical editions, including the Nestle-Aland[25], are not significantly different from the edition of Westcott–Hort, which did not have access to any papyri. He therefore concludes (and laments)

---

[12] P.Egerton 2 is cited only at John 5:39 in the Nestle-Aland[27] apparatus. This is one of few apocryphal texts—if not the only one—cited in the critical apparatus. See discussion below.

[13] See S.E. Porter, 'The Greek Apocryphal Gospels Papyri: The Need for a Critical Edition.', in *Akten des 21. Internationalen Papyrologenkongresses Berlin, 13.–19.8.1995* (ed. B. Kramer, W. Luppe, H. Maehler and G. Poethke; 2 vols.; Archiv für Papyrusforschung Beiheft 3; Stuttgart and Leipzig: Teubner, 1997), II, pp. 795–803

[14] See, for example, J.H. Charlesworth and C.A. Evans, 'Jesus in the Agrapha and Apocryphal Gospels', in *Studying the Historical Jesus: Evaluations of the State of Current Research* (ed. B. Chilton and C.A. Evans; NTTS 19; Leiden: Brill, 1994), pp. 491–532, esp. pp. 491–95, 497.

[15] See, e.g., H. Koester, *Ancient Christian Gospels: Their History and Development* (London: SCM Press, 1990) *passim*; J.D. Crossan, *The Historical Jesus: The Life of a Mediterranean Jewish Peasant* (San Francisco: HarperSanFrancisco, 1991), pp. 427–34 (who also puts P.Egerton 2, P.Vindob. G 2325, P.Oxy. 1224, the *Gospel of the Hebrews*, and the Cross Gospel from the *Gospel of Peter* in this category); R.J. Miller (ed.), *The Complete Gospels* (San Francisco: HarperSanFranciso, 1992), p. 6; R.W. Funk, R.W. Hoover and the Jesus Seminar, *The Five Gospels: The Search for the Authentic Words of Jesus* (New York: Macmillan, 1993), p. 18.

[16] See the helpful comparative chart of dates in Aland and Aland, *Text of the New Testament*, p. 81.

that the papyri have not been incorporated in a significant way into New Testament textual criticism.[17] Even the more radically revised Nestle-Aland[26] (identical to the 27th edition) is only changed in 176 places, rejecting 980 possible places where the earliest papyri have another reading, including a number from 𝔓45, 𝔓46 and 𝔓66.[18] Lectionary manuscripts, even if they are earlier than either (as a few are; see below), are virtually dismissed because they clearly do not meet the criterion of continuous text from the beginning to end of a given biblical book.[19]

Some of this strongly categorical thinking has been exacerbated by the firm line drawn between giving a text a Gregory-Aland number and not—although the line is not as firm as one might think, and should probably be even less firmly drawn. A certain status is conveyed by the classification. This kind of disjunction was certainly not found in the ancient world, since it has been shown that the scribes in what appears to have been a scriptorium in ancient Oxyrhynchus worked on a variety of manuscripts. For example, the copyist of 𝔓22 (P.Oxy. X 1228) is also apparently that of P.Oxy. IV 654 (Gospel of Thomas).[20] The volume by van Haelst, although a different kind of volume, with different purposes (and its own limitations), in some ways overcomes these classificatory difficulties by bringing all of the evidence together in one volume and its own numbering system.[21] Even though this volume recognizes different relative status for the documents involved, there is a tendency to level out differentiations among manuscripts, so that necessary differentiation is lost.

---

[17] Epp, 'Papyrus Manuscripts', pp. 13–14. Cf. also his 'The Twentieth-Century Interlude in New Testament Textual Criticism', *JBL* 93 (1974), pp. 386–414; repr. in E.J. Epp and G.D. Fee, *Studies in the Theory and Method of New Testament Textual Criticism* (SD 45; Grand Rapids: Eerdmans, 1993), pp. 83–108, here pp. 84–85.

[18] See P.W. Comfort, *The Quest for the Original Text of the New Testament* (Grand Rapids: Baker, 1992), pp. 123, 125.

[19] On the neglect of the lectionaries, see C.D. Osburn, 'The Greek Lectionaries of the New Testament', in *Text of the New Testament* (ed. Ehrman and Holmes), pp. 61–74, here pp. 63–64.

[20] See Comfort, *Quest for the Original Text*, p. 60; cf. E.G. Turner, 'Scribes and Scholars of Oxyrhynchus', in *Akten des VIII. Internationalen Kongresses für Papyrologie Wien 1955* (ed. H. Gerstinger; MPER, NS 5; Vienna: Rohrer, 1956), pp. 141–46.

[21] J. van Haelst, Catalogue *des papyrus littéraires Juifs et Chrétiens* (Université de Paris IV Paris-Sorbonne série 'Papyrologie' 1; Paris: Publications de la Sorbonne, 1976).

I am not advocating that the Gregory-Aland system should be completely eliminated, since some system is desirable (and this one is probably better than most). What I am saying is that it is important to see these New Testament and related documents within their larger historical and text-critical context and not to let the Gregory-Aland numbers create an artificial barrier around their utilization. Scholars have recognized problems with the categorization scheme for some time. For example, even though Epp contends that the papyri are continuous-text manuscripts in contrast to the lectionaries, it is questionable whether, for example, all of the papyri or parchments are continuous text, and whether even some of the so-called lectionaries or other manuscripts are not at least as long a portion of continuous text as some of the papyri and parchments. We do know that some of the papyri are continuous-text manuscripts, especially those that have more than one book represented in what we might recognize as canonical order, or some variation of it. However, the number of papyrus manuscripts with more than one biblical book is surprisingly small. Only eleven papyri have the text of a portion of more than one book (𝔓4, 𝔓64, 𝔓67 [if these three belong together], 𝔓30, 𝔓45, 𝔓46, 𝔓53 [but see below], 𝔓61, 𝔓72 [but see below] 𝔓74, 𝔓75, 𝔓84, 𝔓92 [but see below]). Very few of the papyri have a complete book (e.g. 𝔓45, 𝔓46, 𝔓59, 𝔓66, 𝔓74, 𝔓75, 𝔓115 clearly meant to, but do not; 𝔓72 has three complete books, but see below), and so I am not as confident as others that we can make the same determination from those manuscripts that only have one text. The argument appears to be that the other side of the papyrus represents the continuous text, and on the basis of the relative length between texts the size of the codex can be determined. But this does not necessarily mean that the manuscript is not a lectionary or other excerpt of some form, and all that we have is quotation of one text at this particular place in the codex. In fact, we may well have more lectionary or liturgical texts and types of excerpts among the papyri and even the majuscules than we think. For one thing, the early lectionary texts (that is, before the eighth century), do not have lexical systems of pericopes that agree with the normal Greek lectionary,[22] so a very small text, such

---

[22] See Aland and Aland, *Text of the New Testament*, p. 167; cf. Osburn, 'Greek Lectionaries', p. 63.

as may be written on only two sides of a small papyrus, may well be a portion of a non-continuous text of the New Testament. In this case, the problem is that we do not have a means of checking simply on the basis of this small text. In other instances, we can check, however. For example, there are a number of Johannine papyri and parchments that have the word ἑρμηνεία, 'translation' or 'interpretation', at the bottom of the page, followed by Johannine-sounding language. These cannot be considered continuous text in the same way as a manuscript that clearly has only the biblical text on it. The translation or interpretation implies that this text had another purpose, and thus was not simply an edition of the continuous New Testament text.

Aland and Aland admit that there is institutionalized confusion regarding which texts have been included in the list of papyri, when they make the following comments in their introduction to textual criticism. They state:

> Among the ninety-six [now roughly 116] items which now comprise the official list of New Testament papyri there are several which by a strict definition do not belong there, such as talismans (𝔓50 [4th–5th century], 𝔓78 [3rd–4th century]), lectionaries (𝔓2 [6th century], 𝔓3 [6th–7th century], 𝔓44 [6th–7th century]), various selections (𝔓43 [6th–7th century], 𝔓62 [4th century]), songs (𝔓42 [7th–8th century]), texts with commentary (𝔓55 [6th–7th century], 𝔓59 [7th century], 𝔓60 [7th century], 𝔓63 [500], 𝔓80 [3rd century]), and even writing exercises (𝔓10 [4th century]) and occasional notes (𝔓12 [3rd century]).[23]

Others should be included in the list of problematic manuscripts as well. These include 𝔓7 (3rd–4th century), which Aland and Aland question whether it is a patristic fragment,[24] 𝔓25 (4th century), which may well be a fragment of the Diatessaron, and 𝔓76 (6th century), which has the words ἑρμηνεία, as noted above. Thus, by the Alands' type of reckoning alone, around twenty of the approximately 116 papyri alone are questionable as reflecting continuous text writing of the New Testament, almost half of them early. There are majuscules as well that should be re-evaluated, including two with ἑρμηνεία (0145 [7th century] and 0210 [7th century])—others are treated

---

[23] Aland and Aland, *Text of the New Testament*, p. 85. Cf. L. Vaganay with C.-B. Amphoux, *An Introduction to New Testament Textual Criticism* (trans. J. Heimerdinger; Cambridge: Cambridge University Press, 1991 [1986]), p. 24, who lists 𝔓3 𝔓4 and 𝔓44 as lectionaries (but see below).

[24] Aland and Aland, *Text of the New Testament*, p. 96.

below. The Alands' explanation of these phenomena is worth noting: "The presence of lectionaries may be explained as due to a
structural flaw in the overall system, the inclusion of commented
texts to the lack of an adequate definition for this genre . . ., and the
other examples are due to the occasionally uncritical attitude of earlier editors of the list."[25]

I believe that it is time that these problems are addressed. There
are several possible solutions that can be proposed.[26] One would be
to restrict the classificatory definitions severely, and to exclude the
texts now seen to be wrongly included. The effect of this, I fear,
would be to further restrict the range of evidence taken into account
when establishing and tracing the development of the text of the
New Testament, and potentially to lose valuable information.[27] Another
would be to expand the definitions, and include at least some of the
texts mentioned above that have been excluded from the broad range
of textual discussion, such as lectionaries or even some apocryphal
documents. The effect of this, however, would be to further confuse
the categories already used and to get farther away from a solution
to the problem outlined.[28] A third solution—one that I first proposed

---

[25] Aland and Aland, *Text of the New Testament*, p. 85. However, it is worth noting that Kurt Aland was responsible for the papyri list from 𝔓48 upwards, and so
at least ten were placed on the list during Aland's tenure. It is also worth noting
that the Alands have, however, deleted a number of documents from their list of
uncials (pp. 107–28). These include, e.g. 0100 reclassified as a lectionary, 0152
described as a talisman, 0153 described as an ostrakon (see below), 0192 reclassified
as a lectionary.

[26] There have been some slight modifications made along the way, such as E.
von Dobschütz haphazardly and unsystematically expanding the categories by including ostraka and talismans (see E. Nestle, *Einführung in das Griechische Neue Testament*
[ed. E. von Dobschütz; Göttingen: Vandenhoeck & Ruprecht, 4th edn, 1923], pp.
86, 97; von Dobschütz, "Zur Liste der Neutestamentlichen Handschriften," *ZNW*
25 [1926], p. 300; 27 [1928], pp. 218–19; 32 [1933], p. 188—however Gregory
already included ostraka in 0153; see *Griechischen Handschriften*, p. 43), and Kurt
Aland adding a category of "varia" to the list of papyri (K. Aland [ed.], *Repertorium
der griechischen chistlichen Papyri. I. Biblische Papyri* [Berlin: De Gruyter, 1976], pp.
10–11), but these have obviously not alleviated the problem. I am grateful to Thomas
Kraus for this information.

[27] This has already happened in some cases, as the case of 0153 below will illustrate. This has already been observed by in Parker, 'Majuscule Manuscripts', pp.
27–28.

[28] The Alands' solution is to simply state: 'But these peculiarities are on the whole
negligible' (Aland and Aland, *Text of the New Testament*, 85). I beg to differ. Roughly
twenty of 116 instances of the papyri alone is nearly 20% of the total, hardly negligible—to say nothing of the other manuscripts mentioned.

in 1998 at the conference and then in print in 2003—is a re-think-
ing of the nature of the categories used to classify manuscripts. I
believe that it is time that these problems are addressed by restruc-
turing the system and providing categories for some of these other
types of documents. I wish to develop that idea further here. I would
like to propose that there be two major lists of New Testament manuscripts, differentiated by whether they are continuous text or not.[29]
One of the lists would be given to those manuscripts for which there
is little to no doubt regarding their being continuous-text New
Testament manuscripts, whether they be papyri, majuscules, or minuscules, and the other would include those manuscripts for which there
is doubt as to their continuous nature but that are manuscripts of
varying degrees of relevance to establishing the New Testament text.
One could divide this second category into a variety of smaller sub-
units, perhaps corresponding to the types of manuscripts that are
discussed below in the third section of this paper. It would most certainly contain the lectionaries, but a variety of other types of manuscripts as well. The tendency—and one that should probably be
resisted in its most extreme forms—would be to be overly regula-
tive in classification. The purpose of this second list is less to be
definitive regarding the nature of the text than to provide a means
of access to other, often neglected, manuscripts that could play a
role in tracing the development of the text of the New Testament
but without the pressure of having to treat them in the same way
as indisputably continuous-text manuscripts. Hence this second category could include lectionary and other liturgical texts, miniature
codices or magical/talismanic documents, apocryphal documents,
commentaries, excerpts (e.g. ostraka), and unknown but possibly New
Testament texts (e.g. the 7Q documents).[30] The nature of the manuscripts in the second category would be that, in the first instance,
they would be considered as a means of helping to establish the text

---

[29] This is essentially a differentiation by content, rather than by writing surface.
For a proposal similar in some ways, see S.R. Pickering, 'The Significance of Non-
Continuous New Testament Textual Materials in Papyri', in *Studies in the Early Text*
(ed. Taylor), pp. 121–40.

[30] I have not included reference to excerpts from the early church fathers or
other authors, but these certainly could be included as well. My purpose here is to
consider those that appear to be in some way independent manuscripts.

of the New Testament and provide evidence for its development.[31] The intermediary nature of the category and the ambiguous nature of some of the manuscripts within it would provide a useful stage in dealing with manuscripts in the process of being assessed for their use within New Testament textual criticism. A document, such as an apocryphal gospel, might be placed within this category and at some time in the future, because of the nature of its text, find its status elevated to the first category, while some manuscript that is discovered to be questionable in the first category could be placed in the second category so that its usefulness for textual criticism could be retained without its maintaining its status as a primary document.[32]

3. Documents to Consider for the Second Category of Manuscripts

In light of the above discussion, it is warranted to suggest several of the types of manuscripts that might be placed within the second category of manuscripts—whether this second category is differentiated or not (or in quite this way). Some of the discussion below involves re-assessment of some of the manuscripts that are currently within the Gregory-Aland list of New Testament manuscripts but probably should not be retained in a first category. Others involve introducing manuscripts that might well prove useful for future inclusion in discussion of the development and establishment of the text of the New Testament.

---

[31] That the movement of manuscript classification can go in the other direction should be noted as well. 𝔓4 was once classified as *l*943 (Gregory, *Griechische Handschriften*, p. 45), but has not only been elevated from lectionary to papyrus, but its date has moved from the sixth to possibly the second century, and it has been linked with 𝔓64 and 𝔓67. Another feature of 𝔓4 is that even though the manuscript is of Luke (parts of chs. 1–6), one page has εὐαγγεωλιον κατά μαθθαι᾽ον on it, although in a different hand. For discussion, see P.W. Comfort, 'Exploring the Common Identification of Three New Testament Manuscripts: 𝔓4, 𝔓64 and 𝔓67', *TynBul* 46.1 (1995), pp. 43–54 and C.P. Thiede, 'Notes on 𝔓4 = Bibliothèque Nationale Paris, Supplementum Graece 1120/5', *TynBul* 46.1 (1995), pp. 55–58.

[32] One of the reasons for such an approach is the fact that the New Testament manuscripts were often found in an environment with a mix of other manuscripts. See E.J. Epp, "The Oxyrhynchus New Testament Papyri: 'Not Without Honor Except in Their Hometown'?" *JBL* 123 (2004), pp. 5–55 esp. pp. 14–16, where he notes some of the variety of theological texts.

a. *Lectionary and Liturgical Texts*[33]

Lectionaries have been a neglected area of New Testament textual criticism, even though several scholars have attempted in various ways to include more information regarding lectionaries in the text-critical discussion, as well as in the textual apparatus.[34] There are at least two apparent reasons that this neglect has taken place, one being the supposed lack of continuous text and the other the alterations that have taken place to create the lections, such as adding incipits. However, these limitations are in some ways artificial, and raise the questions of what constitutes a lectionary text and what constitutes continuous text. The reasonable presumption is that the vast majority of our New Testament manuscripts were copied for use within a Christian community. In many instances, there are larger sections of text extant in some lectionary texts than is present on some supposed continuous texts. Some of the recognized lectionaries have a significant amount more continuous text than the papyri that we have. For example, papyri with five or fewer verses include 𝔓2 𝔓7 𝔓12 (with a single verse!; see below) 𝔓18 𝔓71 𝔓73 𝔓76 [see below] 𝔓78 [see below] 𝔓80 [see below] 𝔓93 𝔓96 𝔓102 𝔓107 𝔓110 𝔓111 𝔓112 𝔓113. It was once thought that lectionaries were of lesser quality because less care was taken in their copying, but this has now been shown to be false in the light of their ostensible use and consistency one to another, even if many represent what is called the Byzantine text.[35] The second type of manuscript is a biblical manuscript with continuous text that has been

---

[33] I have borrowed freely from my 'The Influence of Unit Delimitation on Reading and Use of Greek Manuscripts', in *Pericope Volume*, 6 [provisional title] (ed. M.C.A. Korpel; Pericope 6; Assen: Van Gorcum, in press) in this section.

[34] See Osburn, 'Greek Lectionaries', pp. 63–71; cf. E.C. Colwell, 'Method in the Study of Gospel Lectionaries', *HTR* 25 (1932), pp. 73–84; repr. in his *Studies in Methodology in Textual Criticism of the New Testament* (NTTS 9; Leiden: Brill, 1969), pp. 84–95; B.M. Metzger, 'A Comparison of the Palestinian Syriac Lectionary and the Greek Gospel Lectionary', in *Neotestamentica et Semitica: Studies in Honour of Matthew Black* (ed. E.E. Ellis, M. Wilcox; Edinburgh: T. & T. Clark, 1969), pp. 201–20.

[35] Osburn, 'Greek Lectionaries', p. 61, citing D.W. Riddle, 'The Use of Lectionaries in Critical Editions and Studies of the New Testament Text', in *Prolegomena to the Study of the Lectionary Text of the Gospels* (ed. D.W. Riddle and E.C. Colwell; SLT-GNT 1; Chicago: University of Chicago Press, 1933), pp. 74–75; Aland and Aland, *Text of the New Testament*, p. 169. Cf. also E.J. Epp, 'Textual Criticism in the Exegesis of the New Testament, with an Excursus on Canon', in *Handbook to Exegesis of the New Testament* (NTTS 25; Leiden: Brill, 1997), pp. 45–98, here pp. 66–67.

appropriated for lectional use. Such a manuscript may well have lectionary headings and other markings added later by a different scribe, as well as the addition of later ekphonetic markings to aid in reading. One particularly interesting manuscript in this regard is Gregory-Aland 0105, a tenth-century biblical manuscript of eight pages that has been marked to indicate lectional use by the addition of headings and Eusebian numbers.[36] However, only some of the pericopes have been marked, not all of them.

In some ways, it may appear at first surprising, therefore, that these lectionary manuscripts have been placed into the second category of manuscripts. One of the assumptions that must be eradicated is that the second category of manuscripts automatically means irrelevant. To the contrary, the second category of manuscripts is distinguished by the fact that the manuscripts are not continuous-text documents of the New Testament. The lectionary texts, because they are not continuous text (but see below) have been relegated so far down the pecking order in the Gregory-Aland listings that they are virtually excluded from serious consideration. One of the reasons for putting lectionary and related liturgical texts into this second category is so that they can be taken more readily into consideration without the pressure of their being treated as continuous text manuscripts.

As a result, a number of manuscripts that might be placed in this category include the following:[37]

𝔓2 (VH 455). This fifth or sixth century single page of a bi-lingual manuscript includes both Greek and Coptic. On the one side is 13 lines of Luke 7.22–26 in Coptic, but on the other is two lines of Luke 7.50 in Coptic, a title and then 8 lines of John 12.12–15 in Greek. The mix of Coptic and Greek in non-continuous fashion, as well as the title, argues strongly for this as a lectionary text.

𝔓3 (VH 412). In Gregory's volume from 1908 that inaugurated the Gregory-Aland system,[38] he notes that at an earlier time 𝔓3 was

---

[36] See S.E. Porter and W.J. Porter, *New Testament Greek Papyri and Parchments: New Editions* (MPER NS 28; Vienna: Österreichische Nationalbibliothek, in press), no. 40.

[37] Below and throughout, unless otherwise noted, I rely upon the descriptions of the manuscripts and opinions gathered by van Haelst, *Catalogue*, with his number given as VH.

[38] Gregory, *Griechischen Handschriften*, p. 45.

considered a lectionary, *l*348. This is no wonder, since 𝔓3, a sixth- or seventh-century manuscript, consists of a single sheet with writing on both sides, but from Luke 7.36–45 and Luke 10.38–42 respectively. It is difficult to see how the manuscript could be continuous writing. As van Haelst notes, this has been suggested by various scholars as a lectionary (Wessely; see also Aland and Aland),[39] a Gospel florilegium (Birdsall), or a page out of a private book (Junack). In support of the lectionary classification is the presence of a title to some of the units.

𝔓44 (VH 365). This highly fragmentary sixth or seventh century papyrus, consisting of a number of fragments from a single sheet, includes passages from a variety of places in Matthew (17.1–3, 6–7; 18.15–17, 19; 25.8–10) and John (9.3–4; 10.8–14; 12.16–18). It appears that there were a variety of relatively small lectional or liturgical excerpts included in this document.

𝔓53 (VH 380). This manuscript consists of two mutilated pages, each apparently from a third century codex of some sort. One of the pages has Matthew on both sides (Matthew 26.29–35, 36–40) and the other, in more fragmentary form, has Acts on both sides (Acts 9.33–38; 9.40–10.1). What is interesting to note and suggests that this may be a lectionary text is that, even though the two pages are written in the same hand, there is the possibility that they are not from the same codex, because such a codex would have been 300 to 350 pages. This raises the question of whether this copyist made two codexes, or whether he made several pages of lectional readings.

*l*1043 (VH 335). By contrast I wish to point out that one of the traditionally recognized lectionary manuscripts has perhaps more to offer to textual criticism than some of these documents cited above, with their current papyrus numbers. This parchment lectionary text of the fifth century, *l*1043, consists of Matthew 3.7–17; 4.23–25. 5.12; 7.13–20; 10.37–42; 9.35; Mark 6.18–29; Luke 2.1–20; 11.27–32; 24.36–38 and John 20.1–18 and 24–27.[40] Many of these units of

---

[39] *Text of the New Testament*, p. 85.
[40] Porter and Porter, *New Testament Greek Papyri and Parchments*, no. 58.

text are longer than those that are found in the papyri above. This is one of the earliest lectionary manuscripts, and it is written in the great codex tradition. It consists of eleven pages. They are clearly not all continuous, yet they provide an early witness not only to the use of the text in liturgy but to the form of the text being used, without any lectionary incipits. A good example is found in Matthew 4.23–5.12. The lectionary does not change the wording at the beginning of the unit to make the sense clearer. It reads: καὶ περιῆγεν ἐν ὅλῃ τῇ Γαλιλαίᾳ διδάϲκων . . . ("and he was going around in the whole of Galilee, teaching . . ."). This follows Codex Vaticanus, whereas most of the major early codexes include reference to Jesus to make clear who was going about Galilee.[41] This latter reading would have made it clearer in the lectionary who the subject of the verb was, but it is not included here. This indicates that at this stage, lectionaries—or at least certain ones such as this one—were less inclined to provide an incipit or introduction to the pericope to ease reading. If this is true, then it would indicate that lectionaries should not be too readily dismissed for their use in textual criticism, since especially early ones may be faithful transmitters of their biblical texts, and utilized in textual criticism.[42] This lectionary supports the reading in Vaticanus and is probably closest to the original. The text-critical history indicates that explicit reference to Jesus was added in some manuscript traditions, quite possibly for liturgical/lectionary reasons, and then retained in the tradition. The issue then became the placement of the noun, not whether it belonged.

b. *Miniature Codices and Magical Papyri/Amulets*

There is significant discussion regarding the similarities and differences between magical papyri and miniature codices. In the ancient world, there were many occasions when documents for private use were written. Some of these were related to magical purposes. As recent discussion has indicated, it is often difficult to tell the difference

---

[41] This lectionary manuscript reads ἐν ὅλῃ τῇ Γαλιλαίᾳ with B, instead οφ ὁ Ἰηϲοῦϲ ἐν τῇ Γαλιλαίᾳ with א* (delete ὅλη) C*, ὁ Ἰηϲοῦϲ ὅλην τὴν Γαλιλαίαν with א¹ D ƒ¹ 33 892 1424 *l*844 *l*2211, or ὅλην τὴν Γαλιλαίαν ὁ Ἰηϲοῦϲ with W ƒ¹³ Majority text.

[42] On the issue of the use of the lectionaries in textual criticism, see Osburn, 'Greek Lectionaries', pp. 3–64.

between these two categories. However, Kruger has provided a useful summary of what he sees as the major characteristics. The magical texts or amulets, which often come with folds so that they can be carried, are usually written on papyrus on one side only, and their content often consists of a biblical citation or some prayer. Miniature codices, by contrast, are usually written on parchment on both sides of the sheet, and their content is often a larger portion of continuous text and includes noncanonical citations.[43]

As noted above, there are some manuscripts that are on the Gregory-Aland list that should probably be placed in this category, and some other manuscripts that could usefully be included here for the purposes of textual criticism.

𝔓50 (VH 482).   This fourth-fifth century papyrus, probably a miniature codex, has text on both sides of four pages, with Acts 8.26–32 and Acts 10.26–31. The pages are virtually complete, so the text cannot be continuous. In fact, the second of the four pages has 8.30–32 and then 10.26–27. The two passages may have been selected for their talismanic value related to Philip and Peter.

𝔓78 (VH 558).   This third-fourth century papyrus with an excerpt from Jude (vv. 4–5 and 7–8) has posed problems. The odd shape (it is wider than it is high) and poor writing, including a number of variant readings, suggests that it was an amulet, but the content as part of the book of Jude suggests that it was part of a miniature codex.[44] Nevertheless, the content does not seem to be continuous.

𝔓105.   That this fifth or sixth century papyrus sheet from Matthew (27.62–64, 28.2–5) is part of a miniature codex is made clear by the fact that a piece of string is still attached to it.[45] The page is bro-

---

[43] M.J. Kruger, *The Gospel of the Savior: An Analysis of P.Oxy. 840 and its Place in the Gospel Traditions of Early Christianity* (TENT 1; Leiden: Brill, 2005), ch. 1, part III. Cf. M.J. Kruger, 'P.Oxy. 840: Amulet or Miniature Codex?' *JTS* 53.1 (2002), pp. 80–94; T.J. Kraus, "P.Oxy. V 840—Amulett oder Miniaturkodex? Grundsätzliche und ergänzende Anmerkungen zu zwei Termini," *ZAC* (forthcoming).

[44] See P.J. Parsons, P.Oxy. XXXIV 2684 (London: Egypt Exploration Society, 1968), pp. 4–5.

[45] J.D. Thomas, P.Oxy. LXIV 4406 (London: Egypt Exploration Society, 1997), p. 12 and photograph. Because of the position of the strings my friend Thomas Kraus thinks the string may have been used to attach the papyrus to the body. If so, then it would be better described as an amulet. See P.M. Head, 'Some Recently Published NT Papyri from Oxyrhynchus: An Overview and Preliminary Assessment',

ken now but would, according to the editor, have contained about 25 lines, so this may well be a miniature codex of the resurrection narrative.

PSI VI 719 (VH 423). This papyrus sheet with biblical writing on one side (a protocol on the other)[46] contains the following passages: John 1.1; Matthew 1.1; John 1.23; Mark 1.1; Luke 1.1; Psalm 90.1; Matthew 6.9.[47] This large amulet from the fourth or fifth centuries contains a cross and then possibly Χ(ριστε) ϛ(ωτ)ερ, then the incipits of the Gospels with John 1.23 interspersed, Psalm 90.1, Matthew 6.9 the beginning of the Lord's Prayer and κα[ὶ τὰ ἐξῆς, a common form of the doxology ending with amen, and then probably χ(ριστο)ϛ and three crosses. The text is run continuously together, probably for incantational purposes—although the individual lines are surprisingly long, with around 70 characters per line, and may have posed a problem for reading purposes. This kind of pattern of biblical quotation is not unknown in other manuscripts, such as P.Vindob. G. 348.[48] This sixth or seventh century papyrus contains writing on one side, with the incipits of the four canonical Gospels in their canonical order, followed by Psalm 90 minus parts of vv. 7 and 8.[49] There are many different manuscripts that have such portions arranged apparently for talismanic purposes.[50]

P.Vindob. G. 29831. A manuscript that might be helpful in illustrating the problematic nature of the singular Gregory-Aland list and

---

TynBul 51.1 (2000), pp. 1–16, here p. 9. Contra Head, the piece of string is still attached in the plate.

[46] See R. Pintaudi, "Per la datazione di PSI VI 719," AnalPap 2 (1990), pp. 27–28.

[47] See the contribution by Thomas Kraus in this volume, where a photograph of PSI 719 is included.

[48] See R.W. Daniel, 'A Christian Amulet on Papyrus', VigChrist 37 (1983), pp. 400–404.

[49] Note that P.Oxy. XVI 1928 contains all of Psalm 90 (noted by Daniel, 'Amulet', p. 400). For a discussion of all of the Psalm 90 manuscripts, see T.J. Kraus, 'Psalm 90 der Septuaginta in apotropäischer Funktion', forthcoming in the published Acts of the 24th International Congress of Papyrology, Helsinki, Finland, 1–7.8.2004; and 'Septuaginta-Psalm 90 in apotropäischer Verwendung: Vorüberlegungen für eine kritische Edition und (bisheriges) Datematerial', Biblische Notizen (forthcoming).

[50] See Pickering, 'Significance of Non-Continuous New Testament Textual Material', pp. 126–29, who discusses in detail P.Vindob. G. 2312 with Psalm 90.1–2, Romans 12.1–2 and John 2.1–2, and lists other, similar manuscripts for John (pp. 133–36). I question whether all of the manuscripts that he cites belong in this category (e.g. P.Egerton 2).

the usefulness of a second list of documents is found is P.Vindob.
G. 29831. Horsley contends that this manuscript, which was originally published as a biblical amulet with John 1.5–6 on it, is the
rejected pages of a miniature codex.[51] He cites a number of examples where he thinks that pages rejected from codices may have been
re-used as amulets (including P.Ant. II 54 [VH 347];[52] P.Oxy. XXXIV
2684, cited above as 𝔓78; P.Yale 1.3, cited above as 𝔓50; P.Osl.
inv. 1661, cited below as 𝔓62; and P.Oxy. II 209, cited below as
𝔓10).[53] On the basis of his reconstruction of the codex, Horsley contends that the codex began with the beginning of John's Gospel.
Therefore, he endorses that a Gregory-Aland number should be given
to this manuscript.[54] One can see the dilemma faced with such a
manuscript. There is clearly a biblical text being cited, but it is
unclear whether the text is continuous or not, and whether the portion cited was simply part of a small codex, or whether it was part
of a larger continuous text of the entire book (although I find the
latter unlikely due to the size). By placing the manuscript in this second list, the manuscript can be taken into consideration without necessarily establishing that it was ever a continuous text manuscript.

c. *Commentaries*[55]

An issue of continuing discussion regarding several Johannine papyri
and parchments is the presence of the word ἑρμηνεία, apparently
centered after the New Testament text and before what appears to
be some Greek words or statements. Scholars have differed regard-

---

[51] G.H.R. Horsley, 'Reconstructing a Biblical Codex: The Prehistory of MPER
n.s. XVII. 10 (*P.Vindob.* G 29 831)', in *Akten des 21. Internationalen Papyrologenkongresses
Berlin, 13.–19.8.1995* (ed. Kramer, Luppe, Maehler, Poethke), I, pp. 473–81.

[52] This third-century manuscript contains part of the Lord's Prayer, Matthew
6.10–12. It is possible that there were more pages at the beginning, but the miniature codex, possibly used as an amulet, breaks off in mid-verse on the last page.
Horsley speculates that the scribed stopped as soon as he realized that he had made
an error in copying the text (Horsley, 'Reconstructing a Biblical Codex', p. 480).
It is clear that it is not continuous text, even though it may have been a rejected
codex that was then re-used as an amulet.

[53] Horsley, 'Reconstructing a Biblical Codex', pp. 480–81.

[54] Horsley, 'Reconstructing a Biblical Codex', p. 479.

[55] This section is dependent upon S.E. Porter, 'The Use of *Hermeneia* and Johannine
Manuscripts', in *Akten des 23. Internationalen Kongresses für Papyrologie, Wien, 22.–28. Juli
2001* (ed. H. Harrauer and B. Palme; Vienna: Österreichische Nationalbibliothek,
forthcoming).

ing what this represents, with some arguing that it is biblical text and commentary[56] and others that the words following have an oracular character, similar to the oracular sayings to be found in the Markan text of Codex Bezae and Johannine text of Codex St. Germain.[57] In either case, the manuscripts may have included all of the book of John but the manuscript itself is not continuous due to this feature. The potential list of manuscripts to include in this list of 'commentary' texts has been disputed, since not all of the Johannine manuscripts actually have the word ἑρμηνεία. With two lists, those that have the word can be put in the second list, while those without can, if they appear to be continuous text (they are all in the Gregory-Aland list already), remain in the first list. Thus 𝔓60, from the seventh to eighth century, with portions of John 16, 17, 18, 19, and 0256, from the eighth century, with John 6.32–33, 35–37, can remain in the first list since the text does appear to be continuous and there is no clear use of ἑρμηνεία.[58]

Manuscripts to include in the second list would include the following:

> 𝔓55 (VH 433), from the sixth to seventh century, with John 1.31–33, 35–38;
> 𝔓59 (VH 429), from the seventh to eighth century, with John 1, 2, 11, 12, 17, 18 and 21;
> 𝔓63 (VH 438), from around 500 to the sixth century, with John 3.14–18 and 4.9–10;
> 𝔓76 (VH 442), from the sixth century, with John 4.9, 11–12;
> 𝔓80 (VH 441), from the third to fourth centuries, with John 3.34;
> 0145 (VH 445), from the seventh century, with John 6.26–31;
> 0210 (VH 443), from the seventh century, with John 5.44 and 6.1–2, 41–42.

Debate remains nevertheless over the understanding of the use of ἑρμηνεία in these manuscripts. Metzger categorically states that 'On

---

[56] Aland and Aland, *Text of the New Testament*, p. 85.

[57] B.M. Metzger, *The Text of the New Testament* (New York: Oxford University Press, 3rd edn, 1992), pp. 266–67; and 'Greek Manuscripts of John's Gospel with "Hermeneiai"', in *Text and Testimony: Essays on New Testament and Apocryphal Literature in Honour of A.F.J. Klijn* (ed. T. Baarda *et al.*; Kampen: Kok, 1988), pp. 162–69.

[58] I note that none of the five recent John manuscripts added to the papyrus list—𝔓106 𝔓107 𝔓108 𝔓109—has the ἑρμηνεία.

the basis of the title, the *opinio communis* has been that the sentences [that follow ἑρμηνεία] are a kind of rudimentary commentary on Scripture'.[59] This opinion is also held by Aland and Aland, as noted above.[60] However, when he edited 𝔓55, Sanz stated that it is 'das Fragment eines Kommentars oder einer exegetischen Homilie zum Johannesevangelium. Da es aber nur reinen Bibeltext bietet, habe ich es hier unter die Biblica eingeordnet.'[61] This manuscript on the verso offers the word ἑρμηνεία only, with no other wording except biblical text. Sanz thus suggested that the recto may have contained a lengthy quotation of John 1.31–33 as part of the commentary on John 1.35–38 that fell under the rubric of ἑρμηνεία.[62] This tentative categorization by Sanz of this manuscript as biblical, in which he felt constrained in his alternatives on the basis of the composition of the manuscript, is perhaps responsible for its originally being categorized as a biblical manuscript, and hence being given a Gregory-Aland number. This perhaps also set the pattern for categorization of subsequently published similar manuscripts. Some editions of later manuscripts, however, apparently recognized the less commentary- or biblical-like and more oracular nature of these portions of the manuscripts. For example, Stegmüller, who published 𝔓63, recognized what he saw as the oracular character of the ἑρμηνεία material, similar to the oracles in the Markan section of Codex Bezae (D) and Johannine section of Codex St. Germain, and even thought that the numbers at the top of each page were either pagination or 'Orakelzahlen'.[63] Hunger, who first edited 𝔓76 in 1959, recognized Sanz's position that the ἑρμηνεία convention might have indicated a commentary, but, noting that it was not strictly speaking a Gospel

---

[59] Metzger, *Text of the New Testament*, p. 266. Cf. Metzger, 'Greek Manuscripts', p. 162, where he states: 'Although not much attention has been given heretofore to this special feature, the *opinio communis* seems to be that such 𝔓 are a kind of rudimentary commentary on the sacred text.'

[60] *Text of the New Testament*, p. 85.

[61] P. Sanz, *Griechische Literarische Papyri Christliche Inhalts I* (MPER NS 4; Vienna: Rohrer, 1946), p. 59.

[62] Sanz, *Griechische Literarische Papyri*, p. 59; cf. H. Hunger, 'Zwei unbekannte neutestamentliche Papyrusfragmente der österreichischen Nationalbibliothek', *Biblos* 8 (1959), pp. 7–12, here p. 10 and n. 7; L. Casson and E.L. Hettich, *Excavations at Nessana*. II. *Literary Papyri* (Princeton: Princeton University Press, 1950), p. 11.

[63] O. Stegmüller, 'Zu den Bibelorakeln im Codex Bezae', *Bib* 34 (1953), pp. 13–22, here pp. 20–21.

commentary, followed Stegmüller and decided that it was a biblical oracle.[64] This opinion was later followed by Quecke, who also drew attention to Codex Bezae in discussing 𝔓76, and van Haelst, who labeled all of the texts with ἑρμηνεία as biblical oracular texts.[65] Thus, whereas some biblical text-critics may have come to the opinion that these manuscripts are commentaries, this is hardly the universal opinion of many of those who have edited these manuscripts. The clear majority of those who have dealt with them consider them to be biblical oracles, possibly influenced by the parallel oracular statements found added to Codex Bezae.

Although it is difficult to state exactly how early the interpretive ἑρμηνεία statements became a part of John's Gospel, it appears that they were very early—earlier than the incorporation of such statements onto other documents, so far as can be indicated from the extant evidence. If John's Gospel were written near the end of the first century, by the third or fourth century such statements were seen to be in some meaningful sense a part of the transmission of the sacred text. Whereas some manuscript traditions seem to have retained an appreciable distinction between text and commentary, even if they were willing later to add commentary to their biblical text, for others such a distinction was not made in the same way, with text and commentary occupying the same manuscript space from nearly the start. The second list of manuscripts makes an attempt to capture this by providing this categorization.

d. *Apocryphal Texts*[66]

Despite the abundance of textual evidence for the Greek New Testament, there are distinct limitations as well. For example, the

---

[64] Hunger, 'Zwei unbekannte neutestamentliche Papyrusfragmente', p. 10.

[65] H. Quecke, 'Zu den Joh-Fragmenten mit "Hermeneiai"', *Orientalia Christiana Periodica* 40 (1974), pp. 407–14; *idem*, 'Zu den Joh-Fragmenten mit "Hermeneiai"' (Nachtrag), *Orientalia Christiana Periodica* 43 (1977), pp. 179–81; and van Haelst, *Catalogue*, esp. no. 429.

[66] The discussion in this section is dependent upon S.E. Porter, 'Apocryphal Gospels and the Text of the New Testament before A.D. 200', in *The New Testament Text in Early Christianity: Proceedings of the Lille Colloquium, July 2000 / Le texte du Nouveau Testament au début du christianisme: Actes du colloque de Lille, juillet 2000* (ed. C.-B. Amphoux and J.K. Elliott; Histoire du texte biblique 6; Lausanne: Éditions du Zèbre, 2003), pp. 235–58. See also T. Nicklas, 'Fragmente christlicher Apokryphen und die Textgeschichte des Neuen Testaments', *ZNW* 96 (2005), pp. 129–42.

late first and early second centuries A.D. are often considered a tun-
nel period in New Testament studies, and similar comments can be
made with regard to the text of the New Testament. One source of
documents that has recently been brought to the fore as providing
potential insight into this period is the Greek apocryphal documents,
especially those of the gospels. A number of these reflect the growth
and expansion of Christian writing, and in their citation of the New
Testament text provide a form of textual witness to it.

There are several considerations for the use of these apocryphal
documents, however. The first is determining which documents belong
in the category of documents to consider for text-critical discussion.
The fact that the documents range from clearly New Testament-like
to abstract theological documents, makes it difficult to draw the
boundary on which documents to include. Further, many of the most
useful documents, such as the apocryphal Greek gospels are fragmentary in nature. Those with a claim to inclusion must, by definition,
have some form of biblical citation, whether it be direct quotation,
paraphrase or even clear allusion (these terms are notoriously difficult
to define).[67] Of the various categories of documents, apart from a
few other documents that may have such occasional citations, the
apocryphal gospels have the largest number that might profitably be
taken into consideration, since their narrative most closely follows
that of the canonical texts.

Even these show a variety of possibilities. For example, three of
the four pericopes of P.Egerton 2 reflect one or more of the canonical gospels. For example, lines 7–10 reflect John 5.39, lines 10–14
John 5.45, lines 15–17 John 9.29, lines 22–24 possibly John 8.59
and/or 10.31, lines 30–31 Luke 4.30, and lines 32–41 the episode
and some of the language in Matthew 8.2–4, Mark 1.40–44 and
Luke 5.12–14 (not present in John's Gospel), lines 45–47 John 3.2,
lines 47–50 possibly the episode in Matthew 22.16–21, Mark 12.13–17
and/or Luke 20.20–25, lines 54–59 Matthew 15.7–9, and Mark
7.6–7 but in a different context, and line 74 John 16.20, among pos-

---

[67] See S.E. Porter, 'The Use of the Old Testament in the New Testament: A
Brief Comment on Method and Terminology', in *Early Christian Interpretation of the
Scriptures of Israel: Investigations and Proposals* (ed. C.A. Evans and J.A. Sanders; Studies
in Scripture in Early Judaism and Christianity 5; JSNTSup 148; Sheffield: Sheffield
Academic Press, 1997), pp. 79–96.

sibly others. The editors of the first edition draw attention to the text-critical possibilities of these verbal parallels, for example in commenting on lines 7–10 that the differences seem to reflect Western textual readings in P.Egerton 2.[68] By contrast, P.Oxy. II 210, which has not of late been considered an apocryphal gospel, though probably should be, has a mix of biblical citations. These include in recto lines 1–3 1 Corinthians 1.26–27, lines 4–7 Matthew 1.24 and Luke 2.10, 12, and verso lines 4–8 the episode in Matthew 19.16ff., Mark 10.17ff., and/or Luke 18.18ff. lines 9–17 Matthew 7.17–19 and Luke 6.43–44, line 17 Johannine 'I am' language, lines 18–19 language like 2 Corinthians 4.4 and Colossians 1.15, line 19 language of Philippians 2.6, line 23 allusion to Romans 1.20, and line 24 perhaps 1 Corinthians 2.6–8.[69] Least helpful is a document such as P.Oxy. V 840, which, though biblical-like in form and shape, does not actually cite the Greek of the New Testament, and hence has limited value for textual criticism. An example is the miniature codex, P.Oxy. 840.[70] It consists of a synoptic-like episode that might be found within the Gospels, since it has elements of the synoptic account, although Kruger finds no sign of direct dependence. He identifies only one place where there may be verbal correlation, in recto line 9 and John 10.23. Nevertheless, the second list allows for such a manuscript to be kept in mind—although only tangentially relevant—for New Testament textual criticism.

A second is the issue of dating, especially relevant for textual criticism. Whereas in many instances scholars wish to argue that the documents reflected are much earlier than the manuscripts, the fact remains that many of the manuscripts themselves are late, and hence of less value for textual criticism than the might be otherwise. A crucial example in this regard is the Akhmim codex of the Gospel of Peter (P.Cairo 10759). The document may date to the second

---

[68] See H.I. Bell and T.C. Skeat, *Fragments of an Unknown Gospel and Other Early Christian Papyri* (London: British Museum, 1935), pp. 16–25, here p. 17.

[69] See S.E. Porter, 'P.Oxy II 210 as an Apocryphal Gospel and the Development of Egyptian Christianity', in *Atti del XXII Congresso Internazionale di Papirologia, Firenze, 23–29 agosto 1998* (ed. I. Andorlini, G. Bastianini, M. Manfredi, and G. Menci; 2 vols.; Florence: Istituto Papirologico 'G. Vitelli', 2001), II, pp. 1095–1108, esp. pp. 1101–1104.

[70] See the new edition and discussion of this manuscript in Kruger, *Gospel of the Savior*.

century, but the manuscript is no earlier than the sixth or seventh century, and perhaps later.[71] Several potential Gospel of Peter papyrus fragments (e.g. P.Oxy. XLI 2949 or P.Oxy. LX 4009) may be earlier, however. Thus, even if there is some text-critical relevance of this document, since it alludes to and even cites New Testament passages within its own narrative framework, it must be treated as would any document from that time.

A third issue in this exercise is to establish the text of these apocryphal documents. This is in fact a much more difficult task than is often realized, but is not too different from that confronted in all papyrological studies, including that of the Greek New Testament. Several of these manuscripts have been edited only once in their editio princeps, with a few having been edited a second or subsequent time. However, for the most part, subsequent 'editions' are often only reprints of the editio princeps, sometimes with changes that are included on dubious grounds. Often what are purported to be new editions are nothing more than those done solely on the basis of photographs. As valuable as photographs are, and as helpful as they can be in editing papyri, they are not a substitute for actual examination of the manuscripts. There is a further problem, however, in the editing of any biblical-like manuscripts, and that is the possible influence of the canonical biblical texts on the decipherment of these apocryphal ones. One of the major questions in the study of the apocryphal gospel papyri in particular is their relationship with the canonical Gospels, as already noted above. In the early days of their publication, it was often (though not universally) accepted that they reflected later gospels that had drawn upon the canonical texts, often evidencing conflation of a number of gospel stories, including even both the Synoptics and John in one document (e.g. P.Egerton 2). However, in more recent times there has been a swing toward claiming that these documents are at least as early as or, in some cases, even earlier than, the canonical Gospels, and that they may in fact contain early and independent gospel accounts of value in analyzing the text of the New Testament.[72]

---

[71] See the most recent discussion in T.J. Kraus and T. Nicklas, *Das Petrusevangelium und die Petrusapokalypse: Die griechischen Fragmente mit deutscher und englischer Übersetzung* (GCS.NF 11 = Neutestamentliche Apokryphen 1; Berlin: De Gruyter, 2004), p. 29.

[72] E.g., as noted above (n. 15), Crossan, *Historical Jesus*, pp. 427–34, places a number of apocryphal and other documents as early as the canonical documents.

In light of these difficulties, the fourth task is to work out an appropriate methodological program for the utilization of these manuscripts in New Testament textual criticism. My proposal of a two-tired system of manuscript classification would allow the potentially valuable evidence that these and related manuscripts contain to be utilized systematically in discussion of the establishment and development of the New Testament textual tradition, but without confusing the situation regarding the manuscripts that form the basis of this text. I suggest that a several stage process be employed in bringing the Greek apocryphal documents to bear in New Testament textual criticism. The first stage is to establish the text of these manuscripts, with as little influence from the canonical texts as possible. This is a necessary task that must be done before the next stages can be pursued with confidence. The second stage is to compare these manuscripts with the canonical text at every point. Attempts along these lines have been made in the past,[73] but here is no systematic examination of the manuscripts in recent discussion, which has tended to concentrate on limited evidence, often found in translation. Where these manuscripts have been used (and this is very rare), the tendency has been to use them in broad scale comparison with the already-established New Testament textual tradition—noting where an apocryphal document is similar to or different from the established text, and to use it to confirm or fill out varying traditions at a given point. The use of apocryphal documents in a second list such as this would facilitate comparison with the readings in other actual manuscripts. The third stage is then to attempt to establish the textual characteristics of these apocryphal documents in light of the range of available evidence, and possibly to chronicle their place in the history of transmission. The fourth stage is to use the apocryphal documents, especially those that are early, as a form of evidence for the readings found in the New Testament text. Early ones might play a more significant role in deciding upon the dating and

---

[73] Examples of limited text-critical use of the Greek apocryphal gospel fragments, besides some of the comments found in the individual published editions (as noted above), include W. Lock and W. Sanday, *Two Lectures on the 'Sayings of Jesus' Recently Discovered at Oxyrhynchus* (Oxford: Clarendon Press, 1897), esp. pp. 7–14; G. Mayeda, *Das Leben-Jesu-Fragment: Papyrus Egerton 2 und seine Stellung in der urchristlichen Literaturgeschichte* (Bern: Paul Haupt, 1946); cf. H. von Schubert, *The Gospel of St Peter: Synoptical Tables, with Translation and Critical Apparatus* (Edinburgh: T. & T. Clark, 1893).

reliability of various readings where the text-critical evidence is limited, while later ones might help to quantify the development of various readings.

e. *Excerpts*

This category is something of a catch-all, since a number of the manuscripts discussed above might well be labeled as excerpts, and could profitably be included in this category. What is meant here are those kinds of manuscripts that clearly contain an excerpt taken from a biblical book, with no intention of producing continuous text. The value of such an excerpt might well be found in how the text is cited—if this can be determined. There may be occasions when textual accuracy is paramount, but there may also be occasions where the excerpt would give insight into the development and transmission of the text as it is adapted to various interpretive contexts. Some manuscripts from the Gregory-Aland list that might well belong here include the following:

𝔓7 (VH 1224 and 1225). Gregory in his volume indicates that there were two papyri with the number 152 in the Kiev archaeological museum collection. One of them had a few words that appear to allude to the Sermon on the Mount (van Haelst says Matthew 6.33–34 and possibly Matthew 7.12, but he labels both papyri and not identified Christian texts), but the other piece has what Gregory calls a speech, homily or a portion of commentary, and then citation of Luke 4.1–2.[74] Van Haelst adds that the Lukan quotation is in quotation marks. This clearly is a citation, possibly in some later patristic commentary or the like, of an excerpt from the Lukan text, but certainly not continuous text. Dates for this manuscript vary, from the third to the sixth centuries.[75]

𝔓10 (VH 490). This fourth-century papyrus is a portion of a writing exercise, as was noted by the original editors, Grenfell and Hunt (P.Oxy. II 209, p. 8) (but not in Gregory's list). The page of papyrus consists of Romans 1.1–7, minus part of v. 6, written in crude majus-

---

[74] Gregory, *Griechischen Handschriften*, p. 46.
[75] See Nestle-Aland[27] p. 684, differing from the later date in Aland and Aland, *Text of the New Testament*, p. 96, and Van Haelst, *Catalogue*, nos. 1224, 1225.

cules on a single sheet, and below the excerpt two lines in cursive writing (see plate II in P.Oxy. II). The very configuration of the document indicates that this is not continuous text, but an excerpt written as part of a writing exercise. It is possible that the same hand wrote the majuscule and cursive portions, as well as a single line on the verso.

𝔓12 (VH 536). The Alands label these excerpts as possibly notes, but there is more to consider.[76] This third- or fourth-century exerpt from Hebrews 1.1 is written in a smaller hand at the top of the second column of three columns of an early Christian letter from Rome (see plate XXV in P.Amh. II; the text is published as P.Amh. I 3). The letter is dated to the third century, although the excerpt from Hebrews may be later. Rather than being simply a note, it was probably added by the recipient or holder of the letter at a later time, possibly as an attestation of the work of God described in the letter. On the verso of the papyrus is an excerpt of Genesis 1.1–5 in Aquila's version, another excerpt (Rahlfs 912).[77]

𝔓18 (VH 559). This third/fourth-century manuscript has Revelation 1.4–7 on one side (P.Oxy. VIII 1079) and Exodus 40.26–32 on the other (P.Oxy. VIII 1075). This may be a scroll fragment to which another text was added later, although it would be difficult to know which one was written first. If the recto were written first, the Old Testament passage, then the New Testament passage would appear to have simply been added to an existing document.[78]

𝔓25 (VH 367). When this fourth- to sixth-century fragment of Matthew 18 and 19 was originally published, it was described by the editor as a fragment of the Greek Diatessaron.[79] It was later

---

[76] Aland and Aland, *Text of the New Testament*, p. 85.

[77] Obviously a similar procedure or reassessing the categories of manuscripts needs to be implemented for the lists used for the Greek Old Testament as well.

[78] Cf. 𝔓13 (VH 537). This third/fourth-century document has a significant portion of Hebrews on one side (P.Oxy. IV 657 and PSI 1292) but a text of Livy on the other (P.Oxy. IV 668). This document may be a scroll to which another text was added later, but the fact that Livy is written on the recto may indicate that the biblical text is simply a set of excerpts—although the length indicates that an attempt was being made to put the entire book of Hebrews on the papyrus.

[79] O. Stegmüller, 'Ein Bruchstück aus dem griechischen Diatessaron', *ZNW* 37 (1938), pp. 223–29.

described as a fragment of Matthew that had been corrupted by Tatianic glosses.[80] This is a good example of a document that should be in a second list (and that argues convincingly for a second list), since it is difficult to place such a document. If one agrees that only continuous text of the New Testament is to be considered for a list of manuscripts, then this one should almost assuredly be removed, but if there is a place for texts that are not continuous text but that bear witness to a text or portion of text, then this one would continue to have importance.

𝔓42 (VH 241). The quotations of Luke 1.54–55, the prayer of Mary, and 2.29–31, the song of Simeon, in this sixth- or seventh-century manuscript are the twelfth and thirteenth canticles in this bi-lingual Greek and Coptic manuscript, which consists of 26 pages.[81] The other eleven songs are found in Exodus 15.1–9 (Moses), Deuteronomy 32.5–6, 9–43, 1 Kings 2.1, 3, 4, 8, 10 (Anna), Jonah 2.3–10, Isaiah 25.1–7, 10, Isaiah 26.1–4, Isaiah 26.11–20, Isaiah 38.9–14, 18–20, Manassah 1–15, Daniel 3:26–45, and Daniel 3.52–26. There are titles in another hand also included. This is clearly an early Christian song- and prayerbook of sorts, which anthologizes various biblical songs and prayers excerpted from the biblical text.

𝔓43 (VH 560). These two passages from Revelation, 2.12–13 and 15.8–16.2, are clearly excerpts found in a sixth/seventh-century manuscript. The first passage consists of four long lines on one side and the other of five long lines on the other side in a different hand.

𝔓62 (VH 359). This fourth-century miniature codex manuscript (with only seven lines to a page) consists of 13 folios, and 26 pages. Pages 3–21 have Matthew 11.25–30 and pages 21–26 have Daniel 3.53–53, 55 (Rahlfs 994). This clearly is not continuous text, for either the New Testament or Old Testament, in this case with the Old Testament excerpt following the New. It is clearly possible that this is a lectionary text.

---

[80] C. Peters, 'Ein neues Fragment des griechischen Diatessaron?', *Bib* 21 (1940), pp. 51–55.

[81] The latest edition of the New Testament portions are to be found in Porter and Porter, *New Testament Papyri and Parchments*, no. 3.

0212 (VH 699). Like 𝔓25, 0212 is usually considered to be a page from Tatian's Diatessaron.[82] A recent study of it, however, concludes that it is not from Tatian's Diatessaron, but instead is a late second-century harmony of the four canonical gospels.[83] The single page (without writing on the back, perhaps suggesting a scroll) contains excerpts from Matthew 27.56–57, Mark 15.40, 42, Luke 23.49–51, 54, and John 19.38. It appears that it was part of a larger continuous text harmony, but clearly is not a continuous text of any of the gospels individually.

0153. This 'manuscript' is no longer listed in the Nestle-Aland Greek New Testament list, and is not included in van Haelst's book.[84] It was, however, listed in Gregory's list of 1908. It consisted of 20 Greek ostraka from the seventh century, all of them with text of the New Testament on them: Matthew 27.31–32, Mark 5.40–42, Mark 9.17–18 (a single word from the latter verse), Mark 15.21, Luke 12.13–15 with Mark 9.3 on the reverse, Luke 12.15–16, Luke 22.40–70 on ten ostraka, John 1.1–9, John 1.14–17, John 18.19–25, and John 19.15–17. It appears that there was some attempt to write a continuous text on ten of the ostraka, but clearly there is not a continuous text of significance from any gospel. This example also well illustrates the importance of having a second list. Once this number was dropped from the Nestle-Aland list, the manuscript has no further role to play in textual criticism, and its information is virtually lost.[85] However, with a second list, without necessarily giving it first list status, the texts that it contains can still be taken into text-critical consideration.

Petrie Ostraka.[86] These thirteen New Testament ostraka, of which one has been previously published O.Petrie/O.Tait. 414 (1 John ?

---

[82] This position has recently been re-iterated by J. Joosten, 'The Dura Parchment and the Diatessaron', *VigChrist* 57.2 (2003), pp. 159–75. Cf. G.D. Kilpatrick, 'Dura-Europos: The Parchments and the Papyri', *GRBS* 5 (1964), pp. 215–25, esp. pp. 222–24; W.L. Petersen, 'The Diatessaron and the Fourfold Gospel', in *Earliest Gospels* (ed. Horton), pp. 50–68.

[83] D.C. Parker, D.G.K. Taylor and M.S. Goodacre, 'The Dura-Europos Gospel Harmony', in *Studies in the Early Text* (ed. Taylor), pp. 192–228.

[84] See above (n. 25), where it is noted that the Aland list does delete a number of uncials.

[85] My description of the content of these ostraka comes from Gregory, *Griechischen Handschriften*, p. 43, who still lists it as an uncial.

[86] C.E. Römer, 'Ostraka mit Christlichen Texten aus der Sammlung Flinders

and 2.12–14, 2.19–22),[87] all have portions of New Testament text
on them. They include: O.Petrie 14: Acts 2.22–24; O.Petrie 15 (Acts
2.25–29, 2.32–36 and 3.1–2), O.Petrie 16 (Acts 15.38–16.1, 16.7–9),
O.Petrie 17 (Acts 16.18 and 19.1, 19.8–9 and +), O.Petrie 18 (Romans
13.3–6, 13.7–11), O.Petrie 19 (Galatians 1.8–11), O.Petrie 20 (Galatians
1.15–18, 2.3–8), O.Petrie 21 (James 2.2–3, 2.8–9), O.Petrie 22 (James
4.11–13), O.Petrie 23 = O.Petrie/O.Tait 414, O.Petrie 24 (1 John
3.17–22, 4.1–3), O.Petrie 25 (1 John 4.10–14, 4.18–21), and O.Petrie
26 (Jude ? and 1–3, 4 and ?). Not all of the ostraka have writing
on both sides, and some have indecipherable writing. An example
such as O.Petrie 17, which jumps from Acts 16 to 19, illustrates that
these are not meant to be continuous text. Nevertheless, the text
that they have can serve a text-critical purpose.

P.Aberd. 3 (VH 590).   This sixth-century ostrakon (not papyrus) is
often considered an unknown apocryphal gospel. However, it is not
a continuous text, but an excerpt written on both sides of the ostrakon
that contains Matthew 3.14, 15, 17 in the baptism of Jesus. Since
this ostrakon seems to belong with a group that includes P.Aberd.
4, 5, and 6, which are hymns, this passage may have been used in
some liturgical context. Even though the text is not continuous, it
appears to follow the text of the Matthean passage that it excerpts
word for word.

𝔓72 (VH 548 and 557).[88]   The Bodmer manuscript within which
𝔓72 occurs, the so-called Bodmer Miscellaneous Codex, in a number of ways raises the question of continuous text of the New
Testament. This third- or fourth-century codex, probably collecting
together works into a single collection from previous independent or
smaller collections, consists of the complete text of 1 and 2 Peter

Petrie', *ZPE* 145 (2003), pp. 183–201 with plates; cf. M.S. Funghi and M.C.
Martinelli, 'Ostraca Letterari Inediti della Collezione Petrie', *ZPE* 145 (2003), pp.
141–82.
    [87] Elliott places this ostrakon with 0153, but this does not fit with the informa-
tion from Gregory.
    [88] I am grateful to Tommy Wasserman for sending to me a copy of his paper,
'Papyrus 72 and the *Bodmer Miscellaneous Codex*', read at the Working with Biblical
Manuscripts section of the 2004 International Meeting of the Society of Biblical
Literature in Groningen, The Netherlands, upon which I depend here for my comments. See also the paper by Tobias Nicklas and Tommy Wasserman on this manuscript in this volume.

and Jude, written by one scribe. Thus, on the one hand, it would appear that this is a continuous text manuscript, since as I have noted above there are numerous papyri and parchments that only contain a single biblical document but that are considered continuous text—this manuscript has three complete New Testament books. However, other factors need to be taken into consideration. One is that there are 11 different books found in this one codex. Besides the New Testament books, they include Nativity of Mary, Apocryphal Correspondence, Ode of Solomon 11, Melito's Homily on the Passion, Apology of Phileas, Psalms 33–34 (LXX), and a hymn fragment. Further, 1 and 2 Peter are not together with Jude, since Jude follows the Ode of Solomon. As a result, there has been speculation that this manuscript was created for private use, or possibly for lectionary or liturgical use though not necessarily in a public service. In any event, it raises questions regarding what constitutes continuous text, with particular poignancy for those manuscripts that are considered continuous text but may not have more than a single book represented.

f. *Unknown*

The last category of document that I wish to include here is that of unknown texts. There are a number of hymns, prayers and other theological and liturgical texts that are simply too far removed from the biblical text to be considered, even if they have a few words that seem to mimic or reflect the New Testament Greek text. However, there are a number of documents that have been suggested as perhaps being fragments of the Greek New Testament, but that have not been accepted as such. Their place in the text-critical context is not clear, but with a two-tiered system there is a place where they can be included without giving them undue influence on textual criticism.

The most well-known of this type of document is no doubt the nineteen Qumran Greek fragments from the seventh cave. Some of these documents have been identified with Old Testament and apocryphal texts (7Q1 = Exodus 28.47; 7Q2 = Baruch/Letter of Jeremiah 6.43–44), but Joseph O'Callaghan and later Carsten Thiede both suggested that at least some of these documents were fragments from the New Testament.[89] O'Callaghan went so far as to identify a large

---

[89] For a summary, see C.P. Thiede, *The Earliest Gospel Manuscript? The Qumran*

number of the documents with a form of the New Testament text. These include: 7Q4 = 1 Timothy 3.16, 4.1, 3; 7Q5 = Mark 6.52–53; 7Q6.1 = Mark 4.28; 7Q6.2 = Acts 27.38; 7Q7 = Mark 12.17; 7Q8 = James 1.23–24; 7Q9 = Romans 5.11–12; 7Q10 = 2 Peter 1.15; 7Q15 = Mark 6.48. Others have made other kinds of identifications of these same manuscripts, usually with Old Testament books.[90]

For a variety of reasons, many of them well-founded but some of them less so, O'Callaghan's hypotheses have been resoundingly rejected on all fronts. No doubt one of the major reasons is that to welcome Greek New Testament fragments in a cave near the Qumran site would potentially overthrow the governing chronological paradigm of New Testament studies. Whatever one thinks of the discussion, it has clearly been disjunctive in nature, with most lining up firmly against O'Callaghan. With a second list, there is a middle ground provided for discussion, in which the manuscript, for example, 7Q5 can be kept in a position of potential consideration without one being compelled to accept or outright reject its significance. For example, it might be worth revisiting the question of the place of 7Q5 if the major textual variant from the tradition that it contains—omission of επι την γην in Mark 6.53—were to appear in another early-manuscript.

4. CONCLUSION

This article begins with the realization that the textual development of the Greek New Testament was highly complex, and involved a number of different types of manuscripts, including those that were

Fragment 7Q5 and its Significance for New Testament Studies (Carlisle: Paternoster, 1992); idem, _The Dead Sea Scrolls and the Jewish Origins of Christianity_ (New York: Palgrave, 2001), pp. 152–81.

[90] Bibliography for the above is contained within Porter, 'Why So Many Holes', pp. 184–85 notes 67, 68. For discussion not included in that article, see J. O'Callaghan, _Los primeros testimonios del Nuevo Testamento: Papriología neotestamentaria_ (Córdoba: Ediciones El Almendro, 1995), esp. pp. 95–145; J. Peláez del Rosal, 'El debate sobre los papiros neotestamentarios de Qumrán: 7Q5 y 7Q4', _EstBib_ 57 (1999), pp. 51–38; T.J. Kraus, '7Q5: Status quaestionis und grundlegende Anmerkungen zur Relativierung der Diskussionum das Papyrusfragment', _RevQum_ 74 (1999), pp. 239–58; E. Tov, 'The Greek Biblical Texts from the Judean Desert', in _Bible as Book_ (ed. McKendrick and O'Sullivan), pp. 97–122, esp. pp. 103–105; H. Förster, '7Q5 = Mark 6.52–53: A Challenge for Textual Criticism', _JGRChJ_ 2 (2001–2005), pp. 27–35.

later to be regarded as canonical, but also those that were not. In textual criticism of the New Testament, the major classification has taken place around the material upon which the manuscripts have been written (although this has not been maintained consistently throughout). I have suggested above that a shift from the type of material to the nature of the content of the manuscripts—whether they are continuous text or not—might provide a way of moving forward in textual criticism. This proposal of one category for continuous text manuscripts and one for those that are not allows reclassification within the current list of manuscripts so that the evidence that certain manuscripts contain will not be lost even if they are reassigned. Perhaps as important, if not more so, is that the second list provides a means of bringing into consideration, but without necessarily altering the nature of New Testament textual criticism, manuscripts that in many cases have been overlooked or marginalized because they have failed to be assigned to the categories currently in use. The above discussion has tried to exemplify what might be included in such a second list by drawing into the discussion a variety of manuscripts, including those currently classified elsewhere and manuscripts and types of manuscripts not currently included. One of the major factors in considering these manuscripts has been to discuss them in terms of their wider context, not just examining the New Testament portion but considering the nature of the manuscript itself. These examples are meant to be illustrative and not definitive. The hope is that discussion can be pushed forward so that a wider amount of evidence can be brought into the equation on similar grounds of consideration.

SELECTED MODERN AUTHORS

ANCIENT SOURCES

IMPORTANT TOPICS